ENGLISH ROMANTICISM AND THE CELTIC WORLD

English Romanticism and the Celtic World explores the way in which British Romantic writers responded to the national and cultural identities of the 'four nations' England, Ireland, Scotland and Wales. The essays collected here, by specialists in the field, interrogate the cultural centres as well as the peripheries of Romanticism, and the interactions between these. They underline 'Celticism' as an emergent strand of cultural ethnicity during the eighteenth century, examining the constructions of Celticness and Britishness in the Romantic period, including the ways in which the 'Celtic' countries viewed themselves in the light of Romanticism. Other topics include the development of Welsh antiquarianism, the Ossian controversy, Irish nationalism, Celtic landscapes, Romantic form and Orientalism. The collection covers writing by Blake, Wordsworth, Scott, Byron and Shelley, and will be of interest to scholars of Romanticism and Celtic Studies.

GERARD CARRUTHERS is Lecturer in Scottish literature in the Department of Scottish Literature at the University of Glasgow. He has co-edited (with Alison Lumsden) *Reliquiae Trotcosienses* (2003) and (with David Goldie and Alastair Renfrew) *Beyond Scotland: New Contexts for Twentieth Century Scottish Literature* (2003).

ALAN RAWES is Senior Lecturer in English at Canterbury Christ Church University College. He is the author of *Byron's Poetic Experimentation* (2000) and co-editor (with Arthur Bradley) of *Romantic Biography* (2003).

ENGLISH ROMANTICISM AND THE CELTIC WORLD

EDITED BY

GERARD CARRUTHERS

Department of Scottish Literature, University of Glasgow

AND

ALAN RAWES

Department of English, Canterbury Christ Church University College

CAMBRIDGE
UNIVERSITY PRESS

PUBLISHED BY THE PRESS SYNDICATE OF THE UNIVERSITY OF CAMBRIDGE
The Pitt Building, Trumpington Street, Cambridge CB2 1RP, United Kingdom

CAMBRIDGE UNIVERSITY PRESS
The Edinburgh Building, Cambridge, CB2 2RU, UK
40 West 20th Street, New York, NY 10011-4211, USA
477 Williamstown Road, Port Melbourne, VIC 3207, Australia
Ruiz de Alarcón 13, 28014 Madrid, Spain
Dock House, The Waterfront, Cape Town 8001, South Africa

http://www.cambridge.org

First published 2003

Printed in the United Kingdom at the University Press, Cambridge

Typeface Adobe Garamond 11/12.5 pt   *System* LATEX 2ε   [TB]

A catalogue record for this book is available from the British Library

ISBN 0 521 81085 X hardback

Contents

Contributors

BERNARD BEATTY is Senior Lecturer in the Department of English Language and Literature at Liverpool University. He edits *The Byron Journal*, has edited two collections of Essays on Byron and is, at present, editing two more, and has written two books on Byron: *Byron's Don Juan* (1985) and *Byron's Don Juan and Other Poems* (1987). He has written numerous articles on Romantic authors, Dryden, the Scriptures, and historicism.

ARTHUR BRADLEY is Senior Lecturer in the Department of English at Chester College of Higher Education. His publications include papers in *Textual Practice, Literature and Theology, The Heythrop Journal, The Aligarh Critical Miscellany, Reinventing Christianity* (ed.) Linda Woodhead (2001). He is the co-editor of *Romantic Biography* (2002). He is working on a monograph entitled *Save the Name: Deconstruction, Negative Theology and Modern French Thought* to be published by Routledge.

WILLIAM D. BREWER is Professor of English at Appalachian State University in Boone, North Carolina. He is the author of *The Mental Anatomies of William Godwin and Mary Shelley* (2001) and *The Shelley-Byron Conversation* (1994). He has also edited three collections of essays and has published articles in *Papers on Language and Literature, Philological Quarterly, Keats-Shelley Journal, Southern Humanities Review* and other journals.

GERARD CARRUTHERS is Lecturer in the Department of Scottish Literature, University of Glasgow. He has published essays on James Thomson, Robert Burns and many other aspects of eighteenth-century culture. He is co-editor of Walter Scott's *Reliquiae Trotcosienses* (2002), and is currently writing a monograph entitled, *The Invention of Scottish Literature During the Long Eighteenth Century*.

CAROLINE FRANKLIN is Senior Lecturer in English at the University of Wales, Swansea. She is author of *Byron's Heroines* (1992) and *Byron, A*

Literary Life (2000), and editor of *The Wellesley Series IV: British Romantic Poets* (1998). She is currently working on a critical guide to Byron and a study of Mary Wollstonecraft.

MICHAEL J. FRANKLIN is Research Fellow in the English Department of University of Wales, Swansea. Since editing *Sir William Jones: Selected Poetical and Prose Works* (1995) and writing the critical biography, *Sir William Jones* (1995), he has been investigating colonial representations of India and their various interfaces with Romanticism. He has edited *Representing India: Indian Culture and Imperial Control* (2000) and *The European Discovery of India: Key Indological Sources of Romanticism* (2001), and has written a series of articles on key members of the Hastings circle which forms the current focus of his research.

MALCOLM KELSALL is Professor of English at Cardiff University. He is the author of *Christopher Marlowe* (1981), *Byron's Politics* (1987, awarded the Elma Dangerfield Prize, 1991), *The Great Good Place: the Country House and English Literature* (1992), *Jefferson and the Iconography of Romanticism: Folk, Land, Culture and the Romantic Nation* (1999) and has just completed a book on the Irish country house under the Union.

DAFYDD MOORE is Lecturer in English at the University of Plymouth. He has written a number of articles on 'The Poems of Ossian' and a book on Macpherson, which will be published later this year.

ANDREW NICHOLSON is Research Fellow in Romantic Studies in the English Department at Bristol University. He is editor of *Lord Byron: The Complete Miscellaneous Prose* (1991) and of various facsimile editions of *Don Juan, Beppo* and other poems of Byron in *The Manscripts of the Younger Romantics* series published by Garland. At present he is editing the letters of John Murray to Byron.

MICHAEL O'NEILL is Professor of English at the University of Durham. He has published widely in the fields of Romanticism and twentieth-century poetry. His books include *The Human Mind's Imaginings: Conflict and Achievement in Shelley's Poetry* (1989) and *Romanticism and the Self-Conscious Poem* (1997). With Zachary Leader, he is currently completing a co-edited edition of Shelley for the Oxford Authors series.

MURRAY PITTOCK holds the Chair in Literature at the University of Strathclyde and is Director of the Glasgow-Strathclyde School of Scottish Studies. He is the author of a number of studies on the Jacobites and on British identities, including *The Invention of Scotland* (1991), *Inventing and Resisting Britain* (1997), *Celtic Identity and the British Image* (1999) and *Scottish Nationality* (2001). He is currently co-editing the Edinburgh History of Scottish Literature and writing a new history of Scotland.

DAVID PUNTER is Professor of English at the University of Bristol. His published work in the Romantic period includes *The Literature of Terror* (1980; rev. edn 1996), *The Romantic Unconscious* (1989), *Gothic Pathologies* (1998), and, as editor, *Blake: Selected Poetry and Prose* (1988), *William Blake: the New Casebook* (1996) and *A Companion to the Gothic* (2000).

ALAN RAWES is Senior Lecturer in the English Department at Canterbury Christ Church University College. He has also taught at the Universities of Liverpool and Strathclyde. He is the author of *Byron's Poetic Experimentation* (2000) and numerous essays on Byron and related topics, and is the co-editor, with Arthur Bradley, of *Romantic Biography* (2003).

J.R. WATSON, formerly Professor of English at Durham University, is the author of many books and articles including *A Handbook to English Romanticism* (1992) and *The English Hymn: a Critical and Historical Study* (1997).

Acknowledgements

The editors are greatly indebted to Dr Kenneth Simpson of the University of Strathclyde for his encouragement and support for this project in its early stages. They would also like to thank Linda Bree and Rachel De Wachter at Cambridge University Press for their patient handling of the book, Cambridge University Press's anonymous readers for their numerous helpful comments and suggestions, the invaluable help of Rhona Brown and the Department of Scottish Literature at the University of Glasgow, whose financial assistance helped the editors in their research for the book at the British Library. A version of Michael O'Neill's chapter was given as the *Pete Laver Lecture* at the *Wordsworth Summer Conference 2000* and subsequently published in *The Wordsworth Circle* with the permission of the editors and Cambridge University Press.

CHAPTER I

Introduction: romancing the Celt

Gerard Carruthers and Alan Rawes

The growth of 'four nations' British literary history in the last decade has brought with it new approaches to the 'Celtic' idea in eighteenth-century and Romantic studies. Yet there is a danger of losing sight of the extent to which Celticism was used as a tool in the construction and expansion of the post-1745 British state. This is one of the central concerns of this volume.

We can see the British use and abuse of the Celtic in its starkest, most jingoistic form in a song by the patriotic English songwriter, Charles Dibdin. At the height of the Napoleonic wars, he writes:

> Fra Ossian to Bruce,
> The bra deeds to produce,
> Would take monny and monny a long hour to scan;
> For mickle were the bairds
> Sung the feats of Scottish lairds,
> When the swankies in array,
> The canty pipes did play—
> 'There never was a Scot but was true to his Clan.'
> . . .
> From Egypt's burning sands,
> Made red by Scottish hands,
> The invincible Skybalds fled, aw to a man;
> For the standard that they bore
> From the keeper's grasp we tore,
> And the French were all dismay'd,
> 'There never was a Scot but was true to his Clan.'[1]

Here we find the confection of Scoto-British Celticism in the service of British military aggression. Ancient history has been overwritten with eighteenth-century literary history as James Macpherson's identification of the legendary 'Ossianic' materials with Scotland rather than Ireland has taken root and this Celtic Scotland is seen as seamlessly antecedent to the Anglophone medieval Scotland of Robert the Bruce.[2] Ethnic distinctions

are erased from historical consciousness. We see another British literary appropriation as the Scots language literary revival of the eighteenth century is
garishly drawn upon (so that Scottish 'bairds' celebrate heroic 'swankies') to
be subsumed within the newfangled British imperial myth of the 'fighting
Jock'.

The gradual establishment during the long eighteenth century, and more
particularly in the Romantic period, of what Stuart Piggott has called
'Anglo-Celtic sanguinity' is by 1866 being given by Matthew Arnold a ge-
netic fingerprint.³ Seeking to unravel the racial pedigree of 'English' poetry,
Arnold suggests that this poetry's 'honesty' is derived from a 'Saxon' source,
its 'energy' from 'Celtic' and 'Roman' sources.⁴ Clearly, such a postulation
was intended to distinguish rather than to devolve English literature and
identity. The import of classical Rome was for Arnold, as father of the
modern upstart discipline of English Studies, a necessary, venerable ingredient. What, though, might help distinguish Britain from the more purely
Teutonic identity to be found in the nation's increasingly powerful imperial rival, Prussia? The 'Celtic' component, particularly its 'turn for natural
magic' was brought to bear here; and this named propensity Arnold found
at the high point of the Romantic movement in England, especially, in the
poetry of John Keats.⁵ Victorian culture, in other words, looked back to
Romantic literature in search of an Anglo-Celtic identity, and what was
available to such a search in the English literature of the Romantic period
forms much of the subject matter of the present volume.

If the incorporation of the Celtic gene within British identity during the
nineteenth century can be aligned very often with militaristic and imperial
aspirations, we might nevertheless suggest that to begin with Celticism had
been appealed to, much more innocently, as part of the attempt to evade
the ideological and internecine strife that had plagued the British polity
from the English Civil War down to the Jacobite rebellions. Such an appeal,
which bore such spectacular fruit, while simultaneously coming under intense scrutiny, in the English writing of the Romantic period, began at least
as early as 1750. Certainly, in that year, William Collins in his 'Ode on the
Popular Superstitions of the Highlands of Scotland' addressed the Scottish
dramatist, John Home, with the injunction to 'wake perforce thy Doric
quill'(p. 56).⁶ Paradoxically, Scotland is seen by this English poet as a land
of simultaneous realism and romance, where 'ev'ry Herd, by sad experience, knows / How wing'd with fate their Elph-shot arrows fly' (p. 57).
This Scotland was to be the ideal site of a revival for an imaginative
sensibility which had become tarnished elsewhere in Britain under the
cultural, economic and doctrinal pressures (all largely encompassing arid

is a rationalism of one kind or another) during the previous century. This
is a Scotland where:

> Ev'n yet preserv'd, how often may'st thou hear,
> > Where to the Pole the Boreal Mountains run,
> > Taught by the Father to his list'ning Son
> Strange lays whose pow'r had charm'd a Spenser's Ear.
> At Ev'ry Pause, before thy Mind possest,
> > Old Runic Bards shall seem to rise around
> With uncouth Lyres, in many-colour'd Vest,
> > Their Matted Hair with boughs fantastic crown'd
> Whether Thou bidst the well-taught Hind repeat
> > The Choral Dirge that mourns some Chieftain brave
> When Ev'ry Shrieking Maid her bosom beat
> > And strew'd with choicest herbs his scented Grave
> Or whether sitting in the Shepherd's Shiel
> > Thou hear'st some Sounding Tale of War's alarms
> When at the Bugle's call with fire and steel,
> > The Sturdy Clans poured forth their bonny swarms,
> And hostile Brothers met to prove each Other's arms.

(p. 57)

Though drawing upon real Scottish Highland source material, particularly
Martin Martin's *Description of the Western Isles of Scotland* (1706), we find
here Collins seeking out, and finding in this highland locus, a site of vital,
charged even, gothic sensibility. Yet the synthetic nature of all this is most
clearly revealed in the stanza above by the reference to 'old Runic Bards'
more properly to be associated with Scandinavia. The Celtic may well be
imaged, by English culture, as a site of renewal, but the image remains an
English construction, and the chapters that follow engage with a number
of specifically Romantic constructions of the Celtic and offer wide-ranging
support for, and expansions of, Howard D. Weinbrot's argument that the
eighteenth-century search for ethnic roots in British literature was creatively
eclectic amid the ferment of new nation building.[7] As we shall see, in the
years leading up to the Romantic period, and most dramatically in the Romantic period itself, this eclecticism is massively increased by the materials
supplied to it by expanding Empire and its attendant 'Orientalism', and
European war.

That England transformed and appropriated the Celtic in the service of
Britishness is, of course, only part of the picture. The addressee of Collins'
poem, John Home, himself indulged in a similar kind of polysemous creativity in his *Douglas* (1757), the text which, more than any other prior
to Macpherson's 'Ossian', located Scotland as the site *par excellence* of

sentimental and noble pathos. Equally, however, dealing with the wars
between Scotland and her ancient foe the 'Norsemen', *Douglas* is full of
Shakespearean echoes, draws upon the old English ballad, 'Gil Morrice', as
a key element in its plot and invokes in the preface written especially for
London performances, the legendary name of Percy as well as Douglas.[8]
Home, the man who had fought on the Hanoverian side during the rebellion of 1745, exemplifies a careful cross-national and cross-political appeal to
remembrance of 'the primitive' past alongside the new and progressive *Pax
Britannica* delivered with the final pacification of Scotland. He also signals a
kind of cross-fertilising cultural dialogue between Anglo and Celtic culture
in which each culture looks to the other for revitalisation. The chapters
of this volume repeatedly foreground and explore instances of precisely
this kind of dialogue in the texts of various Romantic and post-Romantic
literary traditions.

The cocktail of primitivism and progress across the Whig and Tory
British divide persisted throughout the rest of the eighteenth and into
the nineteenth century. High Tory Walter Scott is the best example of its
survival into the Romantic period and beyond. In *Waverley* (1814), Scott
presents an oxymoronic configuration close to Collins's depiction of the
'bonny swarms' of clansmen, as the result of the misfiring gun of Jacobite
figure, Evan Dhu:

A thousand birds of prey, hawks, kites, carrion-crows, and ravens, disturbed from
the lodgings which they had just taken up for the evening, rose at the report of the
gun, and mingled their hoarse and discordant notes with the echoes which replied
to it, and with the roar of the mountain cataracts.[9]

Here in this dangerous but sublime landscape, we find a particularly subtle
version of the 'colonising, animating gaze' (p. 151) to which Murray G. W.
Pittock in his essay in this volume alerts us. Pittock provides an incisive
definition of the primitivism of the age and points to its characteristic
influence on relations between English Romantic culture and the Celtic
world. It is, he says:

... a profound commitment to the past, but one depoliticised in the context either
of the frisson of *Rauberromantik* (bandit romanticism) tourism, or in a commitment to contemporary ideas of liberty which owed more to the hermeneutics
through which primitive simplicity was codified than to a historicised grasp of its
reality (p. 153)

As the present volume frequently reveals, in the English writing of the
Romantic period, the Celtic is simultaneously reinvented for, reappropriated by, and yet excluded from, the historical and political British present.

On the other hand, in poems such as 'The Vision' (1786), Robert Burns demonstrates the aesthetic largesse and political and cultural idealisation that is also implied by Pittock.[10] Here Burns dovetails gothically or supernaturally endowed Celticism with contemporary discussions of 'genius'. The primordially sublime spirit of Coila appears in a dream to the narrator who is tired out in mind and body after a hard day's exertions farming. 'The Vision' is divided into 'Duan First' and 'Duan Second' after the manner of Macpherson's Ossianic production, 'Cath-Loda', as the suitably ethnic framework into which Coila steps to grant the narrator bardic instruction. A Coila who has been reading Virgil explains:

> Know, the great *Genius* of this Land,
> Has many a light, aerial band,
> Who, all beneath his high command,
> > Harmoniously,
> As *Arts* or *Arms* they understand,
> > Their labors ply.
> > (145–50)

Burns here shows himself more than capable of complicity with the creation of the kind of image of the Celtic world that English culture frequently projected on to it in the name of Britishness. Aside from the Habbie Simson stanza form, Burns does not invoke in the course of the poem his great predecessors in the eighteenth-century Scots poetry revival, Allan Ramsay and Robert Fergusson, nor the usual Scots martial heroes, Wallace and Bruce (though, ironically, the title of the poem may be derived loosely from Allan Ramsay's medieval 'forgery', 'The Vision' (1724), a work celebrating William Wallace). Instead 'The Vision' attempts to negotiate a very diffuse British heritage. Such negotiations form a fundamental focus of this book. In the case of 'The Vision', the exemplary poets of 'this land' are the self-consciously British poets James Thomson, for his landscape-painting ability, and James Beattie, for his examination of the growth of primitive poetic faculty in 'The Minstrel' (1771–4). The great military men explicitly name-checked are contemporary soldiers in the service of modern Britain (though the narrator is also given a sign of 'Scotland's' pre-medieval military greatness in being shown the tomb of Coilus, 'king of the Picts').[11] Utilising the stanza form that it does, its 'Celtic' machinery is yoked to a language which has much in common with the diction of Shenstone and Gray (both of whom are mentioned in the poem). The creation of Britishness is not simply an English imposition rooted in English imperialist drives, then, and another of the principal concerns of this volume is the crucial role played in

English, Romantic-period constructions, cementings and problematisings of British identity by Scottish, Irish and Welsh writers.

Yet the volume is not only concerned with Romantic negotiations of a British heritage and Romantic-period constructions of a British identity. Other kinds of Anglo-Celtic dialogue make themselves heard in the chapters that follow. One key area of interest, for instance, is the part played by Celtic culture in the genesis of Romanticism as a literary phenomenon. Indeed, Burns's poetry is a crucial precursor of, and influence on, the *Lyrical Ballads* of Wordsworth and Coleridge, though lacking the sureness the latter text exemplifies where, in Pittock's phrase, this 'marked the exaltation of the spirit of the people in the most poor and remote provinces' and becomes 'the voice of the true human spirit' (p. 154). It is somewhat ironic that it is the English poets, Wordsworth (who draws in a sustained way on the 'poetical' character of Scotland, as Pittock shows in this volume) and Coleridge, who are able to operate ethnically much less self-consciously than Burns after Celtic-engined primitivism has permeated British culture.

If Burns's poetry was a crucial influence on English Romanticism, so were James Macpherson's 'Ossian' productions. As Daffyd Moore elucidates in this volume, notwithstanding the many enthusiastic engagements with 'Ossian' by Blake, Coleridge and others, Macpherson has been far too readily excluded from 'the grand parade of English literary historiography' (p. 50). In his careful stripping away of prejudiced critical assumptions, Moore highlights the fact that there is much more significance to the 'Ossian' texts than merely their confectionary nature: 'whatever we might make of the tradition Macpherson is seen as fostering, however we wish he had done things differently, we should not ignore the threat that this tradition, and the very possibility that *Ossian* holds out that such traditions exist, has posed to whiggish English literary historiography' (p. 50). In other words, even as it fits awkwardly into the supposed scheme of British literary progress towards the 'authenticity' of the Romantic age, 'Ossian' represents a fertile source of the 'otherness' which is so much caught up in the search for the authentic for the ages of Sensibility and Romanticism. It is a key document for English, British and European Romanticism, as Moore shows in numerous examples, so that, as Pittock describes it, the 'Ossian' texts set up a dialogue between an older disappearing world and a new late eighteenth-century world so central to that which we would we now call 'the Romantic'.[12]

While engaging with Anglo-Celtic dialogues that are significant at British and European levels, this volume also considers more localised Anglo-Celtic dialogues. Andrew Nicholson's finely particular reading of the interaction between Byron and Scott reveals an extended dialogue between this self-consciously, but problematically, 'English' writer and the 'wizard of the north' that displays a deep appreciation by the former of the latter's innovatory propensities in concrete poetic form as well as a shared concern with the more nebulous quality of 'right' poetic feeling. Previous hostility on Byron's part to Scott in *English Bards and Scotch Reviewers* (1809), which itself instances an anti-Scottish attitude of the period in the face of a rather rigidly neo-classical reviewing academy in Edinburgh represented by Francis Jeffrey and the Whiggish *Edinburgh Review*, was eventually replaced by deep appreciation.[13] Byron's designation of Scott as 'the Ariosto of the North' referred not to Scott's British location, but his location rather as a northern European more generally and sprang from Byron's appreciation that Scott's Scottish medievalism was an act of 'mainstream', rather than peripheral (wizard-like), Celtic restoration. As Nicholson records, Byron saw that Scott 'was now numbered amongst Chaucer, Spenser, Dryden and Pope as one who had "neatly grafted" "New words" "on a Gallic phrase" and "by force of rhyme" "enrich'd our islands' ill-united tongues" ' (p. 131). In theme, diction and form (especially, specifically, in his retrieval after Swift and Butler of the tetrameter), Byron saw Scott as engaging with history in a more real and complex fashion than has usually been appreciated by criticism before or since. We might say that Scott for Byron is crucial in the British restoration of, in William Collins's phrase, 'Strange lays, whose pow'r had charm'd a Spenser's Ear'.

A very nice identification of a further Byronic dialogue, this time with himself, is made in Bernard Beatty's chapter. Here what is at stake is the relation of Scotland to the rest of European culture in a mind strongly influenced by, but never limited to, Anglo-centric notions of Britishness. In spite of Byron's distancing of himself from his Scottish background, especially in *English Bards and Scotch Reviewers* (a chiastic title suggestive of Byron's defiance in this context), in wholly Byronic fashion, he still advertises his repudiated origins. In Beatty's reading, a Byron emerges whose cosmopolitanism is marked by a species of negative capability, where nationhood is concerned. Byron's gradually increasing recognition as his poetic career progresses of his Celtic-Scottish cradle, nurtured to some extent by his reading of Scott's novels, is an empathetic, and fundamentally Romantic, reclamation primed by his recognition of the cultural 'other' in his cosmopolitan peregrinations in Europe.

The most incendiary type of dialogue between a Celtic periphery and a British centre might be expected to occur in the case of Ireland. The chapters by Bradley, Kelsall and O'Neill combine, however, to offer an account of the ongoing dialogue between Irish literary culture and English Romanticism that undercuts this expectation.

Nationalism in Ireland, at the hightide mark of the rebellious 1790s, tended to follow a prosaic rather than what Arnold might have called a 'Celtic' pattern. Notoriously, Theobald Wolfe Tone, showing irritation at the festival of Belfast harpists in 1792, expressed the desire that these new bards 'be hanged'.[14] Ironically enough, Tone, to escape the indignity of the gallows after the failure of the United Irishmen uprising, slit his own throat and through this act invested himself with an Ossianic-like glamour. That year, 1798, may have been invested elsewhere through the impact of the *Lyrical Ballads* with the idea of 'real language', but in Ireland plain political speaking began to disappear under an often hagiographic Celtic nationalism. As Katie Trumpener records of William Drennan, a founder-member of the United Irishmen and previously a forceful political poet, '[his] strong dissatisfaction with the 1801 Act of Union ... finds expression not in a resumption of revolutionary plotting but rather in the composition of poetic strains of almost Ossianic melancholy'.[15]

Complex relations existed, then, not simply between the Celtic and the Anglo, but between the distinct Celtic cultures themselves. Here a text that became a literary building block of Britishness suggests a consoling mode of poetic composition to anti-British Celtic culture. The problematic literary relationships between Irish periphery and British centre, however, are not so easily pinned down. P. B. Shelley's critique of the oppression of Ireland, for example, is unravelled here by Arthur Bradley who traces the 'intriguing parallels between Shelley's representation of Robert Emmet and Laon and Cythna' (p. 125). Bradley points to Emmet's admonition, 'Let no man write my epitaph' (p. 126) while Ireland remained unfree, words attributed to the revolutionary when in the dock for high treason in 1803. Bradley draws a very striking comparison between Emmet's outlook and what Laon 'calls America: "An epitaph of glory for the tomb / Of murdered Europe may thy fame be made"' (p. 128). We see Shelley through the example of an Irish revolutionary, then, expressing the desire for a new kind of *Ancien Régime* – shaking revolution that is the polar opposite to what we glimpsed in the utterance of Charles Dibdin. Yet for Shelley, according to Bradley, 'Ireland is seen as merely a local example of an international phenomenon, and Irish politics is just a stepping stone on the path to globalised reform' (p. 118). In Shelley's Romantic representation of Ireland, Celtic 'otherness' and Britishness are both subsumed into, and negated by, a much larger, if only potential, universality.

Shelley's exuberant combination of Celticism and Romantic Orientalism, however, serves to remind us of the ultimately stagnant nature of the
Irish dynamic he represents. Thomas Moore's *Lalla Rookh* (1817) is also in
some of its aspects, perhaps, an allegorised reading of the Irish situation,
but is all too obliquely so, coming as it does from the pen of the man
who was Ireland's national lyrist in the first third of the nineteenth century.
The roots of modern Irish independence are to be found in a more recent,
late nineteenth-century wave of Celtic nationalism common, at least in
certain forms of cultural expression, to Scotland, Wales and other parts of
the British Isles. And, as Malcolm Kelsall shows in his analysis of Charles
Lever's *Luttrell of Arran* (1865), this nationalism can sometimes seem to
be 'divided between... the old, dying world of Burkean conservatism and
Byronic revolt on the one hand, and, on the other, a new world struggling
to define selfhood and place' (p. 185). Within this scenario, the character
of Tim O'Rorke represents 'the mindless mantra of old-style Jacobinism,
now yoked to racial hatred'. For Lever, the one-nation Tory, the residue
of old political nationalism now dangerously combined with Celtic ethnicity makes for a 'historically regressive' phenomenon (p. 189), when the
pressing social problem of the day is posed by the blight of the potato
famine. Describing Lever's attitude, Kelsall tells us that '[s]piritually he
belongs with those late Romantics of what Shelley called (in the preface to
The Revolt of Islam) "the age of despair" which followed the Enlightened
dream in the bloody realities of the revolutionary wars of the Napoleonic
era' (p. 189). We might certainly suggest that the dark and sceptical ironies
of *Luttrell of Aran*, which refuse to idealise either past or present for Celtic
Ireland, are akin to, if less humorously voiced than, the sceptical ironies
that resist idealisations of all kinds in Byron's *Don Juan*.

And this refusal to idealise surfaces again as Michael O'Neill deals
with the response of contemporary Irish poets to the English Romantic
canon. These poets frequently stand in ironic affirmation of 'the capacity of
Romantic poetry to enact and criticise longing and desire [as] part of its
fascinating doubleness' (p. 196). Seamus Heaney here is exemplary, feeling,
as O'Neill reminds us, that he has 'no rights on / The English lyric' (p. 202).
Equally, strongly inculcated with Wordsworthian notions of childhood, of
the moment and of imaginative education as he is, Heaney, writing from
within the troubled Ulster and Irish locus ultimately lays 'claim to a... state
of poetic autonomy, a state that has exacted sacrifices but is alive to possibilities' (p. 203). Yet Heaney's bog-poems, juxtaposing the contemporarily
troubled Ireland and pre-Christian Jutland allowing the poet to conclude
wryly that he feels 'Unhappy and at home', bring us full circle as we see

(quite literally earthed) the Celtic sensibility schooled in Romantic ethnic symbolism.

One of the distinctive features of this volume is its focus on the fertile relationship between late eighteenth-century Welsh culture and English Romanticism. Here the volume extends the ground-breaking work of Katie Trumpener on Anglo-Celtic relations in the period. Unfortunately, Trumpener's discussion of Anglo-Welsh relations is brief – her principal interest being in Anglo-Scottish and Anglo-Irish cultural relations – while her study is centred on the Romantic Novel. Here sustained attention is given to the relationship between Anglo-Welsh relations and English Romantic poetry.

The influence of Welsh culture extended far beyond England in the period, of course: as Caroline Franklin points out, Glamorgan on its own 'produced radical Dissenter Dr Richard Price, an adviser to the new American republic, and the Deist David Williams, who had been invited to advise France on drawing up its new constitution' (p. 74). Yet the Welsh influence on English Romantic poetry emerges as seminal. The influence of eighteenth-century Welsh nationalism, and its revival of Welsh legends such as that of Madoc – indeed its transformation of those legends along increasingly radical lines – are here traced through to various English reworkings of those legends during the Romantic period by poets such as Southey and Hemans. A Welsh context for Coleridge's and Southey's Pantisocracy is uncovered. Wordsworth's sense of Snowdon, and of North Wales more generally, as a place of symbolic resonance is traced back to the re-imaging of Welsh landscapes that occurred in the numerous travel guides of the eighteenth century by both Welsh and English writers. The roots of Southey's, Byron's and Shelley's 'Orientalism' and of their occupation with tensions between nationhood and empire are traced back through William Jones to the work of the Welsh revivalists, their interest in alternatives to the classical tradition, their simultaneous centralising and exoticising of marginalised Celtic culture, their feeding and encouraging of 'the Romantic hunger for the primitive and the exotic' (p. 26), their pivotal role in the shift between the culture of the Enlightenment and that culture we usually call Romantic, and their invaluable reinvigoration of the 'classical gentility of English poetry' with materials drawn from Celtic (and, in the case of Jones, Oriental) sources: allowing, for example, Southey, through his exotically Welsh detailing in *Madoc*, to stylistically assault the 'classical epic as the highest form of poetry' (p. 80).

The work and influence of key Welsh individuals are also discussed in some detail. The subject of Michael J. Franklin's chapter,

William Jones, whose *Grammar of the Persian Language* (1771), Franklin suggests, 'inaugurated Romantic Orientalism' (p. 28) is shown to be a pivotal figure in the movement towards Romantic reversals of (imperialist) English notions of centre and periphery, as offering an early example of what would become central Romantic anxieties about nationhood and empire, as a key influence on Romantic constructions of 'the East', and as a direct influence in numerous ways on the work of Southey, Byron and Shelley.[16] Evan Evans's *Specimens* (1764) is foregrounded as a 'pioneering work of lasting significance for the Celtic revival both for appropriation and imitation in England, and in the reanimation of bardic nationalism in Wales' (p. 26). Edward Williams, one of 'that older generation of antiquarians, folklorists and etymologists who bridged the gap between Enlightenment historiography and the Romantic primitivism of Southey's generation', is brought into view as a 'brilliant forger' to place alongside Macpherson and Chatterton whose Welsh mythmaking was massively influential on subsequent English, and Welsh, culture (p. 71); as is Owen Pugh's enormous influence on Southey, the lasting influence of 'ancient Britain interpretators' such as Byrant, Davies and Stukeley, and the revolutionary influence of Lewis Morris and 'the Morisiad' – an influence pivotal in the creation of an ancient Welsh cultural tradition distinct from England's classical inheritance and rooted in a politicised, poetic Bardic tradition, and one that informs the work of English writers from Blake to Southey, Wordsworth and Hemans.

Nevertheless, the volume is not solely concerned with Celtic influences on English Romantic writing, but with also acknowledging the Celtic-Romantic relationship as more complex and dynamic than a process of straightforward, one-way influence. It seeks to explore further the dynamics of Anglo-Welsh cultural relations in this period. How, for instance, was Welsh culture transformed in its use by English Romantic-period writing? And what influence did English Romanticism have on subsequent Welsh culture?

Here matters of consumption, reception, appropriation and ideology come to the fore and a number of the contributors to this volume get to grips with these. And various kinds of English appropriation of Welsh culture emerge very strongly – appropriations in the service of Romantic, Christian, British and Imperial ideologies.

The English Romantics were handed a highly politicised Welsh inheritance. William Jones, friend of Benjamin Franklin, strongly influenced by Locke, and a precursor of Paine and Godwin, was a radical Whig whose 'On the Gods of Greece, Italy and India' transformed 'for many Welsh, and indeed English, Tories', 'the Druidic Oak into the liberty tree' (p. 32).

Edward Williams, 'the authority of the day on Welsh culture' (p. 71) and a 'radical in the Blakean mould' (p. 71), offered, in works such as *Poems, Lyrical and Pastoral* (1794), 'a vision of the Welsh bardic tradition in which poetry...became a vehicle of theological, political and moral instruction' (p. 72), and, despite having his work branded by the *Gentleman's Magazine* as 'a heterogeneous and unnatural mixture [of] poetry and politics' (p. 78), described a Bardic tradition stretching to his own day in which bards hailed 'the Goddess of liberty' (p. 79). Evan Evans, too, offered his readership a politicised image of this Bardic tradition: in his 'A Paraphrase of Psalm CXXXVII, alluding to the Captivity and Treatment of the Welsh Bards by King Edward I', for example, he has the Welsh Bards resist Edward's tyranny by hanging up their harps and 'silently disobeying the order to entertain their captors' (p. 27), while Lewis Morris looked back to his own Welsh ancestors as 'brave people...who struggled so long with a superior power for their liberty' (p. 24). Each of these writers, in their own way, alongside 'the eighteenth-century emigration movement' (p. 70) in Wales that inspired a newly Millenarian revival of the legend of Madoc, produced images of Welsh culture and history that 'encouraged politicised interpretation' (p. 22).

Sometimes, English Romantic writers accepted the invitation offered to them: J. R. Watson's chapter on Wordsworth argues that North Wales, for example, with 'its defiance of the Roman or English conquerors' suited 'well with Wordsworth's own resistance to tyranny and metropolitan dominance' (p. 96), and shows the poet's use of figures such as Llewellyn the Great often to be a 'celebration' not only of Welsh national defiance, but also 'of what *The Prelude* calls "independence and stern liberty"' (p. 97). In a different way, as William D. Brewer shows us, Hemans's bards retain their 'traditional values and patriot feelings' (p. 180), but in various ways, these writers also display that Romantic, ideological tendency, famously described by Jerome McGann, towards

extreme forms of displacement and poetic conceptualisation whereby the actual human issues with which the poetry is concerned are resituated in a variety of idealised localities.[17]

As Watson shows, Wordsworth's *Ecclesiastical Sonnets*, for instance, 'reveal much of interest to the student of Celtic influences on Wordsworth' and 'beneath the steady progress of Christianity' they describe, 'there is an undercurrent of sympathy for the ancient Druids' (p. 98). Yet, as Watson goes on to demonstrate, while the Druids were 'inspirational' figures who 'encouraged the people of Anglesey in their resistance to the Roman invasion'

(p. 97), and despite images of the Druids offered by Edward Williams, for example, in which the rituals of the Druids of the Romano-British Era are described as 'linked to the Jewish Cabbala and Brahminism . . . entirely by-passing institutional Christianity' (p. 74), they become in Wordsworth's account of the Christianisation of the British Isles, 'auxiliars of the Cross. Wordsworth sees the ancient religion as somehow incorporated into the new reign of Christianity, and the Druids have turned incongruously into [Christian] crusaders' (p. 100). Figures that belong to a 'concrete and particular' historical context have been 'resituated' by Wordsworth in these sonnets 'in an idealised',[18] ideological, Christian 'locality' in 'what seems more like an exercise in pleasing the Sir George Beaumonts of this world than an engagement with the Welsh experience of earlier years' (p. 100).

In a different way, for Hemans, the subject of Brewer's chapter, bardic patriotism becomes a desirable, universal (rather than specifically Welsh) attribute. In Hemans's Bards, that is to say, we see a 'conceptualisation' that involves the loss of that 'concrete and particular' context (or contexts – one ancient, one eighteenth-century, both in tension with another, more powerful culture) that originally generated the images she is drawing on, and the resituating of those images in an 'idealised', ideological, location of international nationalism. Bardic figures dramatising inter-national tension are transformed into models of an international 'cosmopolitanism' that, for Hemans, offer universal dignity, integrity and harmony.

Here Brewer's analysis continues the debate recently opened up by Kirsteen Daly about 'how the tenets of benevolent Enlightenment cosmopolitanism were retained, renegotiated and reformulated in the Romantic Period'.[19] Equally, however, Brewer's analysis of Hemans's poetry suggests that the radical Whig attitudes that latched hold of and transformed the figure of 'the Welsh Bard' in the eighteenth century are notably displaced in Hemans's bardic figures by something more 'spiritual and aesthetic' – and in Wordsworthian ways. Hemans's bards, patriots though they are, are valued primarily for a bardic genius that exemplifies 'an eye that can see Nature, a heart that can feel Nature, and a boldness that dares follow Nature' (p. 175). Hemans's ancient bards, 'resemble the Druids celebrated in Wordsworth's *Prelude*'(p. 174) – indeed for Hemans, Wordsworth was a 'True bard and holy' (p. 175) – and do so precisely because Hemans has transformed her own bards according to, and in the service of, a Wordsworthian Romantic ideology. Hemans transforms the bards of the eighteenth-century Welsh Revival into so many Wordsworthian worshippers of Nature and in doing so forces them to undergo a version of that ideological reinvention described by 'Tintern Abbey' – a reinvention that involves the 'spiritual displacement' of the historical and political and a resituating of conflict 'out of a socio-historical context and into an ideological one'.[20] In Hemans's bards, we might say, historical experience has disappeared in 'the transformation of fact into idea, and of experience into ideology'.[21] Here is an ever more precise understanding of what we mean when we say that Celtic culture was 'Romanticised' in the Romantic period.

The appropriation of the eighteenth-century Welsh Revival by a British, imperialist ideology is described in Caroline Franklin's chapter on Southey's *Madoc*. Drawing on and expanding Lynda Pratt's important recent reconsideration of Southey's *Madoc*,[22] Franklin further opens up the discussion of poetic precedents of, and parallels to, the novelistic appropriations of Celtic culture in the service of British Imperialism that are discussed at length by Trumpener.

Franklin shows that the revival of the Madoc legend was rooted in a Welsh, radical, nationalist response to capitalist English colonialism in Wales: Edward Williams's 'beloved Glamorgan', for example, 'was being transformed out of all recognition by the Bristolian imperialist capitalism from historic rural landscape … to furnace and mine' (p. 73), and this produced in him, as in many others, a dedication 'to the preservation of the Welsh language, literature and culture now seemingly on the verge of extinction with the onset of industrialisation and consequent Anglicisation' (p. 71). Other pressures, too, fed the Welsh nationalist feeling behind the Madoc revival: the influx of thousands of English workers, England's declaration of war 'against revolutionary France and the reactionary backlash against Jacobinism' that followed (p. 75), the success of Burkean reactionaries at the eisteddfodau of the 1790s (p. 75), religious repression across the board (the denial of full civil rights to Dissenters as well as the fact that 'Welsh Anglicans' were 'prohibited from practising their religion in their native language'[p. 79]), and a growing sense of 'the colonial dependence of Wales' (p. 73). In such circumstances, the Madoc legend 'allowed the Welsh … to envision escaping their own colonisation by "the Saxons" through embarking on their own (post)colonial adventure' (p. 79) and offered 'a retreat encoded as an advance' (p. 80).

As Franklin shows, in Southey's hands, a paradox already inherent in the Welsh reworkings of the myth – 'that their American republican paradise was founded on slavery and the suppression of indigenous peoples' (p. 80) – 'soon became apparent' (p. 80). But Southey's 'fascination with military violence in a just cause' (p. 81) and his 'support for the state church as the cornerstone of the British constitution' (p. 81) led easily into the ideological transformation of the myth. In Southey's version of it, the expedition is no longer radical or nationalistic but carries 'the white man's burden of bringing the enlightenment of Christianity to the dark continents of the world, and by the sword if necessary' (p. 82). The emphasis of the poem is on 'the necessity of the Welsh extinguishing the natives' barbaric religious rites' (p. 82).

Religion is the justification for Empire, but it is Southey's appropriation of the Welsh myth of Madoc to ram this point home – and his transformation and Anglicisation of this radical, anti-English and, in some ways, anti-colonial myth – that is of central interest here: firstly, in terms of what it reveals about the internal dynamics of the specific relationship between English Romanticism and the culture of late eighteenth-century Wales, but secondly in terms of what it tells us about the larger internal cultural dynamics of the British state in the Romantic period – about the negotiations within the relationship between the cultures that made up that state. And here we begin to glimpse another kind of English appropriation of Welsh culture during the period – the appropriation of Welsh culture by ideologies of Britishness.

Here the volume intervenes in what Weinbrot calls the 'ongoing discussion of the making of a British nation'[23] – a discussion that was given renewed momentum in the 1990s by the work of commentators such as Weinbrot himself, Robert Crawford, Colin Kidd, Pittock[24] and, perhaps most famously, Linda Colley, whose *Britons: Forging the Nation 1707–1837* explored the extent to which 'the invention of Britishness was . . . closely bound up with Protestantism, with war with France, and with the acquisition of empire'.[25] But sustaining that invention necessitated the displacement of past enmity with myths of originary unity, and this is one of the key issues at stake in David Punter's chapter on Blake.

As Punter shows, Blake's poetry offers one example of this kind of displacement, indeed, Blake's poetry, as illuminated by Punter, offers both a good example of, and a commentary on, some of the mechanisms by which one of Benedict Anderson's paradoxes of nationalism are set in place – that between 'the objective modernity of nations to the historian's eye' and 'their subjective antiquity in the eye of the nationalist'.[26]

Taking the work of Gilles Deleuze and Felix Guattari, Benedict Anderson and James Whittaker as points of departure,[27] Punter focuses our attention on a 'strain that runs right through Blake's work' in which 'modern history is underlain . . . by . . . a history that is an essential founding myth of the British nation state' (p. 55), pointing out that 'the perceived

necessity of elaborating a myth of Britishness' in the late eighteenth century
was 'fostered by the need to consolidate national identity in the context of
international imperialism and European war'(pp. 55–56). Blake's response
to this perceived necessity and its effects is a 'complex revisualisation of
the historical and geographical problematic that is "Britain"' (p. 56) that
highlights some of the key features of the wider, Romantic-period appropriation of Wales – indeed of the Celtic more generally – into an ideology
of Britishness.

Blake offers, for example, a 'mapping' of 'contested territories' that locates the Celtic nations 'on the brink of an overwhelming extinction'
(p. 57) but also 'as the guardians of the guardian, as the outer bulwarks
of the state, as protection' (p. 57) *and* 'a specific staging post on the route of
a diaspora, a point from which a new grouping can be promulgated' (p. 58).
Equally, the 'apparent symmetries that inflect' (p. 60) Blake's portrayal of
Britishness do not hide the hierarchies imposed by Britain's appropriation
of the Celtic. There 'is always here a centre and a periphery, a controlling figure and a set of "figures" to be controlled: the Celtic nations are
placed on the fringes, whether as guardians and protectors or mere adjuncts'
(p. 60).

By foregrounding such features of the British appropriation and revisualisation of the Celtic, Blake offers, Punter suggests, a vision of 'the fallen
state which is the "state" of the sleeping Albion': a state that does not strive
'to embody national aspiration' so much as 'suppress national difference. . .
deny peripheral power and. . . bend everything into the service of an ever-
expanding state' (p. 61).

But, as Punter shows, Blake also suggests an absolute limit to the state's
ability to 'obscure the ruins that are all that remain' of what 'it has erased'
(pp. 65–66) by embodying, in the figure of 'Gwendolen', 'the impossibility, indeed the inconceivability, of a resolution' of the task of forming the
British state 'into a smooth space' and ridding it 'of internal contradictions,
to achieve the fantasised goal of "intraconsistency"' (p. 61). For in Blake's
Gwendolen, we see the Celtic nations 'remain as haunting memories, as that
which continues to challenge the *absence of memory* which is the essential
ground for the foundation of the state' (p. 65). Punter's analysis suggests,
then, that, for Blake, the Celtic remains as 'a set of impossible transformations that bite at the heels of the state' (p. 66). Indeed, Blake's vision of
the British appropriation of the Celtic ultimately highlights 'Britain's "war
with itself" during his lifetime as well as problems associated with enlightenment, modernity, progress' (p. 66): problems that powerfully inform a

wide range of relationships between English Romanticism and the Celtic world, and surface repeatedly in this volume.

In the eighteenth century, as the foregoing suggests, Wales reinvented itself only to be then reinvented, in various ways, by an English, Romantic audience. The image of Wales carried forward into the Victorian period is a combination of these two reinventions, but moves forward, of course, only to be reinvented further by other interactions between the cultures of England and Wales. Edward Williams's 'mythology of Celticism', for example, 'was cut adrift from its radical origins and appropriated by a new reactionary generation of respectable Anglicans and gentry, whose picturesque and sometimes grotesque Romantic nationalism seemingly acted as a harmless safety valve for discontent with the colonial status and industrial exploitation of Wales' (p. 84). Indeed, a kind of cultural 'dialogue' between the cultures of England and Wales – an unequal dialogue fundamentally concerned with the colonisation, appropriation and exploitation of Wales and with the defence of Wales against these – that predates, underlies and makes possible that between late eighteenth-century Welsh culture and early nineteenth-century English culture – a dialogue that in some respects initiated the eighteenth-century Welsh reinvention of itself – makes itself loudly heard in the chapters of this volume.

Firstly, as Trumpener has noted, 'Welsh nationalists' in the period were 'driven by a resentment of hegemonic Englishness' (p. 15) and this volume offers numerous examples of this drive and the literature it helped to generate – the construction of a Welsh national identity by Lewis Morris and others that had its roots in a Bardic tradition and inheritance quite distinct from the classical parentage claimed and celebrated by 'Augustan' England could stand as a typical example here. Secondly, we have already seen the intimately related reaction against the immediate effects of English capitalism and imperialism that was a generative influence in the Madoc revival.

But the imaginative reconstructions of Wales that are involved in these responses to a hegemonic and imperial England are themselves in a dialogue with England and Englishness, contributing, for example a reconstruction of Englishness to the ongoing dialogue between the two cultures. For the Wales that is invented by the Madoc legend and by Lewis is defined by its difference from an England figured as unrelentingly imperialistic and tyrannical. Only against this 'other' does Wales become the land of resistance and the fight for liberty. England reconstructs Wales as a colony, Wales responds by reconstructing England as a tyrant and defines itself against that reconstruction, only to find its self-definition reappropriated into England's reconstruction of itself as the centre of Britain and an expanding empire. But even before Wales is reappropriated by English culture, we hear the voice of English culture in its own self-inventions. For England is one of principal intended recipients of, and target audiences for, Wales's self-refashioning. Here 'restraint had to be exercised in the transmission of "alien" cultures' (p. 22), and the efforts of many Welsh Revivalists to win 'consumer approval'(p. 22) in England powerfully mark their constructions of Welshness. Edward Williams's *Poems, Lyrical and Pastoral*, for example, offer images of Wales and the Welsh Bardic tradition 'calculated to appeal to aristocratic subscribers like Elizabeth Montagu, and writers such as Anna Barbauld, Francis Burney Anna Seward' (p. 77), while Evan Evans does not imitate his own Bards in their 'refusal to be culturally appropriated by the dominant power': instead, Evans writes 'in English... supplying footnoted allusions to Milton, Dryden and Goldsmith' and handing the poem's climax over to Gray (p. 27).[28] As a result of such compromises and capitulations, eighteenth-century popular Celticism and literary (and to varying degrees anti-English) Welsh nationalism often produce a Wales paradoxically shaped by English literary tastes and, in the process, politically neutralised – perfectly packaged, we might say, for the English Romantic depoliticisation and/or appropriation of it.

The Wales of the Celtic Revival, then, is often the product of this kind of dialogue between Welsh impulses and English tastes. But equally, the Welsh impulses themselves are shaped by an earlier, ideological dialogue with England. For we can frequently hear the distinctive idiom of Whiggism – an idiom of 'liberty', 'independence' and 'resistance' against 'corruption' and 'tyranny' – in the Revival's celebrations of Welsh history: in Lewis Morris's celebration of his ancestors' struggle 'with a superior power for their liberty' (p. 24), in the 'resistance' against English 'tyranny' of Evan Evans's bards, in the powerful influence of Locke on William Jones's *Principles of Government, in a Dialogue between a Scholar and a Peasant* (1782) as well as in his one-time aim of writing 'a verse epic of tremendous scope' to be called 'Britain Discovered' and 'intended as a poetical panegyric on our excellent Constitution,... as a national epic' (p. 35). Figures of Welsh history are frequently either appealing because of their seeming closeness to the Whig ideal, or reimagined through the ideals of English Whiggism. To a considerable extent, in other words, Wales's eighteenth-century self-reinvention is a reconstruction of the Welsh past along ideological lines laid down by an English political tradition.[29] As a result, its assimilation into various English agendas in the Romantic period – a period in which English writers as diverse as Wordsworth and Byron could think of themselves as in some way belonging to the Whig tradition – was all the easier to achieve.

But then, this kind of cultural interaction, in which Wales is colonised, appropriated or exploited – economically, culturally and spiritually – by English ideologies and agendas, but responds by refashioning itself in self-defence, only to be recolonised, reappropriated and re-exploited, has a long history. The history of the Madoc legend marks out key stages of this cultural history: not least its 'original status as wish fulfilment after the principality's subjugation by Edward I, and the crushing of the subsequent rebellion of Owain Glyn Dwr' (p. 83) and its co-option 'to the service of promoting colonialism' in 'Tudor times' (p. 83).[30]

Similar histories can be traced, of course, in the Anglo-Irish and Anglo-Scottish dialogues that run parallel to this Anglo-Welsh history. But this volume is concerned with those dialogues between all the four nations of Britain that powerfully informed, and that were, in their turn, powerfully informed by, English Romantic writing. In the case of all of the territories of England, Ireland, Scotland and Wales, and at both the sites of Romanticism and Celticism we see negotiated dialogues where complicated questions of aesthetics, cultural politics and nation are asked, and answered in equally complex fashion. It is as a contribution to the mapping out of these multiple late eighteenth- and early nineteenth-century British cultural territories and inter-national dialogues that this volume offers itself to the reader.

CHAPTER 2

Sir William Jones, the Celtic Revival and the Oriental Renaissance

Michael J. Franklin

The Celtic Revival and the Oriental Renaissance have complex cultural, ethnological, political and poetical interconnections; each maximised the prestige of the peripheral and the colonial, establishing relationships with the 'English' coloniser which had the power to fascinate or repel, to consolidate or fragment metropolitan self-absorption. This cultural colonisation of the Occident by the Orient and of the Anglo-Saxon by the Celtic created an important part of the agenda for Romanticism and will constitute the area explored by this chapter.

William Jones, the Welsh Orientalist, argued that a Europe poetically saturated with a classical past should look eastward for new inspiration. His Enlightenment concern for accuracy of translation and comparative linguistic method created a demand for genuine Eastern products whilst significantly adjusting racial and political stereotypes. 'On the Poetry of the Eastern Nations' (1772) established Jones as a precursor of the Romantics, and his revision of pastoral involved not faint shepherds but the full-blooded Bedouin of the *Moallakát* (1782). In their irrepressible resistance to despotic power, the proud Yemeni nomads recall Gray's Welsh Bard, providing an Oriental displacement of Jones's Celtic genealogy. The infusing of a primitivist energy into the genre anticipates Wordsworth's *Preface to the Lyrical Ballads*. Similarly, Jones's 'On the Arts, commonly called Imitative' (1772) is remarkable for its proto-Wordsworthian definition of poetry as 'originally no more than a strong and animated expression of the human passions', an emotionalist concept of art prefiguring Romantic subjectivity.

Sir William Jones accomplished Oriental Renaissance in the West and cultural revolution in India. The powerful combination of Hastings's Orientalist government policies and Jones's long-held ambition to initiate Europe into the vast literary treasures of the East inaugurated a series of translations from the Sanskrit which radically adjusted metropolitan conceptions of Hindu culture, introducing disturbing notions of relationship between coloniser and colonised.

The Hastings/Jones nexus inevitably implicated this Oriental Renaissance in current political debate concerning the government of 'British' India. Orientalism now was more than a fashion, it embraced an emergent structure of power as Britain perfected its own variety of Asiatic/ Enlightened despotism through the transformation of the East India Company into the role of 'merchant-sovereign and sovereign merchant'.[1] The American revolution and the long years of the Hastings impeachment intensified controversies concerning the nature and control of imperial power and the gulf between contrasting cultures which problematised colonial government. Permanent settlements, however, were also being sought in places much closer than India. The mid-century saw the military reduction of Highlanders as well as Marathas; racial, religious and political prejudice against the beleaguered Celtic cultures to the North and West of a strengthening Metropole underlined the tensions of internal colonialism, which were to be further exacerbated by Britain's exposure to Eastern mythologies.[2]

The Highlander James Macpherson, nephew to the infamous Jacobite Cluny Macpherson, was born in 1736 at Invertromie uncomfortably close to Ruthven Barracks. In the years between the blood-letting of Culloden in 1746 and George IV's tartan tour of Edinburgh in 1822 the threat to internal security was replaced by a cultural invasion of the glamorised third-century Highland warrior-poet. In rehearsing "barbarous" Celtic matter in and to the Hanoverian English, the Ossianic poems, as Fiona Stafford has shown, re-enact at a romanticising and safe distance a cultural confrontation only too real to the young Macpherson.[3]

His three collections of prose-poetry published between 1760 and 1763 represented a timely challenge to the Augustan imagination which erupted into the greatest literary sensation of the eighteenth century as private doubts concerning authenticity gave way to public controversy. There was a widely perceived need for fresh imagery.[4] What was most important was that the classical gentility of English poetry might be exposed to reinvigorating traditional materials whether from Celtic or Oriental sources; authenticity was for many a secondary consideration. William Collins had admired the 'rich and figurative' manner of Middle Eastern poetry, but his *Persian Eclogues* (1742) had proved only pretended translations. Macpherson's fabrications came to represent the quintessence of primitive and heroic verse, a distinguished poetic achievement for which he could necessarily only enjoy a reflected glory.

William Jones, however, born ten years after Macpherson and a generation removed from his own ancestral roots in Druidic Anglesey,

established his reputation as Orientalist upon translation of authentic originals, colourfully illustrating Middle-Eastern literature in French, Latin
and English, and urging Europeans to learn Arabic and Persian.[5] Elizabeth
Montagu spread Ossian's fame amidst Bluestocking circles, contributing to
Macpherson's research trip to the Gaelic Highlands. Such patronage was
duly extended to Persian Jones, and Mrs Montagu, unconcerned as to
whether her senses ached to the productions of Asiatic or Jonesian imagination, writes to Scottish poet and critic James Beattie:

> There is a gayety & splendor in the poems which is naturally derived from the
> happy soil & climate, of the Poets & they breathe Asiatick luxury, or else Mr Jones
> is himself a man of most splendid imagination. The descriptions are so fine, &
> all the objects so brilliant, *that the sense aches at them*, & I wish'd that Ossians
> poems had been laying by me, that I might sometimes have turn'd my eyes from
> ye dazzling splendor of the Eastern noon day to the moonlight picture of a bleak
> mountain. Every object in these pieces is blooming & beautiful; every plant is
> odouriferous; the passions too are of the sort which belong to Paradise.[6]

Enlightened consumer approval such as this testified to the success with
which both Macpherson and Jones had finely judged metropolitan tastes.
Novelty and difference were marketable features, but restraint had to be
exercised in the transmission of 'alien' cultures. Readers had been alienated by what Thomas Warton termed the 'tincture of horror' in Runic
imagery.[7] It was a problem that was to exercise Jones's ingenuity in his
cultural translation of Hinduism, notably in Kālidāsa's *Śakuntalā* and particularly Jayadéva's erotic allegory, *Gitagovinda*.[8]

The Ossian controversy and Jones's Oriental translations encouraged
scholarly research into the relationships between poetry, history, and national character. Jones, seeking to dispel stereotypes of Asian despotic deca-
dence, gives a prose translation from Saʿdī's *Bostân* of King Nushirvan's
advice to his son Hormuz; such sentiments 'a century or two ago, . . . would
have been suppressed in Europe, for spreading, with too strong a glare,
the light of liberty and reason'.[9] The Ossianic texts also positively encouraged politicised interpretation. Productions of the Celtic fringe could be
fashionably received as primitive and violent in the reader's search for the
Rousseauistic and the sublime, or nationalistically promoted as civilised
and humane in the polemicist's desire to elevate Scotland. Hugh Blair,
the Scottish academic, advocates both the ethnic and poetic superiority
of the primitive oral epic: 'In humanity, magnanimity, virtuous feelings
of every kind, our rude Celtic Bard' contrasts with the moral shortcom-
ings of the heroes of Homer and Virgil.[10] Whether the glorification was of

third- or eighteenth-century Scotland, few Northern Britons could resist involvement in 'the great national question of Ossian'. Walter Scott, a non-believer, confessed, almost half a century later:

[W]hile we are compelled to renounce the pleasing idea, 'that Fingal lived, and that Ossian sung', our national vanity may be equally flattered by the fact that a remote, and almost a barbarous corner of Scotland, produced in the eighteenth century, a bard, capable not only of making an enthusiastic impression on every mind susceptible of poetic beauty, but of giving a new tone to poetry throughout Europe.[11]

In the 1760s the impetus that both Ossianism and the perceived need to refute Macpherson's imposture had given to the expansion of the canon, the popularising of research into native antiquities and textual history, and intensifying Celtomania demonstrated that even fake antiquarianism can nonetheless prove powerful politics.

In a remote but remarkably 'civilised' corner of Wales, Lewis Morris (1701–65) powerfully presided over a resourceful group of amateur scholars who were painstakingly uncovering the wealth of a heritage which they claimed as pre-Roman, Druidic, a classical tradition independent of Greece and Rome.[12] This influential Anglesey circle, the Morisiad, included his brothers Richard and William Morris, Williams Wynn, Goronwy Owen and Evan Evans. Pioneering prime movers of a Welsh renaissance, they acknowledged the inheritance of two key and interconnected traditions. Firstly, they took into account the antiquarian projects of Edward Lhuyd (1660–1709), Keeper of the Ashmolean Museum and author of *Archæologia Britannica* (1707), and of Moses Williams (1685–1742), his pupil, who had proposed to publish important Welsh manuscripts languishing in private libraries. Secondly, and even more vitally, they respected their bardic patrimony, convinced that the Welsh poetic tradition was unbroken; a conviction which their mastery of the old rules reinforced as they linked medieval and modern Welsh poetry in the strict metres of *cynghanedd* supposedly inherited from Druid times. This cultural inheritance was formally manifested in The Honourable Society of Cymmrodorion, founded by the resourceful Richard Morris in 1751, but despite its ambitious aims for research and patronage, the London Welsh often proved more concerned with conviviality than culture.[13]

Lewis Morris was surveyor of the western coastline of Wales for the Admiralty, a man of rare intellectual versatility, whose wide-ranging interests embraced the practical: mining, mineralogy, farming, carpentry; the scholarly: a respected antiquarian, a correspondent of Thomas Carte, Samuel

Pegge and Thomas Warton (who admitted his indebtedness to Morris in *History of English Poetry* (1774–81); and the creative: a talented poet and composer, who could make a harp and compose the *penillion* (harp stanzas) to be sung to it.[14] His interest in the pedigrees of old Welsh families, intensified by his awareness of an increasingly Anglicised gentry, almost justifies Vanbrugh's description of Wales in *Aesop* (*c*.1697) as 'a Country in the World's back-side, where every Man is born a Gentleman and a Genealogist'.[15] On New Year's Day 1748 he wrote to his old friend William ap Sion Siors (son of John George), known in London as William Jones, FRS, 'Longitude Jones', celebrated mathematician, and father of the future Orientalist:

It was a custom among the Ancient Britons (and still retained in Anglesey) for the most knowing among them in the descent of families, to send their friends of the same stock or family, *a dydd calan Ionawr* [on New Year's Day] a *calennig* [New Year's gift], a present of their pedigree.[16]

This family tree demonstrates that the Morrises and the Joneses were closely related and that, despite their yeoman origins in the significantly named Llanfihangel Tre'r Beirdd (The Parish of St Michael, Town of the Bards), they shared an ancestry deriving from Hwfa ap Cynddelw and the princes of Gwynedd.[17] '[T]he very thought of those brave people', continues Morris, 'who struggled so long with a superior power for their liberty, inspires me with such an idea of them, that I almost adore their memories'.

The Anglesey predilection for 'the descent of families' was to mark the careers of both Lewis Morris and William Jones. For the Admiralty surveyor of the coast of Wales the emphasis was upon classical genealogy, for Oriental Jones, surveying the coast of India, it was Biblical genealogy and speculations concerning linguistic families that occupied his mind. And the results of Jones's investigations were destined to redraw the map of European thought.

For Lewis Morris and his circle it was intense awareness of cultural distinctiveness that sharpened their interest in the rehabilitation of the ancestral past. Anxious to support the authenticity of Geoffrey of Monmouth's work, he elaborated a thesis that the original genius behind *Historia Regum Britanniae* was a seventh-century saint named Tysilio, whose writings Geoffrey had both embellished and mangled.[18] Lewis appreciated that Wales boasted several possible national and transnational lineages, and, not unnaturally, the image of wild Celtic tribesmen resisting Caesar was eclipsed by a prestigious pedigree of pre-Roman antiquity.[19] Following the empirical comparative method of his equally patriotic mentor, Edward Lhuyd, he reinvigorated the tradition, stemming from Nennius and Geoffrey's source, which traced the origin of the Britons to Brutus, great-grandson of Aeneas, entitling the Welsh to claim noble descent from the same royal Trojan line that founded Rome. This invented tradition produced a potent enabling vision of a separate and superior Welsh history. Furthermore, the Morris circle, centred as it was in the atmospheric Ynys Môn, acknowledged the Druidic origin of the Welsh Bards with its alternative classicism, the Bardic system of poetry.

Adopting what James Clifford has termed the 'salvage paradigm', and only too aware of the decline of traditional patronage in the face of an absentee or Anglicised gentry, the Morrises anticipated what was to become Herder's emphasis upon poetic liberation and regeneration, rejecting cultural enslavement, whether it be to England or classical antiquity.[20] For them Wales possessed an autonomous cultural authority, separate from England, and its own intimate links with the civilisation of the South and the ancient wisdom of the East; a tradition whose venerable ancestry rendered classical ancients modern. Wales had its own 'Ancients', and an unbroken Bardic tradition binding the nation together across time with links as intricate and powerful as the interlocked consonantal-chiming of *cynghanedd*. Lewis Morris wrote to Evan Evans in 1756:

As for your sheltering under Horace's wings, I mind it as nothing. He was a stranger to our methods, handed down to us by his masters, the Druidical bards, who knew how to sing before Rome had a name. So never hereafter mention such moderns as Horace & Virgil, when you talk of British Poetry, Llywarch Hen, Aneurin, and the followers of the Druids, are our men and Nature our Rule.[21]

But for 'Persian' Jones, writing in 1768 to Charles Reviczky, the Hungarian Orientalist, it was the poetry of the Middle East that was displacing his classical inheritance:

From my earliest years, I was charmed with the poetry of the Greeks; nothing, I then thought, could be more sublime than the Odes of Pindar, nothing sweeter than Anacreon, nothing more polished and elegant than the golden remains of Sappho, Archilochus, Alcæus, and Simonides: but when I had tasted the poetry of the Arabs and Persians...[22]

Sixteen years later in Calcutta, Jones's discovery of the beauties of Sanskrit literature proved a revelation which he was anxious to communicate to the European reading public:

I am in love with the *Gopia*, charmed with *Crishen*, an enthusiastick admirer of *Rām*, and a devout adorer of *Brimha-bishen-mehais*: not to mention that *Jūdishteīr*, *Arjen*, *Corno*, and the other warriours of the *M'hab'harat* appear greater in my eyes than Agamemnon, Ajax, and Achilles appeared, when I first read the Iliad.[23]

He records his enthusiasm for a translation of one of the *Purānas*: 'it is by far the most entertaining book, on account of its novelty and wildness, that I ever read'.[24] Both Jones and his colleagues of the Asiatick Society and the Morris circle can be seen as purveyors of wildness and novelty, feeding the Romantic hunger for the primitive and the exotic. Certainly, Jones's excitement is remarkably similar to that of Lewis Morris, almost three decades earlier, in the uncovering of the cultural riches of the *Cynfeirdd* (early poets), as he writes to the scholar and poet Edward Richard:

Who do you think I have at my elbow, as happy as ever Alexander thought himself after a conquest? No less a man than Ieuan Fardd [Evan Evans], who hath discovered some old MSS. lately that no body of this age or the last ever as much as dreamed of. And this discovery is to him and me as great as that of America by Columbus. We have found an epic poem in the British called Gododin, equal at least to the Iliad, Aeneid, or Paradise Lost.[25]

It had been Lewis Morris who inspired Evan Evans (Ieuan Fardd [Bard], Ieuan Brydydd Hir [Tall Bard]; 1731–88) with both a love of the old Welsh metres and the zeal of the antiquarian. Second only to Goronwy Owen as a classical poet, Evans channelled his energies and the scant resources of a series of forty pound a year curacies into the location and copying of important manuscripts mouldering in the attics of Anglicised gentry. Evans's *Some Specimens of the Poetry of the Antient Welsh Bards* (1764) was the first substantial selection of the poetry of the *Cynfeirdd* and of the *Gogynfeirdd* ('fairly early poets', court poets of the medieval princes) to be printed. Including a thirty-page Latin treatise, 'Dissertatio de Bardis', from which Gray was to draw for his 'The Triumphs of Owen', 'The Death of Hoël', 'Caradog' and 'Conan', this was a pioneering work of lasting significance for the Celtic revival both for appropriation and imitation in England, and in the reanimation of bardic nationalism in Wales.

In this connection it is interesting to observe the self-reflexive relation-ships on the one hand between scholarly and popular Celticism, and on the other between literary nationalism and political neutralisation in re-sponse to the discoveries of Welsh cultural revival. Evans, in a later poem, 'A Paraphrase of Psalm CXXXVII, Alluding to the Captivity and Treatment of the Welsh Bards by King Edward I', provides his own Biblical gloss to the invented tradition of Edward 'bardicide' by presenting the exiled bards in Babylonian captivity hanging up their harps by 'the willowy Thames', silently disobeying the order to entertain their captors. Their refusal to be culturally appropriated by the dominant power is admired but not imitated by Evans, writing in English and supplying footnoted allusions to Milton, Dryden, and Goldsmith; their Druidic defiance is ventriloquised by Gray, who also provides the poem's climacteric:

> Gray's pale spectre seems to sing,
> 'Ruin seize thee, ruthless King.'[26]

In addition to its intrinsic interest to the young Jones, newly elected to a Bennet Fellowship at Oxford in 1764, Evans's *Antient Welsh Bards*, through its use of Welsh, English and Latin, provided a model of multi-levelled and international appeal; it located an audience for authentic translations from verifiable texts included within the volume. This was the readership, equally eager for the scholarly and the extravagant, upon which Jones was to focus, with increasing shrewdness, during the next thirty years. Furthermore, Evans pointed the way by indicating imaginative similarities between the Celtic and the Oriental:

For there are not such extravagant flights in any poetic compositions, except it be in the Eastern, to which, as far as I can judge by the few translated specimens I have seen, they bear a great resemblance.[27]

Although Ossian demonstrated that among ancient Britons 'poetry shone forth with a light, that seems astonishing to many readers', Evans reveals his doubts concerning the Gaelic offerings by appearing puzzled that unlike sixth-century or even medieval Welsh poems, the third-century Ossian's are 'perfectly intelligible'. Where Lewis Morris had labelled Macpherson 'a rogue sheep-stealer', and demanded to see the originals, Evans adopts a scholarly, sceptical stance. In a letter to Thomas Percy, he remarks: 'The Scots have made it a national affair, and therefore what they say in its plea ought to weigh the less', but he is well aware of the nationalistic relevance of his own discoveries, both in terms of Celtic rivalry and centre-periphery relations.[28]

Encouraged by the interest of Gray, a long and mutually beneficial dialogue with Percy, and the negotiations of the antiquarian, Daines Barrington with Dodsley, Evans's *Antient Welsh Bards*, dedicated to Sir Roger Mostyn and the Morris brothers, brought him scholarly prestige, the approbation of Johnson, but little cash.[29] Here the contrast with Jones appears particularly sharp. Jones's first major publication (excluding a prestigious commission from Christian VII of Denmark, *Histoire de Nader Chah*

(1770), which brought no financial reward) was his *Grammar of the Persian Language* (1771), a text which simultaneously inaugurated Romantic Orientalism and represented a work of utility in the training of East India Company writers. The doors of the Turk's Head and the Royal Society were open to Persian Jones while Ieuan Brydydd Hir could not even obtain a living. Bishop Percy and Johnson attempted to recommend Evans but had no acquaintance with the bishop of St Davids.[30] It was all about connections, and Jones had them in abundance. Via the Spencers, he had an entrée to the world of Whig magnates; Percy was a companion at the Literary Club; Justice Daines Barrington, a colleague on the Welsh circuits; Sir Roger Mostyn invited Jones to dinner whereas Evans might only aspire to the library.[31]

From 1775 to his Bengal Supreme Court appointment in 1783, William Jones practised on the Welsh circuits where he encountered Anglicised landowners, rack-renting squirearchy and the capricious power of magistrates. Jones's egalitarian principles aligned him with the under-privileged, frequently representing the colonised Welsh without a fee. His letters to the Spencers describing the almost feudal oppression of the Welsh 'peasantry and lower yeomanry' applied a powerful corrective to contemporary patrician conceptions of Wales as a little-visited haven of pastoral content, an appealing retreat of quietude and quietism where a contented pauper peasantry managed to combine independence with obedience.[32]

The barrister's social mobility and ethnic hybridity (his mother was English) allowed a multiple perspective; it was as the grandson of an Anglesey sheep-farmer that Jones deprecated rural tyranny, but it was with the ease of a London Welsh celebrity-scholar that he socialised with the more enlightened gentry.[33] While Evans was railing at the 'Anglo-Welsh bishops', as he termed them, for their hostility to Welsh culture, and their ignorance of the language, Jones was courting Anna Maria, the eldest daughter of the nepotist, pluralist, and English, Bishop of St Asaph, Jonathan Shipley.[34] While Curate Evans was tramping the damp byways of Wales, his leather satchel stuffed with books, anxious to gain admittance to yet another gentleman's library, Jones, on his grey mare or later in his chaise, recounted the delights of the Welsh picturesque to his former pupil, Viscount Althorp. Such a straightforward contrast is complicated, however, by Jones's radical Whig politics. He also sent his aristocratic correspondent poems such as 'An Ode in Imitation of Alcæus' (1781), shortly to have a huge popular audience through its publication by Major Cartwright's Society for Constitutional Information as a single leaf octavo to be distributed gratis. 'I composed [these verses] in my chaise between Abergavenny and Brecon and wrote them down in the mountains of Trecastle'. In answer to the rhetorical question of the first line, '*Althorp*, what forms a state?' Jones declares:

> Men, who their duties know,
> But know their rights, and knowing dare maintain,
> Prevent the long-aim'd blow,
> And crush the tyrant, while they rend the chain;
> These constitute a state.[35]   (13–17)

Evans, meanwhile, continued to lament the flimsy intellectual basis for Celtic revival and the arrogance of Anglophone Welsh bishops. He wrote to Lewis Morris from the Denbighshire depths of Llanfair Talhaiarn:

I am afraid, if I continue here much longer, I shall commence a downright savage, so few persons are there in this country that relish anything of learning, or are in any way encouragers of it: and, to complete my misfortune, our Bishops look upon me with an evil eye, because I dare have affection for my country, language, and antiquities, which, in their opinion, had better been lost and forgotten, and which some of them have had the front to maintain in their sermons . . .[36]

Significantly when he composes a poem in Gwent (two years earlier than Jones's Brecon ode), he chooses to write *englynion*, the oldest Welsh metres, to the court of Ifor ap Llewelyn (Ifor Hael), the celebrated patron of Dafydd ap Gwilym. Standing amidst the ruins of the court at Basaleg, in the company of the controversial Druid-democrat, scholar and inventor of tradition, Edward Williams (Iolo Morganwg), he mourns the decline of Welsh bardism and the ancient patronage system which maintained it:

> Llys Ifor Hael! gwael yw'r gwedd, – yn garnau
> Mewn gwerni mae'n gorwedd;
> Drain ac ysgall mall a'i medd,
> Mieri, lle bu mawredd.
>
> Yno nid oes awenydd – na beirddion
> Na byrddau llawenydd,
> Nac aur yn ei magwyrydd,
> Na mael, na gwr hael a'i rhydd.[37]
>
> Ifor Hael's court, wretched sight,
> A ruined pile amidst the alders.
> Thorns and thistles inhabit there,
> And bramble where once was majesty.
>
> No Bard is there, no poets,
> No feasting tables,
> Nor gold inside these walls,
> No bounty, no free-handed generosity.

There are mordant ironies surrounding the fact that when William Jones met Evans in Carmarthen in the spring of 1779, the barrister was on his circuit and the curate was learning Hebrew and Arabic, two languages in which Jones excelled, at the Presbyterian Academy. When Sir Watkin Williams Wynn heard of this apparent neglect of Welsh studies, he short-sightedly withdrew Evans's pension of twenty pounds a year, proving that in 'preferring actors, musicians, and conjurers to men of learning', he was no Ifor Hael.[38] Evans describes Jones as 'gwr mwyn a rhadlon' (a gentle and gracious man), and Jones gave him an address to correspond. The opportunity of availing himself of Jones's connections was apparently missed, and Evans returned to a damp room at Aberystwyth, more concerned with the dangers this represented to his precious manuscripts than to his fragile health.

In his scarce leisure time, Jones, inspired by the researches into the *Cynfeirdd* and *Gogynfeirdd* undertaken by his Anglesey relations, fellow Cymmrodorion, and London Welshmen, could indulge in recreational Celticism. He initiated the society of the 'Druids of Cardigan', in which his facility for virtually extempore composition suited him for the role of *pencerdd*, or chief Bard, and his growing reputation as a jurist allied him to the learned, legislating Druids. The playful hedonism of an early lyric such as 'Damsels of Cardigan' (1779) links the Celtic and the Romantic by both reflecting Lewis Morris's interpretation of the Druidic tradition (quoted above) in which 'Nature [is] our Rule', and anticipating the theme of Wordsworth's 'Expostulation and Reply' and 'The Tables Turned':

> Leave Year-books and parchments to grey-bearded sages,
> Be Nature our law, and fair woman our book.
> ('The Damsels of Cardigan', lines 48–9)[39]

Another Anglo-Welsh poem written for the Cardigan Druids, 'Kneel to the Goddess whom all Men Adore' (1780), a mock-heroic address to Muslims, Christians, Hindus, Parsees, pagan Greeks and Romans who all worship the same goddess be she called Diana, Mary or Astarte, reveals Jones's Enlightened deism, recently appalled by personal experience of the anti-Catholic Gordon riots in early June 1780:

> What means all this frensy, what mad men are they
> Who broil and are broil'd for a shade in religion?
> Since all sage inspirers one doctrine convey
> From Numa's wild nymph to sly Mohamed's pigeon.
> Then Druids arise,
> Teach the world to be wise

And the grape's rosy blood for your sacrifice pour,
Th' immortals invoke,
And under this oak
Kneel, kneel to the Goddess whom all men adore.[40]

(1–10)

Here, 'on the brink of old Teifi', Jones humorously flags the syncretic approach he would adopt in his path-breaking essay 'On the Gods of Greece, Italy, and India' (1784) which tempered comparativism with relativism to establish the classical dignity of the Hindu pantheon on a par with Olympian heathenism.

When dark visag'd Bramins obsequiously bow
To the rock whence old Ganges redundantly gushes,
They feign that they bend to the form of a cow,
And save by this fiction the fair maiden's blushes;
But from Sanscritan Vedes
The discov'ry proceeds
That her aid, whom we honor, e'en Bramin implores;
Like us wildly they dance,
Like us lightly advance,
And kneel to the Goddess whom all men adore.

(31–40)

Aware of the traditions associating Druids and Brahmans, he stresses monotheistic similitude, and the identity of Oriental and Occidental enthusiasm in the repeated 'Like us'. The Vedas describe the purifying Ganges as flowing from the beautiful head of Śiva, as depicted in Jones's 'Hymn to Gangā' (1785), but the reference to saving 'the fair maiden's blushes' (symbolising Occidental sensibilities) would seem to indicate that these Brahmans are bowing to *Bīja*, or semen, which is worshipped as the Ganges flowing from the head of the *Śiva-linga*. The expurgating 'fiction' with which he credits the 'Bramins' ironises what was to prove one of Jones's major tasks in domesticating the overt eroticism of Hinduism. The reference to the Vedas as providing a source of enlightenment foreshadows his later discoveries concerning the comparability of Vedic and Platonic thought, prefiguring that cultural tact with which he was later to avert European eyes from the 'monstrous gods and demonic devotees' of the popular cults upon which the Evangelicals and utilitarians focussed with a horrified delight.

Despite the playful tone and occasion of this poem, contemporary efforts to renew ancient customs of Bardic congresses and eisteddfodau exercised more than a literary fascination for Jones:

See, Teifi, with joy see our mystical rite
On steep woody marge after ages renewed;
Here once Taliesin thou heard'st with delight,
But what was his voice to the voice of our Druid?[41]

(61–4)

The penultimate stanza of the poem as we have it prepares to reveal Druidic
mysteries, the profane are banished, leaving only a select congregation of
passionate lovers, whose devotion is mirrored in the stillness of nature.
Revelation, however, is denied the reader through lack of closure; the
incomplete manuscript yields only the half-line, 'The young oak is an
emblem...'

For many Welsh, and indeed English, Tories, Jones was transforming the
Druidic oak into the liberty tree. *The Principles of Government, in a Dialogue
between a Scholar and a Peasant* (1782), written at the Paris house of his old
friend Benjamin Franklin to convince him that the mysteries of the state
might be made intelligible to the working man, involved industrialising
Flintshire in a notorious episode in the history of the reform movement.
Developing Lockean concepts of voluntary association, Jones observed that
'a free state is only a more numerous and more powerful club, and that he
only is a free man, who is a member of such a state', maintaining that the
qualification for membership was the property which every man possessed
in his own life and liberty.[42] With its tripartite emphases upon popular
education, parliamentary reform, and cooperative association, anticipating
the works of Paine and Godwin, the work was seized upon by Major
Cartwright and the SCI published it as a free pamphlet. When William
Shipley, Dean of St Asaph, and Jones's future brother-in-law, reprinted this
agitational tract at Wrexham in January 1783, the High Sheriff of Flintshire,
Thomas Fitzmaurice, promptly prosecuted Shipley for publishing a paper
'seditious, treasonable, and diabolical'. Jones's radicalism had delayed for
five years his departure for Calcutta. Ironically, however, while Fitzmaurice
was attempting to blacken his name in Flintshire, Fitzmaurice's brother,
Lord Shelburne, was at Windsor, recommending Persian Jones for the
Indian judgeship.

As the case came forward at Wrexham before two of his former circuit
colleagues, Lloyd Kenyon and Daines Barrington, the newly married and
knighted Sir William Jones was nearing Bengal. By the time of Shipley's
acquittal in November 1784, hailed by his eminent Whig counsel, Thomas
Erskine, as a victory for the cause of liberty, and the rights of the jury to
decide on the libellous tendency of any publication, Jones was established
on the Calcutta bench and his prestigious but egalitarian Asiatick Society

was ten months into its research programme. The north Welsh radicals, branded by a contemporary cartoon entitled 'The Triumph of Turbulence, or Mother Cambria Possessed' as prancing 'Welch goats', boosted the audience of Jones's pamphlet beyond the ten thousand copies distributed by the SCI, by incorporating the text, together with a history of the trial into an *anterliwt* (interlude) to be performed at fairs and markets to the literate and illiterate alike.[43] The robust language of *Barn ar Egwyddorion y Llywodraeth, mewn Ymddiddan rhwng Pendefig a Hwsmon,* 'Gan Fardd anadnabyddus o wynedd' (*A Judgement on the Principles of Government, in a Dialogue between a Gentleman and a Farmer,* 'By an obscure Poet of Gwynedd'; 1784), argues the authorship of Thomas Edwards (1739–1810), Twm o'r Nant, or TE Nant as he pointedly styled himself, whose writings combine a populist political message with an abiding interest in the Welsh bardic tradition which had been nurtured by Evan Evans.[44] The stock *anterliwt* characters Llawenddyn y Ffwl (Merriman the Fool) and Siôn Gybydd (John Miser) take the parts of the Gentleman and the Farmer respectively, and Jones's pamphlet is given a forceful colloquial translation:

> *Ff*. Pe mynnei'r Brenhin wneud deddfe ei hun
> Au troi wrth ei wyn pan fynne.
> *Gyb*. Ei droi ynteu allan fydde raid'n hollol.
>
> (p. 21)
>
> *Fool*. If the King should wish to make his own laws
> And alter them as he pleases.
> *Miser*. He too must be turned out.

This polemic version of a radical Whig text subsequently given a new English edition in the wake of the Peterloo massacre (1819) and another Welsh translation at the height of the Chartist movement of the 1840s makes Oriental Jones the author of the first Welsh political tract.

Further West, Ireland, the original home of Druidism according to the deist John Toland, was also looking Eastward for its cultural roots.[45] Politicising a genealogy which had much exercised the imaginations of Englishmen as different as the antiquarian Stukeley and the laureate Pye, the colonised Irish Celts claimed the colonising and cerebral Phoenicians as their ancestors.[46] The most prominent member of the Royal Irish Academy, the Celtomane Englishman, and correspondent of William Jones, General Charles Vallancey (1721–1812), whose enthusiasm and empathy outmatched his scholarship, emerged as the leading proponent of Phoenicianism. Reading this genealogy in the glare of Celtic nationalism the Romans resembled the tyrannical English imperialists, and in the words of Joseph Leersen, 'the relationship between Ireland and England is viewed as an avatar of the enmity between Carthage and Rome'.[47] In *An Essay on the Antiquity of the Irish Language* (1772), Vallancey dismisses the distortion of histories written from the conquerors' perspective: 'Almost all Carthaginian Manuscripts were committed to the flames, and the History of this brave and learned People, has been written by their most bitter Enemies, the Greeks and Romans; in this too they resemble the Irish.'[48]

Phoenicianism constituted an Orientalist tradition which reversed received stereotypes of Celtic barbarity, spelling out the civilising effects of Eastern culture, all too frequently destroyed by Western barbarism. In the same way Ossian had represented to many evidence of a genius superior to that of Graeco-Roman culture. In 1763 the elderly William Stukeley had written to the 'translator' that this text illustrates 'the expiring remains of that very great people, who came from the East 3000 years ago':

Like other old Britons, Ossian borrowed neither from Greece nor Rome, but before them, in time... from the east; and the poetical descriptions are produc'd by a similar genius.[49]

The victimised and vanquished Celts were presented with a venerable ethnology and a tradition rich in alternative culture, both of which might transform nostalgic consolation into patriotic opposition in the heady Patriot decades of the 1780s and 1790s.[50] Like the Morris Circle in Wales, Vallancey was anxious to rehabilitate manuscript histories denounced as forgeries or fantasies, but his etymologies were becoming wildly speculative, ultimately maintaining that Irish was the language of Eden.[51] When Vallancey's *A Vindication of the Ancient History of Ireland, Proved from the Sanscrit Books* (1786) arrived in Calcutta, Jones was scathing in his condemnation of its erroneous etymology and abuse of Indology: 'it is very stupid.... I conceive [it] to be visionary'.[52]

Meanwhile, by means of a new historical and comparative *a posteriori* linguistic method, Sir William Jones in Bengal was simultaneously laying the foundations of modern comparative philology and consigning Phoenicianism to the backwaters of ethnological enquiry. On 2 February 1786, Jones delivered his 'Third Anniversary Discourse' to the Asiatick Society, linking East and West in an Indo-European paradigm which was to revolutionise colonial relations:

The *Sanscrit* language, whatever be its antiquity, is of a wonderful structure; more perfect than the *Greek*, more copious than the *Latin*, and more exquisitely refined than either, yet bearing to both of them a stronger affinity both in the roots of verbs and in the forms of grammar, than could possibly have been produced by accident;

so strong indeed, that no philologer could examine all three, without believing them to have sprung from some common source, which, perhaps no longer exists: there is a similar reason, though not quite so forcible, for supposing that both the *Gothick* and the *Celtick*, though blended with a very different idiom, had the same origin with the *Sanscrit*; and the old *Persian* might be added to the same family.[53]

History has vindicated Jones, reducing Vallancey to the level of speculative blunderer, but each was concerned to establish a cultural link between East and West wherein the colonised, whether Hindu or Celt, might appear in a superior light to the coloniser. Vallancey's influential but unreliable scholarship illustrated an important connection between Celtomania and Indomania, which was to be given 'scientific' substance by Jones's linguistic discoveries. As Trautmann has emphasised: '[F]or all its learned foolishness, the conjuncture of Celtomania and Indomania in Vallancey's later writings rests on one item of fact beneath all the fancy, for Sanskrit and Irish are near kin as members of the Indo-European language family'.[54] The Celtic tongues shared a common proto-Indo-European parent with the classical languages of the Mediterranean and of the Indus. Vallancey's theories concerning that key triad of both the Celtic Revival and Oriental Renaissance: 'nation', 'language' and 'race' were straws in the prevailing Easterly wind.[55]

In 1787 the intemperate lowland Scottish historian, John Pinkerton claimed that 'this may be called the Celtic Century, for all Europe has been inundated with nonsense about the Celts'.[56] It was also the century of Indology when Europe became acquainted with Indian culture and Hindus became worthy to be acknowledged as Aryan cousins. In terms of cultural colonisation the only phenomenon comparable to the Europe-wide craze of Ossianism was the Indomania of the Oriental Renaissance.

As a poet Jones himself was not averse to appropriating the literary potential of the Phoenician tradition in his desire to write himself into the canon of the British epic. He could appreciate arguments, used by patriot Englishman and Celtomane alike, that the Tyrians were intriguing and useful ancestors considering their dual priorities in commerce and letters. In 1770, Jones had sketched out 'a verse epic of tremendous scope' entitled 'Britain Discovered', a work 'intended as a poetical panegyric on our excellent Constitution,...as a national epic...'[57]

The plot involved the colonisation of Albion by a company of enterprising Phoenicians, led by prince Britanus of Tyre, who, disgusted by the cruel polytheism of his compatriots, and guided by a vision of a beautiful nymph representing Liberty, sets sail for the 'beautiful isle in the west', the object of his colonial desire. Britanus, voyaging by way of Egypt, Cyprus, Crete, Gibraltar and Gaul, evades the diabolical temptations of arbitrary power, oligarchy, anarchy and the pursuit of treasure, to gain the cliffs of Dover, and the arms of Albina: a marriage, as Jones has it, 'of royalty with liberty', but also a marriage which reverses the stereotyped polarities of East and West. Neither sensual nor supine, the Levantine Britanus is as energetic, rational and decisive as any Westerner.

At Calcutta in 1787, Jones renewed this Phoenicianist emphasis in a revised plan: 'The discovery of the BRITISH ISLES by the *Tyrians*, is mentioned by *Strabo, Diodorus, and Pliny*; and proved as well by the *Phœnician* monuments found in IRELAND, as well as by the affinity between the *Irish* and *Punic* languages.'[58] Determined to compose the first Anglo-Indian epic, Jones's new plan incorporated the machinery of the Hindu pantheon, much more sympathetically portrayed than the Phoenician polytheism of the earlier version.[59] The goddess Gangā, for example, betrays the entirely reasonable fear that Britanus will establish:

a wonderful nation, who will possess themselves of her banks, profane her waters, mock the temples of the *Indian* divinities, appropriate the wealth of their adorers, introduce new laws, a new religion, a new government, insult the *Bráhmens*, and disregard the sacred religion of *Brihmá*.[60]

A key role is played in the projected final book, however, by Britanus's attendant spirit, a Druid, complete with harp and oaken garland, who, like Jones, 'recommends the government of the Indians by their own laws'.[61] The enlightened intervention of a Druid on behalf of the Brahmans is reminiscent of classical and contemporary efforts to establish links between Oriental and Celtic philosophers and law-givers. This imperial epic simultaneously celebrated the Hastings policy in which Jones was playing a central role as codifier of Hindu and Muslim laws, and problematised notions of European superiority by representing the eponymous hero of Britain as an Oriental colonist urged to empathy with Hindustan by a Welsh 'descendant of a tribe of Brahmins'.[62]

The myth of origins contemplated in Jones's epic complicates the question of British self-definition in regard to the Middle East, India and the Celtic periphery in a celebration of the heterogeneous and the hybrid. Furthermore the figure of the Druid links the Celt and the Indian in diverse and disturbing ways which reflect the link between European languages and the Sanskrit, underlining the cultural centrality of both Western and Eastern peripheries, and complicating the multiple relationships between knowledge and power.[63] Prefiguring Romanticism's reversal of centre-periphery polarities in its engrossment with British imperialism, Jones foregrounds the ancient Eastern wisdom of the Druid as the 'tutelary Power' of colonialism.[64]

He knew that the Celtic Druid might serve both as an exotic Other and as a central icon in the nation's historical Self-definition. Thus it is the Celt and not the Saxon who nurtures the seeds of that constitutional balance of freedom and sovereignty in his training of a Tyrian prince:

> What Chief, what Sage, what Hero, train'd by thee
> To wisdom, first on this delightful isle
> Struck his advent'rous prow? That sacred form
> Of state, self-balanc'd, harmony sublime,
> Freedom with sov'reignty in sweet accord,
> Who constituted first? The Prince of TYRE
> Long wand'ring, long depress'd, yet e'er impell'd
> Right onward, till fair triumph bless'd his toils,
> By godlike worth and beauty's heaven'ly charm.[65]

As both linguist and poet Jones stressed those interconnections between nation formation and empire building which were to occupy the anxieties of Romanticism. In helping to construct the Romantic mythical image of India, Jones was simultaneously reintroducing Indians to their own cultural heritage. Cultural revival was central to patriotic resistance for Celt and Indian alike as both colonialist and colonised pursued authentic self-determination.[66]

In 1760 Lewis Morris had written of English antiquaries who would accord alien status to Celtic poets: 'they would mind no more to hear of Taliesin, Aneurin, Wawdrydd and the Triades, than if they were Hottentots from the Cape of Good Hope: and would get affidavits inserted in the public papers that these were mere infidels that came over with the East India ship, to the great danger of the Church and Constitution'.[67] Within three decades East Indiamen were importing Kálidása, Jayadéva, and *Asiatick Researches*, genuine 'infidel' knowledge to be reprinted and pirated across Europe. The success of Jones's cultural translation introduced a period of Indomania which could relish a domesticated Hinduism 'safe for Anglicans'. This was more than reverse acculturation, it was a conquest of the metropole by alien wisdom and exotic poetry; the *dharmaśástra* of Manu and Visnu's Kūrma Avatára (Tortoise Incarnation) invaded St Paul's on Bacon's colossal statue of Jones.[68] Flaxman in his University College, Oxford monument depicts three native scholars sitting at the Orientalist's feet, but Jones's anti-Eurocentric reversal of these roles best illustrates that the production of colonial knowledge might prove a pluralist dialogic process in which Celt and Indian both participated.

CHAPTER 3

The critical response to Ossian's Romantic bequest

Dafydd R. Moore

I

The Poems of Ossian were published between 1760 and 1763, to great ac-
claim and great controversy.[1] The supposed remains of the third-century
Gaelic warrior and poet Ossian, son of Fingal (or Fionn as he is more
usually known in Gaelic), *Ossian* stands as a nexus between a variety of
cultural and literary idioms and value systems. Of particular interest in the
present context is the position of the poems as one of the first works of
European Romanticism and as a major source for ideas of the Celtic within
modern literary and wider cultural consciousness. This essay is particularly
interested in the ways in which *Ossian*'s influence upon the literary world
has been portrayed within conventional scholarship. I am going to argue
that for a variety of reasons, some sinister, some not, the true nature of
Macpherson's importance has been obscured. I want to suggest that there
is a tendency to marginalise Macpherson, even in the act of mentioning
him, and indeed that such references frequently seem specifically designed
to obscure, not reveal, *Ossian*'s place in the Romantic pantheon.

A cursory consideration may lead to the conclusion that this is an un-
warranted claim. After all, Samuel Monk, in his still classic examination
of eighteenth-century ideas of the Sublime observes that 'everyone who
read, read *Ossian*, nothing could have been more on a level with the taste
of the age' while more recently as notable a Romantic scholar as Jerome
MacGann has suggested that '*Ossian*'s influence on the literary scene of
the late eighteenth century eclipsed all others'.[2] Indeed if the wider literary world is aware of *Ossian* at all, it is probably in terms of the '*Ossian*
Wars' over the authenticity of the poems, and a vague awareness of *Ossian*'s
importance, for a short time at least, to the young Romantics. Indeed,
these two dimensions of the *Ossian* story provide the structuring principle for G. F. Black's 1927 bibliography to *Ossian*, which splits its contents
into works concerned with 'controversy' and with 'influence', a structure

maintained by John Dunn in his 1971 update.[3] These bibliographies are testament to the relatively large if very diffuse body of articles, notes and half-chapters devoted to exploring the nature of Ossianic relationships. More remarkably, while it has only been in the last fifteen years or so that other areas of Macpherson scholarship (the place of *Ossian* within wider Scottish Enlightenment contexts, for example) have managed to emerge from the long shadow cast over *Ossian* studies by the 'authenticity issue', these bibliographies are evidence of work on literary relations of a far older pedigree.

In the face of this what follows aims to make two major points. Firstly, it will fill out what I mean by the marginalising tendency within, in particular, mainstream literary history that has paid lip-service to *Ossian*'s role without considering it seriously. Secondly it will look at some of the central assumptions in the work on *Ossian*'s bequest and argue the need for their reassessment. In the final part of the chapter I shall tie some of these points together and suggest some reasons for the state of affairs I have outlined. These reasons are both general and specific: specific in the sense that some arise from *Ossian*'s – and the idea of the Celtic's – traditional location within Anglo-Scottish cultural politics that, for a variety of reasons has left the poems as something of literary foundlings, and general in the sense that Macpherson's difficulties may be symptomatic of marginalised figures and the long process of revising literary history to take account of them. Both these dimensions are of concern to the revisionist project a collection such as the present is engaged within.

2

This section considers the spirit and intention of work on the debt owed to Macpherson by later writers. It looks at the shape of Macpherson scholarship in this area and at the meta-narratives constructed to account for Macpherson's influence. As I suggested earlier, these narratives tend to marginalise and minimise *Ossian*'s place within 'the Romantic movement'.

I suggested earlier that a relatively large body of scholarship devoted to Macpherson's literary bequest existed within conventional literary historiography. Yet there is no published work of substantial length devoted to the subject. A comparison with the state of scholarship in the non-Anglophone world makes the point succinctly. On the one hand we have, amongst others and most notably, Rudolph Tombo's *Ossian in Germany* (1901) and Paul Van Teigheim's two volume *Ossian en France* (1917); and on the other a small collection of articles and chapters in books, Robin Flower's 1928

pamphlet *Byron and Ossian*, and an unpublished doctoral thesis by John
Dunn. Works such as those of van Teigheim and Tombo – both of which
frequently have the adjective 'magisterial' applied to them – can offer mixed
blessings for the revisionist. Howard Gaskill notes that there has developed
in Germany an assumption that if Tombo was silent on the subject of an
Ossianic affinity then there was nothing to say, and never mind the fact
that Tombo's published work represents only the initial stages of his own
investigation.[4] Nevertheless, at least these monuments of earlier scholarship and endeavour exist, in sharp contradistinction to the situation in the
Anglophone world, where, until very recently, very little of the serious work
carried out has crossed into 'mainstream' literary circulation.

The fact that serious British *Ossian* scholarship in this area is slim and
scattered to the four winds – a note here, an article there, half a chapter in a
book on something else – reflects a sustained marginalisation within more
mainstream references to Macpherson's work. Simply put, there appears to
be a dynamic within scholarship that, if interested in Macpherson at all,
either only pays patronising lip-service or looks to invoke *Ossian* only within
an argument designed overall to reinforce the poem's marginalisation. For
example, in the introduction to the tenth volume of *The Oxford History of
English Literature*, the late John Butt ponders alternative titles to *The Age
of Johnson*:

a historian with an eye on the achievements of the early nineteenth century might
have been embarrassed by the choice of a suitable forerunner – Akenside, or Gray,
or Cowper, or (with increasing desperation) Macpherson – as a banner holder.[5]

Why 'with increasing desperation'? Three names and a fourth included in
'desperation' hardly suggests an 'embarrassment' of choice. As if by some
Pavlovian reflex Macpherson has been evoked only in order to be put down,
even at the risk of undermining the central point of the critic. One might
argue that this is a throw-away comment in a work of general reference and
that it is unfair or inappropriate to subject it to such analysis. Yet in some
ways this is precisely the point: it is upon such comments in such works
that *Ossian*'s reputation, in the wider scholarly world, has rested.

This accords with the suspicion that attempts to explain *Ossian*'s relationship with any given figure is less a legitimate engagement with, and
more an attempt to explain away, that relationship. If Macpherson's name
is mentioned at all that is. It is a notable feature of the most sympathetic
works that they frequently include having to wade through the extremes
others have been willing to go to in order to ignore Macpherson. Gaskill
notes that this includes ascribing the phrase 'the joy of grief' to Young's

Night Thoughts – whatever *Ossian* owes to Young, it does not owe this expression – and Dunn considers the critical game of round the houses indulged in by those who, for whatever reason, are unwilling to consider the convincing Ossianic analogue for 'Kubla Khan' 's 'And mid this tumult Kubla heard from afar/Ancestral voices prophesying war'.[6] Source-hunting can be a rather reductive business of course, and those looking for a single correct answer have probably missed an important point somewhere along the way. But the point here is less the possibility that *Ossian* provides the 'right' answer than the inability of previous critics to entertain an Ossianic possibility.

The alternative to ignoring *Ossian* has proved hardly more sympathetic. This involves adopting (usually) one of two versions of a narrative of obsolescence, the 'adolescent influence' thesis and the self-obsolescence line. The latter of these suggests that *Ossian* is of minor importance because later writers did what he did only better. Ironically, the most lucid version of this is found in Dunn's 'The Influence of Macpherson's *Ossian* on British Romanticism' and its account of 'our indifference' to a man who played such a vital role in 'shaping the spirit of the [Romantic] age' (p. v):

Macpherson's achievement has been obscured by the fact that the artistic direction that he took so early was followed by men of far greater talent than he was ever able to develop. (pp. iii–iv)

For Dunn's part this is not an excuse to ignore Macpherson: as he puts it in 'The Influence of Macpherson's *Ossian* on British Romanticism', on the question of *Ossian*'s prosody 'more accomplished artists followed him and far surpassed him as a stylist, but they followed a direction that he had been the first to take' (p. 261). However, this has bequeathed a sense in less sympathetic circles of a certain pointlessness in studying *Ossian* when the best of the poems were done better by more familiar faces in less messy circumstances.

The second, and in many ways more powerful, thesis types *Ossian* as an adolescent influence, and reconfigures the casting off of a fondness for *Ossian* as a litmus test of artistic and moral maturity. William Wordsworth's comments on the influence of *Ossian* in the 'Essay, Supplementary to the Preface' (1815) represent one of the more influential examples of this critical manoeuvre when he denied the Macpherson was an influence on anyone 'in the least distinguished' with the exception of the 'Boy Chatterton', the broken reed.[7] Fiona Stafford has deconstructed Wordsworth's attitude to Macpherson in terms of his own career and psycho-pathology, and along with John Robert Moore has provided corroborative evidence for Blake's mischievous suspicion that someone other than the poet Wordsworth was responsible for the 'Essay'.[8] The inconsistencies Stafford and Moore highlight in Wordsworth's attitude, and the 'unacknowledged debt' they uncover remind us that, whatever the merit of the 'immaturity' thesis (and I am not suggesting it lacks any credibility), it is an argument that relies on simply taking at face value the opinions of writers – not only Wordsworth, but Scott and Goethe also spring to mind – on the subject of one of their own formative literary experiences. Francis Lamport's recent work on *Ossian* and Goethe demonstrates the subtlety required in unpicking the complicated strands of affinity and antagonism that make up *Ossian*'s role in *Die Lieden des jungen Werthers*, an understanding and subtlety overdue in other areas of the field.[9]

Some, notably Blake, Byron and Hazlitt, fail to fall so neatly into this narrative that sees *Ossian* cast off with the rest of the man of letters childish things. The message that emerges from scholarship is the same though: somehow the figure in question is never himself when demonstrating a fondness for the Ossianic, the 'aberration' which, in the words of Robin Flower, 'so long kept Byron from his proper work'.[10] Thus in what I believe is the only article in the English language exclusively devoted to Byron and Ossian (hence my focus on what might otherwise seem too easy a target) Flower is satisfied with describing the evidence of a relationship between the two as 'the false romanticism or the peevish subjectivity of that Byronic Byron to whose composition I have supposed, something of the Ossianic contributed its share' (p. 18). If the reader detects some tentativeness in this, it should be noted that Flower has already:

hastened to say that I make no claim for any direct influence of Macpherson upon Byron's matter or style. The one great English poet whose style suffered the infection of Ossian is Blake. (p. 5)

The rights or spectacular wrongs in point of fact are again less the reason for citing this comment than its being a *reductio ad absurdum* of the twin desires to minimise Macpherson's influence *and* to blame him for perceived infelicities in a 'great' writer. In Blake's case, Flower holds the influence of *Ossian* responsible for the change from the 'piercing intensity' of the lyrical work to the 'muffled rhetoric' of the prophetic books. Needless to say more enlightened Blake criticism is suspicious of the ideological agendas behind dismissals of the Prophetic Books, yet still the sense that Blake's art is damaged by his fondness for the Ossianic remains: for example, David Fuller describes *Tiriel* as 'hollowly rhetorical', 'a more Ossianic and less explicitly symbolic work than Blake's later mythological poems'.[11]

I should hasten to add that none of this is to say that *Ossian*'s influence could not have been detrimental on some figures, or that others did not assimilate, incorporate, greatly improve on, change their minds about or otherwise move on from Macpherson's unadulterated Ossianic vision. To suggest otherwise would be silly. As Stafford points out in 'Dangerous Success', there may be good psychological reasons why the Ossianic melancholy appeals particularly to those in their late teens (p. 60). But it seems a narrow and naive conception of artistic development (not to mention grossly patronising) to believe that this is the end of the story, that this is all there is to say, and to dismiss *Ossian* entirely as a (conscious) enthusiasm of youth, particularly when the major source of evidence for the limits of this enthusiasm is the writers in question themselves. Equally, that *Ossian* may only have been a phase in the formative development of other Romantic poets does not explain or excuse the disdain with which the poems are treated. In short, there is a need to ask some searching questions about the unexamined assumptions contained in histories of *Ossian*'s reception, and to wonder from whence comes this tone of contempt and dismissal. When, for example, did 'Ossianic' become a standard term of abuse, and what agendas does it serve?

Not surprisingly given the present context, I suspect that now, as then, the Celticism (I want just for the moment to use the word in an unproblematic sense) of *Ossian* bears on the issue. I want to consider, as a brief case study, James Merriman's *The Flower of Kings: a Study of the Arthurian Legend in England between 1485 and 1835* (1973). Merriman's study is a painstaking and meticulous charting of the career of King Arthur far from reluctant to visit some of the dustier corners of literary history. He traces the beginnings of the return of Arthur to what he terms the pre-Romantic period, a period he characterises, judging by his comments on John Leyden's *Scenes of Infancy* (1803), as one of 'Celtic primitivism' and 'Ossianic grimness and fatalism of atmosphere'.[12] It was however during this time that the Arthurian story was, according to Merriman, importantly divorced from pseudo-history, a move which paved the way for the reanimation of the story during the Romantic period proper. Merriman particularly points to Richard Hole's *Arthur: or, the Northern Enchanter* (1789), which, despite being a 'cultural potpourri' of allusions to Virgil, *Ossian* and Northern mythology, was important in this process (p. 105). In a number of places *Ossian* hovers on the edge of Merriman's narrative (Hole, he observes, was a sometime versifier of *Ossian*) without ever being addressed outright. But then Merriman clearly wants to deny that Celticism has any part in the Arthurian revival as he wishes to define it: he makes the revealing comment on Heber's unfinished *Morte d'Arthur* (1810–12) that the 'sort of epic poem' makes mention of 'Celtic glories' and Cuchullin despite the fact that 'neither Irish story nor Celtic antiquities have any place in the chivalric romance of a mythic king who rules an essentially feudal realm' (p. 171). While the cultural and ethnic typing of Arthur is up for grabs from the twelfth century onwards, and the Arthurian story has more to do with Anglo-Norman narratives of assimilation and control than Celtic resistance, to divorce Arthur so absolutely from the Celtic milieu from whence he sprang is at the very least a reckless move. One would only have to point Merriman in the direction of the Celtic mysticism still evident in Chrétien de Troyes's 'chivalric romance of a mythic king who rules an essentially feudal realm' or that which echoes around in the strange business of Gawain's strength, which waxes at mid-day and wanes through the afternoon.[13] More than that it may smack of the very process of cultural appropriation itself. In other words, while Merriman implicitly records how enthusiasm for *Ossian* plays a role in the revival of interest in Arthur – it would seem that the Ossianic (perhaps only temporarily) provided a vocabulary to revivify Arthur, to present him in familiar clothes – this fact is played down, and Ossianic pre-romanticism damned with faint praise. After all, to do any other brings into play a disruptive baggage of Celticism into the representation of an Arthur apotheosised in Tennyson's blond-haired and blue-eyed hero.[14] When Arthur returned from 150 years of neglect his image was surely more up for grabs than Merriman's narrow determinism is willing to allow, and it is a function of a whig literary historiography to remove 'Celtic primitivism' from the picture by retrospectively typing it as a blind alley temporarily taken.

I will return to some of these issues in the final section. For the moment, having considered the narratives of marginalisation created for Macpherson I want to turn my attention to some of the myths about *Ossian* that prevent a full understanding of the impact of the poems. Again we shall see an at times suspicious naiveté of scholarly approach, and again the aim will be to argue that the case needs to be reopened.

3

This section concentrates on two of the false assumptions that prevent a full understanding of the nature of *Ossian*'s standing between 1765 and 1830. By far the greatest assumption, and most damaging myth, is that the authenticity of the poems was the pre-eminent issue in the reception of *Ossian*. Only two years ago Jonathan Wordsworth confidently pronounced that 'had

Ossian not been thought to be authentic, it would have had few readers then, and fewer now'.[15] It is possible to argue that this statement begs too many questions to be profitably offered up for analysis (it not only depends, for example, on what is meant by 'authentic' but even 'then'). However there is a simpler objection: it is not true. The publication history of the poems in no way bears it out, since there were more British editions published in the thirty years after 1805 than there had been in the previous forty.[16] The significance of 1805 is that this year saw the publication of both Malcolm Laing's so-called debunking edition of the *Poems* (in which he traced every conceivable – and many inconceivable – Macphersonian borrowings in order to 'prove' the work to be Macpherson's, a bizarre but influential enterprise) and the Henry Mackenzie headed *Report of the Committee of the Highland Society of Scotland Appointed to Enquire into the Nature and Authenticity of the Poems of Ossian*. Taken together, these documents made it hard for all but the most committed Ossianist to continue to believe in the absolute authenticity of the poems, yet this had no impact on demand for editions of *Ossian*. Equally this means that the conventional image of an Ossianic craze in the 1770s that was over by the turn of century is wide of the mark.[17]

However, we don't have to rely on number crunching. Stafford has noted, in 'Dangerous Success', the frequency with which an acknowledgement of the dubiousness of Macpherson's claims is accompanied with an admission of admiration.[18] To her list can be added Byron's comment that 'while the imposture is discovered, the merit of the work remains undisputed, though not without faults' (cited by Flower, p. 5). This is not to say that the issue did not figure, but that, as might otherwise be expected, readers were capable of making differentiated and subtle responses. Famously, Hazlitt believed that:

If it were indeed possible to shew that this writer was nothing, it would only be another instance of mutability, another blank made, another void left in the heart, another confirmation of that feeling which makes [Ossian] so often complain, 'Roll on ye dark brown years, ye bring no joy on your way to Ossian!'[19]

Not only is Hazlitt unwilling to allow his appreciation of *Ossian* as literature be clouded by the question of authenticity, he corrals that question into his appreciation. More cautiously, Walter Scott agreed with Anna Seward 'that the question of authenticity ought [not] to be confounded with that of [*Ossian*'s] literary merit' while at the same time feeling that a lack of authenticity removes an alibi for the poems' more extravagant touches (since these could no longer be put down to a third-century primitive poet)

and 'destroys that feeling of reality which one should otherwise *combine*
with our sentiments of admiration' (my emphasis).[20] The merit and admiration remain however. As late as 1875 Tennyson was borrowing from
George MacDonald a copy of the so-called Gaelic *Ossian* (the 1807 back-
translation of Macpherson's English that interested parties – bearing in
mind that Macpherson had been dead eleven years at the time – attempted
to pass off as the original) in order to read its parallel text in Latin: 'he
had never believed *Ossian* was a reality', reported Greville MacDonald 'but
seemed a good deal more ready to believe in him when he had read a few
lines, with which he was delighted'.[21] Make what we will of MacDonald's
gloss or Tennyson's desire to flatter his hosts, the fact that the sixty-six-year-
old Tennyson was reading *Ossian* in Latin (regardless of his proficiency in
the language) despite not believing the claims made about them surely
knocks on the head the idea that the poems' value relied on a willingness
to be taken in by their claims. This emphasis on authenticity is not an in-
nocent red-herring. Andrew Hook, in noting the absence of any vehement
authenticity debate overseas, has wondered how much the *Ossian* Wars,
and their prominence within scholarship, is indicative of agendas within
Anglo-Scottish cultural politics.[22] In this particular context, emphasising
authenticity is an instrument whereby attention can be detracted from a
more substantial engagement between *Ossian* and other writers. As late as
1991, John Valdimir Price came to the conclusion that 'if Scottish readers,
critics and theorists in Scotland's Age of Enlightenment had occasionally
resisted Enlightenment, later readers did not'.[23] In itself this represents a
fiction for Anglo-centric histories of eighteenth-century ideas, implying as
it does a fallibility on the part of the Scottish Enlightenment *intelligentsia*.
In a wider sense, the issue has given the question a tone of moral righteous-
ness. In ' "Ossian" and the Canon', Price has arguably even bigger claims
to make as he ends his article with the ringing assertion that 'the literary
canon responds by withholding its imprimatur from the writings of authors judged guilty of such a deception [as that practised by Macpherson]'
(p. 127). But can literary canons be thought of as operating in such a morally
providential way? Are we not more interested in the cultural and ideological agendas behind the marginalisation of certain figures and texts within
literary historiographies? Doesn't Price's conception of the canon obscure
such processes of marginalisation and exclusion to the extent that it may
be complicit with them?

  Authenticity is then a spoiling manoeuvre operating on a number of
fronts. It deflects attention away from more serious engagement between
literary figures, and it turns *Ossian* into a stick with which to beat the

Scottish Enlightenment. We might even feel that the obsession with the issue demonstrates a singular failure to understand the nature of literary or artistic appreciation, or indeed literature or art itself, but then this is the beauty of the tactic since, if *Ossian* is a fraud, if it is not 'real', then it *is* not literature or art, and so can be treated without reference to the standards of the discipline. Thus with a comforting circularity an illegitimate methodology is justified by its own findings.

A final point on the question of authenticity involves noting the substantial work of Katie Trumpener in uncovering the debt owed by the Romantic Regional Novel to *Ossian*.[24] Yet in its emphasis on the importance of the *Ossian* Wars – Trumpener convincingly argues that later novels internalised Johnson's critique of *Ossian* and thereby anticipated and forestalled criticism – *Bardic Nationalism* in some measure perpetuates the myth, albeit in positive terms, that authenticity was primarily what the *Ossian* craze was about. In other words Trumpener's fine analysis needs complementing with work on other aspects of this relationship to present a fuller picture. As a general point this illustrates how high the stakes are here, how these assumptions find their way into even the most sympathetic of revisionism, and of how the very basis of current *Ossian* revisionism is up for grabs in this issue.

The other myth I wish to address here is less sinister but no less limiting, and concerns literary form. It has been generally assumed that *Ossian* was read and understood as epic poetry. For reasons that are important but need not detain this article, it was Macpherson's – and Hugh Blair's – claims for *Ossian* as epic that raised, indeed some might argue created, the stakes over the poems' provenance.[25] But just because Macpherson wished *Ossian* to be read as epic, and just because literary and cultural polemicists such as Blair and Johnson fought over the image of the epic *Ossian*, this does not mean that the epic *Ossian* was either the only or most important *Ossian* in the late eighteenth century.[26] Certainly *Ossian*'s popularity must have played a part in what Stuart Curran has called the 'unprecedented proliferation' of epic writing witnessed in England between 1780 and 1810, an obvious link being Richard Hole, whom I touched upon in the previous section as a sometime versifier of *Ossian* and author of *Arthur: or, the Northern Enchanter*.[27] Equally *Ossian*'s notoriety and influence clearly owed something to the continuing cultural currency of epic over romance and ballad. But along side this there need to be considered the other ways in which *Ossian* was mediated to its readership.

First of all the most popular parts of *Ossian* were the shorter poems, particularly those such as the 'Songs of Selma' constructed out of short monologues. Indeed the *Fragments of Ancient Poetry* were in many quarters the most highly regarded of Macpherson's productions. This emphasis is reflected in the fact that foreign translators concentrated on versions of these short poems, with translations of the epics *Fingal* and *Temora* disproportionately belated, even taking into account the increased time and effort required to produce them.[28] In this context it is worth noting that Macpherson's 1773 revision of the *Works* significantly reorders the poems. It is possible to interpret the effect of this reorganisation in a number of ways (Macpherson's own claim that it put the poems in chronological order is about the least convincing), but it certainly works to make the epics less prominent within the volumes. Equally, anthologies and reading guides such as the 1824 *A Second Evening's Entertainment in the Library* presented *Ossian* as a series of affecting monologues extracted from particular poems to be read, or to be read aloud, in short sharp bursts for moral and polite edification (for example, 'Ossian's address to the Sun' (from 'Carthon'), 'Ossian's address to the Moon' (from 'Dar-thula'), 'Ossian Mourning the Death of Oscar' (from 'Temora')). The anthology-friendly nature of the shorter works over the epic poems ensured their wider circulation, and, to an extent continues to do so.

Neither were adaptors slow to recognise the dramatic potential of Macpherson's poems: it is fitting that Coleridge's major Ossianic piece was to have been an opera based upon the *bel inconnu* romance 'Carthon', given the number of stage adaptations produced.[29] These adaptations catered to a wide range of audience. At one end of the spectrum we are offered the 1791 *New Ballet Pantomime (Taken from Ossian) called Oscar and Malvina; or, the Hall of Fingal*, at the other the 1792 *Comàla: a Dramatic Poem, from Ossian, set to Music by Miss Harriet Wainwright*. While the latter preserves Macpherson's text (and even some of his footnotes) in a faithful rendering, the former represents a Music Hall version, based around no identifiable single *Ossian* poem and containing rustic songs and turns from Music Hall favourites. *Ossian*'s stoic confrontation and facing down of 'dark-brown years' who bring 'no joy in [their] course' (as Ossian has it at the end of the 'Songs of Selma') is rendered thus:

> They surely are thick-headed asses,
>   Who know that youth's gone in a crack,
> Yet will not enjoy, as it passes,
>   The season that never comes back.[30]

This is not to say that the likes of Coleridge, whose eclectic borrowing from, and the 'casual quality' of his allusions to, *Ossian* is evidence, according to John Dunn, of a large-scale and in-depth acquaintance with the poems, were not exposed to *Ossian* in two-volume complete works.[31] But at the same time we do need to recapture a sense of *Ossian* not merely as eight-book epic poetry which one pored over with one's Homer and Milton close at hand, but also as a lyric, performative experience. Equally, the uses the poems were put to outside the context of the two-volume complete-works setting may offer clues to the ways the poems were read within that setting (particularly since many of the stage 'adaptations' merely split the poems into speeches).

This revision of our sense of what *Ossian* meant for readers at the turn of the nineteenth century helps to explain why the poems were read with such enthusiasm then and yet are considered unreadable now. However, it should also be part of a larger reassessment not only of where we might find Ossianic footsteps but also what those footsteps actually look like. Seen in this light scholarship has thus far touched upon only the expressive accidentals of what the Ossianic meant at the end of the eighteenth century, and has only just begun to consider that ruined, mossy castles and the other features of the Ossianic landscape of the Sublime are only the most obvious elements bequeathed by Macpherson.[32] For example, I believe that in formal terms *Ossian* has something to contribute to the story of the rehabilitation and modification of the romance through its pioneering use of retrospective narrative and inset tale, key elements of the High Romantic romance. It may even be possible to see *Ossian* in terms of changes in the way that art is appreciated and understood during the Romantic period. In *The Flower of Kings*, Merriman suggests that the return of King Arthur during the Romantic period is down to the growth of a 'full belief in the poetic imagination as a way of knowing, [a] full faith in its own imagined creations' but is short on a mechanism whereby this came about (it is also striking that he can point to no good Romantic Arthurian poem) (p. 176). Might it not be that part of this change in artistic sensibility came about on account of the challenges offered by reading *Ossian*, a text which confounds simplistic concepts of truth, authenticity and reality?

4

It seems then that Fingal's lament to Swaran that provides the title of this chapter – that fame in song is poor substitute when one is unable to defend oneself – has proved ironically prescient, as *Ossian*'s critical fate stands as striking testimony to the elisions and silent liquidations of national literary historiographies. The sad tale of the critical treatment of Ossian's Romantic bequest is not, I am sure, unique: there are a number of secret histories of Romanticism revolving around writers whose contribution to the literary and intellectual climate of their age has been obscured on account of their gender, class or ethnic background. Equally, the problems I have identified are in many ways symptomatic of the long process of revisionism: fifteen years is not long to overturn 250 years of misrepresentation and misunderstanding, and I am confident that in another fifteen many of the above complaints will have disappeared. The lip-service paid to Macpherson's influence within accounts aimed at minimising his importance is one symptom of a marginalised literary figure who has too frequently had to rely on the kindness of scholarly strangers. There is, after all, a natural tendency within, say, Byron scholarship to emphasise the distinctness rather than the debts. The problem with cases such as *Ossian* is that Macpherson has had too few fighting his corner; there have been too few telling the story from an Ossianic starting point.

Macpherson's is, though, a particularly invidious position. I have suggested that the condescension with which Macpherson is treated may be down to his reputation as a liar and a cheat. What is worse, he is a Scottish liar and cheat, and this works doubly to exclude him from the grand parade of English literary historiography. To add insult to injury, Macpherson also, directly and indirectly, made a fortune out of *Ossian*. His crime, in the eyes of the literary establishment, is to have been a success, and a somewhat vulgar one at that. 'Fingal' Macpherson, political fixer and polemicist, given to announcing that while he hated John Bull he loved his daughters, no more fits the Romantic and post-Romantic view of a poet than he did the increasingly aghast Scottish literati's idea of proper 'North British' behaviour in London. The distaste felt by the literary establishment concerning the fact not only that there is something fishy about *Ossian* but that it also made its author a great deal of money survives to the present, if in slightly different form: Peter Murphy's (otherwise) sensitive criticism of *Ossian*, for example, contains the assertion that Macpherson 'wanted from oral culture only what he could get, and let the consequences fall where they may' and that 'his contempt for form is a contempt for real literary beauty, and the divine emptiness of Ossian's poems is the result'.[33] *Ossian* so the argument runs, is not literature but literary opportunism, and highly damaging opportunism at that. The charge can be defended on two counts. Firstly, it is a retrospective fallacy: if the Highlands and the Celtic became fashionable in the second half of the eighteenth century, *Ossian* created rather than benefited from the fashion. Secondly *Ossian*'s role in the preservation and exploitation, the privileging and the misrepresentation of Gaelic culture defies such a simplistic judgement (see, for example, Gaskill (1986), p. 140). Thus Dáithí Ó hÓgáin, while well aware of the violence done to genuine tradition, can decide that 'credit cannot be denied [Macpherson] for bringing Fionn (albeit a barely recognisable Fionn) into the mainstream of European culture for the first and only time in the long saga of this hero of the Gaelic world', and see Macpherson as 'instrumental in bringing into being what we now know as Celtic studies'.[34]

We have moved into the territory of Macpherson's place within Anglo-Celtic cultural politics. Of crucial importance here is the love-hate relationship that has existed between Scottish revisionists and Macpherson. This means that *Ossian*'s otherwise natural allies against an Anglo-centric historiography have often been 'otherwise engaged' at crucial moments. Despite Andrew Hook's warning in 1984 that to hang Macpherson out to dry as a cultural quisling may play into the hands of English cultural imperialism, it is fair to say that many Scottish cultural commentators have been suspicious of, or antagonistic towards, Macpherson, leading to what Murray Pittock has recently labelled an 'equality of misrepresentation'.[35] The arguments denouncing Macpherson's misty past of doomed Celts as what Hook (in resisting this interpretation) calls the source of everything 'that is corrupt and debilitating, sham and distorting, in the Scottish cultural tradition' have been rehearsed frequently enough without going over them again.[36] Equally, there is a growing body of work which seeks a more subtle model of cultural translation, interpretation and resistance to apply to Macpherson's activities.[37] Perhaps the dissemination of such views may lead to a greater willingness to reinstate Macpherson, in all his complexity, within literary history.

In the final analysis it seems ironic for the modern-day cultural nationalist to want to wash his hands of *Ossian* given that Macpherson is denigrated within conventional literary history precisely for being a cultural nationalist. We saw this with Merriman's marginalisation of 'Celtic primitivism' and it is even clearer in Flower's beef with Macpherson. Flower claims that before Macpherson a notion such as the 'Celtic note in literature' 'would not have been possible' (p. 6). For Flower, Macpherson is the 'forerunner' of Romantic self-consciousness about cultural nationhood that manifests itself as the 'ambition of every people to have a national tradition marked with a separate and distinctive note' (p. 6).[38] Of course, Macpherson's 'Celtic Note' has proved open to deconstruction as, or assimilation within, an Anglo-British agenda of cultural imperialism, but if Flower is right, then we also owe to Macpherson at least part of the roots of the intellectual discourse that sees the need to make such judgements in the first instance.

At the same time it is worth noticing the uneasiness in this observation of Flower, particularly as he himself looks to dissolve such distinctions. Immediately following his comment about national literary self-consciousness, he compares a passage of 'Dar-thula' with Jerome Stone's translation of the verse tale of Froach (a bizarre choice of translation, but passing over that), commenting:

in drawing out this contrast I would not wish to deal in terms of movements and schools, to say that one is romantic and the other classical, the one Celtic and the other pseudo-Celtic, I would rather say simply that the one is good, and the other bad, poetry. (p. 8)

In good humanist style Flower seeks to smooth differences in national or historical sensibility into a single and universal scale of 'good' and 'bad' poetry. Macpherson is a rowdy, inconvenient and despised figure because he insists on the opposite, he insists on, and his work implies, alternative national traditions. Of course Macpherson was hidebound by a set of cultural assumptions that made his alternative national tradition look suspiciously familiar: the Celtic epic is, it transpires, remarkably similar to the neo-classical (though I think similarities have been over-emphasised at the expense of genuinely different elements). But we should at least entertain the possibility that this may represent as much a failure of artistic imagination as it does cultural imperialism, and anyway we should not lose sight of the fact that one critic's assimilation within a literary mainstream is another's appropriation of – or attempt to appropriate – that mainstream. In short, whatever we might make of the tradition Macpherson is seen as fostering, however we might wish he had done things differently, we should not ignore the threat that this tradition, and the very possibility that *Ossian* holds out that such traditions exist, has posed to whiggish English literary historiography. 'My enemy's enemy is my friend' is at best a dubious approach to anything, but it is not necessary to go that far in order to observe, and perhaps explore, the fact that the literary canon 'we have it in for', 'has it in for' Macpherson too.

I want finally to address a different objection to the project I am outlining here, and one less easy to dismiss, concerning the whole notion of validating a figure in relation to the literary canon he may or may not be seen as influencing. In other words, might this actually be working to cement an Anglo-centric perspective that values Scottish literature only to the extent that it impacts on English literature?[39] If that were indeed the point of the exercise, then this objection would be insuperable. But my aim has been to reveal the ways that traditional literary historiography has kicked over the traces of Macpherson's place within literary history. It has not been to imply that Macpherson's influence is the only thing of value about *The Poems of Ossian*. I believe that *Ossian* would be a valuable work of literature and unique cultural artefact had the poems been read by and influenced not one writer subsequently; but the fact is that, despite the efforts of conventional literary historiography to either ignore or pay only lip-service to the fact, they were and they did. Thus it seems to me that this objection should inform any project of tracing Ossianic influences but not block it: it seems better to debate questions of power relations within these links of influence having established their existence than to allow such doubts to prevent them being brought to light. The danger with the latter response, in the case of Macpherson at least, is that it allows the free passage of, or unwittingly conspires with, the distancing, marginalising and excluding agenda of English cultural hegemony.

Ultimately, the story of the critical treatment of James Macpherson's literary influence is one of importance to those studying literary canons from a number of revisionist positions, not only the 'Four Nations' perspective. The distaste for the literary curio *Ossian* and the 'opportunist' Macpherson evident in some quarters ought to be of interest to those exploring the Romantic-bourgeois mystification of literature as a cultural product. I hope however that this outline of the story of *Ossian*'s literary afterlife, and the methodological and theoretical problems encountered in telling it, even in such outline form, is of particular interest to 'Four Nations' revisionists seeking to emphasise not only the importance of the 'Celtic fringe' within literary history but also the ways in which that importance has been obscured.

CHAPTER 4

Blake and Gwendolen: territory, periphery and the proper name

David Punter

On the subject of Celts and the Celtic, Blake maintains a voluble reticence. That is to say, nowhere in his writings does he mention them by name; yet we know, from a whole panoply of intratextual and extratextual sources, of his close involvement with speculative antiquarianism, with the 'matter of ancient Britain', with the whole issue of historical explanation, especially as intertwined with a particular tradition of Biblical exegesis.

For example, there is throughout his work a continuing and evolving topos that links the history of Britain with the twelve tribes of Israel, making of Britain a nation that is at the same time an inalienable homeland and an unending diaspora, a foreign body in and to itself, an envelope for displacement that is at the same time a *fons et origo*, a partially obscured hieroglyph, the challenge of which for the interpreter is to restore it to its putative previous legibility. There is, to take a more specific example, the lost painting 'The Ancient Britons', the account of which in the exhibition advertisement of 1809 begins with a verse that has been shown to be a translation from the Welsh Trials:

> In the last Battle that Arthur fought, the most Beautiful was one
> That return'd, and the most Strong another: with them also return'd
> The most Ugly, and no other beside return'd from the bloody Field.[1]

On the basis of these lines, and more particularly of remarks about them by Southey, it has been supposed that Blake had some acquaintance with the apostle of Welsh culture William Owen Pughe.[2] On better grounds, derived from numerous references in the poetry, we know of Blake's familiarity with Ossian, and also that he knew of – whether by reading or by conversation – such antiquarian and 'ancient British' interpreters as Jacob Bryant, Edward Davies and William Stukeley. Always behind his historiography there lie the great promulgators of the British national legend – Gildas and Geoffrey of Monmouth, principally – so it would be fair to say that there is a Celtic strain that runs right through Blake's work, a scenario in which modern history is underlain – and underwritten – by a history of previous legendary conflict, a history that is an essential founding myth of the British nation state.

The most significant recent contribution to the further understanding of Blake's engagement with this terrain on which history and legend meet and intertwine has been Jason Whittaker's book *William Blake and the Myths of Britain*, published in 1999. Whittaker sets out to explore 'Blake's use of British mythology... the antiquity of Albion and his association with the biblical patriarchs, the legend of a lost Eden in Atlantis and the relations within this primal family'.[3] He sets Blake in the context of other approximately contemporary writers – Gray, Macpherson, Chatterton – who were elaborating related myths, and he deals in detail with Blake's conception – eccentric but nonetheless firmly of his time – of the bards and the Druids. Whittaker also brings a further inflection to the field:

Where Blake differs... from the gentleman scholars of his day, who were as likely to include a Gothic reference in their writings as preserve a Roman curiosity in their cabinets, is in the intensity he confers onto these legendary figures by combining them into a politically and religiously radical figure. More than just the myths of Britain, this book is concerned with *the* myth of Albion as father of the nation, even the species.[4]

Blake's cabinet, we may therefore suppose, is hardly made of crystal, but of sterner stuff; yet there is an irony here, which Whittaker points out but without following to its fullest conclusion: namely, that this search for authentication – a search which was Blake's own but was also deeply embedded in eighteenth-century British culture – was predicated throughout on the inauthentic and the forged.[5]

Ossian, of course, has come down to us as the outstanding example of this process,[6] but there were plenty of other examples, especially scattered through the Welsh efflorescence of those years, of what one might at least call a tendency towards over-enthusiasm in the discovery of ancient sources. A certain search for origins became, therefore, self-vindicating and self-fulfilling; if sources there had to be, then sources had to be found/founded, discovered even where no discovery was possible, established as a cover story for a certain absence, a lack or loss of textual materials that proved intolerable to the cultural-political climate of the times.

What is crucial here, as Whittaker points out, is the way in which the perceived necessity of elaborating a myth of Britishness is fostered by the need to consolidate national identity in the context of international imperialism and European war. Thus the apparent paradox by which Blake the radical was also – or perhaps has been reconstructed as – the patriot Blake of 'Jerusalem' falls into place; the salvific myth of Britain, dependent at every point on the establishment of a Celtic heredity, relies simultaneously on a notion of being rescued from contemporary social oblivion and exploitation *and* the assertion of a primal British greatness that in fact goes well beyond the historical and geographical borders of Britain to embrace and provide a continuing home, an 'eternal city', for the roots and later routes of Christendom.

My purpose here, however, is not precisely to forward understanding of Blake's relation to this Celtic/British topos with which he was clearly so deeply engaged. It is rather to think through Blake's 'Celticism' in terms of a particular frame, a frame that would concentrate on landscape, on territorialisation, on 'geodesy'; the frame advanced by Gilles Deleuze and Félix Guattari in their 1980 book, *A Thousand Plateaus*. In saying this, I do not mean to suggest that I have room here to make out a major case for this collocation, or indeed to suggest that the terrain of the 'Celtic' would be the ideal place to do so; indeed, the difficult archaeological work in this area is currently being carried out by my colleague Alan Nicholson.[7] My purpose here is altogether more limited: it is to examine a restricted set of Celtic allusions in Blake's work – almost entirely in *Jerusalem* – to see whether we can thereby conjure a further glimpse of the extraordinary topography of the Prophetic Books and their complex revisualisation of the historical and geographical problematic that is 'Britain'.

Let us begin with two lines from *Jerusalem*:

> Hereford, ancient Guardian of Wales, whose hands
> Builded the mountain palaces of Eden, stupendous works!
> (46. 3–4; K, p. 676)

The story of these lines, as extrapolated by W. H. Stevenson, involves the grandeur of Hereford cathedral; the town's status as 'historic gateway to South Wales' (though where from?); Thomas Johnes, the Welsh antiquary who built Hafod House near Aberystwyth; and Johnes's own youth in Herefordshire.[8] In other words, in order to understand such lines it is apparent that one must, as Deleuze and Guattari continually advocate, draw a map, and a map is to be differentiated (in terms that Blake would doubtless have referred to under the heading of the imagination) from a tracing:

What distinguishes the map from the tracing is that it is entirely oriented toward an experimentation in contact with the real. The map does not reproduce an unconscious closed in upon itself; it constructs the unconscious. It fosters connections between fields, the removal of blockages on bodies without organs, the maximum opening of bodies without organs onto a plane of consistency.[9]

We can paraphrase parts of this neo-Spinozistic discourse by saying that a map is more than the sum of its parts: in its establishment of hierarchies and descriptions, in its addition of the aptly named 'legend' to the mapped terrain, it reproduces and develops desire. Thus Wales here cannot 'be' itself; instead it flickers and warps, becomes simultaneously too distant to be seen clearly and too close, with a proximity that threatens to remove its identity altogether (as Hafod becomes Hereford):

The law of the painting is that it be done at close range, even if it is viewed from relatively far away. One can back away from a thing, but it is a bad painter who backs away from the painting he or she is working on. Or from the 'thing' for that matter: Cézanne spoke of the need to *no longer see* the wheat field, to be too close to it, to lose oneself without landmarks in smooth space. Afterward, striation can emerge: drawing, strata, the earth, 'stubborn geometry', the 'measure of the world' . . . (D and G, p. 493)

In all of these latter terms, of course, we hear the ring of Urizenic geodesy, we see the compasses measuring and dividing, and this will inevitably and fatally inflect any attempt to 'get to grips' with Blake and the Celtic. What, after all, is a space without landmarks, and what will it take to produce within and on top of that space a localisation, a territorialisation? The question of the Celtic in Blake will always be a question of 'becoming', of mapping contested territory, of what one might refer to as a wilful rejection of perspective.

Where, then, are the Celtic realms located? In *America*, they are situated on the brink of an overwhelming extinction:

The plagues creep on the burning winds driven by flames of Orc,
And by the fierce Americans rushing together in the night,
Driven o'er the Guardians of Ireland, and Scotland and Wales.
(15. 11–13; K, p. 202)

Ireland, Scotland and Wales stand – or fall – here as elsewhere as the guardians of the guardian, as the outer bulwarks of the State, as protection and anxiety. But this geographical arrangement too shifts and flickers, for according to a different but related geodesy in *Milton*, a druidic geodesy, Ireland occupies a rather different position:

> Thence stony Druid Temples overspread the Island white,
> And thence from Jerusalem's ruins, from her walls of salvation
> And praise, thro' the whole Earth were rear'd from Ireland
> To Mexico & Peru west, & east to China & Japan . . .
>
> (6. 20–3; K, pp. 485–6)

Here Ireland is a specific staging-post on the route of diaspora, a 'point' from which a new grouping can be promulgated, a grouping that will necessarily rearrange the earth's surface, that may even serve specifically to set in place hitherto unsupposed connections – the singularly challenging connection here, for example, between Ireland and Japan, which is repeated and consolidated in *Jerusalem*:

> . . . & the Wings spread from Japan,
> Where the Red Sea terminates the World of Generation & Death,
> To Ireland's farthest rocks, where Giants builded their Causeway,
> Into the Sea of Rephaim, but the Sea o'erwhelm'd them all.
>
> (89. 48–51; K, p. 735)

A history, we might say, that is not a history, an absence of textuality; that which exists is that which (in Atlantean fashion) has already been overwhelmed, erased; the map is, as perhaps a map can only be, a map of *that which is no longer there*, that which the map itself serves to obliterate under the sign of a reterritorialisation, a reterritorialisation that will necessarily, as Deleuze and Guattari say, have

two notable effects: *a reorganisation of functions and a regrouping of forces*. On the one hand, when functional activities are territorialised they necessarily change pace . . . [The] other effect, which relates not to occupations but to rites and religions, consists in this: the territory groups all the forces of the different milieus together in a single sheaf constituted by the forces of the earth. The attribution of all the diffuse forces to the earth as receptacle or base takes place only at the deepest level of each territory. (D and G, pp. 320–1)

It is Blake's search for this 'deepest level', I would suggest, that eventuates in the production of the form of Albion, and that converts the question of the Celtic from a search for a 'solution' to a prevailing historical and geographical dilemma into a more complex recognition both of absence and of rhizomatic spread. What does it mean to say that there are druidic temples in Japan? It can *mean* only, I suggest, in the context of the 'single sheaf', which we might also figure as something akin to Freud's dream-knot,[10] the point at which all the strands are ravelled together and there is no possibility of further dissection. It is this point, we might surmise, that Urizen (or the Romans, in the alter-native context of Romano-British struggle) must always disavow; for Urizen Japan, the Red Sea and the Giants' Causeway must always be separated, or at least separable – as also, in some of their incarnations, for the Druids themselves; but then the Druids in Blake, it would seem, know not what they do, they are capable of uttering a greater truth, of acting as a 'receptacle or base' for that which goes on in despite of all their condemnable ritualistic activity.

But then these rituals, this reliance on number, division, classification, all of this imperialistic control of conceptual and geographical territory is ambivalent in Blake. The Celtic must, of course, play its part in a numerological territorialisation:

> Here Los fix'd down the Fifty-two Counties of England & Wales,
> The Thirty-six of Scotland & the Thirty-four of Ireland,
> With mighty power, when they fled out at Jerusalem's Gates
> Away from the Conflict of Luvah & Urizen, fixing the Gates
> In the Twelve Counties of Wales, & thence Gates looking every way
> To the Four Points conduct to England & Scotland & Ireland,
> And thence to all the Kingdoms & Nations & Families of the Earth.
> (*Jerusalem*, 16. 28–34; K, p. 637)

The territories must be nailed down, assigned a numerological status, related to the cycle of the year (fifty-two weeks, twelve months, four seasons), to the twelve tribes of Israel, and so on; but what is the political or, as it might be better put, administrative force of such operations? Interestingly, Deleuze and Guattari completely contradict themselves (or, for all we know, each other) in their inspection of the question of number. They attempt to distinguish between the (pre-existing, primitive – we might in this context say 'Celtic') *nomadic* and the (supervening, modern, Urizenic) *State*. 'Nomad organisation', we hear, 'is indissolubly arithmetic and directional; quantity is everywhere, tens, hundreds, direction is everywhere, left, right: the numerical chief is also the chief of the left or the right' (D and G, p. 390).[11] Yet also 'arithmetic, the number, has always had a decisive role in the State apparatus: this is so even as early as the imperial bureaucracy' (D and G, p. 389). Number, then, is even more ubiquitous than is required for the sustaining of a distinction: the number of the lading bill, the number of camels on the desert trading trip, the number of 'natives' to be supervised, inspected, controlled, the number of counties as administrative units, the number of tribes you need to make up a diaspora ... yet number, as Deleuze and Guattari also point out in terms that cannot fail to remind us of Biblical lineages and of all that Blake derived from them, is also a primary mode of inscription on the land:

The earth is before all else the matter on which the dynamic of lineages is inscribed, and the number, a means of inscription: the lineages write upon the earth and with the number, constituting a kind of 'geodesy'. Everything changes with State societies... The archaic State envelops a *spatium* with a summit, a differentiated space with depth and levels, whereas modern States... develop a homogeneous *extensio* with an immanent centre, divisible homologous parts, and symmetrical and reversible relations. (D and G, p. 388)

Geodesy: 'that branch of applied mathematics which determines the figures and areas of large portions of the earth's surface, and the figure of the earth as a whole' (*OED*) (a 'geode', as it happens, is a kind of crystal cabinet). Blake's texts, we might say, are a terrain on which this conflict between *spatium* and *extensio* is acted out. They embody a conflict that summarises a field of encroaching modernity, wherein the Celtic figures not merely as a fantasy of priority but also as a presentiment of order, and at the same time as a different – and *differentiated* – mapping, measurement, survey of the earth. What emerges is a territorialisation that is simultaneously a textualisation, an inscription – even, as with the Welsh Triads, a translation, albeit a translation where the authenticity of the 'original' questions is 'not in question', is under a singular erasure.

Yet, of course, the apparent symmetries that inflect the portrayals of the 'states of Britain' in *Jerusalem* and elsewhere are not necessarily equivalences; there is always here a centre and a periphery, a controlling figure and a set of 'figures' (in all senses) to be controlled. In the case of Albion as an anthropo-geography, for example:

> London is between his knees, its basements fourfold;
> His right foot stretches to the sea on Dover cliffs, his heel
> On Canterbury's ruins; his right hand covers lofty Wales,
> His left Scotland; his bosom girt with gold involves
> York, Edinburgh, Durham & Carlisle, & on the front
> Bath, Oxford, Cambridge, Norwich; his right elbow
> Leans on the Rocks of Erin's Land, Ireland, ancient nation.
> (*Milton*, 39. 39–45; K, p. 531)

Or, in *Jerusalem*: 'Wales and Scotland shrink themselves to the west and to the north!' (5. 11; K, p. 623). There is no doubt that the Celtic nations are on the fringes, whether as guardians and protectors or as mere adjuncts (you can only get to Wales via Hereford): the vantage point is the site of imperial control, the holder of the axioms of command, and compared with the obscured, troubled but sacred locations of London and its environs the Celtic is in the position that Deleuze and Guattari describe as 'minoritarian'. Minorities, they say, 'are not necessarily defined by the smallness of their numbers but rather by becoming a line of fluctuation, in other words, by the gap that separates them from this or that axiom constituting a redundant majority' (D and G, p. 469).

The power of the minorities is not measured by their capacity to enter and make themselves felt within the majority system, nor even to reverse the necessarily tautological criterion of the majority, but to bring to bear the force of the nondenumerable sets, however small they may be, against the denumerable sets, even if they are infinite, reversed, or changed, even if they imply new axioms or, beyond that, a new axiomatic. (D and G, p. 471)

An axiomatic we may think of as a body of 'self-evident truths', or we may alternatively think of it, as Blake may have done, as that 'other man's system' by which he was determined not to be enslaved;[12] it would be in this sense that the apparent accuracies of number (or figure) would have a further side, would point beyond themselves, would function to disturb the self-evident (the self-evident truth, for example, of the proposition that the British are not Israelites).

  Or we may think of it (the axiomatic) as the ideological arm of the State, a State we may now wish to figure not as that which strives to embody national aspiration but rather as that which seeks to suppress national difference, that which seeks to deny peripheral power and to bend everything into the service of an ever-expanding centre. This, certainly, is the case with the fallen State which is the 'state' of the sleeping Albion, as Blake makes clear in one of his most expressive condemnations of machinic labour:

> Scotland pours out his Sons to labour at the Furnaces;
> Wales gives his Daughters to the Looms; England, nursing Mothers
> Gives to the Children of Albion & to the Children of Jerusalem.
> From the blue Mundane Shell even to the Earth of Vegetation,
> Throughout the whole Creation, which groans to be deliver'd,
> Albion groans in the deep slumbers of Death upon his Rock.
>
> (*Jerusalem*, 16. 22–7; K, p. 637)

Scotland and Wales, to be sure, are not the only localities to be subjected to this process of proto-industrial expropriation, but they are nonetheless emblematic of a subdued periphery, of a map on which they can only be borders, where they are indicated by the direction *from* an assumed English centre. This, of course, is one version of what one might call a political harmonic; the State is, after all, according to Deleuze and Guattari,

a phenomenon of *intraconsistency*. It makes points *resonate* together, points that are not necessarily already town-poles but very diverse points of order, geographic, ethnic, linguistic, moral, economic, technological particularities. It makes the town resonate with the countryside. It operates by stratification: in other words, it forms a vertical, hierarchised aggregate that spans the horizontal lines in a dimension of depth... The question is not to find out whether what is retained is natural or artificial 'boundaries', because in any event there is deterritorialisation. (D and G, p. 433)

'Town-poles', in this terminology, would not be the towns themselves; like Hereford, they would be assemblages, accumulations of value, symbolic and economic. The effort of pulling these 'poles' (which might also be region-poles or nation-poles) together is the effort of the formation of the State, as it is the effort of the formation of a phantomatic body to replace Albion in his absence – which might be better 'figured' as a continuing deferral of presence, the 'groans' of his slumber indistinguishable from the groans of those bent to his unknowing service, or from the groans of the machinery labouring to maintain the territory in being, to prevent its relapse into the primitive (Celtic) earth, to prohibit its reterritorialisation into a land of sacred groves from which, like more recently beleaguered rain-forests, neither profit nor meaning can be extracted.

Where the kind of 'schizoanalysis' proposed by Deleuze and Guattari can truly help with Blake, I think, is in its attempt to move beyond polarities into a realm of multiple 'poles of energy'; similarly, they depict the 'state' of war in terms not of an opposition, an enmity, an outbreak or continuation of hostilities, but in terms of a 'war machine'. That war machine, they claim, originates (if it can be said to 'originate') not within the State: it

is of nomadic origin and is directed against the State apparatus. One of the funda-mental problems of the State is to appropriate the war machine that is foreign to it and make it a piece in its apparatus, in the form of a stable military institution; and the State has always encountered major difficulties in this. (D and G, p. 230)

It would seem to follow from this account that any mobilisation of the war machine in pursuit of specific objectives (the suppression, as it might be, of minorities, Celtic or otherwise) will tend to release quite other forces:

The war machine is not uniformly defined, and comprises something other than increasing quantities of force... *The other pole* seems to be the essence; it is when the war machine, with infinitely lower 'quantities', has as its object not war but the drawing of a creative line of flight, the composition of a smooth space and the movement of people in that space. (D and G, p. 422)

If I interpret these sentences correctly, then it would seem to follow that the State-at-war is always – ineluctably, resonantly, frustratingly – at war *with itself*; its attempt to fight, to rid itself of the other, becomes, seen from an 'other' perspective, an aspect of its own desire to form itself into a smooth space, to rid itself of internal contradictions, to achieve the fantasised goal of 'intraconsistency'. When Blake searches for an emblem to express the impossibility, indeed the inconceivability, of a resolution for this task, he finds and dwells upon a figure that is indubitably Celtic. It is also multiple, and so it is hard to give it a single 'figure' or a single name, but the closest we might come to such a name would be 'Gwendolen'.

> Then laugh'd Gwendolen, & her Laughter shook the Nations & Familys of
> The Dead beneath Beulah from Tyburn to Golgotha and from
> Ireland to Japan: furious her Lions & Tygers & Wolves sport before
> Los on the Thames & Medway...   (*Jerusalem*, 63. 32–5; K, p. 698)[13]

One path which I do not have space to follow here would be Gwendolen's relation to the notion of 'becoming-animal'; another would be this further explosion of the increasingly tantalising and energetic relation between the 'nation-poles' of Ireland and Japan. Instead, I want to focus on Gwendolen's (s)laughter, her unpronounceable exultation at the mobilisation of the war machine. She and her sister Cambel (Cambria, Campbell, a naming for the fringe, an altogether 'improper' name, in the context of which to invoke Geoffrey of Monmouth (another 'improper' name) is altogether to evade the complexities of this specific nominal mapping of the unconscious) laugh; they drink; they dance; they are, singly or together, in some sense Boadicea, with the blood of their/her enemies running from the chariot wheels.[14] But also, they work; they are apparently in the service of the State, but they are also – everywhere, and not merely on the periphery – working, but to a different machinic rhythm:

> Plinlimmon shrunk away: Snowdon trembled: the mountains
> Of Wales & Scotland beheld the descending War, the routed flying.
> Red run the streams of Albion: Thames is drunk with blood
> As Gwendolen cast the shuttle of war, as Cambel return'd the beam,
> The Humber & the Severn are drunk with the blood of the slain.
>   (66. 59–63; K, p. 703)

One might wonder how 'routed' is to be pronounced, or whether it is (also) unpronounceable. The 'historical' (legendary) Gwendolen drowned herself in the Severn. 'Wales & Scotland alone sustain the fight!', we gather a few lines later (67), wondering all the while against what actual or threatened revolution this military/productive activity is being mounted.

> In beauty the Daughters of Albion divide & unite at will,
> Naked & drunk with blood. Gwendolen dancing to the timbrel
> Of War, reeling up the Streets of London, she divides in twain
> Among the Inhabitants of Albion...   (58. 1–4; K, p. 689)

The Celtic cannot be kept at bay, it erupts in the very heartland, the country comes to the city and reterritorialises it 'at will', timbrel becoming tumbril, dancing, laughter and slaughter, but there is of course more to it than this; there is also the question of lineages scripted on the earth, the question of who, or what, begets whom, or what, the question of 'becoming-woman', which is also a question, as we have already seen Blake put it, of what might happen to shake the families of the dead (those dead whose burial place was supposed to be in Annwfn, in that 'west' represented variously by Wales and Ireland, by the farthest infernal reaches of the Celtic periphery).[15]

The war machine entertains a relation to families that is very different from its relation to the State. In the war machine, the family is a band vector instead of a fundamental cell; a genealogy is transferred from one family to another according to the aptitude of a given family at a given time to realise the maximum of 'agnatic solidarity'. Here, it is not the public eminence of a family that determines its place in a State organism but the reverse; it is the secret power (*puissance*), or strength of solidarity, and the corresponding genealogical mobility that determines its eminence in a war body . . . collective bodies always have fringes or minorities that reconstitute equivalents of the war machine . . . (D and G, p. 366)[16]

Indeed they do: and here the 'Celtic fringe' incarnates that war machine through a vicious parody of 'the machine' itself which is indissolubly bound together with a 'becoming-woman'. 'Agnatic': related on the father's side only. This would seem to be true and not true of the 'familial' relationships Blake depicts throughout *Jerusalem* between the sons and daughters of Albion. Certainly Albion is their only origin; he is, in all senses, the 'state' in which they live, their father, environment and commanding absence. But here too there is a violent and fluctuating sisterhood, a female nomadry, held partly in the 'classification', the catalogue, and partly not – as the 'figures' (the impossible numeration of anima)[17] shift and change.

> These are united into Tirzah and her Sisters on Mount Gilead,
> Cambel & Gwendolen & Conwenna & Cordella & Ignoge.
> And these united into Rahab in the Covering Cherub on Euphrates,
> Gwiniverra & Gwinefred & Gonorill & Sabrina beautiful,
> Estrild, Mehetabel & Ragan . . .   (*Jerusalem*, 5. 40–4; K, p. 624)

These figures for a feminised (but nomadic and warlike) 'ancient Britain' cannot be fully separated, they are bound together (like a sheaf), their beauty is not to be held within the hard edges and lines of imperial control:

Gwendolen & Cambel & Gwineverra
Are melted into the gold, the silver, the liquid ruby,
The crysolite, the topaz, the jacinth & every precious stone.
(9. 22–4; K, p. 628)

It would be delightful, it would be the fulfilment of a tremendous desire, to pause for a moment on this 'liquid ruby', to check whether we are looking here at a jewel, at a drop of blood, at a melting of the feminine... but of course we cannot, because the war machine is moving on. That war machine, according to Deleuze and Guattari as well as to Blake, has a particular relation to the feminine, in the specific shape of the 'girl'. On this point though, fraught with complicated desire as it is, Deleuze and Guattari are unwilling to 'trust' their own politically troubling forward movement and refer us instead to a well-kept secret in the form of Trost, a 'mysterious author', who

painted a portrait of the girl, to whom he linked the fate of the revolution: her speed, her freely machinic body, her intensities, her abstract line or line of flight, her molecular production, her indifference to memory, her nonfigurative character – 'the nonfigurative of desire'. Joan of Arc? The special role of the girl in Russian terrorism: the girl with the bomb, guardian of dynamite? (D and G, p. 277)[18]

Gwendolen? Her *alter ego*, her alibi, Cambel? Cambria or Scotia, offspring of the 'kings of Britain'? A sinister Celtic sisterhood:

'O sister Cambel', said Gwendolen, as their long beaming light
Mingled above the Mountain, 'what shall we do to keep
These awful forms in our soft bands, distracted with trembling?'
(*Jerusalem*, 80. 83–5; K, p. 723)

But this would not be the only construction of family we might be able to locate within the body of Albion, within the relation between, for example, London and the Celtic periphery:

London is a stone of her ruins, Oxford is the dust of her walls,
Sussex & Kent are her scatter'd garments, Ireland her holy place,
And the murder'd bodies of her little ones are Scotland and Wales.
(*Jerusalem*, 29. 19–21; K, p. 653)

Everywhere present in the fantasised and reconstructed past, the Celtic nations remain as haunting memories, as that which continues to challenge the *absence of memory* which is the essential ground for the foundation of the State. The State deals in invented memories, it deals in its own essential monumentalisation, it sets its own heroes in 'stone' in order to obscure

the ruins that are all that remain of what the State has erased.[19] Every
State is founded in a wilderness; if there was anything there before, it has
been murdered, thrown to the winds, 'figured' as a non-inscription. What
Deleuze and Guattari never seemed to realise – but perhaps Blake did – is
that there is *no nomad*, it would be 'mad' to think otherwise; what there is
is a fantasy of the nomad, an idea that there was a prior territorialisation;
but this prior territorialisation was *prior to all territorialisation*, it did not
think in those terms, its resistance to expropriation derives from its freedom
from 'propriation' in the first place, its absence of propriety, the absolute
difference from lines, grids, numbers, that can only be recaptured through
the reinscription of text which is, in the strict sense, an epitaph for a lost
minority (which would also be the 'minority', the age of irresponsibility, of
a State that can only figure itself as born adult, as having had no latency,
no 'dark age', no 'Celticism').

In this condition, all that remains would be a haunting, a set of impossible
transformations that bite at the heels of the State and its mobilised machinery and that seem to rise up in letters upon the otherwise uninscribed and
pristine 'stone':

> Reuben return'd to Bashan; in despair he slept on the Stone.
> Then Gwendolen divided into Rahab & Tirza in Twelve Portions.
> Los rolled his Eyes into two narrow circles, then sent him
> Over Jordan; all terrified fled: they became what they beheld.
> (*Jerusalem*, 34. 51–4; K, p. 661)

This is the (t)error occasioned by the minority; that one might lapse, that the
terror of absence might become too much, might come to participate in the
transgression, the excess that previous territorialisations might represent.

Whether it be the infinite set of the nonwhites of the periphery, or the restricted
set of the Basques, Corsicans, etc., everywhere we look we see the conditions for
a worldwide movement: the minorities recreate 'nationalitarian' phenomena that
the nation-states had been charged with controlling and quashing. (D and G,
p. 470)

Deleuze and Guattari here, of course, refer to a contemporary scenario, and
do so in what are perhaps unduly optimistic terms; but the perspectival sense
of 'everywhere we look', the insistence on the parodic, phantomatic role
of the 'nationalitarian', these are categories that we can apply to Blake,
aspects of the fear of Albion that, firmly located as they are in Britain's 'war
with itself' during his lifetime, refer us also to a broader set of problems
associated with enlightenment, modernity, progress and all that (Celticism)

which continually prevents us from achieving the Edenic without having to deal with its prior existence, its Atlantean loss.[20]

Proper and improper naming would here then be crucial: a putative distinction between a naming that might set itself to an impossible task – to sever the roots of the past, to allow for modernisation, to banish the phantom – and a naming that might seek to gather up these older resources into poles of energy – Hereford, Albion, Gwendolen – or might indeed find itself more accurately at the mercy of all which accrues silently to the utterance of the 'proper' name. 'The proper name does not indicate a subject; nor does a noun take on the value of a proper name as a function of a form or a species. The proper name fundamentally designates something that is of the order of the event, of becoming or of the haecceity' (D and G, p. 264).

Naming in Blake is, I suggest, largely improper, for all manner of reasons. It is improper because it mixes incompatible mythologies; it is improper because it perpetuates the history of forgery and fraudulence; it is improper because it tests memory, Blake's own as well as his reader's; it is improper because, as Blake intuited, the 'English' language is itself 'improper', it cannot be reduced to a monolithic (monotheistic) code (inscribed on a single 'lith', stone). What we find inscribed on the words as we use them is scandalous, it 'bespeaks' our mixed heritage, it reactivates long-forgotten conflicts, it sets in motion all kinds of 'absent' war machines.

Such naming, fraudulent, legendary and resonant, coagulates around the Celtic, around the 'warlike naked Britons' as much as around 'London stone', around periphery and centre; it tests the possibility of 'description' – and particularly, for us, the description of an absent object or painting, and one that purports to touch on the vexed question of 'antiquity', and thus we might reasonably doubt the veracity of a 'descriptive catalogue' while at the same time needing to quote it in the search for a certain 'authenticity'. We might need to hear of

...all the fables of Arthur and his round table; of the warlike naked Britons; of Merlin; of Arthur's conquest of the whole world; of his death, or sleep, and promise to return again; of the Druid monuments or temples; of the pavement of Watling-street; of London stone; of the caverns in Cornwall, Wales, Derbyshire, and Scotland; of the Giants of Ireland and Britain. (*A Descriptive Catalogue*; K, p. 577)

But the question would then be what tongue, what speech, what comprehensibility will attend upon this recounting, this rememoration which will always be a dubious translation, an antiquarian exercise in which the origins are never guaranteed, the validity of peripheral memory (like peripheral vision) will always be 'subject', in the strongest sense, to central control. Deleuze and Guattari have a thought on that, which is a thought also, although it cannot know itself as such, on Blake. It is cast, as often in *A Thousand Plateaus*, as an instruction, as a psychopolitical recommendation:

> Gain some time, and then perhaps renounce or wait. The necessity of not having control over language, of being a foreigner in one's own tongue, in order to draw speech to oneself and 'bring something incomprehensible into the world'. Such is the form of exteriority, the relation between brother and sister, the becoming-woman of the thinker, the becoming-thought of the woman: the *Gemüt* that refuses to be controlled, that forms a war machine... Is it by chance that whenever a 'thinker' shoots an arrow, there is a man of the State, a shadow or an image of a man of the State, that counsels and admonishes him, and wants to assign him a target or 'aim'? (D and G, p. 378)

What comes to mind most obviously in Blake is *The Song of Los*, and his superbly ironic economic advice that the 'Councellor' should 'throw his curb / Of Poverty on the laborious' while 'the privy admonishers of men / Call for fires in the City' (6. 15–16, 19–20; K, p. 247); what is perhaps more important, though, is the idea of 'being a foreigner in one's own tongue', which could be described as the perpetual condition of the minoritarian or the diasporic but might in Blake's context also be seen as related to a question of usurpation of language, a question of what language in which to speak. This is not at all to suggest that Blake could have been 'master' of any tongue other than the Cockney in which he wrote and, no doubt, spoke; but it is to be reminded that every 'tongue' is haunted by other tongues, that every territorialisation is haunted by its own renunciation of the terrifying thought of origins, that the very site of Albion is uncannily already occupied by that which must therefore be pushed out to the Celtic periphery (*where*, after all, is the name 'Albion'?) – rather, perhaps, as a primal horde might push out the father to (what might be too easily described as) a wilderness.

But the Celtic is, of course, not the only proper name under which to consider these flights, these trajectories, these reterritorialisations. There is, after all, also the question of Blake and Derbyshire, with which too Gwendolen has a special relation – related, yet different; but perhaps illuminated by these 'closing words':

> These were his last words, relapsing
> Hoarse from his rocks, from caverns of Derbyshire & Wales
> And Scotland, utter'd from the Circumference into Eternity.
> (*Jerusalem*, 23. 26–8; K, p. 646)

CHAPTER 5

The Welsh American dream: Iolo Morganwg, Robert Southey and the Madoc legend

Caroline Franklin

Walter Savage Landor once remarked patronisingly of Bristol, 'I know of no mercantile place so literary.'[1] But it was precisely because the largest British metropolis outside London at the beginning of the eighteenth century was the gateway to imperial trade, that Bristol produced writers engaged in questioning both colonialism and the industrial revolution whose capital investment derived from the profits of that empire. Tumultuous Bristol was famous equally for its riots and for the self-defeating conservatism of its Corporation. West-Country Dissenters and Evangelicals campaigned against its slave trade and a vigorous peace movement opposed the war against revolutionary France until 1797. This context favoured poetry inspired by that turn, which heralded British 'Romanticism', away from Enlightenment narratives of the inevitable progress of reason, commerce and civilisation. Turning away also from the classical genres and styles associated with the Roman empire on which Britain modelled herself and which therefore formed the basis of male ruling-class education, the new poetry demonstrated sympathy instead with primitive or vernacular cultures which had been or were in the process of being superseded.

Thomas Chatterton steeped himself in the Middle Ages, forging for Bristol the romance of her own pre-industrial past. Hannah More was another Bristolian mimic whose anti-Paineite *Village Politics* (1792) by carpenter 'Will Chip' ventriloquised the vernacular broadsheets of pedlars. Her one-time protégée, the Bristol milkwoman Ann Yearsley, the genuine working-class article, wrote as 'Lactilla', challenging the assumptions of Virgilian pastoral. Mary Robinson (née Darby), a former pupil at the More sisters' school, articulated the anguish of the marginalised: whether deserted woman, Negro slave, maniac or prisoner. But most famous to posterity was the circle which formed around Bristolian Robert Southey in 1794 and which saw the publication of William Wordsworth and Samuel Taylor Coleridge's *Lyrical Ballads* by the Bristol publisher Joseph Cottle in 1798.

Joseph Cottle later famously recounted the story of his first meeting with the young writers Robert Southey, the Quaker Robert Lowell (author of *Bristol, a Satire*, 1794), George Burnett and Coleridge who were planning to emigrate to the banks of the Susquehanna with the Fricker sisters and others, to found a community based on the ideals of Pantisocracy.[2] His High Street shop became the centre of their literary circle, and he engaged to publish their poetry while Coleridge and Southey began earning money for the venture by giving a series of public lectures in rooms above the Corn Market: Coleridge on political and moral subjects and Southey on history. Coleridge challenged not only the reactionary Burke but also those Paineite Jacobins content to leave the industrialised lower classes out of account. He has been described as then 'a revolutionary, egalitarian, Christian pacifist'.[3] When Cottle wrote his reminiscences, both Coleridge and Southey had become political reactionaries, so Pantisocracy was tactfully passed off as quixotic youthful idealism. But actually the dream focused their writing for many years, even when Coleridge eventually settled for the Somerset village of Nether Stowey and Southey substituted Neath for the American wilds. Neither was Pantisocracy exceptional, being only one of many such emigration schemes being organised by Dissenters, Unitarians and freethinkers who were fleeing the reactionary backlash against radicals.[4]

Joseph Priestley, whose home and laboratory was destroyed by a Church and King mob, was one of thousands to settle in Pennsylvania. In Wales, many of whose Quakers had accompanied William Penn in seventeenth-century colonisation of America, the eighteenth-century emigration movement was so strong it inspired a revival of the legend of Madoc, a twelfth-century Welsh prince who supposedly discovered America before Columbus. In its newly millenarian manifestation the myth encompassed travellers' tales of 'white' native Americans who spoke some Welsh, perhaps the descendants of Madoc's colony who had themselves fled monarchical tyranny and could form the kernel of a New World Utopia of Liberty.

This legend became the subject of the long poem Robert Southey intended to be his masterpiece, on which he worked intermittently for a decade and which he finally published in 1805. The poem was of autobiographical significance, not only in enshrining what Pantisocracy had originally meant to the poet, but in dialogising his evolving views on colonisation. (By 1813 Southey would support an Evangelical campaign for a change in the law to permit missionaries to proselytise Christianity in India.) So far did his emphasis change that *Madoc* succeeds in laying disconcertingly bare the paradoxes on which the original myth itself is based, producing in the process an artistic failure, yet a poem of great interest to the cultural historian. For the discordant voices in Southey's *Madoc* illustrate not only Southey's personal journey from pacifist Jacobin to militant imperialist, but, more interestingly, the way in which Welsh post-colonial construction of a myth of nationhood has been adopted to provide material for English romantic writing – which paradoxically adapts it to serve the cause of the British empire.[5] To illustrate this process, we will first look at the way the myth was presented by Southey's Welsh contemporaries and sources.

Not only prominent in the extensive notes, but also making a cameo appearance as a character in the story itself was Edward Williams (who wrote in Welsh under his bardic name of 'Iolo Morganwg' which translates as 'Ned of Glamorgan'). Born in 1746 in Llancarfan in the Vale of Glamorgan, he was of that older generation of antiquarians, folklorists and etymologists who bridged the gap between Enlightenment historiography and the Romantic primitivism of Southey's generation.[6]

Williams was one of a group of autodidact Welsh artisans dedicated to the preservation of the Welsh language, literature and culture now seemingly on the verge of extinction with the onset of industrialisation and consequent anglicisation. Like many of his friends he was also a fiery radical in the Blakean mould – the product of cults of religious Dissent rather than the cult of Reason. From 1791–5 Williams made an ultimately unsuccessful attempt to survive as a professional writer in English in London, acting as chief promulgator of bardic, Druidic fantasies to the Jacobin circle of Joseph Johnson as well as to the Gwyneddigion society of the London Welsh.[7] A stonemason by trade and a pedestrian both by necessity and principle (he refused to accept rides in rich men's carriages), he had tramped all over Wales in search of manuscripts and made himself the authority of the day on Welsh culture. In 1797 Southey was writing to Williams's colleague William Owen (later-Pughe) for antiquarian information. By August 1805 he could recommend Williams to Cottle, who was also composing a Romantic Welsh poem, *The Fall of Cambria* (1809), assuring him that the latter would 'tell you all that either history or tradition has preserved'.[8] Not only had Williams been in person, by letter and in print a primary source of information for *Madoc*, but (unbeknown to Southey) he had actually supplied many of the notes for other histories Southey had cited, such as William Owen (-Pughe)'s *Cambrian Biography* (1803) and William Warrington's *The History of Wales* (1786).[9]

Of course, Southey did not realise, nor even any of Williams's more sceptical contemporaries, that Williams was not only a meticulous scholar and a fine poet in Welsh in his own right, but also a brilliant forger. Far more convincing than Chatterton (with whom he was fascinated) or Macpherson, it

took major twentieth-century scholarship to sift his 'discoveries' of lyrics by
Dafydd ap Gwilym from the genuine fourteenth-century poems published
in *Barddoniaeth Dafydd ab Gwilym* (1789), co-edited by the unsuspecting
Owain Myfyr and William Owen (-Pughe). Moreover, as he was the main-
stay of Welsh antiquarianism for much of his long life and since everything
he touched was liable to imperceptible embellishments and manipulation
of evidence, his mythmaking sank deep into the psyche of Welsh nationalist
consciousness just as it was forming. His invented *Gorsedd* ceremony was
in 1819 incorporated into the National Eisteddfod (a newly patriotic revival
of the defunct tradition of local poetry competitions) where it remains a
disconcerting spectacle of bogus Celticism to this day.

Johnson's dictionary gives two meanings for 'forge': 'the act of the forge'
in making as well as 'the crime of falsification'. A poet was a 'maker' in the
days of the medieval poetry Williams wanted to preserve; the meetings of
the bards he wanted to revive in his 'gorsedd' ceremonies had been guilds,
where the secrets of the wordsmiths' complex crafting of the patterning
of sounds were passed on. A craftsman in stone, Williams learnt to craft
poetry in the ancient Welsh forms by imitation, and, like Samuel Beckett
in our own century, chose the further distancing discipline of writing in his
second language (English was the language of his home). He called himself
a bard not a poet, signifying the social and political role of remembrancer
of national culture rather than a writer concerned primarily with his own
subjectivity. He probably felt that forgeries were acceptable if replicating the
spirit of the authentic authors, or even merely of the particularly national
characteristics of the culture; that his myth-making was truer to the spirit
of Wales than narratives conforming with accepted English versions of 'history'. The profusion of scurrilous political squibs and lampoons amongst
his unpublished manuscripts suggests that he even took an amoral Brechtian
delight in subverting the 'superstructure' of orthodox scholarship, believing
that he could thus bring about ideological change more quickly, and that
his own radical ends justified the means. Ian Haywood convincingly links
the rise of literary forgery with the onset of capitalist notions of authorship
in the eighteenth century, enshrined in the 1709 copyright act which first
defined art in terms of intellectual property.[10] In contrast to the modern
cult of the authorial personality, Williams stressed in his *Poems, Lyrical and
Pastoral* (1794) that 'poetry, in the hands of the bards, became the vehicle
of theological, political, and moral instruction'.[11]

Bristol is also significant in Williams's story. It was the economic capital
of South Wales for Swansea was only a small port and Cardiff a village. As
well as a flourishing literary culture with its own publishers, newspapers
and ancient public lending library, Bristol had an important artistic circle

with a distinct, prolific school of carvers of monuments and sculptures.[12] It was therefore a prime source of work for a stonemason, and Williams was so often in Bristol that he mentions in a letter to his wife on 29 November 1794 that he kept books and papers on literary projects stored there to work on.[13] This essay will suggest that the twin economic roles of Bristol as metropolis of Wales and the West and chief port of the British Empire is a key to understanding the shaping of Williams's extraordinary literary personality, especially with reference to the changing character of his home county of Glamorgan – whose centrality to Welsh culture he was determined to establish.

As a metropolis, Bristol dominated trade with South Wales chiefly through the exchange of the raw materials of the Welsh countryside for the manufactured and imported goods of the city.[14] Bristol's economic relationship with long-conquered Wales was therefore arguably colonial like that with the West Indies. Bristol provided a huge market for Welsh agricultural produce, while its manufactories finished Welsh woollen, leather, lace goods and tinware. The next inevitable stage was Bristol's function in providing capital for investment and thus bringing about the industrial revolution. The profits of the slave trade found their major outlet in opening up the heavy industries of South Wales. It was Bristol merchants who financed the Welsh copper, then iron and coal industries: in places such as Dowlais, Merthyr, Machen, Basaleg and Ebbw Vale. Most of the copper, brass and tinplate and some iron was in turn exported back to the West Indies.[15] Edward Williams's beloved Glamorgan was being transformed out of all recognition by Bristolian imperialist merchant capitalism from the historic rural landscape he had hymned in 'Davona's Vale' in 1777 to the despoliation of furnace and mine. The fate of the new industrial workers inspired Coleridge in his Bristol lectures to compare them with the slaves of the colonies: '... the necessity of twelve hours daily toil, would make my *soul* a slave, and sink *the rational* being in the mere animal'.[16] Bilingual Glamorgan had evolved its own particularly hybrid culture: its coastal vale had absorbed linguistic and cultural influences from the Romans, Vikings and Normans; the name of Williams's home village of Flemingston (sometimes written 'Flimston') indicates later foreign settlers. But now as the English flooded in by the thousand to work in the new industries, Glamorgan seemed a microcosm of the precariousness of the whole of Welsh culture in all its ancient diversity, subject to the homogenisation of English imperialist power on the one hand and self-immolation through Methodism on the other.

Williams was only one of many Glamorgan scholars and thinkers galvanised by a new awareness of the colonial dependence of Wales into campaigning for the preservation of the ancient Welsh language which consequently underwent a South Walian revival. He himself had been taught by local lexicographers Thomas Richards of Coychurch and John Walters of Llandough.[17] As well as other autodidact intellectuals like the Deist John Bradford, poet Lewis Hopkin, and the Unitarian Edward Ifan, the county had also produced radical Dissenter Dr Richard Price, an adviser to the American republic, and the Deist David Williams, who had been invited to advise France on drawing up its new constitution.[18] It was the contempt of North Walians of the *Gwyneddigion* for Glamorgan Welsh which had inspired Edward Williams to pioneer research into South Walian dialects; it was when the renowned scholar Evan Evans ('Ieuan Fardd') showed him the ruined house of Ifor Hael (patron of Dafydd ap Gwilym) at Basaleg that he made the South Walian noble 'Ivor the Generous' the subject of so many (sometimes forged) encomiums that the newly founded workers' benevolent society, the Ivorites, came to be named after him.[19]

Though the English capitalist exploitation of Glamorgan was the trigger, Williams's cult of Celticism aimed at the ultimate emancipation of the whole of Wales. His politics was, like Blake's, born out of religious radicalism. He campaigned for the rights of Dissenters, portraying the Church of England as linguistically and culturally alien to Wales. He preached peace even during the war against revolutionary France. He proselytised natural religion: he described himself as 'the oldest Unitarian in Wales'[20] and in 1802 helped found the movement in Merthyr Tydfil. His belief that Wales had a more ancient history of Christianity than England was the core of his nationalism. He created new cultural institutions of the Folk (though in the guise of revivals), such as the *Gorsedd*, or Order of the Bards of Great Britain, which he orchestrated first in 1792 at Primrose Hill, London. This colloquium of a Welsh intellectual élite, was intended to spearhead the revolution through educating the people in their proud history and gave poets the role of acknowledged legislators. In articles in the *Gentleman's Magazine* in 1789 and the posthumously published *Cyfrinach Beirdd Ynys Prydain* (1829) he declared the guilds of Medieval bards had evolved from the rituals of the Druids of the Romano-British era, which he asserted were pacifist in nature and linked to the Jewish Cabbala and Brahminism, having been originally handed down from the Patriarchs themselves, entirely by-passing institutional Christianity.[21] Keeping the knowledge of ancient Welsh culture alive thus took on the appurtenances of religion.

Williams was a brilliant showman but the London Welsh as a whole were gripped by Utopianism in the 1790s. Influenced by the pageantry of secular festivals choreographed by David to celebrate the triumph of Liberty in the

French Revolution, the *Gwynweddigion* had even ordered the medals for the 1789 *Eisteddfod*, revived to act as a Welsh Academy, from the engraver to the French National Assembly.[22] It was this Millenarian radicalism which produced a revival of the Madoc legend, intensifying when England declared war against revolutionary France and a reactionary backlash ensued against Jacobinism, and especially when compositions by Burkean reactionaries like Gwallter Mechain and David Thomas ('Dafydd Ddu Eryri') began to scoop the prizes at the eisteddfodau of the early 1790s. To Welsh radicals, Madoc became a mythic Welsh Moses; America the Promised Land of Liberty. The myth had been kept alive through the Dissenting culture of the American Welsh in the eighteenth century, witness poems such as Richard Lewis's *Upon Prince Madoc's Expedition*, published in *The American Weekly Mercury* No. 739 (19–26 February 1734), and inscribed to 'the worthy Society of Ancient Britons, meeting at Philadelphia, March 1st'.[23] But it was reignited in Wales itself by Dr John Williams's *An Enquiry into the Truth of the Tradition concerning the Discovery of America by Prince Madog ab Owen Gwynedd about AD 1170* (1791). This inspired the Voltairean folklorist and healer, William Jones, Llangadfan, to make an impassioned address at the Llanrwst eisteddfod that year, exhorting all 'indigenous Cambro-Britons', especially oppressed tenant-farmers like himself, to quit their slave-masters and emigrate to the land of Liberty. He later suggested that Madoc might even have been the first Inca emperor, having discovered Mexico and Peru, for 'Mango Capae sounds very like ap Madog, & Mango by a very easy transition becomes Madog'.[24]

A month later, Edward Williams was writing on the subject in the *Gentleman's Magazine*, and by March 1792, he and William Owen (-Pughe) had come up with such an amount of 'evidence' elaborating on the original thesis that Dr John Williams had to bring out a second edition to incorporate it.[25] All Iolo Morganwg's scholarly genius went into the amassing and manipulating of convincing evidence (including thirty travellers' accounts of Welsh-speaking Indians); so much so that he prepared a paper 'to be laid before... but... not to be publicly read' to the Royal Society,[26] artfully taking advantage of the Nootka Sound dispute with Spain to stress the colonialist opportunities for sponsors of an expedition to find the Welsh Indians:

Query? Is not the investigation of this subject, a more proper object of national attention to <u>Britain</u> than exploring the mountains of Abyssinia in search of the Nile. Our claim it seems, to <u>Nootka Sound</u> has been allowed by Spain, the <u>River of the west</u> or Oregon goes up into the country of these civilised Indians... our brethren – and amongst whom... we might soon establish a <u>flourishing settlement</u>...[27]

In another draft, he went further:

... it might be of great advantage to commerce, the wide continent would take vast quantities from our hands of <u>British manufacturers</u>, we should obtain many valuable commodities... perhaps silver and gold.[28]

He wrote in quite a different strain, of course, when proposing a similar expedition to the Americans themselves:

I have from the beginning been an enthusiastic admirer of your glorious and successful struggles for <u>Liberty</u>, your Republican principles, your excellent Constitutions of Government.[29]

Like Southey, Coleridge and the other enthusiasts for Pantisocracy, Edward Williams decided to emigrate to America, and, like them, he never got there.[30] Gwyn A. Williams has told the story of the Utopian expedition planned by Williams, William Owen (-Pughe) and David Samwell (poet 'Dafydd Ddu Meddyg', surgeon to Captain Cook) to seek the Welsh Indians on the banks of the Missouri. Though he embarked on a rigorous training programme for survival in the wilds, Williams succumbed to a breakdown in health, abandoning his disciple the young John Evans to undertake the unsuccessful enterprise alone, and endure countless hardships in the service of Spain and the Welsh West-Indian adventurer Jacques Clamorgan before his death at the age of twenty-nine.

As the tide of reaction turned at home, some Welsh Jacobins had little choice *but* to flee to America, such as the Glamorganshire Baptist minister Morgan John Rhys in 1794.[31] Rhys had translated Volney into Welsh, pioneered Sunday schools, and set up the first periodical in Welsh in 1793, after returning from France where he preached that the Revolution was the work of God against tyranny. Hounded out of Wales, Rhys travelled throughout America, championing the rights of the Negroes and campaigning for peace with the native Americans before founding the *Gwladfa* (Welsh national home) for persecuted Dissenters at Beulah in Pennsylvania. Meanwhile by 1797 Edward Williams was organising a more utilitarian emigration scheme: a 'South Wales association for the more easy providing of a passage to America' for 120 men, women and children.[32] He also proposed a 'Beneficent Society for communicating to the Indians of North America the benefits of a peaceful and friendly intercourse with the Dominions of Great Britain', urging: 'How many of these nations, once numerous, have been extirpated by those who, under the pretence of converting them to Christianity, have only their own interest in view...'[33]

He also speculated to himself:

Who knows but that I shall one day or another take it into my head to imagine that I am able to write as good an Epic poem as the <u>Iliad</u> of <u>Homer</u> on the discovery of America by <u>Madoc Prince of Wales</u>.[34]

In the event, the task was undertaken by Robert Southey. But when Williams published his English poetry, *Poems, Lyric and Pastoral*, 2 vols. (1794), from which the Bristolian would quote extensively in notes to *Madoc*, he announced on the first page of the preface:

I had, and still have, an intention of going to America, partly to fly from the numerous injuries I have received from the boasted laws of this land . . . [and] to ascertain the truth of an opinion, prevalent in *Wales* . . . that there are still existing, in the interior parts of the American continent, the remains of a *Welsh Colony* that went over there in the twelfth century under the conduct of Madoc . . .

The collection had been delayed by Williams's breakdown, which, though exacerbated by poverty and laudanum addiction, was probably triggered by the persecution he and other radicals suffered at the outbreak of the war with France. 1793–4 saw a coalition between Pitt and the conservative Whigs to stamp out Jacobinism; the treason trials which Williams attended; and the suspension of Habeas Corpus. Government spies reported on Williams, spreading rumours he would depart to America with his subscription money, and his wife wrote fearfully begging him to curtail his Jacobin writings. In these circumstances, *Poems, Lyric and Pastoral* is an extraordinary production, evidencing all Williams's genius in controlling heterogeneous readers' responses – through ventriloquising a range of poses. The list of Subscribers is in itself testimony to his personal charm and showmanship. Who else could boast both the Prince of Wales and Thomas Paine! The poems are declared to be the 'real unsophisticated productions of the self-tutored Journeyman Mason' (xiii) and Williams insisted in dressing the part even to carrying his tools in his audience with the prince. The collection is dominated by conventional pastoral verse extolling the joys of peasant life in Glamorganshire, calculated to appeal to aristocrat subscribers like Elizabeth Montagu, and writers such as Anna Barbauld, Francis Burney, Ann Yearsley, Anna Seward and the orientalist, Sir William Jones. But the history of bardism elaborated in poems and voluminous notes in the second volume was more than picturesque Celtic costume: it attempted to rehabilitate the Bard (and Williams claimed to be the last one) as true historian of his culture. Moreover, acerbic notes to many poems, especially those on the horrors of war and in praise of America suggest such a role could be oppositional, explaining the presence of subscribers like General Washington, Drs Priestley and Price, Citoyen Jansen

and John Horne Tooke. Nevertheless, the way the author portrays himself
as a solitary, melancholy eccentric in the preface and as an 'oddity' (p. 95)
perhaps defused any qualms of Evangelical subscribers such as 'Humanity's
Wilberforce', the Bowdler family and Hannah More that such radicalism
was any more than quirky eccentricity. *Poems* was widely and favourably
reviewed, despite the *Gentleman's Magazine*'s disquiet at the 'heterogeneous
and unnatural mixture [of] . . . poetry and politics'.[35]

Williams wrote drily to John Walters on 21 January 1794:

The Notes on my Ode on converting a sword into a pruning hook and those on
the [modern] war song of British Savages are the most obnoxious, but unluckily,
I fear not sufficiently so . . . I hope however they will make some noise from the
circumstances (which some have called impudence) of their being dedicated to the
Prince.[36]

He says he wishes he could be another Thomas Paine in his writings but
cannot for the sake of his family:

I will not endeavour to be so until I am in America, and there I will publish my
Kingcraft versus Christianity: with a plan for abolishing the Christian religion as
being inimical to the rights of Kings.

Note the language of inversion of orthodox doctrine which E. P. Thompson
points out as characteristic of the demotic tradition of Radical Dissent
which had survived since the seventeenth century, surfacing in the 1790s.[37]

In 'Address to the Inhabitants of Wales, Exhorting them to Emigrate,
with William Penn, to Pennsylvania', Williams actually ventriloquises a
seventeenth-century Dissenter or 'enthusiast'. But he takes care to set up a
discrepancy between the speaker's impassioned appeal to 'Britain's ancient
race' to emigrate since 'Tyranny . . . Enslaves your native plains' and the
present-day 'translator' and 'editor' who parades his scholarly objectivity in
that Enlightenment frame to the Romantic poem, the footnote:

The Church of England, in those days . . . was, it must be confessed, of a persecuting
spirit; but this error it has, long ago, seen, acknowledged, and reformed; its present
moderation is but little short of exemplary . . . (*Poems*, ii. 51).

It is up to the reader to choose whether to swallow this whole or to take
it as heavy sarcasm, bearing in mind that Dissenters were still deprived of
full civil rights, following the failed attempt to repeal the Test and Corporation Acts for Protestant Dissenters in 1790. Controversy was at its height
on the question from 1792–3, and in Wales resentment at the payment of
tithes by Dissenters denied their civil rights was particularly sharp.[38] The
reader may prefer to endorse the emigrant's vehement denunciation of 'The

soul-enslaving Priest' (stanza 9) and the draconian laws which had in Charles II's time forbidden five or more persons meeting for a non-Anglican service, on pain of fines, imprisonment and even transportation. The speaker's direct address to his/her monarch to remember the loyalty of the Welsh who supported the Royalist cause, cleverly constitutes an indirect appeal to the Princely dedicatee of Williams's collection, who was allied with the Whig opposition at this time against the King who opposed toleration. The 'editor' notes that it is not surprising Nonconformity thrives in Wales since Welsh Anglicans are still prohibited from practising their religion in their native language as had been pre-Reformation Catholics. In contrast to the warmongering motherland they are leaving (and the contemporary reader could make his/her own comparison with Britain's declaration of war against republican France in 1793), Penn's Quaker followers are 'the Sons of Peace' (st.15), and their 'laws are nought but HEAV'N'S command (stanza 17). Penn's journey recapitulates the original migration by Madoc himself, who had fled medieval civil war caused by monarchy: as alluded to by the speaker and elaborated by the editor. The new Eden of America is the true *gwladfa*, already inhabited by Madoc's descendants, 'A free-born race, of manners mild' (stanza 32).

The Madoc legend was also the subject of 'Sonnet to Hope, on resolving to emigrate to America' (ii. 186) and alluded to in the 'Ode on the mythology of the ancient British Bards' (ii. 193). The latter associated the ancient Welsh bards with the culture of Protestantism by claiming that because the Celtic church predated Roman Catholicism in Britain, the Bards were at 'perpetual war with the Church of Rome' (ii. 193). Meanwhile the present-day Bards hail the Goddess of Liberty and weep at 'Britain's foul disgrace' (of the slave trade) in contrast to America's 'Madocian plains' where 'government [is] founded on the true principles of *Liberty, Justice*, and the *Rights of Humanity*' (ii. 212).

These examples of Edward Williams's writing make clear the role the Madoc legend played in allowing the marginalised Welsh to romanticise themselves as a lost tribe – the ultimate in Rousseau's natural man – whilst also claiming to be the inheritors of the most ancient culture in Europe; and to envision escaping their own colonisation by 'the Saxons' through embarking on their own (post-)colonial adventure.[39] So comforting was this fantasy to the principality, that, as late as 1858, the adjudicators of the Llangollen Eisteddfod, refused to award the prize to Thomas Stephens's outstanding essay simply because, when setting the well-worn topic of Madoc, they could not countenance the scholarly demolition of the myth.

For both Williams and the enthusiasts of Pantisocracy at Bristol, the flight of Radicals to America represented retreat encoded as advance. Moreover, all were pacifist opponents of the slave trade (see Southey's preface to his *Poems* [1797]; and when a briefly a shopkeeper in Cowbridge in 1797, Williams famously advertised *East Indian sweets uncontaminated with human gore*).[40] Yet all failed to confront the paradox that their American republican paradise was actually founded on slavery and the suppression of the indigenous peoples. The legend of Madoc, however, circumvented the problem by identifying the Welsh with the Indians. As Robert Southey set to work on his new poem in 1794, just after Williams's *Poems* had appeared, the paradoxes soon became apparent.

In 1803 Southey wrote to Charles Danvers that *Madoc* had been

... projected in 1789 and begun in prose at that time; then it slept till 1794 when I wrote a book and a half – another interval till 97 when it was corrected and carried on to the beginning of the fourth book and then a gap again till the autumn of 1798. From that time it went fairly on till it was finished in your mother's parlour on her little table.[41]

The 1794 draft was lively though clumsy, the hero being a Man of Feeling, and like Southey's earlier *Wat Tyler* and *Joan of Arc*, the medieval setting provided a historical pedigree for its straightforward denunciation of tyrannical monarchy and support for the ideals of the French Revolution. Between 1797 and 1799 he had completely revised the poem and extended it to the fifteen-book version described to Danvers as 'finished'. Lynda Pratt has pointed out that Southey's Jacobin intentions for this version also included literary innovation, for the exotically Welsh detailing in the poem was part of a stylistic assault on classical epic as the highest form of poetry.[42] Any similarities between the story of the Welsh prince and the Trojan founder of the Roman empire were only intended to point up the contrast between the martial values of Aeneas and those of the high-minded Welsh champion of social justice, whose followers (in the 1797–9 version) were 'not of conquest greedy, nor the sons / Of Commerce, merchandising blood'. Moreover, as Pratt's study shows, Southey even experimented in this version with a radical departure from the conventional epic hero in a failed attempt to combine the character of the mythical prince Madoc with that of the Inca emperor Mango Capac, who was believed to have given over a third of the realm to the people to hold in common. We have already seen how William Jones, Llandgadfan and Edward Williams had speculated on such an identification. Pratt points out that Southey was influenced by the idealisation of Mango Capac in Joel Barlow's *The Vision of Columbus:*

a Poem (1787). Such a hero would have been ideal to celebrate the values of pantisocracy, but in the end Southey had not Iolo Morganwg's stomach for making his sources fit in quite so blatantly with his ideology:

It was my design to identify Madoc with Mango Capac, the legislator of Peru; in this I have totally failed, therefore Mango Capac is to be the hero of another poem.[43]

Despite Coleridge urging him to publish, Southey procrastinated. Not only had his project for a new kind of hero failed, but his pacifist Jacobinism was becoming striated by a fascination with military violence in a just cause. Eventually, he made further substantial revisions in 1803–4. Significantly, this was the year he decided he could no longer contribute poems to the liberal *Morning Post*.[44] 1803–4 saw the revival of sectarian conflict over whether the state church should have a monopoly over social control in the guise of education: in missionary work both amongst the working classes at home and the subjugated races in the colonies. In 1804 the British and Foreign Bible Society was founded. Both Coleridge and Southey were shortly to become the principal literary supporters of the state church as the cornerstone of the British constitution. The final version of *Madoc* shows the nature of Southey's ideological transformation.

From the beginning, the 1805 version stresses the Christianity of the Welsh expedition: on their safe return to Wales, the voyagers' first action is to pray.[45] In Madoc's account of the first encounter with the American natives, he depicts them as childlike: 'beardless' 'fearless' (*PWRS*, vol. v, p. 37), steeped in 'lethargy of life' (*PWRS*, vol. v, p. 42). It is a defining moment when the child Lincoya is made to ask the Welsh 'to conquer and protect' (*PWRS*, vol. v, p. 41) and the High Priest acknowledges them 'a race ... mightier than they, and wiser, and by heaven / Beloved and favour'd more' (*PWRS*, vol. v, p. 44). The Hoamen, having been conquered by the King of Aztlan, are 'reft of ... realm' (*PWRS*, vol. v, p. 44), their effeminacy and helplessness symbolised by their monarch being an old woman. Southey's Madoc is no Quaker but a militant Christian. He informs the Aztec King that he comes to do God's holy bidding (*PWRS*, vol. v, p. 51) in his mission to prevent the Aztecs' bloody sacrifices and oppression of the Hoamen. The narrator takes pride in the superior weaponry of the Welsh (*PWRS*, vol. v, p. 54) but they pragmatically adopt a policy of moderation after their military victory, 'That love shall mingle with their fear ... Ye shall be / As gods amongst them' advises an old man (*PWRS*, vol. v, p. 55).

The ideological contradiction at the heart of the poem is nowhere more apparent than in this military victory over the Aztecs to force upon them the adoption of Christian peace. 'Old Iolo' is depicted accompanying Madoc to superintend the ceremony (after the battle) of burying the sword (*PWRS*, vol. v, pp. 60–8), during an elaborate *gorsedd* ceremony.[46] This section is larded with Iolo Morganwg's theories of bardism, details of Welsh myths of the Land of the Departed and examples of Welsh triads (adapted and sometimes invented). Another unassimilated incongruity is the intriguing dramatic irony of Madoc returning home to Wales to find that in his absence his own country has lost her independence to the Saxons: 'We are a fallen people!' (*PWRS*, vol. v, p. 72), and that the English now intend to raise a holy crusade against the infidel. But rather than exploring the ambiguities created by such parallels, Southey merely turns back to justifying the moral necessity of the Welsh finally extirpating the natives' barbaric religious rites when they return to America.

There is no need to belabour the point that the poem has been transformed to justify colonialism by depicting it originating as 'the white man's burden' of bringing the enlightenment of Christianity to the dark continents of the world, and by the sword if necessary. We see here how an Enlightenment critique of priestcraft and superstition as the opium of the people has metamorphosed into a determination to stamp out paganism in the name of progress. Southey's letters of the time support introducing Christianity into India, South Africa and the South Sea islands 'to produce the greatest possible good' by ending the barbaric practices like polygamy, human sacrifice and infanticide.[47] The paganism of the Incas defaces Madoc's American Eden: it is represented as the worship of an enormous serpent, fed on children by unscrupulous priests. Madoc has to declare war 'to enforce / Obedience' that the natives worship only his god (*PWRS*, vol. v, pp. 253–4), and he now openly exults in the righteous vengeance of feeling 'his good sword again' (*PWRS*, vol. v, p. 323).

Southey unselfconsciously boasted of giving *Madoc* to posterity (*NLRS*, vol. 1, p. 113); of how much money it would make (*NLRS*, vol. 1, p. 117); how it would provide for his family after his death (*NLRS*, vol. 1, p. 206); stating pompously that 'On a great work like *Madoc* I should think ten years labour well bestowed' (*NLRS*, vol. 1, p. 181). When it was finished, he declared, 'I am satisfied with it; and, die when I may, my monument is made'.[48] Unfortunately, a year after publication in sumptuous quarto for two guineas, it had only made £3 17s 1d profits. The volume was dedicated to Southey's Welsh patron Charles Wynn, younger brother of Sir Watkin Williams Wynn, the rack-renting squire who had trebled the rent of 'the Welsh Voltaire' William Jones, Llangadfan, between 1786 and 1795.[49] It was reviewed in fourteen journals, and though praised by Landor, Walter

Scott and William Wordsworth, most critics found the protagonists mere righteous ciphers. Even more disturbing, the pacifist tone of the opening, when Madoc turns his back on war-torn Wales and attempts to bring peace to the priest-ridden Aztecs in America, seems completely undermined by the Gothic relish with which the Christian military defeat of the Aztecs is recounted in part two, before God himself pronounces on their civilisation by immolating it under a volcanic eruption and earthquake. The *Eclectic Review* declared, 'We are sickened almost in every page...' and deplored 'such deification of a marauder, possibly almost as savage as the Indians themselves'. Significantly, it was only the *Imperial Review* which felt '*Madoc* would hardly yield to *Paradise Lost*'.[50]

The use by Robert Southey of the Welsh myth of Madoc to justify the British Empire is hardly surprising. Indeed the history of the myth shows English colonialism to be an essential component of the forces which brought it into being in the first place. Gwyn A. Williams has explored the way the original Welsh legend originated as obvious wish-fulfilment fantasy after the principality's subjugation by Edward I, and the crushing of the subsequent rebellion of Owain Glyn Dŵr which had generated the first glimmers of national consciousness in Wales. But it was not until Tudor times that the myth appeared in print and became elaborated to prove Madoc's destination was definitely America. This was because the legend was co-opted to the service of promoting colonialism, providing a handy historical basis for challenging Spanish hegemony in the New World. The Welsh could at best console themselves with the Welsh origin of the Tudor dynasty, who had completed their loss of national autonomy by imposing on them the English shire system and English as the official language. They could also bask in reflected glory that their myth was the justification in establishing the Queen's title to the West Indies through the writings of Welshman Sir John Dee and Richard Hakluyt. Gwyn A. Williams comments: 'Madoc first effectively entered history as an instrument of imperial conflict. His story henceforth was to follow the ebb and flow of imperialism...'[51] In the light of this, it is hardly surprising that a Bristolian poet should revert to the appropriation of Welsh myth to imperialist purposes. After all the city of Bristol had taken the most prominent part of all in the original exploration, trade and colonisation of the new World. From the fifteenth century onwards it had been involved with trade with the search for the northwest passage and trade with Newfoundland and the Caribbean.

It was not only Southey whose views had metamorphosed. In the principality, too, the brief but heady era when Welsh Romanticism fused with

Jacobinism was over. Edward Williams's mythology of Celticism was cut adrift from its radical origins and appropriated by a new reactionary generation of respectable Anglicans and gentry, whose picturesque and sometimes grotesque Romantic nationalism seemingly acted as a harmless safety-valve for discontent with the colonial status and industrial exploitation of Wales.[52]

Edward Williams himself did not change, however. Southey had once jokingly claimed that writing *Madoc* should 'entitle me to the Poet Laureateship of the principality'.[53] When his support for church and king actually earned him the post of British Poet Laureate in 1813, Edward Williams commented to his son of Southey: '[H]e is gone to the Devil'.[54] Williams was not speaking metaphorically. He continued 'I have some thoughts of preparing an ode for the new year under the signature of <u>Auxiliary Laureat</u> [*sic*] the subject will be the Battle of Armagedon [*sic*] wherein all the Kings of the earth are gathered together see Revelns ch. XVI vs 13, 14, 15, 16.' The text is as follows:

And I saw three unclean spirits like frogs come out of the mouth of the beast, and out of the mouth of the false prophet. For they are the spirits of devils, working miracles, which go forth unto the kings of the earth and of the whole world to gather them to the battle of that great day of God Almighty.

CHAPTER 6

Wordsworth, North Wales and the Celtic landscape

J. R. Watson

I

Wordsworth's *Descriptive Sketches* of 1793 is a record of his tour of the Alps with Robert Jones in 1790. It was preceded by a dedication to Jones in the form of a letter, ending with a polite reference to Jones's own country:

> With still greater propriety I might have inscribed to you a description of some of the features of your native mountains, through which we have wandered together, in the same manner, with so much pleasure. But the sea-sunsets, which give such splendour to the vale of Clwyd, Snowdon, the chair of Idris, the quiet village of Bethgelert, Menai and her Druids, the Alpine steeps of the Conway, and the still more interesting windings of the wizard stream of the Dee, remain yet untouched.

Wordsworth went on to say that he was 'apprehensive that my pencil may never be exercised on these subjects', although of course it was. As a discrete and significant part of his work, the treatment of North Wales in his work has never received the attention which it deserves: it has been overshadowed by the encounter with Tintern Abbey and the river Wye on the one hand, and the Lake District landscape on the other. And yet North Wales is important in Wordsworth's work, and its cultural significance is part of the complexity of response to the external world which is found in his poetry. He made two visits there, in 1791 and 1793, and a later one in 1824.

His first visit was dated by Mark Reed as lasting from late May to mid-September.[1] The fact that this first summer after Cambridge should have been spent there indicates that Wordsworth may have been using the opportunity of his friendship with Jones to spend an agreeable summer away from London and to see another mountainous landscape. He had revisited the Lake District in 1788 and 1789; then came the summer in the Alps; and then Wales. In what geographers call the 'mental mapping' of Wordsworth's experience of different regions, Wales, together with Scotland, must have figured on his list of places to be seen. No doubt Jones had told him something of the Welsh landscape in Cambridge or during the Alpine tour, much as Wordsworth himself was given to 'enthusiasm' about the north of England.[2] Wales was therefore a natural progression from the landscapes of the previous summer; and Wordsworth would have been welcome and comfortable with Jones and his sisters at Plas-yn-Llan, at Llangynhavel, near Ruthin. As Dorothy jokily put it, 'Who would not be happy enjoying the company of three young ladies in the Vale of Clewyd and without a rival?'[3]

During this visit, Wordsworth and Jones went on a walking tour to see the mountain landscapes referred to in the 1793 dedication: Snowdon, Cader Idris, Beddgelert, the Menai Straits and Conway, and the River Dee. It is not possible to determine exactly what was seen, at what time, or in what order: a walker's logic would suggest starting with the Dee, then going west across mid-Wales to Dolgellau and Cader Idris, north to Beddgelert and Snowdon, followed by the Menai Straits and the Conway. A more southerly crossing of Wales would have allowed them to pass through Machynlleth, Aberystwyth and the Devil's Bridge (which they would have wanted to compare with its name-sake, the Teufelsbrücke, which they had seen in the Alps). Walkers as active as Wordsworth and Jones would have had no trouble in covering the distance in the six weeks between 17 June and 3 August (Reed's dates of the tour): indeed, this length of time suggests that this was the time of the visit to Aberystwyth (rather than 1793), and that they took the more southerly route. The distance between the significant mountains, however, would have made for long days in undulating but not sublime scenery, and in the *Guide to the Lakes* Wordsworth comments on the Lake District's 'concentration of interest' which 'gives to the country a decided superiority over the most attractive districts of Scotland and Wales, especially to the pedestrian traveller'.[4]

Moorman refers to the dedicatory letter of 1793, with its final 'yet untouched', in order to make a somewhat fanciful play upon words: 'was this because Wordsworth himself remained "untouched" by their beauty?' As she points out, when he revisited North Wales many years later (in 1824), he said of the mountains that 'either my memory or my powers of observation had not done them justice'.[5] He said that he was surprised in later life by their beauty, and yet the 1793 letter speaks of 'so much pleasure': the names that are cited speak of a mind that was actively engaged. This essay attempts to understand that engagement.

2

Wordsworth went to Wales because the opportunity presented itself: Jones's home was open to him, and the mountains were not far away. But the attractions of North Wales would have been based on more than free board and lodging with scenery. He would have wanted to visit Wales, as other eighteenth-century travellers did, because of its complex historical, cultural and poetical associations, and because it was becoming a place of serious interest to the Romantic traveller. Paul Sandby, as a young artist, visited it in 1771, in company with Sir Watkin Williams Wynn, of the great aristocratic family in the Welsh Borders; Sandby published his depictions of Wales in 1778, after a second tour. Samuel Johnson visited Wales, in company with the Thrales, in 1774 (Mrs Thrale had been born in North Wales, and lived there as a child), although he was more interested in churches, houses and castles than in the scenery ('We went down by the stream to see a prospect, in which I had no part' . . . 'We then went to see a cascade. I trudged unwillingly, and was not sorry to find it dry').[6] His diary remained unpublished until 1816, but the journey itself, though punctuated by Johnsonian grumbling, is evidence of a growing interest in an area that had been thought of as remote and primitive. Johnson found it unwelcoming. On the way back, when they reached the house of the hospitable Sir John Middleton at Gwaenynog, near Denbigh, he noted that it was 'the first place . . . where we have been made welcome'. He saw there a wood which he described as 'diversified and romantick',[7] but apart from that his diary has little evidence of an interest in landscape, or in Welsh history and poetry (although he subscribed to a collection of Welsh poems, *Gorchestion Beirdd Cymru*, published in Shrewsbury in 1773).[8]

Johnson's visit is curious, and evidence of a growing interest in Wales, but it is unlikely that he would have travelled there without the company of the Thrales, or the chance to visit Lichfield on the way there and Oxford on the way back. He certainly failed to appreciate the Welsh landscape and its associations. His response to Thomas Gray's *The Bard* of 1757, written a few years after the Welsh tour, is revealing: in its obtuseness it suggests a mind that had not considered Welsh history with any seriousness, and which had not been affected in any way by the landscape or the local culture. *The Bard* was one of those compositions 'at which the readers of poetry were at first content to gaze in mute amazement'; its third stanza contains 'the puerilities of obsolete mythology', and the weaving of the warp and woof by the slaughtered bards is described as 'a fiction outrageous and incongruous'. In a dismissive sentence he asserted, myopically: 'I do not see that *The Bard* promotes any truth, moral or political.'[9]

The contrast between Johnson and Gray in their response to Wales could hardly be greater. Between 1755 and 1758 Gray studied Celtic poetics seriously, and (as William Powell Jones has pointed out) wrote articles on early English poetry and on Welsh lore: entitled in his Commonplace Book

'Cambri', they were concerned with Welsh poets, with prosody, and with history. In Jones's view:

He discovered that instead of a barbarism Welsh poetry was full of sophistication and of a richness that, as he expressed it, 'appears both for variety and accuracy to equal the invention of the most polish'd Nations'.[10]

Jones argues that the style and language of *The Bard* were affected by Gray's study of Welsh poetics, and by his attempt to incorporate some of their features in an English Pindaric Ode. He points to Gray's note on the internal rhyme at line 43, 'No more I weep. They do not sleep':

The double cadence is introduced here not only to give a wild spirit and variety to the Epode; but because it bears some affinity to a peculiar measure in the Welch Prosody, called Gorchest-Beirdh, i.e. the *Excellent of the Bards*.[11]

In addition to his study of Welsh prosody, Gray made extensive enquiries into Welsh history, using the *Descriptio Cambriae* of Giraldus Cambrensis and Thomas Carte's *General History of England* (1750), in which he found the account of Edward I's order to slaughter the Welsh bards (for the bards themselves he relied on Bishop Thomas Tanner's *Bibliotheca Britannica* of 1748). His voluminous reading was exceptional, but Gray was an unusually scholarly man: his treatment of Welsh history in *The Bard* baffled eighteenth-century readers, including Johnson. Gray had begun the poem in 1755, but then laid it aside;[12] his difficulties with the poem were swept aside in 1757 by what Wordsworth was later to call the 'power of music'. The visit to Cambridge by John Parry, the blind harper to Sir Watkin Williams Wynn, caused a sensation. According to Gray, he 'scratch'd out such ravishing blind Harmony, such tunes of a thousand year old with names enough to choak you, as have set all this learned body a-dancing'.[13]

Parry started something of a rage for Welsh harp music: Joseph Cradock hired a harper on the night before he ascended Snowdon in 1770, presumably to get into the right frame of mind.[14] Gray's enthusiasm for Parry's music carried him through to the end of the poem, which he sent to William Mason in 1757. Mason's edition of Gray's poems, 'To which are Prefixed Memoirs of his Life and Writings' (York, 1775) was familiar to Wordsworth from his schooldays (he later owned the 1776 edition), and much loved by him. Gray's description of his visit to the Lake District in 1769 would have been one reason for this, but (as Moorman points out) Gray's account of Switzerland influenced the decision to go to the Alps in 1790 and the choice of route.[15] Wordsworth used Gray when composing *An Evening Walk*, and it seems very possible that he would have known *The*

Bard and some of Gray's letters to Mason about Wales. Mason printed a letter of 1756 from Gray to himself, whimsically responding to a letter about Mason's plans for his Welsh tragedy, *Caractacus*: Gray facetiously saw his imagination as sitting on Snowdon and nodding to Mason's imagination on Anglesey:

I see, methinks, as I sit on Snowdon, some glimpse of Mona and its haunted shades, and hope we shall be very good neighbours. Any druidical anecdotes that I can meet with, I will be sure to send you when I return to Cambridge; but I cannot pretend to be learned without books, or to know the druids from modern bishops at this distance. I can only tell you not to go and take Mona for the Isle of Man: it is Anglesey, ... Forgive me for supposing in you such a want of erudition.[16]

Mason's *Caractacus* (1759) contains a chorus of bards and a cast of druids, in addition to the principal characters of Caractacus, his son Arviragus and his daughter Evelina; and it portrays Mona, or Anglesey, as the seat of religion and virtue, as well as of British independence:

> Mona! thy grove is Virtue's throne;
> To Peace, to Piety alone
>   Thy central Oak its shade extends;
> Here, melting in Devotion's fires,
> Thy soul, sublim'd, to heav'n aspires,
>   Its dross subsides, its gold ascends.
>
> (I. vi)

Mason's play is evidence of an interest in druidism which was widespread during this period, and of an imaginative concern with British culture. Perhaps the oddest example of this was the work of William Stukeley (1687–1785), doctor and antiquarian, who published *Palaeographia Sacra* in 1738 and *Stonehenge, a Temple restor'd to the British Druids* in 1740, and who described druidism as 'the original patriarchal religion' (Stukeley was known as 'the arch-druid of the age').

But although Gray was so fired by Parry's music that he finished *The Bard*, he did not visit North Wales. His last summer tour, of 1770, was through the border counties of Worcestershire, Gloucestershire, Monmouthshire, Herefordshire and Shropshire, but he seems to have gone no further west. In this, he was not unusual. Henry Penruddocke Wyndham, in his *Tour through Monmouthshire and Wales*, recording journeys in 1774 and 1777, noted:

The romantic beauties of nature are so singular and extravagant in this principality, particularly in the counties of Merioneth and Caernarvon, that they are scarcely to be conceived by those who have confined their curiosity to other parts of Great Britain. Notwithstanding this, the Welsh tour has been, hitherto, strangely neglected; for, while the English roads are crowded with travelling parties of pleasure, the Welsh are so rarely visited, that the author did not meet with a single party of pleasure, during his six-weeks' journey through Wales.[17]

Wyndham knew Gray's work, and he makes reference to *The Bard*: he heard a Welsh harper (the only one) at Conway, but was consistently unlucky with the weather in Snowdonia, describing Beddgelert as a 'miserable town', and claiming never to have had sight of the summit of Snowdon. He was also sceptical about druidical remains:

which had nothing either certain or wonderful in them, and under the sanction of which name, as Mr Bryant observes, we shelter ourselves, whenever we are ignorant and bewildered.[18]

The reference is probably to Jacob Bryant's *A New System, or, an Analysis of Ancient Mythology* (1774), sub-titled 'wherein an attempt is made to divest tradition of fable; and to reduce the truth to its original purity', although that book is concerned mainly with the religions of the near East, and I can find only one reference to druids in its three ponderous volumes. Nicholas Owen's *A History of the Island of Anglesey* (1775) has more to say about them. They were, he writes, 'well versed in geometry, astronomy, natural philosophy, and geography':

they were also supreme judges in all causes, ecclesiastic and civil, from whose determination there lay no appeal; and whoever refused to comply with their edicts was reckoned impious and forthwith excommunicated.[19]

To Owen's brief history was added *Memoirs of Owen Glyndowr*, 'originally written by Mr Thomas Ellis, Rector of Dolgelle, in Merionethshire', which prints a Welsh poem in praise of Owen, 'written by his Poet Laureat, Gruffyth Llwyd, A.D. MCCC'. A version of this poem appeared in Thomas Pennant's *A Tour in Wales* (1778–81), the most important stimulus to visiting Wales by what Wyndham called 'parties of pleasure' in the late eighteenth century. Pennant began by emphasising his own Welshness: 'I now speak of my native country, celebrated in our earliest history for its valour and tenacity of its liberty'.[20] The first volume started in Flintshire, with the well-known beauty-spot of Holywell (which Johnson had also seen), followed by the northern marches, including the 'wizard stream of the Dee', and then Merioneth, which was famous for its associations with Owen Glyndwr. His house, Sycharth, was 'a sanctuary for bards', and Pennant quotes one of them, 'agreeably paraphrased by a bard of 1773':

Cambria's princely eagle, hail!
  Of Gryffyd Vychan's noble blood!
Thy high renown shall never fail,
  Owain Glyndwr, great and good!

The second volume of Pennant's *Tour* begins with an Advertisement, stating 'This book contains a journey from my own house to the summit of Snowdon, and takes in almost the whole of our Alpine tract.' Its additional title page is 'The Journey to Snowdon, 1771'. Since Pennant lived at Downing, near Whitford in Flintshire, his journey to Snowdon was from East Wales to West Wales, and was an anticipation of Wordsworth and Jones's summer tour twenty years later. Like them, Pennant went to Beddgelert, and climbed Snowdon by night from the west:

I took much pains to see this prospect to advantage: sat up at a farm on the west till about twelve, and walked up the whole way. The night was remarkably fine and starry: towards morn, the stars faded away, and left a short interval of darkness, which was soon dispersed by the dawn of day. On this day, the sky was obscured very soon after I got up. A vast mist enveloped the whole circuit of the mountain. The prospect down was horrible. It gave an idea of numbers of abysses, concealed by a thick smoke, furiously circulating around us. Very often a gust of wind formed an opening in the clouds, which gave a fine and distinct visto of lake and valley.[21]

Similarly William Sotheby, who published *Poems: Consisting of a Tour through Parts of North and South Wales* in 1790 described how he climbed Snowdon with a guide, a discharged soldier who had been at the siege of Gibraltar:

Thee *Snowdon*! king of *Cambrian* mountains hail!
With many a lengthen'd pause my ling'ring feet
Follow th'experienc'd guide; a Veteran maim'd
With glorious wounds, that late on *Calpe*'s height
Bled in his country's cause.

Sotheby saw

mountains on mountains pil'd,
And winding bays, and promontories huge,
Lakes and meand'ring rivers, from their source,
Trac'd to the distant ocean ...

Wordsworth and Jones climbed in different conditions, although they also used a guide: their night was foggy and misty until they climbed out above the low cloud, and found themselves under the shining moon. Nevertheless, the climbing of Snowdon, and the brilliant description of it in *The Prelude*, was the climax of a Welsh experience in which Wordsworth must have been aware of a complex series of predecessors and images: mountains, druids, bards, Welsh history; all amounting to a strong sense of locality, of place, of Welshness. From Milton's *Lycidas* came the famous druids, and the 'wizard stream' of the Dee (Wordsworth applied the word 'wizard' to the Derwent in *An Evening Walk*); from Gray came the history of liberty, and the defiance of the bard; from Sotheby, if Wordsworth had read it, came the concept of the sublime prospect, and the climbing of Snowdon; from Pennant came the celebration of Owen Glyndwr and, again, the suggestion of the climbing of Snowdon. Wordsworth and Jones visited Pennant, probably in 1791, and also his friend Thomas Thomas at Pennant Melangell in Montgomeryshire, where Wordsworth got into an argument with a Welsh priest that ended in the priest threatening him with a knife.[22]

What the argument was about, and why it reached such a dangerous intensity, we do not know; it is a reminder, perhaps, of a certain *farouche* element in Wordsworth at this time, which is detectable (as Moorman has suggested) in the rejected stanza of *Peter Bell*, where he describes meeting the travelling tinker near Builth Wells in 1793, and 'both hung back in murderer's guize':

> 'Twas thou that wast afraid of me
> And I that was afraid of thee, . . .[23]

If the quarrel with the Welsh priest took place in 1793, it may also be relevant to recall that this was the year in which Wordsworth read Richard Watson's *The Wisdom and Goodness of God in having made both Rich and Poor* and composed his angry reply to it, the 'Letter to the Bishop of Llandaff'. But it could have been about anything (supposing the priest not to have been violent or mad, which of course he may have been): the French Revolution, the church, the English and Welsh, language, politics, religion. The reason for mentioning it here is two-fold: it may (whatever its explanation) seem a pointer to some quality of Welsh-ness, its difference, its independence; and it may serve as a reminder of the imaginative territory into which Wordsworth was entering in 1791 and 1793. That part of North Wales had become a newly travelled place: it had associations with liberty, and a history of repeated conquest and defiance. Its rulers, such as Glendwr, supported the bards; its conquerors, such as Edward I, slew them. Similarly, according to Nicholas Owen, the Romans destroyed the druid groves on Anglesey.

North Wales was a territory of the mind for Wordsworth, as well as a place to visit. We may observe it as emerging, in the second half of the eighteenth century, as a place to be discovered: a place with mountains, harpers, bards, druids, castles, ruins. Travellers such as Sir Richard Colt Hoare of Stourhead went there repeatedly in the 1790s.[24] He also edited *Itinerarium Cambriae*, the account of Archbishop Baldwin's journey through Wales in 1185 (1804). Wordsworth would have brought to North Wales an enquiring mind, and one which would have been enriched by reading Gray and others (perhaps in the Jones's house at Plas-yn-Llan). His approach to landscape was always complex and multi-layered: he speaks in the Preface to *Lyrical Ballads* of the poet 'who considers man and the objects that surround him as acting and re-acting upon each other, so as to form an infinite complexity of pain and pleasure'. In that process, the external world is understood by bringing to it what Wordsworth calls 'a certain quantity of immediate knowledge' and also his sympathies – 'looking upon the complex scene of ideas and sensations, and finding everywhere objects that immediately excite in him sympathies.' This is the response to landscape which modern humanistic geographers would call 'geographical space':

composed of whole complexes of visual, auditory and olfactory sensations, present circumstances and purposes, past experiences and associations, the unfolding se-quence of vistas and the various cultural and aesthetic criteria by which we judge buildings and landscapes.[25]

North Wales, in Wordsworth's experience, was a classic example of the way in which 'mental images help to shape the geography of the land'. It was a place to which he brought 'immediate knowledge', the understanding of history and tradition, and also a heady mixture of sympathies. The most important of these were his appreciation of the natural scene in a mountain-ous country, and his love of what he later called 'National Independence and Liberty'.

3

The landscape becomes a text to be read and interpreted. The understanding of it can be visual, geomorphological, historical, associative, each of these depending on inherited assumptions – how to see a landscape (as sublime or picturesque), how to relate it to history (castles, druid stones). The landscape-text also becomes a site for competing interpretations: different views supplement and modify one another. When it is written about, or painted, it becomes a text which is refigured on each occasion, each writing or painting in dialogue with the previous ones. William Sotheby, who has already been mentioned, saw North Wales in traditional terms of the

Sublime, contrasting it with South Wales:

> Fled are the fairy views of hill and dale;
> Sublimely thron'd on the steep mountain brow
> Stern Nature frowns[.]

Similarly Turner, visiting North Wales two years after the publication of Sotheby's poem, exploited its possibilities in the sublime mode. Every traveller modifies the landscape: so Turner, in 1792, developed Richard Wilson.

Wordsworth, for his part, was aware of Gray, and his references to Wales are written over against *The Bard*. The bard-figure, found in Blake, and in Scott's minstrel, is Wordsworth's prophet from the end of *The Prelude*:

> Prophets of Nature, we to them will speak
> A lasting inspiration, sanctified
> By reason, blest by faith: what we have loved,
> Others will love, and we will teach them how[.]
> (*The Prelude*, XIV. 444–7)[26]

Wordsworth assumes the bardic stance, and he does so after all the experiences related in *The Prelude*, culminating in the climbing of Snowdon in Book XIV. That event, held back to form the last great 'spot of time' (and therefore spot of place) is the greatest legacy of the Welsh visits to his poetry. Not only does it show Wordsworth's descriptive and narrative powers at their best; it also invokes the mountain landscape as symbolic. It is symbolic, but also Celtic: Snowdon is named. Once it is named, it brings with it all the associations of North Wales at this time: Gray's *Bard*, Pennant's *Tour*, the druids, Mason's *Caractacus*, Merioneth and Owen Glyndwr, and all the other Welsh history which Wordsworth may have come across – the Roman invasion, Archbishop Baldwin's itinerary with Giraldus Cambrensis in 1185, Llewellyn the Great in the thirteenth century; that heady mixture of religion and rebellion that made up the 'infinite complexity' with which the external world interacted with the internal mind. And to that grandeur of conception is added the moment itself: an evening in 1791, that moment which Wordsworth prayed to remember always:

> In one of those excursions (may they ne'er
> Fade from remembrance!)
> (*The* Prelude, XIV. 1–2)

The early part of the climb is filled with little details, trivialities: the cottage, the summoning of the guide, the 'short refreshment', the shepherd's dog barking at a hedgehog. Then comes the silence of the climb, each traveller conscious of the others yet also wrapped up in himself (the syntax slips tellingly between 'we' and 'I'). The poet remembers himself leading the climb at that point:

> When at my feet the ground appeared to brighten,
> And with a step or two seemed brighter still;
> Nor was time given to ask or learn the cause,
> For instantly a light upon the turf
> Fell like a flash, and lo! as I looked up,
> The Moon hung naked in a firmament
> Of azure without cloud, and at my feet
> Rested a silent sea of hoary mist.
>
> (*The Prelude*, XIV. 35–42)

Wordsworth's exciting description of coming out of the cloud to find the mist below him, and 'a hundred hills' raising their dark summits around him, is succeeded by the portrayal of the moon, full-orbed,

> Who, from her sovereign elevation, gazed
> Upon the billowy ocean, as it lay
> All meek and silent, save that through a rift –
> Not distant from the shore whereon we stood,
> A fixed, abysmal, gloomy, breathing-place –
> Mounted the roar of waters, torrents, streams
> Innumerable...   (XIV. 54–60)

This would be enough in itself to give an impression of the sublime night landscape; but Wordsworth takes it further by an inspired conjecture, in which the sublimity becomes emblematic. He admits it as conjecture – 'it appeared to me the type / Of a majestic intellect'. That intellect is one

> That feeds upon infinity, that broods
> Over the dark abyss, intent to hear
> Its voices issuing forth to silent light
> In one continuous stream[.]
>
> (XIV. 71–7)

In the presence of such power, even the 'least sensitive' of men 'see hear, perceive, / And cannot choose but feel'. And that same power resembles 'that glorious faculty / That higher minds bear with them as their own'. The power which Wordsworth goes on to describe at length is that of the imagination, prompted by 'sensible impressions' (those of the world of the senses) but not held in thrall by them, so that their 'quickening impulse' directs the mind to a higher world:

> To hold fit converse with the spiritual world,
> And with the generations of mankind
> Spread over time, past, present, and to come,
> Age after age, ...
>
> (xiv. 108–11)

It would be absurd to claim this as concerned with Welsh history: the whole point of the climbing of Snowdon passage is that it begins in a time and a place only to transcend both. But that time and place are so well delineated, that the reader can be justified in marking them as coming from a North Wales situation, a Celtic environment, rich with its tradition of sublimity and individuality.

Its defiance of the Roman or English conquerors is well recorded, and suits well with Wordsworth's own resistance to tyranny and metropolitan domination. His admiration for the 'statesmen' of Westmorland and Cumberland was a part of his love of independence and his consistent admiration for those who stood for liberty, from Milton to Toussaint l'Ouverture. In this context, the visit of 1793 contains an important moment, recorded in *The Prelude*, when in the church of a Welsh village he found it impossible to pray for victory against the French Republic. He even rejoiced in the defeat at Hondeschoote (8 September 1793)

> When Englishmen by thousands were o'erthrown,
> Left without glory on the field, or driven,
> Brave hearts! to shameful flight.
>
> (*The Prelude*, 1850, x. 286–8)

This may have been the same visit in which Wordsworth so angered the Welsh priest. And it must have been in 1793, as Moorman points out, that Wordsworth found himself in church

> like an uninvited guest,
> Whom no one owned,
> and 'fed on the day of vengeance yet to come'.
>
> (x. 297–9).[27]

The battle between the British and the infant Republic would have been for Wordsworth a re-enacting of an old pattern – of an oppressor attempting to stifle independence and liberty. The fact that the news of Hondeschoote came to him in North Wales would have added to its import. In the same spirit, many years later and in another cause, he invoked another figure from Welsh history, Llewellyn the Great, who died in 1240. In *The Convention of Cintra* (1809) he writes of local history: 'Love and admiration must always push themselves out towards some quarter: otherwise the moral man is

killed.' The 'quarter' which he has in mind is the past of a nation, of
the kind which Edward I tried to destroy with the killing of the Welsh
bards:

Perdition to the Tyrant who would wantonly cut off an independent Nation from
its ineritance in past ages; turning the tombs and burial-places of the Forefathers
into dreaded objects of sorrow, or of shame and reproach, for the Children! Look
on Scotland and Wales: though, by the union of these under the same Government
(which was effected without conquest in one instance), ferocious and desolating
wars, and more injurious intrigues, and sapping and disgraceful corruptions, have
been prevented; and tranquillity, security, and prosperity, and a thousand exchanges
of amity, not otherwise attainable, have followed; – yet the flashing eye, and the
agitated voice, and all the tender recollections, with which the names of Prince
Llewellin and William Wallace are to this day pronounced by the fire-side and
on the public road, attest that these substantial blessings have not been purchased
without the relinquishment of something most salutary to the moral nature of
Man: else the remembrance would not cleave so faithfully to their abiding-place
in the human heart.[28]

Wordsworth's fierce eloquence suggests a deeply held regard for local loyal-
ties, and his remark in the parenthesis about Scotland is a reminder of his
feeling for the contrasting importance, moral and spiritual, of Welsh history. His admiration for Wallace (found in Book 1 of *The Prelude*), is here
given added lustre by the reminder of Welsh defiance, and the celebration
of what *The Prelude* calls 'independence and stern liberty'. It is the Wales
of Gray's poem, here brought into the argument of 1809.

Wordsworth uses heroic and prophetic figures to embody this ideal,
drawing on the long tradition of bardic and druidic power. The druids
were gifted and knowledgeable, as we have seen, in geometry, astronomy
and other subjects: yet they also gave out laws, and encouraged the people
of Anglesey in their resistance to the Roman invasion. They were also
inspirational, and the source of religious power. In 'To the Clouds', he
specifically links them with the Orpheus legend:

> Where is the Orphean lyre, or Druid harp,
> To accompany the verse?
>
> ('To the Clouds', 60–1)

The answer is that it is found in the landscape itself, even as the mind of
man is found in the experience of Snowdon:

> The mountain blast
> Shall be our *hand* of music; he shall sweep
> The rocks, and quivering trees, and billowy lake,

And search the fibres of the caves, and they
Shall answer, for our song is of the Clouds,
And the wind loves them; ...

('To the Clouds', 61–6)

It is not surprising, therefore, that Wordsworth celebrates druids: a footnote
to the 1793 *An Evening Walk* tells the reader about the druid stones at
Broughton in the Lake District, as if Wordsworth had been awakened to
their significance by his 1791 visit to Wales.

The most sustained treatment of Welsh religion and the druids, however,
is found in the first series of *Ecclesiastical Sonnets*, which surprisingly reveal
much of interest to the student of Celtic influences on Wordsworth. They
suggest a strangely divided loyalty: Wordsworth wrote the sonnets as a
memorial of walking with his great friend of the middle years, Sir George
Beaumont, looking for a site for a new church on his estate; but beneath
the steady progression of Christianity, which is the avowed subject of the
sonnets, there is an undercurrent of sympathy for the ancient druids. It
is as though the Wordsworth of 1821, bound by ties of friendship to the
respectable Beaumont, has overlaid the Wordsworth of thirty years earlier,
who walked round Wales, frightened the travelling tinker, and had a fight
with a Welsh priest.

Part 1 of the *Ecclesiastical Sonnets* is sub-titled 'From the Introduction of
Christianity into Britain to the Consummation of the Papal Dominion',
and it demonstrates a considerable knowledge of druidical tradition:
Sonnet 3, for example, describes the 'Trepidation of the Druids', beginning with the scream of the white sea-mew and the coming of the cor-
morant, a bird of ill omen. 'The Bard' is haughty (as an echo of Gray's
defiant figure, perhaps), and seems impervious to the coming of Christianity: but Wordsworth suggests that the 'meek doctrines' of Christianity
will 'blight / His transports'. This will come about by a process which
Wordsworth would in earlier times have found repellent – the Roman
conquest of Anglesey:

But all shall be fulfilled; – the Julian spear
A way first opened; and, with Roman chains,
The tidings come of Jesus crucified.

The excuse for this union of compulsion and conversion is that the druids
were themselves tyrannical, as the fourth sonnet, 'Druidical Excommu-
nication', makes clear. The 'Outcast', in this primitive society, is 'cut off
by sacerdotal ire' from human sympathy (as Nicholas Owen had noted –
'whoever refused to comply with their edicts was reckoned impious and

forthwith excommunicated'). The origins of Christianity, however, are lost, in Sonnet 5, 'Uncertainty':

> seeking, we are lost
> On Snowdon's wilds, amid Brigantian coves,
> Or where the solitary shepherd roves
> Along the plain of Sarum . . .

These places (Wales, the north of England and Salisbury Plain) contain confusing evidence, but (it is argued) this does not matter if the coming of the early church is still visible, even if from a later date:

> Nor these, nor monuments of eldest name,
> Nor Taliesin's unforgotten lays,
> Nor characters of Greek and Roman fame,
> To an unquestionable source have led;
> Enough – if eyes, that sought the fountain-head
> In vain, upon the growing Rill may gaze.

The inclusion of Taliesin, the sixth-century Welsh bard, is an indication that Wordsworth had been reading Sharon Turner's *History of the Anglo-Saxons*, which has much to say about the distinction between Celtic and Gothic, and which also describes druids in some detail. Chapter 5 of Turner's pioneering history describes the destruction of Ancient Bangor (near Chester), and the flight of the king of Powys, Brocmail: he was one of the patrons of Taliesin, whose poem is quoted by Turner in a footnote.[29] The sack of the monastery of Old Bangor is the subject of Sonnet 12, in which Wordsworth laments the '*unarmed* Host', the monks who were praying against Ethelforth, and therefore seen as his enemies and killed. More heartening is Sonnet 10, 'Struggle of the Picts against the Barbarians', in which Mason's hero reappears:

> The spirit of Caractacus descends
> Upon the Patriots, . . .

and King Arthur, with 'the virgin sculptured on his Christian shield', is supported by the druids and the bards, who throw down their harps and take up swords:

> from Cambrian wood and moss
> Druids descend, auxiliars of the Cross;
> Bards, nursed on blue Plinlimmon's still abode,
> Rush on the fight, to harps preferring swords,
> And everlasting deeds to burning words!

The druids have now become 'auxiliars of the Cross': Wordsworth sees the ancient religion as somehow incorporated into the new reign of Christianity, and the druids have turned incongruously into crusaders. From now on, the danger will come from the pagan Anglo-Saxons (before the coming of Augustine), as the destruction of the monastery of Bangor makes clear.

Wordsworth's incorporation of the druids into the early stages of his poetic history of the church in Britain is evidence of his continuing interest in Celtic tradition and Welsh history. The *Ecclesiastical Sonnets*, however, while apparently treating of Welsh matters in the manner of Gray, seem more like an exercise in pleasing the Sir George Beaumonts of this world rather than an engagement with the Welsh experience of the earlier years, and their rich political and historical suggestions.

4

Wordsworth made one further visit to Wales, in 1824, with Mary and his daughter Dora. Dorothy, who wrote to Lady Beaumont from Rydal Mount about it, described Robert Jones as having 'travelled with them everywhere', but now, in his unathletic middle age, 'with his car and servant'.[30] Wordsworth described the whole route to Beaumont in a letter from Radnor dated 20 September. They had taken a boat from Liverpool to Bangor, thence to Caernarvon and Snowdonia, and then eastwards to Corwen and Llangollen. Having, with due propriety, visited 'the ladies of Llangollen' (Lady Eleanor Butler and the Honourable Miss Ponsonby: Wordsworth wrote a sonnet to them), they turned westwards again to the Vale of Clwyd and Beddgelert, which Wordsworth thought changed for the worse: 'a smart hotel has taken the place of the lowly public-house in which I took refreshment almost thirty years ago, previous to a midnight ascent to the summit of Snowdon'.[31] They then made their way to Aberystwyth, and from there to the Devil's Bridge. In Dorothy's words, they were 'thridding that romantic country through every quarter'.[32]

The sonnet written 'To the Lady E.B. and the Hon. Miss P.', which was sent to Beaumont in Wordsworth's letter of 20 September, is one of three written during this short tour (the Welsh visit yielded nothing like the extensive harvest of other tours in the later years). The first, 'Composed among the Ruins of a Castle in North Wales' affirms the beauty which time has conferred upon the remains; the second, 'To the Torrent at the Devil's Bridge, North Wales, 1824' is of more interest, after a feeble octave. The sestet picks up the reference in the title to the date, 1824:

There I seem to stand,
As in life's morn; permitted to behold,
From the dread chasm, woods climbing above woods,
In pomp that fades not; everlasting snows;
And skies that ne'er relinquish their repose;
Such power possess the family of floods
Over the minds of Poets, young or old!

The 'family of floods' refers to other waterfalls, mentioned in the octave of the sonnet; the purpose of the poem is to explore the way in which waterfalls have a power over the imagination. Wordsworth struggles to recapture that imaginative response to landscape that he possessed in earlier years: the echoes of the description of the Simplon Pass (not then published) are witness to an imaginative reaching out to the waterfall, at that time, in that place, revisiting the scene of 1791, or possibly 1793.

The revisiting of landscapes, from Tintern Abbey to Yarrow, was an important element of Wordsworth's imaginative life and its response to the external world. The result is an extreme sensitivity to change, as in the reference to the inn at Beddgelert; and a strong sense of the self – the checking, as it were, of the self against the landscape, the past self and the present self seen against the woods, and snows and skies. Wordsworth actually thought that he had forgotten how beautiful the Welsh landscape was: he told Jane Marshall, later in the year, that 'the beauties of North Wales much exceeded my expectations as regulated by the impaired remembrance of thirty three years'.[33]

The 1824 visit is of little interest to the student of Wordsworth's poetry, except that it throws into relief the earlier visits of 1791 and 1793. By 1824, Jones had become a contented and overweight clergyman, and Wordsworth a respected friend of the Beaumonts, Butlers and Ponsonbys of this world. Not much walking was done in 1824. In 1791 and 1793, by contrast, the visits to Wales were by a young and unconventional poet, an explorer of a country that was just beginning to awaken interest as the home of liberty and art. It was a place that would have helped to politicise his poetry. It was also a land in which a young man could climb mountains and find an echo of the Alpine sublimity that had intoxicated him in 1790. Above all, perhaps, it was different – Welsh, Celtic: North Wales was the land of the druids, priests of an ancient religion and culture; it was the land where the bards had defied the tyranny of the English conquest, and been put to death because they were the guardians of national identity and feeling. It was a place where the recent awakening of interest in its history and culture – Mason's *Caractacus*, Parry, Gray, Pennant, Colt Hoare, and others – allowed a response from a poet who was struggling, in these years, to find himself, and whose greatest poetry is dominated by two things: the awareness of the self in relation to the external world, and the importance of 'national independence and liberty'. North Wales had much to give to Wordsworth in both of these areas of human and poetic sensibility.

CHAPTER 7

The force of 'Celtic memories' in Byron's thought

Bernard Beatty

Byron is customarily thought of as an English poet and not infrequently claimed as a Scottish poet but, despite Matthew Arnold's insistence that the 'Celtic passion of revolt' is titanically embodied in Byron, he is not normally thought of as a Celtic poet.[1] This volume prompts us to ask if there is any useful sense in which he might be thought to be one, and whether Byron himself entertained this possibility?

A passage in Byron's last major poem, *The Island* (1823), seems to give a wholly positive answer to our second query:

> And Loch-na-gar with Ida looked o'er Troy,
> Mixed Celtic memories with the Phrygian mount,
> And Highland linns with Castalie's clear fount.
>
> (II. 290–3)[2]

Byron recalls in these lines the first ten years of his life in Aberdeen where he wore the Gordon tartan[3] of his mother's clan and felt 'at home with the people lowland & Gael'.[4] Especially he recalled his summer holidays, from the ages of eight to ten, at the farmhouse of Ballaterich on Deeside. Here he rambled on hill and mountains, such as Loch na Garr, swam, and heard Gaelic spoken.[5] When he was at Cambridge, he wrote a poem, 'The Adieu. written under the impression that the author would soon die'. This poem identified the sources of his personality and Muse as Harrow, Cambridge, the Highlands, Newstead Abbey and Southwell. The Highlands here are in a ratio of 1:5 as sources of his poetry and this is pretty much the rough impression made by his first major publication: *Hours of Idleness* (1806). In the introduction to this volume he declares with his customary nicety:

Though accustomed, in my younger days, to rove a careless mountaineer on the Highlands of Scotland, I have not, of late years, had the benefit of such pure air.[6]

What is interesting here is the indirection. Byron nowhere suggests that he is actually a Scot, either Highlander or Lowlander, in any sense. He was

103

just 'accustomed... to rove' in the Highlands. In *English Bards and Scotch Reviewers* (1809) – a much more meditated appearance before the audience he intended to reach, he in effect denies his Scottishness altogether. The original working title of the poem was *British Bards*,[7] but Byron now presents himself as an English Bard traduced by barbarous Scotch Reviewers. Scotland itself is put into the position of Pope's queen of Dulness:

> Thus having said, the kilted Goddess kist
> Her son, and vanished in a Scottish mist.
>
> (526–7)

References to England in the poem all suggest that the author, like the reader, is wholly English and certainly has no 'Celtic memories'.[8] The quotation, too, goes out of its way to elide Highland and Lowland muses in a single denunciation. In a note to these lines Byron says that 'I could not say Caledonia's Genius, it being well known there is no Genius to be found from Clackmannan to Caithness'.[9] He makes similar points in *The Curse of Minerva* (1811) where he compares Scotland to Boeotia (130). In *Beppo* (1817) too, the contrast of the poem is between Venetian and English, not British, manners (e.g. 336, 344, 369, 461, 473, 685). The author is an Englishman abroad. So too is the author of *Don Juan* (1819–23) for most of the poem (see V, 460). It is only when we get to Canto X (written in 1822) that Byron admits he is 'half a Scot by birth, and bred / A whole one' (135–6) and repeats in the next canto that he is 'half English... (To my misfortune)' (94–5).

We must assume that Byron self-consciously distanced himself from his Scottish sources of inspiration in much the same way that he cast off his Scots accent when he came to England in 1798 where, he said, 'I had been hatched'.[10] Karl Elze asserted that the young Byron 'insisted on being called George Byron Gordon'.[11] Byron's father was obliged to accept the additional name of Gordon as part of the marriage settlement and certainly sometimes called himself 'John Byron Gordon of Gight'.[12] The tenth laird, Marie Gordon, was a woman and this step was taken in order to preserve the name of Gordon.[13] His godfather was the Duke of Gordon but Byron was brought up to believe himself to be descended from a better and older branch of the Gordons and also from the Royal Stewarts. When he convalesced and holidayed in the Highlands near to Loch na Garr, he must have opened deeply to this association of a dark noble history and the wild energies of an ancient landscape. By then, this vision of authenticating Gaelic ancestors is fused with his reading of Ossian:

Clouds, there, encircle the forms of my Fathers,
They dwell in the tempests of dark Loch na Garr.
('Lachin Y Gair', 23–4)

So far as I can determine, Byron did not have full-fledged 'Gaelic' or Highland ancestors but they were 'Gordons', had a castle in the Highlands, and
as a family had supported the exiled Stuarts. In the early part of his parent's
marriage, bagpipes were played within their house.[14] This was sufficient. Yet
by the time of writing these lines, 'George Bayron Gordon' (his name as entered in Aberdeen school)[15] had long since turned himself into Lord Byron,
an English public schoolboy and Cambridge undergraduate of aristocratic
Norman lineage. He now primarily recognised a different set of ancestors
derived from the father bracketed by his mother and himself when a child.
'On Leaving Newstead Abbey', which is put first in the *Hours of Idleness*
collection, begins like this:

> Thro' thy battlements, Newstead, thy hollow winds whistle;
> Thou, the hall of my fathers, art gone to decay[.]

These 'fathers', we must presume, largely drove out the first maternal set.
Certainly they seem wholly expunged when he writes back to John Murray
in March 1820 who had used the phrase 'like our Saxon ancestors'. Byron
replies quite tartly: 'they are <u>not</u> my ancestors, nor yours either, for mine
were Normans, and yours I take it by your name were <u>Gael</u>'.[16] In October of
the same year, writing again to Murray, he revealingly gives quite contrary
indications in a single letter. He begins by thanking Murray for sending
him Scott's *The Abbot*:

The Abbot will have more than ordinary interest for me; for an ancestor of mine
by the mother's side, Sir J. Gordon of Gight, the handsomest of his day, died on a
scaffold at Aberdeen for his loyalty to Mary.[17]

We note here Byron's close association between reading Scott's novels and
accepting his own Scottish ancestry. But later in the letter he seems to
distance himself from this identification by describing his mother's pride
in her lineage and commenting: 'notwithstanding our Norman, and always
masculine descent, which has never lapsed into a female, as my mother's
Gordons had done in her own person'.[18] The word 'our' here is strongly
contrasted with 'my mother's Gordons' as though they have nothing to do
with him. This contrast seems to contradict his earlier phrase 'an ancestor
of mine by the mother's side' and his own note thirteen years earlier to
'Lachin Y Gair' where he refers to 'my maternal ancestors, the "Gordons"'
and to Sir William Gordon whom 'I have the honour to claim as one of my

progenitors'.[19] But in the conclusion of the letter to Murray, it is as though he is no longer George Byron Gordon. Indeed, in 1821, on the death of his wife's mother, he, like his father before him, added her name to his and became Noel Byron, thus apparently effacing the Scottish ancestry that he has begun to re-acknowledge.[20]

These details are worth tracking because Byron's poetry is a poetry of ancestry in a way that is not true of any of his great contemporaries, even Scott. None of them were very interested in their great grandparents or assumed that this had much to do with their writing. An aristocrat is someone who knows their own ancestry as a public fact. Byron is self-consciously such. In a different but parallel way, he always regards himself as genetically fated. Why then, we must ask, does Byron never set any of his poems in Scotland and only use a sustained English setting when he comes to write the last cantos of *Don Juan* where, at last, he acknowledges publicly that he is 'half a Scot' and 'half-English'?

It is clear that we must talk not only of 'a poetry of ancestry' but also of an abandonment of ancestors. He is always 'Lord Byron' but he becomes a Greek who learns Romaic, a Venetian who talks the local lingo, he wears an Albanian costume, sets himself to learn Armenian from an Armenian, prides himself on the accurate detail of his Turkish Tales, and writes Hebrew Melodies for a Jewish composer. Poetically, he openly declares and defends his poetic ancestors, Pope and Dryden, against the parricidal attacks of Bowles, Wordsworth, Coleridge and Keats. At the same time, he gains new Continental forbears by borrowing something for *Manfred* from Goethe's *Faust*, translating Pulci as well as Horace, imitating Alfieri's tragedies, and deriving the manner of *Don Juan* as much from Casti as from Hookham Frere. He takes an epigraph from *Le Cosmopolite* to introduce *Childe Harold's Pilgrimage*, for Byron is, of course, a cosmopolitan, that is to say, a man without ancestors. This is why he can speak out of the countries whose histories and ancestors he has adopted. He is, and has always been acclaimed as, a great European and World poet. If he abandoned his Scottish ancestors when he came to England, then he seemed to have abandoned his English ones when he went to and then settled on the Continent. But we can read the evidence in more than one way.

It was, after all, perhaps that initial movement from bourgeois Aberdeen to the neighbouring Highlands that gave him both the 'infant rapture' that made him a poet, and the imagined contact with his shadowy ancestors in the tempests and 'Scottish mist' that he was later to ridicule. The same association of imagined ancestors and the gift of poetry marks 'On Leaving Newstead Abbey'. The gift of speaking out of authentic but imagined ancestors is successively established here and then broadened out into a pan-European identity with what Manfred calls 'the great of old' (III. iv. 39). Byron's very first assay into poetic ancestry is in an early poem turning Ossian's address to the Sun in 'Carthon' into Popeian couplets. This is where he first tried out the vocabulary of 'Northern tempests howl along the blast'[21] which he will later apply to his Gordon ancestors. Byron, we may say, learns how to have ancestors and how to abandon them. It is no accident, perhaps, that his first poem on the house of his ancestors should be entitled 'On <u>Leaving</u> Newstead Abbey'.

That is one side of things. But there is another and it is voiced in those remarkable lines on Byron's relation to Scotland, addressed to Walter Scott, which Andrew Nicholson discusses elsewhere:

> And though, as you remember, in a fit
> Of wrath and rhyme, when juvenile and curly,
> I railed at Scots to shew my wrath and wit,
> Which must be owned was sensitive and surly,
> Yet 'tis in vain such sallies to permit,
> They cannot quench young feelings fresh and early:
> I '*scotched*, not killed' the Scotchman in my blood,
> And love the land of 'mountain and of flood'.
>
> (*Don Juan*, x. 19)

Byron's only other poetic use of Theobald's brilliant reading of Macbeth's lines is in *Marino Faliero* where one of the conspirators says to the Doge: 'Would that the hour were come! we will not scotch, / But kill' (III. ii. 268–9). The context here is that the Doge is to lead a revolt against his fellow Patricians and kill all of them. In a wonderful scene at the beginning of the same Act, the Doge has arranged to meet a conspirator in front of an equestrian statue. He suddenly announces that they are overlooked. The conspirator says that the statue is only 'a tall warrior's statue' but the Doge replies: 'That Warrior was the sire / Of my Sire's fathers' and he insists that there are eyes 'in death' which behold this betrayal (III. i. 86, 89–90, 94). Hence the phrase 'not scotch But kill' implies eradicate your kin and your ancestors completely. In the lines 'I "*scotched*, not killed", the Scotchman in my blood' we can therefore detect Byron's admission that he has tried to do the same, but unsuccessfully. He is always aware of ancestral eyes in death which, in the end, reclaim him. Most of Byron's political plays depend upon this pattern. Sardanapalus, for instance, knowingly rejects his ancestors who reclaim him in a dream (*Sardanapalus*).

Again we can read the evidence in two ways. In part we can suggest that Byron's open acknowledgement of his presumed Gaelic, Scottish and

English roots seems to occur, almost in the manner of a recantation, in
the 1820s at whose outset we have still found evidence of the opposite
tendency.[22] In a conversation with Medwin, whom he first met in late 1821,
he tidies the whole thing up. He says that he initially loved Scotland, then
went off it because of the Edinburgh Review critique of *Hours of Idleness*
so that 'I transferred a portion of my dislike to that country; but my affection for it soon flowed back into its old channel'.[23] This is true but the
word 'soon' may mislead. It is only in 1822 that, for the first time, he sets a
substantial part of a major poem in England whilst simultaneously admit-
ting his half-Scottishness. Almost certainly the effect of constantly reading
Scott's novels – which themselves dramatise the tensions between Scots and
English, Lowlander and Highlander – brought his earliest memories back
to him and, as it were, 'authorised' them, as we have seen. We will first
need to establish this. But secondly, we can detect the working presence of
Byron's expunged ancestors throughout his poetry.

The evidence for Byron's late acknowledgement of Scotland is explicit
in the cited passages from the late cantos of *Don Juan* and *The Island*.
We could add in some amusing lines from the end of *The Age of Bronze*
(1823) where Byron mocks the attempts of George IV, stage-managed by
Scott himself, to present himself as heir to the Stuarts and thus prince of
the Highlands as well as Lowlands. The Lord Mayor of London (maker of
sea-biscuits at Wapping) sailed with the king to Scotland and 'had *celtified*
himself on the occasion':[24]

> My Muse 'gan weep but, ere a tear was spilt,
> She caught Sir William Curtis in a kilt!
> While thronged the chiefs of every Highland clan
> To hail their brother, Vich Ian Alderman!
> Guildhall grows Gael, and echoes with Erse roar,
> Whilst all the Common Council cry 'Claymore!'
> To see proud Albyn's tartans as a belt
> Gird the gross loins of a city Celt[.]   (767–74)

There is a mockery of Highland tushery here but, unlike *English Bards and
Scotch Reviewers*, the mockery is mainly at English rather than Scottish
pretensions. The satire presupposes a proper inviolability in kilts and
tartan with which, however lightly, Byron identifies himself, and a betrayal of this by the Highland chiefs' acclamation of 'a city Celt'. Byron
quotes approvingly Jennie Deans's phrase that his 'heart warms to the
tartan', and he would again wear the Gordon tartan when he returned finally to Greece.[25] All these texts occur from 1822 onwards and suggest a

knowingly resumed identity at this time. But there are less explicit indicators too.

In Norman Abbey, Byron returns to his first, long since abandoned, poetic theme – his own house, Newstead Abbey, and its ancestors. But there is a disjunction. In the early poems, Byron's Norman ancestors flit Ossianically about the ruined building. 'On Leaving Newstead Abbey' ignores the monks who built the monastery and tries to suggest that Byron's knightly medieval ancestors have somehow always been associated with the abbey. When Byron makes that remarkable poetic return to his old subject-matter in Canto XIII of *Don Juan*, the business of ancestors and ownership is foregrounded and a clear division is made between religious and secular ownership in the significantly named 'Norman Abbey'.

There are in effect four possible claimants for the house and estate. The first is the present owners, the Amundevilles, whom we see organising the property and stage-managing its social occasions in order to exercise political social control over the neighbourhood. Their Norman name elides with the name of the house and progenitors of the abbey but their suzerainty is limited:

> Amundeville is lord by day,
> But the monk is lord by night[.]
> (XVI, 357–8)

So the 'monk' is the second claimant of the property built originally for him. But there is a stage even before this, though fused with it, we could call it 'nature' though this is usually a word that Byron is wary of in its new Romantic sense. Byron activates it very deliberately. The old house sings like an Aeolian harp in harmony with the elements (XIII, 62–3) and it is intensely receptive to its surrounding landscape (XV, 15). The ownership lies primordially here. Far more profoundly perhaps than this, the house and landscape belong to the Catholic orphan Aurora Raby in whom the two more fundamental layers of ownership – natural and spiritual – rise up and assail Juan even, and precisely, though she does not seek to exercise ownership. What, if anything, is Celtic about all this?

I have searched through Byron's works looking for any displayed interest in Druids but, not surprisingly, have found very little. Collins famously called Thomson a Druid,[26] and Byron borrows the term for Rogers[27] but, though an 'English Bard', Byron customarily eschews both bardic properties and the kind of interests succinctly described in A. L. Owen's *The Famous Druids*.[28] That is part of his customary anti-Romantic stance. He mocks the new status of the word by using 'druid' to stand for a scribbler in

English Bards and Scotch Reviewers and *Hints from Horace*.[29] There are two
significant references in *Don Juan*, however, one humorously dismissive
(XI, 193), and the other deeply thoughtful. It is situated right at the beginning
of the Norman Abbey section and describes its placing:

> It stood embosom'd in a happy valley,
> Crown'd by high woodlands, where the Druid Oak
> Stood like Caractacus in act to rally
> His host, with broad arms 'gainst the thunder-stroke;
> And from beneath his boughs were seen to sally
> The dappled foresters – as day awoke
> The branching stag swept down with all his herd
> To quaff a brook which murmured like a bird.
>
>   (XIII. 56)

The image of Caractacus 'in act to rally' and fused with the oak tree's broad
arms is striking. It suggests some particular source but I cannot find one.
What the image does do, however, is present a layer of secular and religious
usurpation (Celts by Romans, Druids by Roman Religion) which antedates
that of the Saxon by the Norman and the monk by the aristocrat. Moreover
'the Druid oak' fuses political, religious and natural reference neatly together
and thus forecasts the concerns of the whole Norman Abbey section. It
does so by associating it with the political resistance of Caractacus. Though
I can't find a protoype for this image of Caractacus himself, there is one
for the Druid Oak and it must be where the idea came from. In Chapter 5
of *Rob Roy* (1817), we suddenly come across Osbaldistone Hall. It is 'a
large and antiquated edifice, peeping out from a druidical grove of huge
oaks'.[30] Osbaldistone Hall is undoubtedly a protoype for Norman Abbey,
and Diana Vernon, its Catholic heroine (a new venture in neo-Romance),
is undoubtedly a protoype of Byron's Aurora Raby. Scott lightly associates
Druid, Catholic, Tory survivals and resistances in the old house in the face
of various usurpations but his emphasis, as always, is on change. Byron,
at the end of his life, broods more deeply and to different ends but in
the same territory. We can see his different direction if we ask where the
'thunderstroke' comes from against which the Druid Oak sets its broad
arms. We will have to search back to Byron in Northern Greece where he
apostrophised Zeus the Thunderer's oak-tree oracle at Dodona:

> Oh! where, Dodona! is thine aged grove,
> Prophetic fount, and oracle divine?
> What valley echo'd the response of Jove?
> What trace remaineth of the thunderer's shrine?
>
>   (*Childe Harold's Pilgrimage*, II. 53)

The imaginative leap from Dodona, via Scott, to Druids at Newstead is another instance of 'Loch-na-Garr with Ida looked o'er Troy'. In *Childe Harold's Pilgrimage*, Byron is concerned elegiacally to mark an erasure but in Norman Abbey, to which both diction and idea are carried, the mystical oak tree is not only recalling a brave but hopeless Celtic resistance to Roman invasion but is active in the present landscape into which it sends its similitude in the 'branching' stag and herd who quench their thirst in the brook which murmurs 'like a bird'. The details are no longer elegiac or masculine. Caractacus, oak tree and stag stand as protectors but the life of the scene is primordially feminine, fecund, delicate and firmly settled. These emphases are repeated in the next two stanzas ('soften'd way', 'nestled', 'brooding', 'like an infant made quiet') and confirmed by the statue of 'The Virgin-Mother of the God-born child' (XIII. 482) who still reigns benignly over the landscape. There is a fusion of natural, spiritual, Celtic, Catholic, and feminine presences who come out of the landscape's past but have not lost any authority.

If we think back to Byron's early presentation of Newstead, we must read this as a displacement of the Norman ancestors whose identity-conferring authority Byron had then accepted. If, at the same time, he begins to boast his Scottish ancestry which, though scotch'd, is not killed, could we not find a reinstatement of those repudiated Celtic ancestors,[31] powerful ghostly presences in a landscape coming to him through his 'mother's Gordons', which are allowed, for the first time, to engage with the Normans of Norman Abbey and claim their more ancient right? This can only be a hypothesis but it is certainly true to the form of Byron's imaginings. The most extreme form of this hypothesis would be that Byron finally allowed his mother, only route to his 'Celtic' ancestors, into his verse. Byron's mother was the most unpoetic of possible muses as far as her son was concerned, but she was a Gordon, from a line of ancestors, putatively 'Celtic', often Catholic,[32] whom Byron, without much evidence, associated with Culloden and,[33] more to our purpose, she was, like Aurora Raby, an orphan. For a time, she lived at Newstead Abbey. We must remember how her own patrimony as heir to the Gordons of Gight had been wholly wasted by Byron's father. The ancestral castle and estates were sold to stave off his debts for a while. Byron was brought up with constant reminders of the despoliation both of this estate and of Newstead itself by Byron's predecessor, the fifth Lord Byron. The last cantos of *Don Juan* are a battleground between various feminine muses (Adeline, Aurora, Fitz-Fulke, associated with Pope, Shakespeare and fashionable light verse respectively) and various conceptions of genre (satire, romance, novel, comedy). From Byron's point of view, this is a struggle between ancestors. Aurora, as a Catholic, is associated with the monastic ghost who is a threat to the Amundevilles, and Fitz-Fulke dresses up as him. These are not Bloomian ancestors open to parricidal misreading. They claim rights, confer fecundity, and rule us 'from their urns' (*Manfred*, III. iv. 41). In the Norman Abbey cantos, he allowed his masculine descent to 'lapse into' a female reading of the continuities of history in the very 'hall of my fathers'. His 'Mother's Gordons' get their revenge on the Norman Byrons at last. The seeds of this possible fusion lay very deep in him. In a letter to Edward Noel Long (16 April 1807), he writes: 'I am an isolated Being on the Earth... Let me but "hear my fame on the winds" and the song of the Bards in my Norman House.'[34] This Celtic/Norman synthesis might seem embarrassingly stagey, but that sense of isolation and mixed ancestry was to flower fifteen years later in the strange music of Norman Abbey's ruined arch, in Lady Adeline's mock-minstrel ballad of the Black Friar, and throughout the greatest section of his greatest poem. It is tempting to explore this further but we have two more tasks. One is to establish the hidden 'Celtic' side to Byron's muse in that period of time when he had apparently abandoned it. The other is to propose a link between the kinds of suppression and reappearance that form part of Byron's poetic ancestry and his understanding of political events.

A good instance of the persistence of the Celtic is Byron's foregrounding of the presence and sound of Highlanders on the Field of Waterloo:

> And wild and high the 'Cameron's gathering' rose!
> The war-note of Lochiel, which Albyn's hills
> Have heard, and heard, too, have her Saxon foes: –
> How in the noon of night that pibroch thrills,
> Savage and shrill!
> (*Childe Harold's Pilgrimage*, III. 226–30)

The two established poems on Waterloo – Scott's 'The Field of Waterloo' (1815) and Southey's 'The Poet's Pilgrimage to Waterloo'(1816) – both mention the activity of Highlanders but Southey's reference is perfunctory, and even Scott, who does mention both 'Cameron' and 'Lochiel' together, makes nothing particularly Gaelic of their presence. Scott refers specifically to 'generous Gordon' who died in the battle.[35] Byron quotes Scott's poem,[36] makes the same sequence of references to the Ball at Brussels and the death of Brunswick as Southey, but omits the references to Gordon dying though he was shown over the battlefield by Major Gordon, a friend of Byron's mother.[37] He puts in new references to the death of his paternal cousin, Major Howard. Nevertheless, more than anyone, he imagines a Gaelic presence as such on the battlefield to which he brings the bagpipes that played nightly in his mother's ancestral castle. As T. S. Eliot noted, the force of these lines came from his 'mother's people'.[38] This is pertinent, but Byron is also seeking out the contrast of Gaelic and modern styles of warfare, just as in the Greek canto of *Childe Harold's Pilgrimage* he deliberately juxtaposes the wild anapæstic battle-song which the Suliotes 'half sang, half screamed' in their highlands (II. 647–8), with his impeccably iambic apostrophe to the Classical Greece of the 'Attic plain' (II. 705). The word 'screamed' is significant here. Byron emphasises the 'shrill' note of the bagpipes. In one version of warfare, armies such as the Roman and navies such as the British pride themselves on their Apollonian self-control in the face of Dionysiac hordes of adversaries. Byron praises and likes the order of the naval ship on which Harold travels to Greece (see stanzas 118–19 of *Childe Harold's Pilgrimage*, II). But Byron is interested in the male shriek which has something of the nature of a battle cry and is ritualised in the bagpipe-playing before and during a battle. One of his most taciturn heroes, Lara, emits a shriek (*Lara*, I. 203–5) and Byron himself, according to Mary Shelley, on a boat in Lake Geneva, asked his companions if they wanted to hear an Albanian song and then gave out 'a strange wild howl' which he declared 'was an exact imitation of the savage Albanian mode'.[39] There is, almost certainly, a Celtic hinterland to this. Ghosts shriek regularly, and heroes occasionally, in Ossian. Mackenzie's *Man of Feeling* popularised male tears but men do not normally shriek or scream in English fictions as women do in Mrs Radcliffe's novels. Highlanders in Scotland do so in fact and in Scott's fictions, and thus present a different mixture of maleness and femaleness to that familiar to 'Saxons'. Edgar Johnson describes how 'Scott presided at a dinner of the Celtic Club surrounded by plaids and claymores. The English officers among the guests, he observed, seemed amazed "at our wild ways... the peculiar shriek of applause so unlike English cheering'."[40]

The division between Lowland and Highland Scotland was the first to engage Byron's imagination and became the template for his encounters with other landscapes and divided histories. Greece, like Scotland, is a blend of both. It is instructive to notice how many times in his letters Byron insists that he is going to make a trip to the Highlands as though to keep alive a buried connection and, at the same time, to preserve his role as a visitor still 'accustomed... to rove'. On an early occasion, he declares to Elizabeth Pigot (11 August 1807): 'I set off for the Highlands... I mean to collect all the Erse traditions, poems & &c & translate or expand the subjects, to fill a volume, which may appear next Spring, under the Denomination of "The

Highland Harp".'⁴¹ Byron presents himself gaily here as a new Macpherson
but he was in fact to transfer much of this endeavour to Greece when he
added extensive notes and appendices on the Romaic language and Greek
and Turkish customs to the first two cantos of *Childe Harold's Pilgrimage*.
Byron often comments on the equivalences of landscape, lifestyle, dress
('kilted clan') and language ('Celtic in its sound') between the two kinds of
Highlands as Andrew Nicholson discusses elsewhere in this volume. When
he sends his Arnaout costume to Mercer Elphinstone, he describes part of
it as 'the camesa or kilt (to speak Scottishly)'.⁴² Byron's celebrated Greek
outfit is a version of the old Gordon one. More striking still is his use of
a quotation from *Waverley* in a letter to Charles Barry in 23 October 1823
describing why he is fighting for Greece: 'I shall "cast in my lot with the
puir Hill Folk".'

If it is true that Byron, with whatever qualification, eschews first his Scottish then his English lineage but these ancestries retain their voice despite
this repudiation and, eventually, he allows them to 'flow into their old chan-
nels', we can fruitfully see this as a version of the norms of those large-scale
historical movements to which Byron, like Scott, so consistently attended.
He sets it out in his 'Address intended to be recited at the Caledonian
Meeting' written the year before Waterloo:

> Who hath not glowed above the page where Fame
> Hath fixed high Caledon's unconquered name;
> The mountain-land which spurned the Roman chain[.]
>   (1–3).

The politics of the poem are quite complicated. These lines sharply distinguish Celts from invading imperial Romans but later he associates
Highlanders with English arms: 'O'er Gael and Saxon mingling banners
shine'(9). Andrew Noble once criticised these lines as 'extraordinary' and
'absurd' insofar as they collude with British imperialism and deny Byron's
elsewhere demonstrated ability to empathise with many different peoples.⁴³
But the grounds of Byron's ability to enter into diverse cultural modes and,
as a 'cosmopolitan', overlook them, is his conscious identification first with
his Scots and then with his English ancestors. Why should we criticise
Byron for going to the trouble of writing a poem in support of a meeting
designed to give financial support to 'the education and support of the children of Scottish soldiers, sailors, and marines who fought for Britain'?⁴⁴
The poem makes no mention of imperial enterprises and, at the time of
writing, Byron and his readers would assume that fighting against Napoleon
was the most likely occupation of British forces. Byron admired Napoleon

but recognised, e.g. in the Spanish section of *Childe Harold's Pilgrimage*, that Napoleon was both tyrant and invading imperialist. Byron's godfather, the Duke of Gordon, established a Highland regiment (later 'the Gordon Highlanders') and, as we have seen, Byron saluted the Cameron Highlanders in his lines on Waterloo. The Report of the Caledonian Meeting for 1814 celebrates the 'brave men' through whom 'the independence of the Empire has been preserved' rather than the expansion of Empire, and E. H. Coleridge's listing of the Scots of the '71st Light Infantry' who fell in the Peninsular War is entirely appropriate to the poem.[45] Ernest Coleridge also spots the echoes of Ossian triggered in this occasional piece.[46] Instead of finding Byron's lines 'absurd', we should note Byron's deliberate emphasis of Celtic opposition to the Romans but eventual alliance with the Saxons. Apart from peripheries like Northern Scotland, the Celts initially opposed but ultimately accepted domination by the Romans. This doubleness does not correspond to a contradiction but to a thought.

We can set that thought out like this. When Byron as a child, moved from 'moderate Presbyterian' Aberdeen (*Don Juan*, xv. 728) to 'the natives of dark Loch na Garr' ('Lachin Y Gair', 16), he moved into a circumambient landscape and to an older way of life. Here he found, imagined and embodied his ancestors. The history of the Celts as it has been understood since the Romans is of precarious minor existence on the peripheries of empires or major subordination within them. Nevertheless they persist, surround and outnumber their conquerors. What they remember exists as traces of their suppressed ancestors who abide as ghosts in narratives, place-names and song. In time these ghosts reassert themselves in later history. Gray's 'The Bard' (1757) is the *locus classicus* of this view of things. This reassertion may be for the benefit of the conquered but also for the conquerors who begin to express nostalgia, as it were by intinction, for the culture which they have displaced. Macpherson's Ossian is 'a sublimated elegy for Jacobite history',[47] a version of the Celtic past designed to appeal to readers of Gray as well as to those Highlanders who will make careers in the 'British' army. Lowlanders, and even makers of sea-biscuits from Wapping, discover the attractions of the kilt. From another point of view, this accommodation may be seen as time's harmonisation of inherited differences or, via Scott, as an Hegelian or Marxist synthesis of dialectically distributed elements. Byron read this exegesis of History by way of Scottish history avidly in the Waverley novels. It was his own history and a clue to all secular and sacred histories. From yet another point of view, to name the ancestor, to reactivate the ghosts of a long subordinated but still circumambient people, is to suggest a revolutionary call to arms. The 'Isles of Greece' poet in

Canto III of *Don Juan* does precisely this. When Byron himself returns to Greece in 1823 as famous English poet, defender of Classical and Byzantine Greece against Oriental Imperialism, sympathetic fellow-Highlander, and European Liberal supporting a small-scale nationalism, he reveals how awareness of such complex oppositions, so central to his activity as a poet, does not in the least preclude a clear and active commitment to useful, rather than gesture, politics. At the end, George Gordon, Lord Byron cast in his lot with 'the puir hill folk' as, in his earliest years, he had done with his ancestors. Whenever we read him, we should always remember his middle name.

CHAPTER 8

Shelley, Ireland and Romantic Orientalism

Arthur Bradley

In Percy Bysshe Shelley's *Laon and Cythna* (1817), Cythna predicts the revolution she leads will spread from the eastern plains of Islam to 'the green lands cradled in the roar / Of western waves'(v. 2263–4).[1] If it is not clear exactly which 'green lands' Cythna is referring to here, a number of factors suggest that the most likely candidates are the British Isles or, to be precise, Britain and Ireland.[2] Romantic Orientalism has historically been written and read from a European perspective. Shelley himself famously described the poem in an 1817 letter as an orientalised displacement of a European uprising. 'It is a tale illustrative of such a Revolution' he writes 'as might be supposed to take place in an European nation'(SL, 1, p. 563–4). Marilyn Butler, in a recent essay on Romantic Orientalism and narrative, interprets the genre as a political allegory for the turbulent situation in Britain in particular.[3] Despite, or perhaps because of, Anglocentric readings like these, though, it is surprising that the Irish context of Shelley's Orientalism has, until recently, remained relatively unexplored. There is, after all, more than *one* green land cradled in the roar of western waves in Shelley's poem. This hidden context has only begun to emerge, ironically, as the study of Romantic Orientalism has shifted away from an exclusively European perspective. Nigel Leask and Mohammed Sharafuddin briefly examine the Irish context of Byron's *Eastern Tales* (1813–16), Moore's *Lallah Rookh* (1817), and *Laon and Cythna* in their work on orientalism but, despite developing some promising lines of enquiry, Leask, in particular, prefers to read Shelley's poem as a quasi-literal exploration of British colonialism in India rather than an allegorical one of colonialism in Ireland.[4] Indocentric readers of the poem can perhaps be forgiven for not exploring Laon and Cythna's 'other island' more easily than their Anglocentric equivalents, but it remains a source of frustration even here because, as Leask brilliantly observes, Shelley drew a number of striking aesthetico-political parallels between the colonial situation in Ireland and the orientalised India of *Laon and Cythna*. In this paper, I would like to explore in a little more detail the interface between Shelley's constructions of Ireland, the Orient and elsewhere by reading *An Address, to the Irish People*, his poems on Ireland and the Irish revolutionary Robert Emmet, and, in particular, his Oriental revolutionary poem *Laon and Cythna*.[5]

SHELLEY AND IRELAND

Shelley's 'Irish expedition' of 1812 has traditionally been dismissed as a youthful folly, but recent criticism acknowledges it as 'a significant stage in the development of would-be political agitator into major poet'.[6] His pamphlets on Catholic Emancipation and the Repeal of the Union articulate a neo-Godwinian position that gradual, individual self-reform, rather than collective violent revolution, is the best means of achieving political progress in Ireland. If they are to choose individual reform over institutional revolution, Shelley argues that the Irish must learn the lessons, not only of the French Revolution, but of their own rebellions of 1798 and 1803. The leaders of these uprisings, Wolfe Tone, and in particular, Robert Emmet, became tragically, and not unheroically, ensnared upon the horns of this national dilemma and the Irish people must learn from their example. But though Shelley's active interest in Irish politics is striking enough for someone of his age and background, the most remarkable and problematic aspect of this whole episode is that he never analyses the Irish question in exclusively national terms. Ireland is seen as merely a local example of an international phenomenon, and Irish politics is just a stepping stone on the path to globalised reform. 'English Romanticism and the Celtic World' is, for Shelley, a strikingly literal proposition.

In *An Address, to the Irish People*, which he largely completed before arriving in Ireland, Shelley publicly declares that his desire was 'to awaken in the minds of the Irish poor, a knowledge of their real state, summarily pointing out the evils of that state, and suggesting rational means of remedy. – Catholic Emancipation and a Repeal of the Union Act' (SPW, p. 8). But in a private letter he also admits that his real aim was to 'shake Catholicism at its basis, and to induce Quakerish and Socinian principle[s] of politics without objecting to the Christian religion, which would do no good to the vulger [sic] just now' (SL, vol. 1, p. 239). Shelley is adamant that the cause of political reform is best served by personal reform: 'O Irishmen, REFORM YOURSELVES' (SPW, p. 25). If his audience had been in any doubt as to exactly which aspects of themselves needed reforming, he thoughtfully goes on to diagnose a whole series of faults in the Irish character. He argues that 'the warm feelings of an Irishman sometimes carry him beyond the point of prudence' and leave him prone to 'drink' (SPW, p. 22), 'mobs and violence' (SPW, p. 22) and religious 'intolerance' (SPW, p. 23). To moderate these tendencies, he continually counsels his audience to develop the habits of 'SOBRIETY, REGULARITY, and THOUGHT'(SP, p. 19). In conclusion, Shelley urges his audience to establish nationwide philanthropic societies and thus conveniently introduces the second of his Irish pamphlets *Proposals for an Association of Philanthropists* (1812).

Unsurprisingly, *An Address, to the Irish People* was given a somewhat mixed reception. Shelley delivered it to a meeting of the Catholic Committee in Dublin on 28th February 1812 and remarked upon 'the hisses with which they greeted me when I spoke of *religion*' (SL, vol. 1, p. 275). His supposedly secret intention 'to shake Catholicism at its basis' was all too obvious and could only have alienated his predominantly Catholic, middle-class, liberal audience. He best proves his own claim that 'Many Englishmen are prejudiced against you' (SPW, p. 23). If the *Address* is not a very realistic picture of Ireland or the Irish, then, it is perhaps more generously seen as Shelley's first aesthetico-political construction of a people apparently on the verge of radical change. The fact that Shelley wrote it before setting foot in Ireland is testament both to his political naivety or presumptuousness *and* his increasing poetic maturation. In *An Address, to the Irish People*, he constructs a mass almost schizophrenically poised between alcoholism and autodidacticism, mob violence and philanthropic reform, religious barbarism and enlightened atheism. This portrait of the 'Irish people' is a likely model for the mighty crowds and restless mobs in later poems like *Rosalind and Helen* (1817–18) and, perhaps most explicitly, *Laon and Cythna*.

If Shelley wanted a specific figure around which his general analysis of Ireland and the Irish could cohere, it appears that he found one in the leader of the abortive Irish rebellion of 1803, Robert Emmet. Shelley's connections with the United Irishmen have already been well documented.[7] He bemoaned the lack of impact his expedition was having amongst current political pressure groups such as the liberal Catholic Committee in a letter to Elizabeth Hitchener, declaring the 'remnant of United Irishmen whose wrongs make them hate England I have more hopes of' (SL, vol. 1, p. 264–5). During his stay in Dublin, Shelley also contacted a number of public figures who had associations with the movement, including the radical publisher Archibald Rowan Hamilton, the newspaper editor John Lawless, the revolutionary activist Catherine Nugent and the barrister John Philpot Curran. But if Shelley's public lectures reveal his sympathy with the non-sectarian, and initially reformist, ideals of the United Irishmen, they also betray an anxiety that those ideals were compromised by the widespread violence of the 1798 and 1803 revolutions. The poet does not refer directly to the Irish uprisings – it would have been politically risky to do so in front of a liberal and reformist Catholic audience – but his references to the French Revolution seem to contain coded references to the United Irishmen's rebellions as well. Shelley draws an obvious parallel between the French and Irish uprisings, for instance, when he argues that the French Revolution was destroyed by the same kind of 'warm feelings' he detects in Ireland: 'The murders during the period of the French Revolution, and the despotism which has since been established, prove that the doctrines of Philanthropy and Freedom, were but shallowly understood' (SPW, p. 51).

In the figure of Robert Emmet, it would seem that Shelley found a specific signifier for this defining political tension between philanthropic rationalism and revolutionary violence in Irish society. Robert Emmet and his followers began an attack on Dublin Castle on 23 July 1803. The attack was intended to provoke a full-scale national uprising but a combination of indecision and confusion led to Emmet's eventual arrest, trial and execution. Emmet has historically been regarded as a tragic romantic visionary, leading a rebellion that was doomed to failure from the outset, but recent work presents us with a more complex and self-contradictory character than this picture suggests.[8] On the one hand, his initially reformist politics, his belief that the rebellion should be conducted in a dignified, almost chivalrous, manner, and his supposed declaration from the dock that his epitaph should go unwritten until Ireland was a free nation, still suggest an idealistic, 'romantic' personality. On the other hand, increasing recognition of his effectiveness as a revolutionary leader, his organisation of a secret nationwide movement, and particularly his understanding of the effectiveness of propaganda and martyrology, reveal a figure simultaneously steeped in the demands of *realpolitik*. In a phrase which aptly captures his ambiguous intentions, Emmet once wrote that he wanted the Dublin uprising to have the 'respectability of insurrection'.[9] Shelley's fascination with Emmet has been documented by Timothy Webb amongst others but the poet's analysis of the Irish national character helps to explain his interest in the figure.[10] This simultaneously realist, romantic, respectable and revolutionary personality embodies the tensions in the Irish political character that Shelley diagnoses and attempt to reconcile in *An Address, to the Irish People*. If Robert Emmet hadn't existed, it is tempting to think that Shelley would have had to invent him.

Shelley wrote two fairly undistinguished poems about Emmet during his time in Dublin. In 'The Tombs', his hagiographical account of Emmet's life and death, the poet's ambivalence towards the Irish revolutionary leader still shows through:

> That the high sense which from the stern rebuke
> Of Erin's victim-patriot's death-soul shone,
>   When blood and chains defiled the land
>   Lives in the torn uprooted heart
>   His savage murderers burn?
>   ('The Tombs', 21–5)

Shelley eulogises the 'high sense' of Emmet but his praise is tempered by the recollection of the violence of the 1798 rebellion and its still more violent suppression: 'When blood and chains defiled the land'. The poet is unable to gloss over the tensions in Emmet's political character, and by extension, in the political character of 'Erin' as a whole. But if Emmet's life embodies what Shelley believes to be the self-contradictions of Irish revolutionary politics, however, his death appears to transcend those contradictions.

Shelley predicted on setting out for Dublin that his expedition would end in either 'the noblest success or the most glorious martyrdom' (SL, vol. 1, p. 246). It seems that the notion of 'glorious martyrdom' continually presented itself to him as a means of resolving the difficulties inherent in radical change. The tensions which bedevil Emmet's rebellion in the 'The Tombs' are partially resolved, or at least conveniently obscured, by Emmet's martyrdom. Emmet compromises his ideals by embracing violent revolution, but it seems that he recovers something of his former dignified status in defeat. 'The Tombs' still ends up characterising Emmet as the 'victim-patriot' rather than the 'savage murderer'. Following that disturbingly graphic image of Emmet's 'torn uprooted heart' (which we will come back to later) the memory of the revolutionary leader's own violent past begins to fade. By peacefully submitting to the judgement of a manifestly unjust tribunal, Shelley's Emmet turns death into martyrdom and failure into moral victory: 'the stern rebuke / Of Erin's victim-patriot'. In 'On Robert Emmet's Tomb' (another rather inappropriate epitaph for a figure who famously claimed that his epitaph should not be written until Ireland resumed her place amongst the nations of the world) it is clear that Shelley feels Emmet's moral victory will ultimately be a political one as well:

> When the storm-cloud that lowers o'er the day-beam is gone,
> Unchanged, unextinguished its life-spring will shine;
> When Erin has ceased with their memory to groan,
> She will smile through the tears of revival on thine.
>   ('On Robert Emmet's Tomb', 25–8)

Shelley's poems on Robert Emmet are juvenilia but the central idea of political martyrdom is something that recurs throughout his poetic career. If the Irish people are the earliest models for the crowds in poems such as *Rosalind and Helen* and *Laon and Cythna*, the Irish rebel Emmet is also a prototype for the tortured revolutionary poet-martyrs in those poems, Lionel and Laon and Cythna themselves.

What role does Shelley's analysis of the Irish question play in his politics more generally? Shelley continually stresses in his work on Emmet, the United Irishmen and Ireland that the Irish Question is not simply a local one but has international ramifications. The Celtic 'world', in Shelley's view, is nothing less than the Celtic *world*. Just as Shelley uses Catholic Emancipation as a Trojan horse for generalised atheism, so he exploits Irish politics as the first step in his plan for globalised reform. 'Thou art the isle on whose green shores I have desired to see the standard of liberty erected' he wrote 'a flag of fire, a beacon at which the world shall light the torch of Freedom!' (SPW, p. 13). The first nation to benefit from the Irish example was supposed to be Britain. In a letter to Elizabeth Hitchener, Shelley explains that his plan to set up philanthropic societies in Ireland is merely the first stage of a wider programme to establish similar societies in Wales, and, eventually, throughout England and asks, in a question curiously resonant of Emmet's oxymoronic desire for a respectable insurrection: 'Might I not extend them all over England, and *quietly revolutionise* the country?' (my emphasis) (SL, vol. 1, p. 264).

France was another obvious target for Shelley's philanthropic zeal. In *Proposals for an Association of Philanthropists*, as we have already seen, Shelley compares the Irish political situation favourably with the recent history of France and argues that France, too, would benefit from the gradual increase in liberty he advocates for Ireland. Ireland is the signifier of quiet gradual revolution, but France is the beacon of a sudden, bloody one: 'Had there been more of these men, France would not now be a beacon to warn us of the hazards and horror of Revolutions, but a pattern of society, rapidly advancing to a state of perfection, and holding out an example for the gradual and peaceful regeneration of the world' (SPW, p. 52). If Ireland can avoid the mistakes the French fell into, then it can go on to assume the exemplary position that France should have occupied. This emphasis on the lessons that Ireland must learn from France, and that France can re-learn from Ireland would not have been lost on an audience who were only too aware of the interconnections between the United Irishmen, the first French Directory and the Napoleonic governments.

But the importance of the Irish example stretches far beyond western Europe. Timothy Webb notes that Shelley wrote a poem in tribute to the establishment of a republic in Mexico during his time in Ireland, which he included in a letter with another set of lines beginning 'O thou Ocean...'. The Mexican poem implicitly compares the 'unextinguished' flames of the martyred revolutionary priest Miguel Hidalgo and Robert Emmet: 'Feel the pulses of the brave / Unextinguished in the grave' (6–7). This adjective 'suggests the interconnection of Emmet and the Mexican revolutionaries' Webb argues 'just as the conjunction of the two poems in Shelley's letter suggests that his concern is with a political phenomenon of international dimensions'.[11]

Perhaps the best example of Shelley's belief in the universal applicability of the Irish example, however, is the case of Asia or the 'Orient'. Nigel Leask notes that Shelley's 'approach to the colonial situation in Ireland touches on his perception of the situation in India'. Shelley's analysis of both situations is deeply indebted to Volney's *Les Ruines, ou méditation sur les révolutions des empires* (1791), and in particular, Volney's rationalist theory of the equivalence of all religions as instruments of socio-political coercion. It is difficult to accept Leask's claim that Shelley saw the religious 'superstitions' of the Irish as 'a useful curb on their passions' – quite the contrary seems the case – but it is easier to sympathise with his view that, for the poet, such superstitions must 'ultimately give way to the rational transparency of the modern state'.[12] In almost all the works he wrote or delivered in Dublin, Shelley is at pains to stress that his message applies equally to Catholics and Protestants alike and he continually cites Muslim and Brahmin comparisons to emphasise its universal implications. The *Address, to the Irish People* professes to have never found a Protestant 'impudent enough to say, that a Roman Catholic, or a Quaker, or a Jew, or a Mahometan, if he was a virtuous man, and did all the good in his power, would go to Heaven a bit the slower for not subscribing to the thirty-nine articles' (SPW, p. 11). 'Were Ireland at this moment peopled with Brahmins' he later proclaims 'this very same address would have been suggested by the same state of mind' (SPW, p. 17). In his *Declaration of Rights* (1812), he argues that 'A Christian, a Deist, a Turk, and a Jew, have equal rights: they are men and brethren' (SPW, p. 58). 'If a person's religious ideas correspond not with your own, love him nevertheless' he continues 'How different would yours have been, had the chance of birth placed you in Tartary or India' (SPW, p. 59). Shelley, in classic Volneyan fashion, continually relativises the religious differences between nations, and stresses the universal sameness that underlies it:

[H]as not your belief been rather the chance result of birth, and of the empire of habit and education? Are you not born Christians on the banks of the Tiber, Mahometans on those of the Euphrates, Idolaters on the shores of India, in the same manner as you are born fair in cold regions, and burnt under the African sun?[13]

If Shelley really saw Irish Catholics and Turkish Muslims as interchangeable members of the same universal family, then there is no reason why *An Address, to the Irish People*, 'On Robert Emmet's Tomb' and so on should not be read in the context of oriental poems like *Laon and Cythna* and vice versa. There is something unShelleyan about insisting upon national distinctions between his political analyses because, as Leask notes, he does not care 'whether the Other is Irish or Italian or Bengali (not to mention female) so long as it can be alchemised into the Same'.[14] This homogenising tendency can be best glimpsed by a reading of *Laon and Cythna*.

IRELAND AND THE ORIENT

Laon and Cythna is the story of Greek siblings, who lead a peaceful revolution against a Turkish Emperor, Othman; the establishment of a radical, atheist new society; Othman's violent and successful counter-revolution; the martyrdom of Laon and Cythna; and their admission into the Temple of the Spirit, a kind of House of Fame for revolutionary heroes. Shelley's poem has been read as a 'beau ideal' (SL, vol. 1, p. 564) of recent French, English and now even Indian political history, but I would argue that it can also be analysed in the context of the Irish revolutionary uprisings of 1798 and, particularly, 1803. This is not to say that Shelley set out with the intention of writing an Oriental allegory of Irish rather than British or French politics – his version of *Lallah Rookh*[15] – but that his perception of the political situation in Ireland overlaps with, and cannot be divorced from, his perception of wider European and even Asian politics. There is a deeply *unheimlich* quality to the poem as images and ideas that are familiar from contemporary European politics constantly turn up in displaced, orientalised forms. In *Laon and Cythna*, Shelley conflates the signifiers of Ireland with those of Britain, France and India under the general sign of an Oriental uprising against a colonial regime.

I want to briefly sketch some possible directions for this reading. It is clear that there are a number of points of convergence between Shelley's constructions of the Greeks in *Laon and Cythna* and the Irish in *An Address, to the Irish People*. In the Preface to his Oriental poem, Shelley analyses the descent of the French Revolution into violence in terms which recall his analysis of the Irish national character five years earlier. The French exhibit what Shelley earlier identified as the distinctive signifiers of Irishness. They are understandably prone to an instinctive warmth and impetuousness of feeling which nonetheless require moderation by rational thought and reflection:

It has ceased to be believed, that whole generations of mankind ought to consign themselves to a hopeless inheritance of ignorance and misery, because a nation of men who had been dupes and slaves for centuries, were incapable of conducting themselves with the wisdom and tranquillity of freemen so soon as some of their fetters were partially loosened. That their conduct could not have been marked by any other characters than ferocity and thoughtlessness is the historical fact from which liberty derives all its recommendations, and falsehood the worst features of its deformity. (S, p. 87)

The Greeks in the poem proper are also characterised by a quasi-Celtic 'ferocity and thoughtlessness' in action. Their supposedly pacific revolution is constantly threatened by the ferocity and thoughtlessness of strong emotions: 'and then revenge and fear / Made the high virtue of the patriots fail: / One pointed on his foe the mortal spear' (v. 1788–90). Interestingly, it is only when Laon stills the revolutionaries' emotions by appealing to their rational sense of fraternity that the revolution regains its peaceful nature: 'Ay, ye are pale, – ye weep, – your passions pause, – / 'Tis well! ye feel the truth of love's benignant laws' (v. 1799–1800). Laon pleads for the vengeful crowd to spare the life of the vanquished Othman by petitioning them to temper their Irish 'warm feelings' with the 'chastened will of virtue':

> 'What call ye *justice*? is there one who ne'er
> In secret thought has wished another's ill? –
> Are ye all pure? Let those stand forth who hear,
> And tremble not. Shall they insult and kill,
> If such they be? their mild eyes can they fill
> With the false anger of the hypocrite?
> Alas, such were not pure, – the chastened will
> Of virtue sees that justice is the light
> Of love, and not revenge, and terror and despite.'
> (v. 2017–25)

In my view, however, there are also intriguing parallels between Shelley's representations of Robert Emmet and Laon and Cythna. Laon is an enlightened radical who must confront and overcome his own inherent propensity for violence as well as the oppressions of an occupying power. He begins by following not merely the obvious examples of the Jacobins, but of Miguel Hidalgo, the Emmetesque protagonist of Shelley's Irish lines upon the Mexican revolution. Hidalgo's cry of ' "Liberty or Death!" ' (10) is reproduced by Laon in Canto 3: 'so I drew / My knife, and with one impulse, suddenly / All unaware three of their number slew, / And grasped a fourth by the throat, and with loud cry / My countrymen invoked to death or liberty!' (III. 1193–7). In Canto 6, too, Laon responds to Othman's counter-revolution by drawing on the historic weaponry of Irish rebellion: 'a bundle of rude pikes, the instrument / Of those who war but on their native ground / For natural rights' (VI. 2444–6).[16]

Laon goes on to eschew violence and in doing so adopts the rhetorical strategies of Emmet's martyrology. The story of Laon and Cythna's capture, self-mythologising and martyrdom contain unmistakable echoes of Emmet's rhetorical attitudinising from the dock. 'Let no man write my epitaph' Emmet supposedly declared at his trial 'When my country takes her place among the nations of the earth, then, and not till then, let my epitaph be written.'[17] Shelley comes perilously close to eulogising Emmet's plea to go uneulogised in the poem 'On Robert Emmet's Tomb': 'No trump tells thy virtues – the grave where they rest / With thy dust shall remain unpolluted by fame, / Till thy foes, by the world and by fortune caressed, / Shall pass like a mist from the light of thy name' (21–4). Thomas Hogg, in his biography of Shelley, also remembers coming across an account and engraving of Emmet's trial in the London hotel room the poet took upon returning from Ireland. 'The principal figure was the unfortunate young man' Hogg remembered 'he was standing at the bar and addressing the bench'.[18] This image of the 'unfortunate young man standing at the bar' seemingly resurfaces in Canto 9 of 'Laon and Cythna' where the hero and heroine mythologise themselves as Emmetesque martyrs. Like Emmet, Laon and Cythna's presently uncommemorated fame – 'None shall dare vouch' – will ultimately outlast the fortunes of their foes: 'That record shall remain, when they must pass':

> And Calumny meanwhile shall feed on us,
> As worms devour the dead, and near the throne
> And at the altar, most accepted thus
> Shall sneers and curses be; – what we have done
> *None shall dare vouch*, tho' it be truly known;
> *That record shall remain, when they must pass*
> Who build their pride in its oblivion;
> And fame, in human hope which sculptured was,
> Survive the perished scrolls of unenduring brass.
>
> (IX. 3739–47, emphases mine)

Perhaps another link between Ireland and Orientalism in the poem are those enemies who 'build their pride' in Laon and Cythna's 'oblivion'. It is clear that there are some important aesthetic and political connections between Laon's foes and the enemies of Emmet. Othman's counter-revolution leads to the onset of a famine that threatens to engulf revolutionaries and reactionaries alike. The powerfully apocalyptic famine scenes are probably influenced by the Europe-wide agricultural depression that began in 1814 but it is worth mentioning that there was an Irish potato blight in the same year that Shelley wrote *Laon and Cythna*. In Canto 10 of the poem, Othman recruits an Iberian Priest to lead and unite the increasingly diverse factions of the counter-revolutionary army he has assembled. The character of the Priest, according to Kenneth Neil Cameron, is at least partially based on Castlereagh who by 1817 had risen from the position of Chief Secretary for Ireland to become Foreign Secretary and architect of the Holy Alliance.[19] If the Iberian Priest clearly mirrors Castlereagh's contemporary role in orchestrating Britain's rapprochement with reactionary Catholic Europe, it would also appear that he reflects the part Castlereagh played in suppressing the United Irishmen's rebellion nineteen years earlier. The connection is confirmed by the reappearance of a particularly gruesome image from Shelley's Irish poems. Shelley says in his poem 'The Tombs' that Emmet's heart was 'torn uprooted' by his English opponents. Another Irish poem called 'The Devil's Walk' (1812) even more graphically asserts that Castlereagh tears Emmet's heart from his chest and holds it in his hand:

> Fat – as the Death-birds on Erin's shore,
> That glutted themselves in her dearest gore,
>   And flitted round Castlereagh,
> When they snatched the Patriot's heart, that *his* grasp
> Had torn from its widow's maniac clasp
> And fled at the dawn of day.
>   (*The Devil's Walk*, 57–62)

This disturbing image – in which colonial oppression and deracination are exacted on a bodily level – turns up again in *Laon and Cythna*. In Canto 10 of the poem, the Iberian-Priest-influenced Othman proposes a disturbingly similar fate for Laon as Castlereagh did for Emmet in 'The Tombs' and 'The Devil's Walk':

> The Monarch saith, that his great Empire's worth
> Is set on Laon and Laone's head:
> He who but one yet living here can lead,

> *Or who the life from both their hearts can wring,*
> Shall be the kingdom's heir, a glorious meed!
>
> (x. 4155–9, emphasis mine)

But the most obvious parallel between the Irish and the Oriental revolutionaries is the manner of their deaths. *Laon and Cythna* concludes with the trial and execution of the hero and heroine. Laon submits to Othman's will in a scene that almost inevitably recalls contemporary accounts of Robert Emmet's trial: 'Before the Tyrant's throne / All night his agèd Senate sate, their eyes / In stony expectation fixed; when one / Suddenly before them stood, a Stranger and alone' (xi. 4338–41). Shelley showed how in 'The Tombs', Emmet's trial speech recovers a moral clarity from the wreckage of revolutionary compromise and defeat: 'That the high sense which from the stern rebuke / Of Erin's victim-patriot's death-soul shone'. Laon likewise succeeds in tempering the 'warm feeling' which endangered his uprising into a rational and reflective eloquence: 'when he spake, his tone, / Ere yet the matter did their thoughts arrest, / Earnest, benignant, calm, as from a breast / Void of all hate and terror' (xi. 4344–7). In the scene where he upbraids an assailant, Laon again strikes a similar note of 'stern rebuke' to Emmet:

> . . . 'What hast thou to do
> with me, poor wretch?' – Calm, solemn, and severe,
> That voice unstrung his sinews, and he threw
> His dagger on the ground, and pale with fear,
> Sate silently – his voice then did the Stranger rear.
>
> (xi. 4400–44)

Laon's act of martyrdom grants him the quasi-religious immortality of predecessors like Emmet. He becomes another 'victim-patriot' whose death at the stake preserves the 'soul' of his republicanism for future vindication. Shelley was already transposing the figure of Emmet on the scaffold into the Shelleyan figure of Laon at the stake in a letter written in February 1813, one year after his Irish expedition: 'the soul' of his Republicanism 'would shrink neither from the scaffold or the stake' he wrote (SL, vol. 1, p. 352). *Laon and Cythna* also transplants the hopes Shelley once had for Ireland to America but it is interesting to note that the new world is described in almost classically Emmetesque terms. Emmet supposedly wanted a free nation to be his epitaph and Laon calls America: 'An epitaph of glory for the tomb / Of murdered Europe may thy fame be made, / Great People' (xi. 4427–9). In the conclusion of the poem, Laon exits the vicious circle of revolutionary and counter-revolutionary violence by his act of political martyrdom and thus takes his place amongst the 'good and great' in the

Temple of the Spirit: 'These perish as the good and great of yore / Have perished, and their murderers will repent, / Yes, vain and barren tears shall flow before / Yon smoke has faded from the firmament' (xii. 4693–4). Laon and Emmet finally sit side by side in the pantheon of revolutionary heroes.

In *Laon and Cythna*, then, Shelley collapses the space between his constructions of Ireland and the Orient to the extent that it becomes increasingly difficult and unnecessary to distinguish between them. If in one sense Laon and Cythna's revolution has yet to reach the 'green lands cradled in the roar / Of western waves' by the end of the poem, in another it has always already arrived there, because it already contains Shelley's reading of the Irish rebellions of 1798 and 1803 within it. The world is always already Celtic. From desert plains to green lands, Shelley's Orient and Shelley's Ireland are less distinctive topographies and more convenient, 'marginal' spaces in which he can begin to construct and enact his homogenising ideology of world reform. In this sense, 'the green lands cradled in the roar / Of western waves' are themselves merely the cradle for Shelley's global political aspirations.

CHAPTER 9

Byron and the 'Ariosto of the North'

Andrew Nicholson

With regard to the 'Ariosto of the North' surely their themes Chivalry – war – & love were as like as can be – and as to the compliment – if you knew what the Italians think of Ariosto – you would not hesitate about that. – But as to their 'measures,' you forget that Ariosto's is an octave stanza – and Scott's anything but a Stanza. – If you think Scot[t] will dislike it – say so – & I expunge. – I do not call him the '*Scotch* Ariosto' which would be sad *provincial* eulogy – but the 'Ariosto of the *North*' – meaning of *all countries* that are *not* the South. (Byron to Murray, 17 September 1817)[1]

In the Romantic period the two writers who stood above the others in pop-ular estimate were not Southey and Wordsworth or Coleridge, or Moore and Rogers or Campbell or Crabbe, but Scott and Byron. This was recog-nised by themselves, their critics, publishers and readers. As early as *Childe Harold* I and II (1812), it was customary for critics to class Byron and Scott together.[2] Throughout their writing lives Byron and Scott were engaged in an unspoken dialogue which cannot be regarded simply as rivalry. True, Scott himself seems to invite such a reading to account for his having re-linquished poetry for the novel, especially in the introductions to the 1830 edition of his poetical works and from a number of comments, such as those to Ballantyne in 1813 – 'James, Byron hits the mark where I don't even pretend to fledge my arrow.'[3] But his letters suggest rather a different story;[4] and he had turned his thoughts to the novel long before Byron arrived on the literary scene (the opening chapters of *Waverley* were drafted in 1805).[5] Byron himself, moreover, invites quite the contrary reading: 'I never risk *rivalry* in any thing'; 'it is my story & my *East* – (& here I am venturing with no one to contend against – from having *seen* what my contemporaries must copy from the drawings of others only)'.[6]

Scott and Byron corresponded with each other from 1812 onwards, be-came friends, read each other's works avidly and supported each other staunchly in public. Byron had first alluded to Scott in a lengthy passage in *English Bards and Scotch Reviewers* (1809).[7] Its mere length (twenty-five lines) is a covert recognition of the stature Scott had already achieved by that time; but the lines themselves are ill-considered and immature. Byron charges him with writing, as he puts it in his long note to this passage, 'for hire'.[8] When he returned from his first tour to the East two years later, however, bearing the first two Cantos of *Childe Harold* and *Hints from Horace,* he presented a different view. In the latter poem Scott was now numbered amongst Chaucer, Spenser, Dryden and Pope as one who had 'neatly grafted' 'New words' 'on a Gallic phrase', and 'by force of rhyme' 'Enrich'd our islands' ill-united tongues'[9] and who had also, following Swift and Butler, successfully re-introduced the tetrameter:

> Though at first view – eight feet may seem in vain
> Formed, save in Ode, to bear a serious strain,
> Yet Scott has shown our wondering isle of late
> This measure shrinks not from a theme of weight,
> And varied skilfully, surpasses far
> Heroic rhyme, but most in Love and War,
> Whose fluctuations, tender or sublime,
> Are curbed too much by long recurring rhyme.[10]

These lines indicate a shift in Byron's tone from the indiscriminate and personally abusive character of the Juvenalian *English Bards* to the more tempered, didacticism of the Horatian model. This is in marked contrast not merely to his own former criticisms but also to those of Scott's reviewers at the time – principally Jeffrey – who, besides other 'unpoetic' and 'unnatural' features of style and subject, and 'blemishes, both of taste and of diction', picked out Scott's versification for particular censure.[11]

One reader's views are instructive here. In a letter of 6 March 1812, Lord Holland told Byron: 'I promise myself great pleasure from Childe Harold I am glad to see that it is in a regular stanza & that stanza of Spensers I should have been very sorry to see the other system sanctioned by your authority & recommended by another powerful writer as well as Walter Scott'.[12] But when Byron himself in his next two major publications, *The Giaour* and *The Bride of Abydos* (both 1813), also deployed the tetrameter and as irregular a stanzaic form as that of Scott, Holland was dismayed. On receiving the former he wrote: 'I must be permitted to lament your infidelity to ten syllable verse (either in heroicks or in stanza's [*sic*]) which as it is the best adapted to every thing high in poetry you will not be offended at my saying, seems better suited to your Muse than the Namby Pamby eight syllable which Walter Scotts careless genius has made so current in the world.'[13] And on receiving *The Bride,* which Byron had dedicated to him, he was even more tellingly disturbed. Though he regarded Scott as 'the great model of irregular poetry or at least the most fashionable seducer of Modern Bards to that practice',[14] he thought that even in this depart-ment Byron outstripped him. This is pertinent not only to the competitive character given to the Scott-Byron comparison at the time, but also to the notion of education. For despite his reservations, Holland still says 'I never read a poem more to my taste in *irregular* verse' and concludes his letter by reiterating: 'I am delighted with the poem, The descriptions the thoughts the story the language the characters & the versification wherever your Moslem predilections allow you to adhere to a Christian metre'.[15] There is surely more than a touch of equivocation in this, suggesting that Holland was largely unsettled by the *novelty* to which Scott and Byron were expos-ing him, but was nevertheless beginning to find Byron's instruction in its attractions irresistibly persuasive. In his reply Byron excused himself with what seems almost equal equivocation:

I merely chose that measure as *next* to *prose* to tell a story or describe a place which struck me – I have a thorough & utter contempt for all measures but Spencer's [*sic*] stanza and *Dryden's couplet* – the whole of the Bride cost me *four nights* – and you may easily suppose that I can have no great esteem for lines that can be strung as fast as minutes. . . . If the public will read things written in that debauched measure – that is their own fault – and if they begin in the present instance – to dislike it – I shall be more happy in curing them – than in adding one to their Philistine Idols[.][16]

Yet the same day he wrote of Scott in his Journal: 'I like the man – and admire his works to what Mr. Braham calls *Entusymusy*'; and eight days later drew up his 'Gradus ad Parnassum' placing Scott at the summit and commenting: 'He is undoubtedly the Monarch of Parnassus, and the most *English* of bards.'[17] Moreover, he was to return to the same measure in *The Siege of Corinth* and *Parisina* (both 1816). Evidently, despite his own apparent distaste for the tetrameter, it none the less had its function and place, and perhaps its own peculiar challenge. As he points out in his Dedication to Moore of *The Corsair* (1814), although he had 'attempted not the most difficult but perhaps the best adapted measure to our language – the good old & now neglected heroic couplet', he nevertheless considered that 'the stanza of Spenser is perhaps too slow and dignified for narrative; though, I confess, it is the measure most after my own heart; and Scott alone, of the present generation, has hitherto completely triumphed over the fatal facility of the octo-syllabic verse; and this is not the least victory of his fertile and mighty genius.'[18]

Having then built his initial discourse of opposition on Juvenal in *English Bards and Scotch Reviewers*, Byron turned to Horace to shape it into instruction, and so qualify himself in the first instance as the arbiter of taste whose office the critics had misappropriated. This required demonstrating not merely by precept – as much the domain of critics whose exhibitions of canonic works upheld a rigidly doctrinaire orthodoxy – but in practice as a poet. He and Scott shared a common adversary. In league together, they might rescue taste from the critics' display cabinet, assert their artistic independence and re-engage directly with their audience.

Writing to his mother from Prevesa in Greece on 12 November 1809 Byron remarked:

I shall never forget the singular scene on entering Tepaleen at five in the afternoon as the Sun was going down, it brought to my recollection (with some change of *dress* however) Scott's description of Branksome Castle in his lay, & the feudal system. – The Albanians in their dresses (the most magnificent in the world, consisting of a long *white kilt*, gold worked cloak, crimson velvet gold laced jacket & waistcoat, silver mounted pistols & daggers,) the Tartars with their high caps, the Turks in their vast pelises & turbans, the soldiers & black slaves with the horses, the former stretched in groupes in an immense open gallery in front of the palace, the latter placed in a kind of cloister below it, two hundred steeds ready caparisoned to move in a moment, couriers entering or passing out with dispatches, the kettle drums beating, boys calling the hour from the minaret of the mosque, altogether, with the singular appearance of the building itself, formed a new & delightful spectacle to a stranger.[19]

What captures Byron's interest here is not so much the palace itself as the multitudes of the people, the various tribes and their striking dresses grouped and arranged with the eye of a painter, the alertness and the sounds, and lingering in the background is 'Scott's description of Branksome Castle in his lay'. This letter feeds the description of Tepaleen Byron gives us in *Childe Harold*, II:

> The Sun had sunk behind vast Tomerit,
> And Laos wide and fierce came roaring by;
> The shades of wonted night were gathering yet,
> When, down the steep banks winding warily,
> Childe Harold saw, like meteors in the sky,
> The glittering minarets of Tepalen,
> Whose walls o'erlook the stream; and drawing nigh,
> He heard the busy hum of warrior-men
> Swelling the breeze that sigh'd along the lengthening glen.
>
> He pass'd the sacred Haram's silent tower,
> And underneath the wide o'erarching gate

Survey'd the dwelling of this chief of power,
Where all around proclaim'd his high estate.
Amidst no common pomp the despot sate,
While busy preparation shook the court,
Slaves, eunuchs, soldiers, guests, and santons wait;
Within, a palace, and without, a fort:
Here men of every clime appear to make resort.

Richly caparison'd, a ready row
Of armed horse, and many a warlike store
Circled the wide extending court below:
Above, strange groups adorn'd the corridore;
And oft-times through the Area's echoing door
Some high-capp'd Tartar spurr'd his steed away:
The Turk, the Greek, the Albanian, and the Moor,
Here mingled in their many-hued array,
While the deep war-drum's sound announc'd the close of day.

The wild Albanian kirtled to his knee,
With shawl-girt head and ornamented gun,
And gold-embroider'd garments, fair to see;
The crimson-scarfed men of Macedon;
The Delhi with his cap of terror on,
And crooked glaive; the lively, supple Greek;
And swarthy Nubia's mutilated son;
The bearded Turk that rarely deigns to speak,
Master of all around, too potent to be meek,

Are mix'd conspicuous: some recline in groups,
Scanning the motley scene that varies round;
There some grave Moslem to devotion stoops,
And some that smoke, and some that play, are found;
Here the Albanian proudly treads the ground;
Half whispering there the Greek is heard to prate;
Hark! from the mosque the nightly solemn sound,
The Muezzin's call doth shake the minaret,
'There is no god but God! – to prayer – lo! God is great.'

Just at this season Ramazani's fast
Through the long day its penance did maintain:
But when the lingering twilight hour was past,
Revel and feast assum'd the rule again:
Now all was bustle, and the menial train
Prepar'd and spread the plenteous board within;
The vacant gallery now seem'd made in vain,
But from the chambers came the mingling din,
As page and slave anon were passing out and in.

In marble-pav'd pavilion, where a spring
Of living waters from the centre rose,
Whose bubbling did a genial freshness fling,
And soft voluptuous couches breath'd repose,
ALI reclin'd[.][20]

Again one notes that it is evening; the crowded scene; the state of poised alertness, the ornamental dresses; the sounds that emanate from everywhere. Note too, the skilful variation in the use of the Spenserian stanza, the verbally-derived and compound adjectives, and the shifts from past to present tense: in each instance the spectacle as presented by Byron in his letter is intensified. We move from the more general, panoramic view of Tepaleen to the people within its precincts who create the atmosphere, and finally to the driving force and epicentre of the whole – 'ALI'.

In a note to this Canto, Byron observes: 'The Arnaouts, or Albanese, struck me forcibly by their resemblance to the Highlanders of Scotland, in dress, figure, and manner of living. Their very mountains seemed Caledonian with a kinder climate. The kilt, though white; the spare, active form; their dialect, Celtic in its sound; and their hardy habits, all carried me back to Morven.'[21] This echoes the second sentence in the letter to his mother and it can hardly have escaped Byron's knowledge and delight in coincidence that in medieval Latin 'Albania' was the name for Scotland. It is appropriate to compare these stanzas with Scott's description of Branksome Castle in the opening stanzas of *The Lay of the Last Minstrel*:

The feast was over in Branksome tower,
And the Ladye had gone to her secret bower;
Her bower that was guarded by word and by spell,
Deadly to hear, and deadly to tell –
Jesu Maria, shield us well!
No living wight, save the Ladye alone,
Had dared to cross the threshold stone.

The tables were drawn, it was idlesse all;
    Knight, and page, and household squire,
Loiter'd through the lofty hall,
    Or crowded round the ample fire:
The stag-hounds, weary with the chase,
    Lay stretch'd upon the rushy floor,
And urg'd, in dreams, the forest race
    From Teviot-stone to Eskdale-moor.

Nine-and-twenty knights of fame
    Hung their shields in Branksome hall;

Nine-and-twenty squires of name
  Brought them their steeds to bower from stall;
Nine-and-twenty yeoman tall
Waited, duteous, on them all:
They were all knights of mettle true,
Kinsmen to the bold Buccleuch.

Ten of them were sheath'd in steel,
With belted sword, and spur on heel:
They quitted not their harness bright,
Neither by day, nor yet by night:
  They lay down to rest,
  With corslet laced,
Pillow'd on buckler cold and hard;
  They carv'd at the meal
  With gloves of steel,
And they drank the red wine through the helmet barr'd.

Ten squires, ten yeomen, mail-clad men,
Waited the beck of the warders ten:
Thirty steeds, both fleet and wight,
Stood saddled in stable day and night,
Barb'd with frontlet of steel, I trow,
And with Jedwood-axe at saddlebow;
A hundred more fed free in stall:
Such was the custom of Branksome Hall.

Why do these steeds stand ready dight?
Why, watch these warriors, arm'd, by night?
They watch to hear the blood-hound baying:
They watch to hear the war-horn braying;
To see St. George's red cross streaming,
To see the midnight beacon gleaming:
They watch against Southern force and guile,
  Lest Scroop, or Howard, or Percy's powers,
  Threaten Branksome's lordly towers,
From Warkworth, or Naworth, or merry Carlisle.

Such is the custom of Branksome Hall.
  Many a valiant knight is here;
But he, the chieftain of them all,
His sword hangs rusting on the wall,
  Beside his broken spear.
Bards long shall tell
How Lord Walter fell!
When startled burghers fled, afar,
The furies of the Border war;
When the streets of high Dunedin

Saw lances gleam, and falchions redden,
And heard the slogan's deadly yell –
Then the Chief of Branksome fell.[22]

From the start, Scott varies his stanza length which, together with the unequal verse line (basically tetrametric), irregular rhyme scheme and assorted
masculine and feminine endings, lends speed and vigour to the formal process of the narration, fixing our attention. This is further reflected in the
narrative itself: its mixture of the past and present tense, which gives a
local urgency to the rhetoric but not, as in Byron's text, an immediacy to
the narration. Note too the blend of odd and even enumeration ('Nine-
and-twenty', 'Ten', 'thirty', 'hundred'); the repetitions ('bower', 'Deadly',
'knights', 'squires', 'yeomen', 'steeds', 'steel'), inversions ('mettle true', 'helmet barr'd', 'warders ten'), nomination ('Teviot-stone', 'Scroop', 'Howard',
'Warkworth', 'Naworth', 'Branksome') and the anaphora, so like a cate-
chism ('Why', 'Why watch', 'They watch', 'to hear', 'To see', 'Such was',
'Such is'). These elemental, incantatory and arcane features all contribute
to the sense of the uncanny which characterises the ballad. All is disposed
with an agility and dignity appropriate to Bardic recitation. Most obvious
of all is the language in which it is couched – demonstrably Spenserian,
courtly, chivalric ('Ladye', 'idlesse', 'wight', 'knights', 'steeds') – which emphasises the historical perspective investing it with a sense of the archaic,
even the anachronistic, yet which is at the same time wholly at variance
with its *un*Spenserian *form*.

In the Byron text, there is no apparent borrowing from Scott though
there is a borrowing from the same *language*; and some words might describe
Scots as much as Albanians – 'kirtled', for instance. But Byron's idiom at
this point is contemporary and studiously avoids Spenserian diction and
vocabulary. Indeed Byron's letter is the only indication we have that a
connection between the two descriptions might be made. It is the general
effect of Branksome Castle that Byron has imaginatively associated with
Tepaleen not the verbal or descriptive details of Scott's poetry itself.

In his prefatory statement to the *Lay* Scott writes: 'the poem was put
into the mouth of an ancient Minstrel, the last of the race, who, as he is
supposed to have survived the Revolution, might have caught somewhat
of the refinement of modern poetry, *without losing* [emphasis added] the
simplicity of his original model.'[23] This crystallises the argument he develops later in his Introduction to the first edition of *The Bridal of Triermain*
(1813) to distinguish between Epic and Romantic Poetry:

Poets, under various denominations of Bards, Scalds, Chroniclers, and so forth, are
the first historians of all nations. Their intention is to relate the events they have

witnessed, or the traditions that have reached them; and they clothe the relation in rhyme, merely as the means of rendering it more solemn in the narrative or more easily committed to memory.[24]

Such strictly speaking is the Epic, and the function of the Epic poet is essentially one of an historian – Scott's principal example being Homer, whose 'purpose was to write the early history of his country'. He continues:

> But as the poetical historian improves in the art of conveying information, the authenticity of his narrative unavoidably declines. He is tempted to dilate and dwell upon the events that are interesting to his imagination, and, conscious how indifferent his audience is to the naked truth of his poem, his history gradually becomes a romance.[25]

And matters so progress until eventually we arrive at 'Romantic Poetry', which 'comprehends a fictitious narrative, framed and combined at the pleasure of the writer', but which dispenses with 'the campaigns and heroes of our days' since they are 'perpetuated in a record that neither requires nor admits of the aid of fiction'. Hence, from an originary fusion, the one growing out of the other, poetry and history dissever and become separate and independent, indeed opposing, 'species of composition'.[26] To a large degree this constitutes Scott's poetical manifesto or *apologia pro poema sua* to account for his own practice of writing *historical romance*: of selecting historical rather than modern or topical subjects but departing from historical fact and rigid traditionary form.

In his note to stanza 38 of *Childe Harold*, ii, Byron said of the Albanians: 'Their very mountains seemed Caledonian with a kinder climate.'[27] He did not say that the Albanian mountains seemed 'like' or 'as if they were' the Caledonian mountains; there is in fact no such tacit simile or metaphor implied at all – they simply 'seemed'. What he sees are the Albanian mountains and the Caledonians together, simultaneously, the one superimposed upon or showing through the other – not identical but sharing an identity, distinctively themselves yet cohabiting the same space: a perfect palimpsest. And here the word 'Albania', as designating both the country of that name and, in medieval Latin, Scotland, provides us with an elucidatory parallel: for just as it unites two separate countries under a single denomination, so the palimpsestic imagination collocates and synchronizes two distinct entities in a single perception:

> The infant rapture still survived the boy,
> And Loch-na-gar with Ida looked o'er Troy,
> Mixed Celtic memories with the Phrygian mount,
> And Highland linns with Castalie's clear fount.[28]

As Ruskin points out, 'Scott and Burns love Scotland more than Nature itself: for Burns the moon must rise over Cumnock Hills, – for Scott, the Rymer's glen divide the Eildons; but, for Byron, Loch-na-Gar *with Ida* looks o'er Troy, and the soft murmurs of the Dee and the Bruar change into voices of the dead on distant Marathon.'[29] Ruskin is exactly right in isolating this as a peculiar poetic quality and way of envisioning history. Yet, while this is what crowns Byron as 'the widest-hearted' of 'the three – unholy – children' of the world's 'Fiery Furnace',[30] Ruskin is not being altogether fair to Scott:

> From clime to clime, where'er war's trumpets sound,
> The wanderer went; yet, Caledonia, still
> Thine was his thought in march and tented ground;
> He dream'd 'mid Alpine cliffs of Athole's hill,
> And heard in Ebro's roar his Lyndoch's lovely rill.[31]

The last line in particular, matching Byron's 'Loch-na-gar with Ida looks o'er Troy,' carries the point, testifying to the same palimpsestic perception in Scott: the Ebro and the Lyndoch do not become synonymous, nor are they substitutes for one another; they remain distinct and individual, yet the one is perceived in the other.

Such a prophetic vision seems to inform Scott's descriptions of landscapes and architecture, as well as the depictions of his heroes and of Scottish personal, familial and clan relationships. Take for example the Tower of Tillietudlem in *Old Mortality* (1816) which, we are told, stood 'upon the angle of a very precipitous bank, formed by the junction of a considerable brook with the Clyde', and from that position 'commanded two prospects, the one richly cultivated and highly adorned, the other exhibiting the monotonous and dreary character of a wild and inhospitable moorland'.[32] The tower, like the author, like the present, looks backwards and forwards, near and far, *commanding* both the past and future. And it is at this 'junction' that the contest between civilisation and barbarity will be decided: retrogression to the 'moorland' or progression to the 'cultivated.' But it is more than this too; for the 'moorland' becomes 'cultivated' under the auspices of the tower: that is, the present cultivates (or *should* cultivate) for the future what comes to it seeded from the past – just as the author moulds his raw material into a work of art. Such towers become recurrent motifs throughout Scott's works as centres of choice, of decision, sites where events take shape; and they are solid and solitary – like Branksome Castle.

Yet, while *romance* may offer such an ideal, history tells a different story: men seldom make an obligation of their choice. For Scott the prevailing evidence of this is dissension: civil, factional, political or religious strife, even personal hostility. In such cases Scott looks back to show that his age is merely *repeating* all the disorders and mistakes of a former age – *rehearsing* not advancing history. And such is precisely Byron's view:

Vide Napoleon's last twelvemonth . . . I thought . . . that all this was not a mere *jeu* of the gods, but a prelude to greater changes and mightier events. But Men never advance beyond a certain point; – and here we are, retrograding to the dull, stupid old system, – balance of Europe – poising straws upon king's noses, instead of wringing them off! . . . A republic! – look in the history of the Earth – Rome, Greece, Venice, France, Holland, America, our short (*eheu!*) Commonwealth, and compare it with what they did under masters.[33]

'But Men never advance beyond certain point' – the year is late 1813, a few months before Napoleon's downfall. Is this really just 'a mere *jeu* of the gods', an unalterable law of Nature? Or is it not rather man himself who is responsible? The question besets Byron unremittingly; and his answer, expressed with increasing vigour over the years, is proclaimed with particular force and clarity in *Childe Harold*, IV. It is 'the moral of all *human* tales' (emphasis added): men make history but that history has '*one* page':

> There is the moral of all human tales;
> 'Tis but the same rehearsal of the past,
> First Freedom, and then Glory – when that fails,
> Wealth, vice, corruption, – barbarism at last.
> And History, with all her volumes vast,
> Hath but *one* page, – 'tis better written here,
> Where gorgeous Tyranny had thus amass'd
> All treasures, all delights, that eye or ear,
> Heart, soul could seek, tongue ask – Away with words! draw near . . .

> The Roman saw these tombs in his own age,
> These sepulchres of cities, which excite
> Sad wonder, and his yet surviving page
> The moral lesson bears, drawn from such pilgrimage.

> That page is now before me, and on mine
> *His* country's ruin added to the mass
> Of perish'd states he mourn'd in their decline,
> And I in desolation: all that *was*
> Of then destruction *is*: and now, alas!
> Rome – Rome imperial, bows her to the storm,

> In the same dust and blackness, and we pass
> The skeleton of her Titanic form,
> Wrecks of another world, whose ashes still are warm.[34]

But '*one* page', the 'same rehearsal' – dramatic images, powerfully uttered, sustained across the whole Canto. Here, the general statement in the first two lines of stanza 108 is followed by a detailing of the specific stages of decline in the next two, which is then followed by the crescendo to the alliterated 'volumes vast', immediately deflated by the '*one* page.' Yet the play of antitheses is never lost sight of, nor the pattern of cyclical inevitability – the whole steadily gaining momentum and intensified as he approaches his final ascent into speechlessness – a second climax as it were – 'Away with *words*.' That single page records nothing but man's 'ruin', 'ravage' and 'destruction'; we merely add to it (*re*hearse it) and pass it on to (rehearse it *for*) the future, 'Rotting from sire to son, and age to age.'[35] The prophetic vision perceives this the poet sees the same page ('the same dust and blackness') as the Roman saw – and indicts us for failing to turn it, for failing to usher in those 'greater changes and mightier events' and so practise history; we may *know* the lesson but we have not *learnt* it, we *reflect* it:

> The 'good old times' – all times when old are good –
> Are gone; the present might be if they would;
> Great things have been, and are, and greater still
> Want little of mere mortals but their will ...[36]

The 'present', 'if they would', 'but their will': but 'would' they? do we ever *will* it? Byron's point is evident enough; it is not just a statement of the case, but a challenge to change it. This challenge is central to Byron's continuing dialogue with Scott – and indeed, the phrase 'The moral lesson' is one counter in that dialogue:

> Yet 'mid the confidence of just renown,
> Renown dear-bought, but dearest thus acquired,
> Write, Britain, write the moral lesson down:
> 'Tis not alone the heart with valour fired,
> The discipline so dreaded and admired,
> In many a field of bloody conquest known;
> Such may by fame be lured, by gold be hired;
> 'Tis constancy in the good cause alone,
> Best justifies the meed thy valiant sons have won.[37]

This is the last of the solemn six Spenserian stanzas with which Scott concludes his otherwise irregular and tetrametric poem, *The Field of*

Waterloo (1815). Its weighted and highly rhetorical first seven lines admonish the present against relaxing into the temporary self-satisfaction of victory, rather than reaping from it what has permanent value in it – the 'moral lesson' of 'constancy' – delivered by contrast so pithily in the final couplet. Compared with Byron's stanzas, this is fearfully ponderous. Byron persuades by his passionate *involvement* – his very present urgency is compelling. But Scott's detached, orotund delivery, proposing no startlingly fresh or invigorating 'moral lesson' at all, hardly inspires conviction. What exactly does he mean by 'constancy'? This is a weak word on which to rest his climax. Herein, lies a major difference between Scott and Byron: Byron is equally at ease when describing Tepaleen for instance, as when commenting upon contemporary affairs; Scott is not. And one explanation for his awkwardness here is that *The Field of Waterloo* is the only major poem Scott wrote that deals directly with a contemporary historical event and real persons (Napoleon, Wellington) and according to his Introduction to *The Bridal of Triermain*, such events belonged to a 'species of composition' *opposite* to those of poetry.

Scott and Byron conducted their dialogue through apparent minor borrowings or echoes which subtextually elaborated more decisive issues – in the same way as a metonymy operates. An instructive example involves the phrase 'the truth in masquerade'. In *The Antiquary* (1816), the antiquarian, Monkbarns and his neighbour Sir Arthur Wardour, with the help of their assistants, 'discover' some 'treasure'. When Sir Arthur recommends it should be kept a secret,

'Why, as to that,' said Monkbarns, 'recommending secrecy where a dozen of people are acquainted with the circumstance to be concealed, is only putting the truth in masquerade, for the story will be circulated under twenty different shapes. But never mind, we will state the true one to the Barons, and that is all that is necessary.'[38]

This is rather more complex than may at first appear: secrecy, concealment, truth, masquerade – the one word Scott has avoided actually using is 'lie'. Yet even he can't conceal its presence, implied unavoidably by the presence of its exact opposite – 'the truth'. In the first place, then, suppressing the truth would, as Monkbarns justly observes, give rise to numerous versions of it ('twenty different shapes'), each of which not being the truth ('the true one') would necessarily be false, viz. a lie. However, the irony here is that the 'treasure' itself has been buried by the impostor Dousterswivel to deceive Sir Arthur and Monkbarns into believing in his divinatory powers. Thus unbeknownst to Monkbarns the very secret to be suppressed is a falsehood (deception); so that the 'story' he proposes telling the Barons is not the 'true one' at all, but a lie in its very essence: himself deceived, he would merely be disseminating his own deception – that is, *his version* of the 'truth' – adding a twenty-first variety to the existing 'twenty different shapes'.

For Scott 'the truth' implies a tacit understanding and agreement between the parties concerned of the precise nature of the question under discussion and the absence of any intention to deceive. The 'truth in masquerade', on the other hand, is but an euphemism for a palpable lie, of which there is a criminal type (deliberate and knowing concealment of 'the truth') and a less culpable type (versioning of 'the truth'), both of which, however, appear to mirror and promote that very 'dissension' Scott deplores in so many of his novels. Truth unifies, lies divide. In all his works, poetry *and* novels, some form of deception, concealment or fraud, and eventual revelation, discovery or exposure plays a fundamental, almost obsessive, thematic role. It is not surprising, then, that this becomes a metaphor for his own fiction and authorial role, and for the ingenious double-bluffs, vindications or disclaimers to which the various personae by whom his novels are written, edited, introduced or transcribed resort.

Byron, who knew all along that Scott was 'The Author of Waverley' though he respected his reserve on the matter, pinches Scott's phrase in *Don Juan*, XI, stanzas 36 and 37:

> our notion is not high
> Of politicians and their double front,
> Who live by lies, yet dare not boldly lie:
>   Now what I love in women is, they won't
> Or can't do otherwise than lie, but do it
> So well, the very truth seems falsehood to it.
>
> And, after all, what is a lie? 'Tis but
>   The truth in masquerade; and I defy
> Historians, heroes, lawyers, priests to put
>   A fact without some leaven of a lie.
> The very shadow of true Truth would but shut
>   Up annals, revelations, poesy,
> And prophecy – except it should be dated
> Some years before the incidents related.[39]

Byron's apparent glibness here hides a serious point. In stanza 36 we are presented with two forms of lying and their distinction is crucial. First, the lie of politicians which is hypocrisy ('double front') and equivocation ('dare not boldly lie') by which they exploit others ('live by lies'). This is the lie of the Dousterswivel variety – manipulative, self-interested, timeserving. By contrast, we next have the much more cryptically expressed lie of women, who lie with such consummate skill that their lie is more convincing – and attractive – than the truth itself. This is the artistic lie; harmless, because whether or not they lie wilfully, incontinently or by nature (and Byron seems reluctant to say which), their doing so is acknowledged and understood as a matter of course by all concerned; it is a social *mos* – there is no deception as such. Indeed, delight is in the very accomplishment, its *artistry*, and the sociability it is capable of diffusing, in direct opposition to the divisive, anti-social lie of the politician.

This prepares us for the elaboration in stanza 37 of the generic lie, deliberately cast in the *social* (carnival) guise of the 'truth in masquerade', in which all who embellish or exaggerate a fact (add 'some leaven of a lie') when recounting an event participate. That is to say *all* of us, because we all have our own versions, or subjective readings, of a story each of which can only approximate, but none of which can be, the 'true' one. Here we are, then, back at the versioning idea we elicited from Scott – but with a big difference. For this time, Byron has not just borrowed Scott's phrase and refined it, but redefined it altogether, turning it right round and applying it to all forms of human discourse. And he has done so in order to emphasize the *relative* nature of truth which is sadly 'true' Truth's necessary condition in this sublunary world. Absolute Truth ('true Truth') is ideal – coessential, it seems, with God or some omnipotent, all-knowing agency – whose existence on Earth would in fact make our own existence superfluous (all *discourse* would cease). The *relative* truth, whose counterpart is the sociable lie of the 'truth in masquerade', is essential to our preservation, a condition of our being; it unites and harmonizes us.

Byron returns to this notion and develops it more distinctly in *Don Juan*, xv, stanzas 88 and 89. Justifying his own inconsistency by asking rhetorically, 'But if a writer should be quite consistent, / How could he possibly show things existent?' (stanza 87), he proceeds:

> If people contradict themselves, can I
>   Help contradicting them, and every body,
> Even my veracious self? – But that's a lie;
>   I never did so, never will – how should I?
> He who doubts all things, nothing can deny;
>   Truth's fountain* may be clear – her streams are muddy,
> And cut through such canals of contradiction,
> That she must often navigate o'er fiction.
>
> Apologue, fable, poesy, and parable,
>   Are false, but may be render'd also true

By those who sow them in a land that's arable.
   'Tis wonderful what fable will not do!
'Tis said it makes reality more bearable:
   But what's reality? Who has its clue?
Philosophy? No; she too much rejects.
Religion? *Yes*; but which of all her sects?[40]

I have preferred the manuscript reading here* over the printed version ('fountains'), as it is as crucial to preserve Truth's singular 'fountain' as against her plural 'streams', as it is to observe that the former is 'clear' and the latter are 'muddy'.[41] For in these two figures we have the exact counterparts of 'true Truth' (Absolute Truth) and the 'truth in masquerade' (relative truth). Byron subtly negotiates his image from the navigational to the agricultural to illustrate how we may approach nearer to the former via the latter. The clear water of the singular fountain of Truth dissipates into the plurality and opacity of her 'streams' (natural) – picked up in 'canals' (man-made) – which Truth must 'navigate' in order to irrigate and fructify the 'land' (the fallen world) which is diversely cultivated by her *relatives* – those poets who are also the 'canals' through whose words Truth's waters flow – who 'sow' not for their own present reward but for the future benefit of others. The whole image at the same time providing the perfect metaphor and analogue for both the process of, and Byron's apology for, poetry: systems (Philosophy, Religion) create absolutes that divide; 'fiction', in all its diverse forms, cultivates – educates, enlightens – or at least makes life more 'bearable' by rendering readers a little less un-certain, or a little more hopeful, or a little more harmonious by the means of the 'truth in masquerade'.

All this is done with such amiable grace and good humour that the text itself becomes the embodiment and measure of the very sociability it seeks to advance. And in this respect, Byron may very well be responding to another feature he found irresistibly potent in Scott – the fact that Scott's novels are densely and diversely populated. His characters are social, their backgrounds are filled in, they belong to a community which itself has a strong sense of its past, and they are extraordinarily garrulous – chattering away almost incessantly and invariably in dialect which happened to appeal particularly strongly to Byron.

In the majority of Byron's poems, however, quite the contrary is the case: all tend to be thinly populated and to focus on the single figure – the Glaour, Conrad, Lara, Manfred. Byron's are isolated, asocial, exiled figures, sullen, surly and generally silent, who bear about with them their own self-sufficiency. For Byron, survival is individual (Napoleon is the figurehead here); his heroes have no roots, show no dependency on others, and do not develop – they simply are: fixed in an eternal present, suffering remorse for some mysterious crime. Until, that is, *Don Juan*; when the *dramatis personae* increase manifold as vocal and individually characterised dramatic presences. Byron certainly did not need Scott to prompt him in this direction; there are plenty of other candidates who can share that honour: Cervantes, Fielding, Swift, Smollett, Sterne, Montaigne, Ariosto, and so on; but for Byron, Scott is in there too. And what seems to have engaged him particularly were his characters, their language, their eccentricities, their 'signatures': Dalgetty, the Baron of Bradwardine, Monkbarns, Edie Ochiltree, Douce Davy Deans – he quotes them all frequently and at random throughout his writings and, more often than not, as if they were real people and their sayings common currency or proverbs. He appears to be much more taken with them than with their convivial narrator – despite the fact that he and Scott, simultaneously but independently of each other, chose the same pseudonym: Byron, Wortley Clutterbuck; Scott, Cuthbert Clutterbuck.[42] And as if to alert us to his presence, only a few stanzas earlier in this same Canto xv (stanza 59), Byron has referred – not for the first time in *Don Juan* – to Scott:

> Methinks we may proceed upon our narrative,
> And, as my friend Scott says, 'I sound my Warison;'
>   Scott, the superlative of my comparative –
> Scott, who can paint your Christian knight or Saracen,
>   Serf, Lord, Man, with such skill as none would share it if
> There had not been one Shakespeare and Voltaire,
> Of one or both of whom he seems the heir.[43]

The very naming is praise in itself; but the repeated exclamation heightens it by lending it cohesion, intensity and increasing emphasis. The effect is incantatory – as if Byron were apostrophizing Scott as his Muse. But why is Ariosto not mentioned? The stanza echoes what Byron had expressed in his letter to Murray of 17 September 1817 ('themes Chivalry – war – & love') which stands at the head of this chapter, and written in stanza 40 of *Childe Harold*, iv; and the citation in the second line here, from *The Lay of the Last Minstrel*,[44] is all the more pointed in so far as it takes us back to Scott the *poet* – the only honourable way Byron can still pledge Scott in public, without betraying him as 'The Author of Waverley'. But Scott's prowess as a *novelist* (indeed, as a poet, dramatist, critic and all-round philologist) is suggested by the united presence of Shakespeare and Voltaire. But why these two *precisely*? Shakespeare is understandable enough: Scott was frequently compared to him by the reviewers – as was 'The Author of Waverley'; but why Voltaire? The hint I should like to follow comes from Scott himself. On receiving a letter from Goethe in 1827, he wrote in his Journal: 'Goethe is...a wonderful fellow, the Ariosto at once, and almost the Voltaire of Germany'.[45] Now Voltaire was a great admirer of Ariosto; and amongst other things he has to say about him in his *Dictionnaire philosophique* is this: 'l'auteur, toujours au-dessus de sa matière, la traite en badinant. Il dit les choses les plus sublimes sans effort, et il les finit souvent par un trait de plaisanterie qui n'est ni deplacé ni recherché. C'est à la fois l'Iliade, l'Odysée, et don Quichotte'.[46] Byron translates this at the end of his *Letter to John Murray* (1821), where, speaking of '*Vulgarity*' as opposed to '*Gentlemanliness*' in writing, he writes: '*Vulgarity* is far worse than downright *Blackguardism* – for the latter comprehends wit – humour – and strong sense at times – while the former is a sad abortive attempt at all things – "signifying nothing." – It does not depend upon low themes – or even low language – for – Fielding revels in both – but is he ever *vulgar*? – No – you see the man of education the gentleman and the Scholar *sporting with his subject – it's Master – not it's Slave*' (these last nine words, which I have emphasized, echo almost word for word Voltaire's 'l'auteur, toujours au-dessus de sa matière, la traite en badinant').[47] So now we have the conjunction of Ariosto and Fielding, and only two months previously in his Journal Byron had referred to Scott as the 'Scotch Fielding, as well as great English poet – wonderful man! I long to get drunk with him'.[48] We have then a rich equation set up between Ariosto and Voltaire and Fielding and Scott, whereby Byron can praise Scott explicitly as a poet, and at the same time, implicitly as 'The Author of Waverley' – the allusion to Shakespeare now perhaps taking on an added subtlety in view of the reviewers' comparison of 'The Author of Waverley' (and Scott, in his named capacity as poet and dramatist) with him.

Thus, if Byron, writing in the 'octave stanza' (his 1817 letter to Murray) of the 'southern Scott' (as he dubs Ariosto in the *Childe Harold* stanza) is in 'comparative' apposition to the 'superlative' of Scott who is 'the Ariosto of the North', then he (Byron) is the southern Ariosto – or, to put it another way, 'half a Scot[t]'. Such is the circularity of his associations, that eventually he and Scott become reflections of each other, – Byron being as much as Scott the 'heir' of Shakespeare and Voltaire, via *Scott*. For in *Don Juan*, XI, Byron has already told us magnificently that he was once 'The grand Napoleon of the realms of rhyme' (55), but that 'Sir Walter reigned before me' (57).

.This brings us back to our point of departure, and to a remarkable reaction of Byron's to one of those reviewers who contributed to uniting him with Scott in the first place. In *Don Juan*, x, Byron devotes nine stanzas (11–19) to literary criticism generally, and in particular to Jeffrey who had recently censured him for savaging Southey:[49]

> And all our little feuds, at least all *mine*,
>   Dear Jeffrey, once my most redoubted foe,
> (As far as rhyme and criticism combine
>   To make such puppets of us things below)
> Are over. Here's a health to 'Auld Lang Syne!'
>   I do not know you, and may never know
> Your face, – but you have acted on the whole
> Most nobly, and I own it from my soul.
>
> And when I use the phrase of 'Auld Lang Syne!'
>   'Tis not addressed to you – the more's the pity
> For me, for I would rather take my wine
>   With you, than aught (save Scott) in your proud city.
> But somehow, – it may seem a schoolboy's whine,
>   And yet I seek not to be grand nor witty, –
> But I am half a Scot by birth, and bred
> A whole one, and my heart flies to my head, –
>
> As 'Auld Lang Syne' brings Scotland, one and all,
>   Scotch plaids, Scotch snoods, the blue hills, and clear streams,
> The Dee, the Don, Balgounie's Brig's *black wall*,
>   All my boy feelings, all my gentler dreams
> Of what I *then dreamt*, clothed in their own pall,
>   Like Banquo's offspring; – floating past me seems
> My childhood in this childishness of mine:
> I care not – 'tis a glimpse of 'Auld Lang Syne.'
>
> And though, as you remember, in a fit
>   Of wrath and rhyme, when juvenile and curly,
> I railed at Scots to shew my wrath and wit,
>   Which must be owned was sensitive and surly,
> Yet 'tis in vain such sallies to permit,
>   They cannot quench young feelings fresh and early:
> I '*scotched*, not killed,' the Scotchman in my blood,
> And love the land of 'mountain and of flood.'

These stanzas exemplify the prophetic vision practising history as sociability. For instead of returning fire with fire, or digging up old resentments and so merely repeating negatively the past, we have before us the *example* of Byron renouncing hostility, *choosing* to forgive and forget wrongs and to heal old wounds through reconciliation – in fulfilment, one might add, of the Curse of Forgiveness announced in *Childe Harold*, IV. 76.[50]

The health, 'Auld Lang Syne!', pledged to Jeffrey in the first instance (but not 'addressed' to him in the second, because in that and its subsequent usages it has assumed its literal meaning of 'long ago' or 'old times' – those personal to Byron alone), recalls Scott by way of metonymy – 'I long to get drunk with him.' Then Edinburgh, then the whole of Scotland, and then its details are brought into view – its characteristic dress, and particular rivers and landscapes, which by metonymy again evoke not just Byron's youth but his 'boy *feelings*', nor just the dreams he '*then dreamt*' but their 'gentler' aspect, which even now as he writes makes him gentle – hence his heart 'flies' to his head because 'flies' suggests the flight both of flying and of fleeing to the succour and nourishment of his head, thus capturing the notion of thought thinking feelingly, delivered from the petty prejudices of reasoning, heart and head at one, in harmony; and, as the poet with himself, so with others. Added to this gentleness is humility: the endearing admission of that 'childishness' which we all have felt and understand, but few would acknowledge so publicly. All this occupies just four sentences, the last of which is spread over two stanzas, thus capturing in the very form itself the immediate presence of thought flowing on, interconnecting and accumulating, ineluctably.

In stanza 19 Byron is even more spacious in his concessions and more open in reprobating and repudiating his earlier hostility to criticism (the reference is to *English Bards* and the review in the *Edinburgh Review* which occasioned it), now characterised in martial vocabulary – 'wrath', 'railed', 'sallies.' We should particularly notice the neat balancing of 'wrath and rhyme' with 'wrath and wit', which are not the same, for the first is the *furor* of the poet which Cicero defines for us,[51] while the second comprises the feelings and faculties Byron should have kept under control. The verse then moves to those initial 'young feelings' upon which he has already expatiated in the previous stanza, allowing them to re-emerge unsmothered by the supervening 'rhyme' and 'wit', to prove *demonstrably* by their very disposition in the stanza, that the world of refinement and urbanity cannot ultimately 'quench' what is natural in the natural state of human nature. They return now, in Macbeth's phrase, '*scotched*, not killed',[52] because indeed they remained 'Scotch' all along; which leads to the resonant pun on 'Scotchman' (superficially jocular, but in truth, deeply poignant), which itself now gathers up the *Macbeth* allusion and the less ostensible *English Bards and* Scotch *Reviewers* allusion, and so on back through the stanzas – 'Scots', 'Scotch', 'Scotland', 'half a Scot', 'Scott' – to fall supremely in the final line – 'the land of "mountain and of flood" ' – on Scott.[53]

And so we have come full circle; with Byron offering the palm of reconciliation held out to Jeffrey, the censor of Byron and Scott, and embracing his compatriot who, by the magic of verbal echoes, is the other 'Scotchman' in his blood that makes him 'half a Scot[t] by birth, and bred / A whole one.'

CHAPTER 10

Scott and the British tourist

Murray G. H. Pittock

The eighteenth-century tourist was often a member of the gentry or aristocracy undertaking the Grand Tour, travel in Continental Europe which 'involved essentially a trip to Paris and a tour of the principal Italian cities, namely Rome, Venice, Florence and Naples'. As the century progressed, there was an 'expansion of foreign tourism' as well as the development of tourism within the British Isles: these formed part of the move towards 'a more widespread consumerism that was general throughout both the social elite and the middling orders', as the advent of a mass advertising market through the expanding print media helped to consolidate a more unified British middle class. In particular, there was a growth of travel for pleasure: a French envoy reported in 1772 that 'leurs voyages n'ayant eu pour objet que leur curiosité'. That curiosity could be satisfied within Britain as well as outside it: and despite the noted lack of tourist facilities, there were several prominent tours of Scotland after the Rising of 1745: Sir William Burrell's in 1758, Thomas Pennant's in 1769 and, most famously, that of Samuel Johnson and James Boswell in 1773. In 1792 the beginning of the Revolutionary war cut off much of fashionable Europe (though Mary Wollstonecraft famously travelled to unfashionable Scandinavia in 1795), and as a consequence it became more likely that tourists would travel within the British Isles.[1]

Both leisured upper-class and more straitened middle-class tourists held in common the idea of the *locus amoenus,* the spirit of place and location. One travelled not only to broaden one's own horizons with variety, but also to encounter and perchance absorb the animating concept, the *geist*, of the society to which one travelled. Other societies represented other values, in many cases a single predominating value: if in crude eyes this was a stereotype and in more cultivated ones an ideal, it was nevertheless arguably a function of the beholder and not the beheld – a colonising, animating gaze. The presence of a multiplicity of Queen's Views (deriving from the Victorian period) in Scotland is a local and temporally located indicator of this practice. Such a relationship has been written about extensively in this and more particularly in other and explicitly imperial contexts, but it is equally if not more important in assessing the surreptitious coalescence of concrete place and abstract value in the literature of the long eighteenth century, which in its turn fed the simplified discourse of the first generations of mass tourism in the nineteenth and twentieth centuries. In other words, some of the most sophisticated edifices of literary creation were built on simple 'tabloid' ideas of the unity of place and value, which in their turn fed a new generation of such ideas with the fertile prestige of their own imaginative ascendancy. Sir Walter Scott is one of the most clear-cut examples of this: an influence on the history of ideas so powerful, that he has either been read or embedded with a sense of history which has so absorbed his ideas that they often seem stale or go unnoticed.

British tourists on the Continent in the eighteenth century often held particularly set views concerning the countries they were visiting. An internalised ascendancy born of island isolation, Protestantism and, as the century wore on, military power, could mean that even what the visitor went to see might be despised, for 'Britain, or for English tourists more clearly, England was best' (Black, *British Abroad*, p. 235). Italy was perhaps the prime exemplar of this as a destination: its admired Roman and Renaissance antiquities were remains indicative of a grander past in a country politically fragmented and dominated by Catholicism, a religion dedicated in Protestant eyes to exalting a veneration of the past while suppressing the present potential of the human spirit. Italy was one giant reliquary of that human spirit, of which the Papacy served as a continuing synecdoche. The country enshrined magnificent art in a series of corrupt and dilapidated contemporary institutions: the Papacy, the Papal States, the Stuart court at Rome, the fading trading cities of Venice and Genoa with their immobile Doges and inadequate political and military structures. In 1763 the Marquess of Tavistock advised a fellow-peer 'to study a little the constitution of the Republic of Venice, in order to inspire you with a proper dread of aristocracy'; the 'corruption, luxury and effeminacy' of the city was noted by Adam Walker in 1787. Dr John Swinton thought that in Genoa 'the population was controlled by Jesuits', while Robert Gray opined that 'the volcanic nature of the country about Rome tends to confirm...that Rome, like Sodom, shall "be utterly burnt with fire"' (Black, *British Abroad*, pp. 221, 227–8, 242, 246). Seventeenth-century English drama had helped pave the way for the tourist's eighteenth-century Italy, from the tragedies of John Webster to Thomas Otway's *Venice Preserv'd* of 1682, itself used as a politically coded play in England.[2] In the Romantic period, a new generation of artists would serve to spread the ideas of stereotyped location to a new set of countries and areas, both within and outwith the British Isles.

Primitivism was of key importance in this development. This complicated and diverse imaginative movement had at its literary core 'a high cultural codification of orally based folk culture, which was beginning to suffer large-scale attrition through improved communications, migration to cities, enclosure, clearances and war'; its expression in the visual arts will be dealt with later in this essay. It combined a profound commitment to the past, but one depoliticised in the context either of the frisson of *Rauberromantik* (bandit romanticism) tourism, or in a commitment to contemporary ideas of liberty which owed more to the hermeneutics through which primitive simplicity was codified than to a historicised grasp of its reality. Yet from Jean-Jacques Rousseau's 'L'homme est né libre, et partout il est dans les fers' to the 'yet though the conscious socialist movement be but a century old, the labouring folk all down the ages have clung to communist practices and customs' of W. F. Skene and the idea of Celtic Ireland as 'a kind of primitive socialist utopia' found in the writings of James Connolly, the utilization of this Romantic construction of the primitive has been of the utmost importance in the critical arenas of post-1789 politics.[3] The withering away of the state in classic Marxism bears something of the same aura about it: Primitivism gathered to itself classical notions of a pastoral golden age among the high cultural tools by which aboriginal simplicity was valued. For Shelley 'The world's great age begins anew, / The golden years return';[4] for John Ruskin and especially William Morris, Socialism in an advanced industrial society was primarily constituted in the abandonment of industrialism, a return in Wordsworthian terms from Luke's 'evil courses' to the 'unfinished sheepfold' of that most golden age of activities, 'shepherding':[5] the foundation-stone of pastoral and 'one of the predominant metaphors of Christian mission'.

The idea that certain cultures preserved in their primitive simplicity values lost in more advanced societies was evident in the writings of Jean-Jacques Rousseau (1712–78). In Scotland it was found in Adam Ferguson's (1723–1816) *Essay on the Origins* of *Civil Society* (vol. 1, p. 767), although Ferguson thought that there were more than enough gains to outweigh the losses of primitive purity, and other Scottish Enlightenment writers appeared to think that there were no losses at all. Perhaps the fact that Ferguson was the only major Enlightenment figure to come from the Gaidhealtachd had something to do with his more even-handed position. Imaginative writers could respond more unequivocally: James Boswell (1740–95) found in the cause of Corsica both a surrogate for a patriot struggle for Scottish independence which was no longer relevant, and also a primitive heroic society of the kind praised by Rousseau, with in Pasquale Paoli, a charismatic leader to boot. Later, Byron and Shelley would find the spirit of liberty in Greece and Blake and Coleridge would see it in America and France, while Southey would link the Welsh to the Aztecs and find in Wallace a spirit of liberty to provide a Scottish counterweight to Thomas Gray's Welsh Bard.[6]

The spirit of liberty was a new spirit, but it was often seen as having its roots in either developing societies or among thinkers who had praised primitive simplicity, with (in Blakean terms) its Orc-like impulsiveness. It was associated both with internationalism and regionalism: in 1798, Wordsworth and Coleridge's *Lyrical Ballads* marked the exaltation of the spirit of the people in the most poor and remote provinces of England as the voice of the true human spirit. In Germany, Johann Gottfried Herder (1744–1803) and the brothers Grimm (Jacob (1785–1863)/Wilhelm (1786–1859)) evidenced a view of nationality inhering in the literature of the people in a manner which could seem to some like the archaeology of what was yet a new ideal: the objectification of the subjective literary will, in Hegelian phrase. Later, Wagner and many more nefarious interpreters were to make much of the ideas of essential and immemorial narratives of the folk sunk deep in the spirit of the German people, who in and through them saw the means of fulfilment and liberty. For Scottish imaginative writers, however, this kind of version of history became associated with a *Gemeinschaft/Gesellschaft* split between the emotive idyll of the Highland past and the contemporary polite and industrialising world of post-Union Britain.

James Macpherson's (1736–96) *Fingal* (1761) and *Temora* (1763) served both to create an intensely nostalgic image of a simpler and more heroic Celtic Scotland, cunningly mediated through the oblique language, of sensibility and an evocative scattering of Jacobite allusion, and also to undermine the status of Scotland's and Ireland's historic connections. Fingal and Ossian/Oisin and Fionn became not the heritage of a common Gaidhealtachd/Gaeltacht, celebrated in locations across Ireland and Scotland, but chiefly the property of Scotland alone. Thus began the creation of 'the cult of Scotland' which 'tied the country to a fixed image'.[7] The development of this 'fixed image' came in three stages: Macpherson's Ossian, Scott's poetry and fiction, and the tartanisation of the Royal Family under Queen Victoria. Each stage was accompanied by the development of tourism: visitors came to see the *Kulturvolk* of, if not the contemporary Highlander, at least the Ossianic image of him: as John

Glendening points out, 'tourism and romanticism were intertwined from the first, growing from the same cultural roots as similar responses to the same social developments'.[8]

As early as 1800, visitors were carving their names in Fingal's Cave in Staffa (Haldane, 'Imagining Scotland', 34, 108). It little mattered whether Fingal had been there or not: as John and Margaret Gold observe, 'given the lack of specific place information contained in Ossian's poetry, there was free range for the imagination'.[9] Yet this was only half the story: the spirit of place was important, but by rendering his Ossian poetry relatively Macpherson had made it extensible: its extension was not one of address, glen or township, but one of feature. Wherever the sublime or the picturesque could be found, wherever sensibility could raise a tear to faded glamour, there was Ossian's Scotland.

In 1757, in A *Philosophical Enquiry into the Sublime and the Beautiful* (of which there were seventeen more editions by 1797),[10] Edmund Burke had defined these two concepts in a way which stressed the awe, terror, majesty and indefinition of sublimity: all features which in some degree could be attached to remote and primitive societies, particularly when living in a suitable landscape, such as the mountains of Corsica or Scotland. Burke's conception was to be powerfully influential on tourist guides in the Lake District from 1770 on, such as Thomas West's 1778 *Guide to the Lakes* ('directed by theory and the theory is Burke's'), and the Irish philosopher left his mark on Hugh Blair's *Lectures on Rhetoric and Belles Lettres* (1783), Wordsworth (who in a letter of 1808 used Burke's title as a description of the Lake District), Coleridge and John Martin.[11] Dugald Stewart, 'Scott's friend and teacher' praised Burke's view of the Sublime,[12] and it was amplified in both a Wordsworthian and Scottish context by William Gilpin's (1724–1804) tours of the Wye, the Lake District and Highlands in the latter part of the eighteenth century.

In 1792, Gilpin published *Three Essays on the Picturesque*, a third category to add to Burke's two, and one chiefly descriptive of 'any scene that would look well in a painting, a natural spot that conformed to the rules of art' (Haldane, 'Imagining Scotland', p.155). There were, however, other important dimensions to the concept: the Picturesque tended to involve travel, being 'a frame of mind, an aesthetic attitude involving man in a direct and artistic relationship with the natural scenery through which he travels' and having also qualities of roughness and irregularity: 'ruins', 'broken ground, rocks, valleys, and cascades' are all picturesque, with a narrow contracted valley being 'an ideal subject for a foreground'. Many of these observations were on the Lakes, where Gilpin also thought that 'in wild, & desert scenes, we are best pleased with banditti-soldiers', a landscape modelled on those of Salvator Rosa (1615–73).[13] In *Essays on the Picturesque* (1794), Sir Uvedale Price (1747–1829) (whom Scott was studying in 1811/13, and subsequently wrote on) emphasised the appropriateness of 'ruins, Gothic architecture, hovels': 'anything in efficient working order is excluded'.[14] For Johnson in 1773, Scotland's ruins had been a sign of national infidelity and decline, but at its peak in the 1790s the Picturesque 'fondness for dilapidation and gloom' was clear. As Robert Heron (1764–1807), one of the 1790s tourists in Scotland, wrote at Dunkeld:

I began to reflect that I was entering the land of Ossian's heroes; the land which presented those few simple, grand, and gloomy objects which give a melancholy cast to the imagination of the past, and supplied that sublime, but undiversified imagery which forms one of the most peculiar characteristics of the ancient Gaelic poesy. (Andrews, *Picturesque*, vol. i, pp. 3, 23, 28, 411)

The practice of the Picturesque has been traced back in Scottish poetry to James Thomson (1700–48),[15] and it 'becomes conspicuous in the 1760s and 70s' (ibid., p. 3). It had already entered the guidebooks, for in the 1769 edition of Daniel Defoe's *A Tour through the Whole Island of Great Britain,* 'a more recognisable picturesque aesthetic' and 'the beginning of a narrative treatment of place ... and some slight foreshadowing of Scott's panoramic, onward-moving style' were visible, while later William Hutchinson's *A View of Northumberland with an Excursion to the Abbey of Melrose in Scotland* (1778) gave indication of Scott's 'stylistic features' (Hutchinson also wrote *An Excursion to the Lakes* [1774]).[16] For Gilpin (as with Macpherson) the quality of what he sought to represent was 'unrelated to any particular place'.[17]

Scott understood the implications of all this: 'his close acquaintance with the theory and practice of the picturesque is well recorded and almost certainly dates from his days at university, if not earlier'; Michel Baridon has gone so far as to suggest that he 'saw himself as a landscape painter *manqué*'.[18] Scott took full advantage of the intensity of Macpherson's representation of the essence of Scotland while modifying the Badenoch writer's lack of specificity with a host of capitalised locations: many of which, however, had in common those same extensible Macphersonian features, amplified by an understanding of the visual appeal of the Picturesque, and with a *frisson of* direct Jacobitism restored in place of Macpherson's obliquity for the benefit of a later age ('Tis Sixty Years Since', as *Waverley* (1814) proclaims) in which its politics were obsolete. The Napoleonic Wars themselves had seen a revival in Jacobite song and symbolism on the occasion of the restoration of the Bourbons in 1814, and this discourse was thus fortuitously available to Scott.[19] As Coleridge remarked acerbically to Wordsworth of Scott in 1810, 'the component parts of the Scottish Minstrelsy' included 'a vast string of patronymics, and names of Mountains, Rivers... all the nomenclature of Gothic Architecture, of Heraldry, of Arms, of Hunting, & Falconry... with a *Bard* (that is absolutely necessary)'.[20] Macpherson had made this last especially necessary in Scotland: as early as 1771, Tobias Smollett had Melford 'look for the suspended harp of that divine bard [Ossian]' in his host's hall in *Humphrey Clinker*, and appreciate 'the brown heath that Ossian wont to tread'.[21] The Ossianic figure of the bard had also been developed by Thomas Gray (1716–71), whose *The Bard* (1757), 'depended on information supplied by Ieuan Fardd' of the 'Cymmrodorion Society'. Gray had made trips to the Highlands in 1765 and the Lake District in 1769.(Pittock, *Celtic Identity*, p. 34; Andrews, *Picturesque*, vol. 1, p. 13). The 'image of the Last Bard, who had killed himself' in 'our Welch Alps' rather than submit to Edward I, was as an earnest of liberty which arguably sustained the idea of a unitary Celtic picturesque: in 1821, when George IV landed at Milford Haven, the *Court Newsman* opined 'The Chief of Wynnstay [Sir Watkin Williams Wynn] intends to summon the bards and minstrels... to give our beloved Monarch a specimen of the manner in which the Antient Britons performed their national music'.[22]

Scott's blend of this visual and literary heritage is visible in the famous passage in chapter 22 of *Waverley* in which Flora MacIvor (as the feminine embodiment of an old and fanatically patriotic Scotland) seduces Waverley himself to the Stuart cause with an apparatus of landscape and sensibility to which any Englishman would (apart from Flora's personal appeal) have probably been oblivious in 1745, before the craze for the Picturesque. Flora meets Waverley in a sublime landscape, where two streams join, one (usually taken as representing British Unionism) 'placid... sleeping in dark blue pools' and the other (Scottish nationalism and the Jacobite cause) 'rapid and furious, issuing from between precipices, like a maniac from his confinement' (pp. 174–5).[23] Waverley follows the latter to a land of romance, a 'narrow glen' (one of Gilpin's preferred Picturesque locations) full of rocks and spanned by a wooden bridge 'which crossed, like a single black line, the small portion of blue sky not intercepted by the projecting rocks on either side' (p. 175). On this thin bridge, Flora appears in the air like the genius of the place. Waverley goes to her, and finds her gazing at 'a romantic waterfall... like one of those lovely forms which decorate the landscapes of Poussin' (p. 176). Nicolas Poussin himself (born in 1612) brought to his art the representation of a displaced, vague landscape, 'toned all down to a prevailing golden brown, through which the greens of the landscape backgrounds and the flesh tints of his figures show dimly' in 'strong light and shadow'.[24] The Picturesque sought to reclaim the landscape ethos of seventeenth-century painters (Hutchinson, following James Thomson, used Claude Lorraine (1600–82) (Ruddick, 'Scott's Northumberland', p. 21)); in this it fed on the existing custom for the Grand Tourist to bring back 'evocative scenes from their tour' by Claude or others (Andrews, *Picturesque*, vol. 1, p. 6).

In this landscape, the roughness ('splintered into rocks and crags') of which not only displays Burke's Sublime but is also a necessary ingredient of Gilpin's Picturesque, Flora gets to work. She is accompanied by an attendant 'holding a small Scottish harp' which had belonged to 'Rory Dall, one of the last harpers in the Western Highlands'. Lest this elegiac hint should be lost, Scott instantly reminds the reader that 'the sun' was 'now stooping in the west': its light is contrasted with 'the full expressive darkness of Flora's eye' (*Waverley*, p. 176) an indefinably sublime and dangerous creature from a primitive world, now fading like the westering sun: Gilpin was interested in the picturesque quality of sunsets (Barbier, *Gilpin*, p. 135–6).

The landscape is sublime; Flora is beautiful ('of such exquisite loveliness…[a] beautiful woman…conscious of her own power' (*Waverley*, p. 177)); the collocation of scene, action and character is Picturesque: a landscape 'of Poussin', decorated by Flora. This is an excellent setting for the 'civilised' gaze to interpret the primitive: three high cultural conceptions of place collocated and reiterated. It is time for Flora to put the capital 'P' in Primitive, and she does not disappoint. She tells Waverley that her country has a 'poetical language' (hence associated with ballads and with the 'real language of men in a state of vivid sensation' from Wordsworth's canonisation of Primitivist assumptions in the 1802 Preface to *Lyrical Ballads*), and that 'the seat of the Celtic muse is in the mist of the secret and solitary hill, and her voice in the murmur of the mountain stream' (p. 177). She then plays on the harp a 'battle-song' in a 'wild and peculiar tone' which gives rise to a 'wild feeling of romantic delight' in Waverley. Lest the Ossianic moniker of the bard should be missed, the last quoted stanza of Flora's song particularly mentions Fionn / Fingal (pp. 177–8, 180), though the direct reference to Jacobitism goes beyond the obliquity of Macpherson. The world Flora conjures up (she is the 'fair enchantress' (p. 177)) is that of a primitive society, aroused for one last time to Jacobite war, even though in Adam Ferguson's terms, society had now moved on from 'that vigour of spirit, which renders disorder itself respectable'. Flora's knowingness, and the deliberate quality of her scene-setting invalidates the struggle for 'domestic liberty' praiseworthy in an earlier age: but it still leaves, in its collocation and bardic exaltation, a delicious sense of readerly involvement in the gloaming of a world about to be lost.[25] It was perhaps passages like this which made 'Victorian travellers' favorite episode of Scottish,' history... the 1745 Jacobite rebellion' (Haldane, p. 271).

In one sense, chapter 22 of *Waverley is* magnificent literature, operating on many levels simultaneously; in another, it is a *mélange* of every crowd-pulling device known to the tourist guides of the day, with Waverley standing, here as elsewhere, for the Romantic Englishman ready to be wooed by primitive glamour. As William Ruddick observes, 'Scott's prose maintains the exactness of reference of the county historians, but vivifies time and place as the ballads had done all in the context of a dramatisation of the picturesque ('Scott's Northumberland', p. 26): almost a gazeteer. By acknowledging the deliberateness of Flora's device (*Waverley*, p. 177), Scott averts attention from his own: and this passage is by no means the only one in which he offers a vision of the past whose factitiousness is concealed by a partial authorial confession to narrative device. In his fiction, the dimness and vagueness of sublimity, the 'colourful, striking, or singular' prospect of the picturesque (Ross, ' "Waverley" ', p. 100) are alike commonplace. As Jana Davis notes with respect to *Guy Mannering:* 'rather than revealed by sunlight, the landscapes are hidden by twilight or darkness, or altered by moonlight, like the suddenly moonlit ruins and silvered beach Mannering views from Ellangowan'.[26] But this feature can also be found in the description of what 'the pale moon, which had hitherto been contending with flitting clouds, now shone out' to reveal at Wolf's Crag in *The Bride of Lammermoor* or the moon on St Leonard's Crags in *Heart of Midlothian*.[27] Similarly, 'the low and setting sun... like a warrior prepared for defence, over a huge battlemented and turreted wall of crimson and black clouds' sets the scene in *Redgauntlet,* while the shadowy image of Burley, 'concealed by the shadow of the rock... dimly ruddied by the light of the red charcoal' at the climax to *Old Mortality* alike combines the red of the setting sun (and of the bloody, 'old' Scotland on which it shines) with the darkness of night in the same wavering, varied and uncertain light by which Flora works her magic in *Waverley*.[28]

Scott had already developed these ideas in his poetry. In *The Lady of the Lake* (1810), landscape and the character of its people are one, where 'The rocky summits, split and rent, / Form'd turret, dome, or battlement.' Just as dark Flora praises 'the solitude of the desert' as a home for the Celtic muse (*Waverley*, p. 177), so the Hermit in *The Lady* had already been defined by Scott in similar terms:

The desert: gave him visions wild,
Such as might suit the spectre's child
Where with black cliffs the torrents toil,
He watch'd the wheeling eddies boil,
Till, from their foam, his dazzled eyes
Behold the River Demon rise;
The mountain mist took form and limb,
Of noontide hag, or goblin grim;
The midnight wind came wild and dread,
Swell'd with the voices of the dead...
Far on the future battle-heath
His eye beheld the ranks of death:
Thus the lone Seer, from mankind hurl'd,
Shaped forth a disembodied world.[29]

Many of the familiar elements are here: solitude, darkness, the hint of the supernatural, the boiling water, the future battle. There is the same forceful attempt to meld the way of seeing the primitive through landscape with the character of the primitive in the landscape. Not long afterwards, Roderick Dhu makes that landscape come alive, as if his Celtic tribesmen (in Scott's construction) are not just intimately bound to the land (like Wordsworth's *Michael*), but actually made of it:

– Wild as the scream of the curlew,
From crag to crag the signal flew,
Instant, through copse and heath, arose
Bonnets and spears and bended bows...
... From shingles grey the lances start,
The bracken bush sends forth the dart,
The rushes and the willow-wand
Are bristling with axe and brand,
And every tuft of broom gives life
To plaided warrior armed for strife.
(*Works*, p. 313)

When Roderick Dhu calls them off, 'It seem'd as if their mother Earth / Had swallow'd up her warlike birth' (p. 314). These Scots are truly children of Nature, fading into and rising from the countryside which bore them in their 'graceful plaid' of 'varied hue'(p. 309). Just in case the potential visitor hasn't got the message that Scotland is a key location of primitive value, Scott occasionally hammers home the point in a direct appeal to the visitor, as here in *The Lord of the Isles* (1814):

STRANGER! if e'er thine ardent step
 Hath traced
The northern realms of ancient Caledon,
Where the proud Queen of Wilderness hath placed,
By lake and cataract, her lonely throne;
Sublime but sad delight thy soul hath known,
Gazing on pathless glen and mountain high,
Listing from where from the cliffs the torrents thrown
Mingle their echoes with the eagle's cry
And with the sounding lake, and with the moaning sky.
         (p. 528)

These are '[t]he fragments of an earlier world' as Scott puts it in *The Lady of the Lake*; 'Caledonia! stern and wild, / Meet muse for a poetic child !' (p. 248) in *The Lay of the Last Minstrel* (1805) and the place where 'tall cliff and cavern lone, / For the departed Bard make moan' 'And rivers teach their rushing wave / To murmur dirges round his grave' in the same poem (p. 76). Most importantly, the character of the Scot is, by a colossal gesture to the pathetic fallacy, in some key sense a function of the character of the place: the emotions roused by the landscape are also those of its people. The primitive children of Nature echo her moods. The moss-troopers are manifestations of this in the Border context, where in *The Lay*

High over Borthwick's mountain flood,
His wood-embosom'd mansion stood;
In the dark glen, so deep below,
The herds of plunder'd England low.
         (p. 66)

Harden's lord (Scott both old and new) is art and part of the character of the landscape he dominates, a verbal picture so composed by his descendant that the agricultural low-lying land of cattle-grazing England lies at the bottom of it. The 'herds of plunder'd England' can only find their grazing far below the mighty mansion which itself is mothered in the wood's bosom: a picturesque *locus amoenus*, and one almost placed in its own sacred grove. So in *Waverley*, the bridge and waterfall are part of the composition of Flora's height 'propped, as it were, in mid air... She stopped upon observing him below, and... waved her handkerchief... He was unable, from the sense of dizziness which her situation conveyed, to return the salute' (*Waverley*, p. 175).

  Just as Waverley climbs higher and higher still in pursuit of Flora (and her Jacobitism), so the English visitor following in his footsteps is invited to believe that he or she will become, for a transitory moment, part of what is being visited, a primitive sublimity of character, not merely of view. This primitive sublimity is linked with Scott's type of 'old' Scotland: the intransigent, impulsive, fanatic patriot manifested in Vich Ian Vohr, Redgauntlet, Burley, Elspeth and many others. Redgauntlet's cottage may no longer stand in its 'cleuch...steep, precipitous and full of trees' in a place 'so narrow...that no ray of the morning sun was likely to reach it' (*Redgauntlet*, p. 53), but it, like Creehope-linn or Burley's yet more dreadful cavern in *Old Mortality* (p. 461), retains in its scenery the sublimity which produced such characters, and from which the visitor may take away not only a vision of landscape, but the delight of having been for a short time exposed to the place of the genesis of a rude people, a voyeur of a rough-bred world who for a moment can fancy its presence a danger, till the very mobility of a gaze which invests another's landscape with such value can reassure itself of its own invulnerability by passing on.

But if Scott's landscape serves as a synecdoche for a nationalist Scottish nationhood, it also (and here is Scott's brilliance) serves as a Unionist paradigm. The flexibility of the Scottish border at the Solway in *Redgauntlet*; the similarity to Scotland of 'mountainous Northumberland' where Scott's 'two short holiday trips...in 1791 and 1792 combined ballad awareness with antiquarian discovery' (Ruddick, 'Scott's Northumberland', pp. 23–4), and the emphasis on similarity of culture (the 'Northern harper rude' who 'Chanted a rhyme of deadly feud' in *Marmion* is a Northumbrian, not a Scot (*Works*, p. 118)), all combine to suggest an idea of a certain historic commonality, one we still accept in the ingrained term 'Border Ballads'. As Francis Jeffrey acidly pointed out in his review of *Marmion*, 'there is scarcely one trait of true Scottish nationality or patriotism...too little pains is taken to distinguish the Scottish character and manners from the English' (Hayden, *Critical Heritage*, p. 42). By these means, Scott could persuade the English reader of the absence of a real cultural and national barrier, while his emphasis on the internal 'border' between Highland and Lowland in Scotland itself serves to further dilute the starkness of Anglo-Scottish division in a manner alien to contemporaries such as James Hogg, who in 'Lock the Door, Lauriston' constructs Border warfare in the ethnic terms of Scot v Saxon.[30] Scott's Primitivism is of a kind which is in full dialogue with Wordsworth's, as indeed the history of the relation of these two writers suggests.

In the stories, told by the servant Ann Tyson, the child Wordsworth had already grown up with a pattern of Border tales which might well have predisposed him to Scott's influence. In September 1803, 'Wordsworth toured the Borders with Scott, just after the latter had in the *Minstrelsy of the Scottish Border* (1802) presented 'an alternative tradition of true poetry' in the manner of Wordsworth, in the latter's own 1800 Preface to *Lyrical Ballads*. Just as Scott was influenced by the idea of the Picturesque, so were the Wordsworths. Dorothy's *Journal* of the 1803 Tour emphasises 'a number of features found in *Waverley* ch. 22 and elsewhere: enchantment, solitude, the outlandish, Rob Roy as the Salvator Rosa bandit; Glencoe's mountains, 'such forms as Milton might be supposed to have had in mind' when he wrote of Satan (cf. Burley as, 'a fiend in the lurid atmosphere of Pandaemonium' (*Old Mortality*, p. 462)) and in all as 'lovely a combination of forms as, any traveller who goes in search of the picturesque need desire'. When the Wordsworths visited Scott, he read them *The Lay of the Last Minstrel*.[31] Dorothy had already in a letter of 1793 likened her brother to Beattie's Minstrel, while *The White Doe of Rylstone* (for which Wordsworth 'scorned historical information offered by Scott'), was an attempt to match *The Lay of the Last Minstrel* with a Northumbrian lay. Fittingly, Wordsworth may have chosen the Scottish packman James Patrick as a model for his Pedlar in *The Excursion* (1814); Scotland was 'the most poetical Country I ever travelled in' in an 1805 letter to Scott. Both writers spent a good deal of time on each other's side of the Border, implicitly or explicitly, Scott's Lake Tour occurring just before the publication of *Lyrical Ballads* just as Wordsworth's Scottish tour followed *The Minstrelsy of the Scottish Border* and trod on the heels of *The Lay of the Last Minstrel* (1805).[32]

When it came to attracting visitors to Scotland, Scott was aided by the death of others in the Napoleonic Wars. The prolonged conflict on the Continent 'made Scotland virtually the only (even partly) foreign place to which English tourists could safely travel at the turn of the century, aside from Gaelic Ireland', and Gaelic Ireland had revolted in 1798. Fed by Scott's presentation of Scottish Enlightenment historiography in a Romantic landscape, the 'tourist had an almost insatiable appetite for stories of... lawlessness and ferocity' (Haldane, 'Imagining Scotland', pp. 6, 273). This caricature of course remains one of the chief means of selling Scotland's history to its visitors, much aided and abetted by cinematic caricature from *Brigadoon* to *Braveheart*. In this, however, cinema may be being truer than it knows to the ideas of Primitivism which influenced it, as Thomas Deegan argues in tracing Scott's influence through Fenimore Cooper on the genre of the Western.[33]

On a more scholarly level, *Waverley* indirectly fed the growth of Scottish history. The recreational Highland primitivism of the early Highland societies and the Highland Games (begun in the 1780s and developed in tourist terms by Victorian patronage) increased after 1814, but so did the historical clubs dedicated to printing the primary texts of Scottish history, of which only two were 'pre-Waverley': Scott himself founded the Bannatyne Club.[34] Historical pride and primitive valour united in texts such as David Stewart's *Sketches of the Highlanders of Scotland* (1822), which themselves helped to feed the Victorian representation of the Scot (particularly the Scots soldier) as huge and hairy, gifted with 'a sort of preindustrial vigour and strength' (Haldane, 'Imagining Scotland', pp. 273, 283). It was that strength which the monarchy itself partook of in its mid-century move to Balmoral. While on holiday in Scotland, the Prince Consort was portrayed amusing himself as Redgauntlet does in the opening chapter of Scott's novel, by spearing fish with a leister; the hunt, particularly the deer-hunt, became a burgeoning means of access to Primitivist value by the gentry and aristocracy of the most powerful modern state. The medievalism which so characterised the Victorian period itself owed much, via *Ivanhoe* and other novels, to 'the fancy-dress school of history pioneered in Scotland'.[35] The deerhound which Prince Albert found a 'perfect companion' had been Scott's favourite dog, and its noble roots in the Ossianic world of the Fianna had doubtless sustained 'the restoration of the breed... by Archibald and Duncan McNeill' by 1825.[36] On the 1842 royal visit, Victoria and Albert were met 'in Crieff... by 100 of the local tenants, dressed in tartan, some with Lochaber axes'; at Dunkeld, 'Atholl Highlanders complete with claymores and battleaxes' turned up (Haldane, 'Imagining Scotland', pp. 30–1). An intensely visual Primitivism was being generated: and it was being generated from the world of the Waverley Novels.

Scott's role in all this was thus of major importance. The visit of George IV in 1822, which he stage-managed with tartan pageantry and the inevitable *frisson* of Jacobitism (which survived 'to a wonderful degree in Scotland' according to Scott), helped not only, via the Grand Ball in the Assembly Rooms, to define 'the kilt as the national dress of all Scotsmen', but led to a massive boom in the market for tartan.[37] By 1831, James Logan's *The Scottish Gael* was offering 'the first descriptive list of "clan" tartans', thus foreshadowing the entire industry and market of today.[38] Likewise, 'from the 1820s the tweeds of Galashiels and the borders were made popular by Sir Walter Scott'.[39]

Scott's sales had already provided the basis for this boom, for he was the novelist 'who discovered the novel as a source of wealth, status and cultural power' (Checkland and Checkland, *Industry and Ethos*, p. 138). By 1815, *The Lay of the Last Minstrel* had gone through fifteen editions; *Rob Roy* sold 10,000 copies in its first fortnight, and *The Lady of the Lake* 'at least

50,000 copies by 1836', *Marmion* 36,000 by 1825. Coleridge described Scott in 1810 as 'a man...familiar with descriptive Poets & Tourists, himself a Picturesque Tourist' (Hayden, *Critical Heritage*, pp. 2, 3, 57).[40] More recent writers have found in Scott not only a tourist, but, explicitly conscious of his sales, realised and prospective, a tour guide. As Ian Alexander notes, 'from, 1805 onwards [the date of the *Lay of the Last Minstrel*], tourists materialised in droves with the poems in their pockets if not in their heads', and 'by the time he came to write *The Lord of the Isles*, published in 1815, Scott was offering cautionary advice, guidebook style, in the course of the actual narrative', e.g. 'Seek not the giddy crag to climb; / To view the turret scathed by time; / It is a task of doubt and fear / To aught but goat or mountain-deer' in Canto IV. vii.[41] In Scott's fiction the tourist's eye can gaze through those of his characters: sometimes this process is almost explicit, as when in *The Bride of Lammermoor* 'our travellers were too impatient for security against the rising storm to permit them to indulge themselves in studying the picturesque' (*Bride*, p. 83).

These concepts endure. In a recent study of the effects of continuing Primitivist assumptions on the outlook of incomers living in Scotland, Charles Jedrej and Mark Nuttall found that a dual definition of 'locals' as 'either, romantic heroes, or heroines, a people of integrity, courage, loyalty' co-existed with a more negative image of their backwardness:

The majority of cosmopolitans who visit or dwell in rural Scotland are attracted by their experience of the scenery as Romantic, and they will, naturally enough, not wish their 'view' to be spoiled by rustic locals, so they will be more likely to people the scenery with romantic figures... It is a short step from being a consumer of tourism looking for facilities to becoming a producer for other tourists.

Those who come to live in rural Scotland still seek 'a landscape of majestic glens, tremendous mountains, awesome cliffs, enchanting sea lochs, magical movements of light and shade, all infused with melancholy memories and ancient legends of dark death and tragic heroism, and inhabited by a deeply spiritual people moved by the landscape to create poetry'.[42] Every single one of these features can be found repeated in Scott, and all but one of them are emphasised in Chapter 22 of *Waverley* alone. Without direct allusion to Scott, contemporary social science thus indicates the enduring hold his compositional arrangement of Primitivism, Enlightenment historiography and the visual aesthetic of the long eighteenth century have had on the image of Scotland. As Historic Scotland tells us 'Scotland is a land of castles. Mighty fortresses on rocky heights, isolated keeps... grim strongholds set on towering sea cliffs'.[43] There are passages in Scott of which this is almost a paraphrase: in *The Bride of Lammermoor* 'the cliffs which overlooked the ocean were hung with thick and heavy mist' round 'the portals of the half-ruinous tower', Wolf's Crag, where 'the sombrous and heavy sound of the billows . . . dashing against the rocky beach at a profound distance beneath, were to the ear what the landscape was to the eye'. From this dreary and lonely place at the beginning of the novel, the body of Lord Ravenswood issues 'to an abode yet more dreary and lonely' (*Bride*, pp. 32, 81).

This solitude is of course of a piece with that of Flora's Celtic muse, and, as Scott's repetitive use of images of darkness in his writing suggests, links solitude to death. That death is, at least on one level, the death of Scotland itself: and hence, in Scott's sustenance of the Scottish image and the Scottish tourist industry lies a paradox of death-in-life and life-in-death, a country created in its uncreation, victorious in defeat, popular in its depopulation and visited by tourists as its land is cleared. In these paradoxes lies the point and counterpoint of most Scottish cultural criticism since 1900. Such is Scott's legacy: but one, I trust this essay has shown, in deep debt and relationship to and with the major influences on English Romanticism.

CHAPTER II

Felicia Hemans, Byronic cosmopolitanism
and the ancient Welsh bards

William D. Brewer

Felicia Dorothea Hemans (1793–1835) considered Wales the 'Green land of [her] childhood, [her] home and [her] dead'.[1] As Peter W. Trinder observes, Hemans 'spent all but the first and last few years of her life [in Wales], and all her happy years'.[2] She composed the poetry for the first number of *A Selection of Welsh Melodies* (1821), addressed Wales and its scenery in such poems as 'Written in North Wales', 'The Vale of Clwyd', 'The Scenes of Conway [Conwy]', 'A Farewell to Wales', and 'The River Clwyd in North Wales', and is included in a series of volumes sponsored by the Welsh Arts Council, *Writers of Wales* (1984). Hemans was, however, neither born in Wales nor of Welsh extraction: she was born in Liverpool to a Venetian-German mother and an Irish father. Moreover, she situated the overwhelming majority of her poems outside of Wales. Unlike the Welsh poet Ann Griffiths (1776–1805), she wrote in English rather than Welsh, although Trinder speculates that 'she could read and understand the Welsh language sufficiently for us to accept that the translations contained in [*A Selection of Welsh Melodies*] may be her own originals rather than paraphrases'.[3] According to Jane Aaron, Hemans's poetry is 'characteristic of English culture' during the Romantic era, and 'the depth of her commitment to the [Welsh] nationalistic cause can be gauged by the fact that the author of "Owen Glyndwr's War-Song" was also the author of "The Stately Homes of England" '.[4] Her celebration of Owain Glyndwr (dramatised by Shakespeare as Glendower in *Henry IV*, *Part One*), who attempted to form a Franco-Welsh alliance against England, also seems inconsistent with her Anglophilic poem to George III published a year earlier, *Stanzas to the Memory of the Late King* (1820), and her quasi-imperialist 'England's Dead' (1823). Although Tricia Lootens asserts 'Few poetic careers can have been more thoroughly devoted to the construction of national identity than was that of Felicia Hemans', she concedes that while Hemans 'wrote bloodthirsty British victory and battle songs,... her martial verse also celebrated (carefully chosen) armies of Greeks, Germans, Moors, Norwegians, Spaniards, and Welsh, among others. However anglicised and homogenised, Hemans's protagonists are nothing if not diverse in "collateral circumstances"...such as "language, literature, manners, national customs".[5]

In fact, Hemans's penchant for locating her poems in exotic locales such as ancient Carthage, Greece, North America and India suggests that she perceived herself as a cosmopolitan writer capable of authentically portraying the emotions and experiences of people from various nations and historical epochs. According to Nanora Sweet, Hemans, influenced by Germaine de Staël's *Corinne* (1807), mounts a 'critique of empire and parallel espousal of Continental cosmopolitanism' in such poems as *The Restoration of the Works of Art to Italy* (1816) and *Modern Greece: a Poem* (1817).[6] Her understanding of non-British cultures came, however, from books rather than firsthand experience. Thus some anglicisation in her works set in foreign countries is inevitable.

Although Hemans's contemporary Lord Byron was, like her, a poet with Celtic roots ('half a Scot by birth, and bred / A whole one'),[7] their conceptions of cosmopolitanism differ greatly. T. S. Eliot has dubbed Byron 'a Scottish poet',[8] but Byron seems to have had an ambivalent attitude toward his Scottish heritage. The speaker of his early satire *The Curse of Minerva* (1811) attempts to appease Minerva's fury against England by telling her that Greece's 'plunderer was a Scot' (line 128), Lord Elgin. The assessment of Scotland that follows is extremely negative:

> well I know within that bastard land
> Hath Wisdom's goddess never held command:
> A barren soil where Nature's germs confin'd
> To stern sterility can stint the mind,
> Whose thistle well betrays the niggard earth,
> Emblem of all to whom the land gives birth;
> Each genial influence nurtur'd to resist,
> A land of meanness, sophistry and mist.
> (lines 131–8)

After his famous pilgrimage to Portugal, Spain, Albania, Greece and Turkey (from 2 July 1809 to 14 July 1811), Byron began to see himself as a cosmopolite with eastern sympathies. To his half-sister Augusta Leigh he wrote that he would 'turn Mussulman in the end',[9] and he announced to his friend Francis Hodgson, 'In the spring of 1813 I shall leave England for ever... Neither my habits nor constitution are improved by *your* customs or *your* climate. I shall find employment in making myself a good Oriental scholar. I shall retain a mansion in one of the fairest islands, and retrace... the most interesting portions of the East' (*BLJ*, vol. II, p. 163, emphasis mine). Byron's cosmopolitanism has a religious as well as national dimension: in his letter to Augusta he jokingly suggests a willingness to convert to Islam, and he sent his illegitimate daughter Allegra to be raised in an Italian Catholic convent. He suggests that in order to be a true cosmopolite one must shed ethnic and religious affiliations, live in various (preferably exotic) cultures, and adopt the broadly tolerant perspective of a citizen of the world. In contrast, many of Hemans's verses celebrate Britain and its military triumphs and can be described as 'devoutly Anglican'.[10] Whereas Byron makes the deceased George III the butt of his satire in *The Vision of Judgment* (1822), Hemans eulogises him as 'a blasted oak, / Sadd'ning the scene where once it nobly reign'd' in *Stanzas to the Memory of the Late King*.[11] While Byron could never quite come to terms with his Scottishness, Hemans became an enthusiastic participant in the Celtic revival movement. In a letter to Mary Russell Mitford she insists, perhaps a bit defensively, that 'the Welsh character is by no means yet merged with the English'.[12]

Byron's responses to Hemans's works reflect his cosmopolitan attitudes. In his assessment of Hemans's anonymously published *Modern Greece, a Poem*, Byron writes 'Modern Greece Good for nothing – written by some one who has never been there – ... besides why "*modern*"? – you may say *modern Greeks* but surely *Greece* itself is rather more ancient than ever it was' (*BLJ*, vol. v, pp. 262–3). According to Byron, only a poet who has lived in a country can write a credible poem about it. Thus since Hemans's pilgrimages were limited to the British Isles, her works set in continental Europe, Asia and the Americas do not have the authenticity or accuracy that Byron valued.[13] Byron also detects some insularity in Hemans's *The Sceptic* (1820), which holds that the dying are miserable without religious consolation. He declares that 'Mrs. Hemans is ... quite wrong – men died calmly before the Christian æra – & since without Christianity – witness the Romans – ... A deathbed is a matter of nerves & constitution – & not of religion; – Voltaire was frightened – Frederick of Prussia not' (*BLJ*, vol. vii, p. 113). In his view, Hemans lacks the frame of reference necessary to make universal generalisations about human nature. For her part, Hemans idolised Byron until she was offended by the extracts from Thomas Moore's *Letters and Journals of Lord Byron: with Notices of his Life* (1830) published in periodicals. According to Henry F. Chorley, 'the details of his continental wanderings shocked her fastidious sense as exceeding the widest limits within which one so passionate and so disdainful of law and usage might err and be forgiven'.[14] In comparison to Byron, Hemans seems insular indeed. This essay will argue, however, that Hemans's poetry explores a different kind of cosmopolitanism – an ancient Welsh or British cosmopolitanism that contrasts with Byron's conception of himself as a citizen of the world. In so doing she constructs a bardic ideology that has its foundation in ancient times and natural sites, subscribes to values endorsed by diverse cultures, and transcends national boundaries and ethnic allegiances.

Hemans's enthusiasm for ancient Wales must be considered within the context of the Celtic revival which began with Ossian and inspired Robert Southey's *Madoc* (1805). As Ernest Bernhardt-Kabisch points out in his discussion of *Madoc*, 'The speculations of Celtomaniacs like William Stukely, Edward Williams, and Edward Davies ... convinced [Southey] ... that the religious "system" of the Medieval Welsh "bards" was the "patriarchal faith" as derived, via the Druids, from the "real and true faith" of the Celtic descendants of Japhet. Wales was the true Britain, the once and future England of Gray's *Bard*.'[15] Southey shared his fascination with Welsh bards in an 1805 letter to Joseph Cottle, who was working on *Fall of Cambria* (1809): 'You will of course have something to do with the Bards ... I myself very much incline to believe that the patriarchal system was preserved more purely by the Bards than by any other race of men; if this could be proved it would add the sanction of faith to a creed which will stand the test of reason.'[16] The legendary hero Madoc (or Madog) is, in some ways, an ancient Welsh cosmopolite. According to legend, he and his brother Rhiryd, sons of the prince of North Wales, sailed westward from their native land in 1170 to avoid taking part in the struggle between two other brothers for the throne. Madog discovered America and, '[h]aving returned home, ... described the fertile countries he had visited'.[17] In 1172 he arranged another expedition but was never heard from again. Southey's *Madoc* describes the title-character's adventures in America, his return to Wales to gather colonists, his defeat of the Aztecas [*sic*], and his establishment of a kingdom in the New World. Although not a bard himself, Madoc reveres 'The Masters of the Song / In azure robes ... that one bright hue / To emblem unity, and peace, and truth, / Like Heaven, that o'er a world of wickedness / Spreads its eternal canopy serene'. His cosmopolitanism is demonstrated by his willingness to leave 'his barbarous country', explore uncharted lands, and learn about, negotiate with, and live alongside cultures which differ profoundly from his own.[18] This does not, however, mean that Madoc is in any sense a cultural relativist: he remains true to Southey's version of the bard's 'patriarchal system' and violently opposes the Aztec ritual of human sacrifice.

Hemans features Madog in *A Selection of Welsh Melodies*, for which she supplied the 'Characteristic Words' and John Parry contributed the 'Symphonies and Accompaniments' in the first number. Trinder describes *Welsh Melodies* as 'a mixture of imaginative recreations of scenes from Welsh history and translations of Welsh poems'. He may mean transliteration rather than translation, because he considers them 'very free versions'.[19] In 'Prince Madog's Farewell', the departing explorer seems more homesick than cosmopolitan: instead of looking forward to his arrival in the New World, he mourns the fact that he will never return to Wales. He has little of the confidence of Southey's coloniser. His Welsh spirit of adventure comes, however, to his aid as he sails westward:

> 'Tis not for the land of my sires to give birth
>   Unto bosoms that shrink, when their trial is nigh;
> Away! we will bear over ocean and earth,
>   A name and a spirit that never shall die.
> My course to the winds, to the stars I resign,
> But my soul's quenchless fire, oh! my country! is thine.[20]

Whereas the Byronic cosmopolite adapts to different cultures until he loses his original national identity and becomes a citizen of the world, Hemans's Madog pledges that whatever course the wind and the stars make him follow his soul will remain forever Welsh.

Like Southey, Hemans venerated the 'patriarchal' Welsh bards. According to the historian E. D. Evans, in eighteenth-century Wales 'Bardic learning, handed down by oral tradition, was waning but far from extinct and it was possible... for Iolo Morganwg to learn his poetic art and acquire a wealth of literary tradition from country poets who lived in Glamorgan'.[21] The Cymmrodorion Society held Eisteddfodau (meetings of Welsh bards) in Wrexham in 1820 and in London in 1822, and Hemans wrote 'The Meeting of the Bards. Written for an Eisteddvod [*sic*], or Meeting of Welsh Bards' for the second Eisteddfod. Her headnote to the poem reveals that she had studied William Owen Pughe's *The Heroic Elegies and other Pieces of Llywarc Hen* (1792). Here, as elsewhere in her writings, she uses the adjectives 'British' and 'Welsh' interchangeably, which reflects her belief (and that of the other Celtomaniacs) that the Welsh are the direct descendants of the ancient Britons who were driven to Wales by the Saxon and Norman invasions:[22]

The *Gorseddau*, or meetings of the British bards, were anciently ordained to be held in the open air, on some conspicuous situation, whilst the sun was above the horizon... The places set apart for this purpose were marked out by a circle of stones, called the circle of federation. The presiding bard stood on a large stone (Maen Gorsedd, or the stone of assembly), in the centre. The sheathing of a sword upon this stone was the ceremony which announced the opening of a *Gorsedd*, or meeting. The bards always stood in their uni-coloured robes, with their heads and feet uncovered, within the circle of federation. (*The Siege of Valencia*, p. 311)[23]

During the London Eisteddfod, Humffreys Parry, the 'Conductor of the Cymmrodorion Transactions', presented the audience with 'an historical outline of these national assemblies from the most ancient notices of their revival by the Welsh Bards, whether as *Gorseddau* or *Eisteddfodau*, down to the era of the present auspicious re-establishment under the patronage of the Cymmrodorion and the Societies of Wales. This being done, the same gentleman read a copy of beautiful verses, written by Mrs Hemans, for the occasion'.[24]

Hemans honours the ancient bards for their honesty, nobility and love of peace. In a 14 May 1823 letter she praises her 'favourite bardic expression, "in the face of the sun, and in the eye of light"' as 'a noble motto for all the proceedings of our ancient Welsh bards'. She also writes that 'the title...which their order assumed – "They who are free throughout the world", has always struck me as being particularly fine... I must try to make you acquainted with their magnificent principles and system'.[25] Hemans continues this discussion in a subsequent letter:

The idea entertained of the bardic character appears to me particularly elevated and beautiful. The bard was not allowed, in any way, to become a party in political or religious dispute; he was recognised so completely as the herald of peace, under the title of 'Bard of the Isle of Britain', that a naked weapon was not allowed to be displayed in his presence. He passed unmolested from one hostile country to another, and if he appeared, in his uni-coloured robe (which was azure, being the emblem of peace and truth), between two contending armies, the battle was immediately suspended. One of the general titles of the order was, 'Those who are free throughout the world', and their motto, 'The Truth against the World'.[26]

This bard is, in some ways, cosmopolitan: he can travel 'unmolested from one hostile country to another' and is 'free throughout the world'. Whereas Byron envisions the citizen of the world as a cultural hybrid who learns and sometimes adopts foreign customs and mores, Hemans's bard is steeped in ancient British rituals and beliefs. He represents, however, the transcultural and transhistorical values of peace and truth, 'The Truth against the World' which Hemans considers absolute rather than relative. This bardic cosmopolite is visionary and idealistic and thus contrasts sharply to Byron's more experienced and cynical citizen of the world.

Hemans's bard derives his power and authority from nature, which is the site of his meetings, songs, inspiration and worship. In 'The Meeting of the Bards' Hemans emphasises the ancient bards' pantheism:

> They met – oh! not in kingly hall or bower,
> But where wild Nature girt herself with power:
> They met – where streams flash'd bright from rocky caves,

> They met – where woods made moan o'er warriors' graves,...
> There throng'd th' inspired of yore! – on plain or height,
> *In the sun's face, beneath the eye of light,*
> And, baring unto heaven each noble head,
> Stood in the circle, where none else might tread.
> Well might their lays be lofty! – soaring thought
> From Nature's presence tenfold grandeur caught...
> Whence came the echoes to those numbers high? –
> 'Twas from the battle-fields of days gone by!
> And from the tombs of heroes, laid to rest
> With their good swords, upon the mountain's breast.
>
> (*The Siege of Valencia*, pp. 311–13)

When Hemans turns from the Welsh bards of the past to the Eisteddfod in Romantic-era London, there is a sense of loss. The nineteenth-century inheritors of this proud tradition do not meet 'Midst the stone-circles, hallow'd thus of old; / Not where great Nature's majesty and might / First broke, all-glorious, on our infant sight; / Not near the tombs, where sleep our free and brave'. 'In these late days', Hemans continues mournfully, 'dark Mona's [Anglesey's] shore, / Eryri's [Snowdon's] cliffs resound with harps no more!' But although the modern bards lack their forebears' oneness with nature and what Wordsworth would call 'the visionary gleam', their dreams 'are haunted by [the ancient bards'] voice of song' and they possess an equally intense 'patriot-feeling' (*The Siege of Valencia*, p. 314). In 'The Meeting of the Bards' Hemans asserts a spiritual and patriotic connection between heroic Welsh bards and her poetic and antiquarian contemporaries. Soon after its re-establishment the Cymmrodorion Society made a similar symbolic gesture by affiliating itself with the most famous living Celtic poet – it enrolled Sir Walter Scott as one of its honorary members.[27]

In her juvenile poem 'Genius' (1808), published fourteen years before 'The Meeting of the Bards', Hemans describes herself composing verses in a 'favourite rustic seat' where 'bards have wak'd the song of other days':

> Some Cambrian Ossian may have wander'd near,
> While airy music murmur'd in his ear:
> Perhaps, even here, beneath the moonlight beam,
> He lov'd to ponder some entrancing theme
>   . . .
> Sweet was the Cambrian harp in ancient time,
> When tuneful bards awak'd the song sublime;
>   . . .
> Oh! Cambria, tho' thy sweetest bards are dead,
> And fairies from thy lovely vales are fled;

> Still in thy sons the musing mind may trace
> The vestige of thy former simple race:
>
> . . .
>
> The wandering harper in plaintive lays,
>
> . . .
>
> Declares the glory of departed days.
>
> (*Poems*, pp. 73–4)[28]

Like 'The Meeting of the Bards', this early poem registers a sense both of loss and of continuity. The modern 'wandering harper', like the nineteenth-century Eisteddfod, cannot hope to recapture the sublimity of ancient times, but he can declare their glory. And the young poet, writing where a 'Cambrian Ossian' may have wandered, imagines his 'strain of plaintive melody' (*Poems*, p. 74) and adopts him as her poetic forebear. She speculates that for the Welsh bards nature was not just a place for meetings and religious ceremonies: it was also the site of poetic and musical creation. In composing her poem under moonlight 'Where pensile ash trees form the green retreat', Hemans continues their tradition.

Hemans's ancient bards, who meet 'where the Druid's ancient Cromlech [i.e., altar] frown'd' (*The Siege of Valencia*, p. 312), resemble the Druids celebrated in Wordsworth's *The Prelude* (1805 version). On 'the Plain of Sarum' (XII. 314) Wordsworth observes 'Lines, circles, mounts, a mystery of shapes / . . . By which the Druids covertly expressed / Their knowledge of the heavens, and imaged forth / The constellations' (XII. 340–7).[29] In 'an antiquarian's dream' he envisions these 'bearded Teachers, with white wands / Uplifted, pointing to the starry sky / Alternately, and Plain below, while breath / Of music seemed to guide them, and the Waste / Was cheared with stillness and a pleasant sound' (XII. 349–53). Wordsworth's Druids, like Hemans's bards, are associated with music and nature, but he makes his 'bearded Teachers' ancient astronomers, whereas Hemans's bards are inspired by 'the battle-fields of days gone by' rather than by scientific curiosity. They are, in fact, contradictory figures, simultaneously representing peace (in their sky-blue robes) and ancient violence. Although not warriors themselves, they sing battle-songs.[30] They reflect a tension present throughout Hemans's poetry, which affirms both the 'ideology of the domestic affections' and 'a masculine code of military glory and individual heroism'.[31]

During the Romantic era Wales was famous as a land of haunting scenic beauty, capable of inspiring modern as well as ancient bards. The last book of Wordsworth's 1805 *Prelude* begins with his ascent of Mount Snowdon, which offers him an inspirational vision of 'The perfect image of a mighty Mind' (XIII. 69). As Hemans writes in her note to 'Eryri Wen' ('White Snowdon'), 'Snowdon was held as sacred by the Ancient Britons... It is still said, that whosoever slept upon Snowdon would wake inspired' (*Welsh Melodies*, 1st Number, p. 59). In a letter to an unidentified correspondent, Hemans praises the 'beauty and grandeur' of 'the country around Llangollen'. She associates this area both with a bardic tale and her own experience there: 'The ruin... on the height of rather a grotesque rock above the valley of Llangollen, was formerly the residence of a distinguished Welsh beauty, and the poem in which the Cambrian bard has with much enthusiasm celebrated the perfections of the fair Myfanwy is still extant. I once passed through that scenery at night, when its sublimity was inexpressibly heightened by the fires which had been lighted to burn the gorse on the mountains. The broad masses of light and shadow which they occasioned gave it a character of almost savage grandeur, which made a powerful impression upon my mind.'[32]

In 'The Rock of Cader-Idris' from *A Selection of Welsh Melodies* Hemans presents another inspirational site in Wales. A note to the poem informs the reader that 'There is a popular Welsh tradition, that on the summit of Cader-Idris, one of the highest mountains in North Wales, is an excavation in the rock resembling a couch, and that whoever should pass a night in that seat, would be found in the morning either dead, raving, or endowed with supernatural genius' (*Welsh Melodies*, 1st Number, p. 12). Hemans associates the word 'genius' with bards, or 'Some Cambrian Ossian', in her poem on the subject, but 'The Rock of Cader-Idris' does not specify whether the first-person narrator is preparing to become a poet, a prophet, or a leader like Madog or Owain Glyndwr. Hemans supplies, however, the bardic definition of genius: 'One of the Welsh poetical Triads thus describes the attributes of Genius: – "The three primary requisites of genius: an eye that can see nature, a heart that can feel nature, and boldness that dares follow nature" ' (*Welsh Melodies*, 1st Number, p. 12). This definition of poetic genius would fit Wordsworth, whom Hemans praises in her poem to him as 'True bard, and holy!... / Who, by some secret gift of soul or eye, / In every spot beneath the smiling sun, / Sees where the springs of living waters lie.'[33] The speaker of 'The Rock of Cader-Idris' describes how he lies 'on that rock where the storms have their dwelling, / The birth-place of phantoms, the home of the cloud', hearing 'The voice of the mountain-wind' and feeling, 'midst a world of dread grandeur, alone'. From a Wordsworthian perspective, nature grants the newly born genius the visionary gleam, which enables him to see nature's 'glory', 'beauty' and '*soul*'. This knowledge gives him 'A flame all immortal, a voice and a power', the ability, presumably, to be a great Welsh bard, perhaps one of the 'Welsh poetical Triads'. But his nocturnal experience is not entirely positive: it is a nightmare teeming with 'dread beings' and 'the mighty of ages departed', who freeze him with their glances and threaten him with death or madness. Nature seems to be harshly challenging rather than benign and nurturing. Paradoxically, although the narrator has received 'a voice and a power', he declares that 'Man's tongue hath no language to speak what [he] saw'. Although the title of the poem locates it 'on the summit of Cader-Idris', the narrator's description of the mountain's physical setting is so vague that it could apply to almost any mountain; in fact, he refers to Cader-Idris at one point as 'the hill'. He can *feel* the 'deep presence' of 'the powers of the wind and the ocean' but does not know 'their forms'. 'The Rock of Cader-Idris' is, then, an extremely nonspecific account of the birth of a genius who receives his visionary voice and power from universal nature and 'the mighty of ages departed', dead heroes whose nationality is not identified. He becomes a pantheistic poet-prophet who cannot describe his visions on Cader-Idris in Welsh or any other human language.

In her discussion of 'The Rock of Cader-Idris', Lootens writes that 'even as she celebrates the Welsh bards' national identity, constituting herself as their heir, Hemans colludes in the dispersion of that identity. To Mary Russell Mitford, for example, she describes the 'Welsh character' as not 'yet merged in the English' character... – rather as if any regional specificity were doomed; and even her nationalistic 'Welsh melodies' implicitly assign a 'brighter lot' to Wales during the period of England's predominance ('The Mountain-Fires'[*Welsh Melodies*, 1st Number, p. 54])'.[34] While Hemans clearly recognised that the Welsh 'character' was threatened by the dominant English culture, Lootens bases her assessment of 'The Rock of Cader-Idris' on a very narrow view of the Welsh bards who, as we have seen, represent transcultural values as well as the beliefs of Ancient Britain. In her poem Hemans forges a connection to them that is spiritual and aesthetic rather than ethnic. Her kinship with the bards is embodied by a natural site associated with their magic and genius rather than Welsh parents. Moreover, while Hemans alludes to the 'brighter lot' of the modern Welsh in 'The Mountain-Fires', almost any lot would be 'brighter' than that of their 'sires' mourning 'the massacre of the British chiefs by Hengist [a Jutish invader], on Salisbury Plain' (*Welsh Melodies*, 1st Number, p. 54 n.).

Perhaps the most famous of Hemans's bardic predecessors is Taliesin, a 'prophet bard' whose voice still 'floats' among the hills of Wales (*Welsh Melodies*, 1st Number, p. 37). Taliesin 'flourished from AD 520 to 570' and 'is ranked in the Triads, with Merddin Emrys and Merddin ab Madog

Morvryn, as the three 'privardd bedydd', or baptismal bards of the Isle of Britain'.[35] In a note to 'Taliesin's Prophecy', Hemans writes: 'A prophecy of Taliesin relating to the Ancient Britons, is still extant, and has been strikingly verified. It is to the following effect:

> "Their God they shall worship,
> Their language they shall retain,
> Their land they shall lose,
> Except wild Wales." '
> (*Welsh Melodies*, 1st Number, p. 37)

'Taliesin's Prophecy' explains how the bard's vision comes to him: 'The path of unborn ages is trac'd upon my soul, / The clouds, which mantle things unseen, away before me roll. / A light, the depths revealing, hath o'er my spirit pass'd; / A rushing sound from days to be swells fitful in the blast.' As in 'The Rock of Cader-Idris', the language is vague and the speaker is disembodied: the vision traces itself on the poet's soul, illuminates his spirit, and takes the forms of clouds, light, and wind. Taliesin prophesies that the 'ancient race' of Britain will be 'Driv'n from their fathers' realm, to make the rocks their dwelling-place'. But they will not be entirely annihilated: 'long as Arvon's Mountains shall lift their sovereign forms, / And wear the crown to which is given dominion o'er the storms, / So long, their empire sharing, shall live the lofty tongue, / To which the harp of Mona's woods by Freedom's hand was strung' (*Welsh Melodies*, 1st Number, p. 37). Whereas Cader-Idris and Snowdon provide inspiration to those who recline or sleep on their summits, Arvon's mountains are associated with ancient Britain's linguistic survival. According to the bards, all Welsh culture has its basis in natural sites: the harp to which 'Freedom's hand' strings Wales's language is located in 'Mona's woods'. The poem also links 'the lofty tongue' of Wales to freedom, which suggests that its continued use will guarantee a degree of cultural autonomy for the remnants of the 'ancient race'. Unlike the Welsh Druid of 'The Lament of the Last Druid', who mourns the extinction of his order by the Romans in 58 AD and the disappearance of 'the lore sublime, / The secrets of primæval Time' (*Welsh Melodies*, 2nd Number, p. 34), the prophetic Taleisin transcends his historical period. Hemans, as one of his poetic successors, repeats and praises the accuracy of his vision. Moreover, his bardic dedication to truth enables him to disregard any cultural and national prejudices he may have and make a pessimistic prediction regarding the fate of his people.

Welsh nationalism is, however, featured in some of the *Welsh Melodies*, most notably in 'The War Song of Owain Glyndwr'. Since Owain Glyndwr

Illustration of Owain Glyndwr, 1.387.b. Reproduced by permission of the British Library.

was born in the 1350s and died around 1415,[36] his career comes long after Taleisin's time (the sixth century AD). As R. R. Davies points out, Glyndwr 'drew on a mythology which was ancient and British; but he, or his advisers, framed their vision in terms which were distinctly Welsh – not the recovery of the crown of London nor the restoration of a single Britain, but the creation of an independent Wales, politically, ecclesiastically, culturally, and educationally'.[37] Hemans's poem is heavily influenced by Thomas Pennant's account in *Tours in Wales* (1778–81), which she paraphrases in footnotes. Pennant emphasises Glyndwr's use of omens and divination and his association of himself with the legendary King Uther Pendragon (*Welsh Melodies*, 1st Number, p. 38). The engraved illustration of 'The War Song of Owain Glyndwr' on the title page of *Welsh Melodies* (1st Number) depicts Glyndwr standing bard-like on a rocky cliff at the centre, gesturing to the comet which inspired the Welsh rebels in 1402. A harp lies propped up on a boulder near his feet; a structure reminiscent of Stonehenge stands to the left of the engraving, below which are the amazed rebels, including a bard playing his harp (see illustration). In 'War Song' he uses the prophecies handed down by 'the seers / And Monarch-bards of elder years, / Who walk'd on earth, as powers', specifically the visions of Merlin (Merddin Emrys), to encourage his adherents to battle the 'Saxon'. Of course Glyndwr is not himself a 'Monarch-bard', and his invocation of them can be seen as a political ruse; as Hemans notes, Glyndwr 'applied' the 'ancient prophecies' of Merlin and others 'to his own cause, and [they] assisted him greatly in animating the spirit of his followers' (*Welsh Melodies*, 1st Number, p. 38 n.).

Glyndwr's patriotism is not, however, inconsistent with the bardic ideology presented in Hemans's writings. 'In the Meeting of the Bards' she identifies 'patriot-feeling' as a sentiment shared by both ancient and modern bards, and in a note to 'The Monarchy of Britain' (or 'Sons of the Fair Isle!') Hemans alludes to a patriotic poem that bards traditionally sang to 'the ancient Welsh Princes': 'The Bard of the Palace... always accompanied the army when it marched into an enemy's country; and, while it was preparing for battle, or dividing the spoils, he performed an ancient song, called *Unbennaeth Prydain*, the monarchy of Britain. It has been conjectured that this poem referred to the tradition of the Welsh, that the whole Island had once been possessed by their ancestors, who were driven into a corner of it by the Saxon invaders' (*Welsh Melodies*, 1st Number, p. 30). Along with truth, peace and a belief in the inspirational power of nature, love for one's country is a bardic virtue. In its noblest form, it represents loyalty, courage and respect for the heroic dead.

Patriotism is not, of course, usually considered a cosmopolitan trait. But as Lootens observes, 'Hemans was deeply committed to a form of Enlightenment thinking that envisioned the glory of nationalism as international... She thus won fame not only as a poet of English patriotism but also as the author of "The Landing of the Pilgrim Fathers"..., and she glorified the courage both of Crusaders and of their Arab opponents'.[38] Moreover, she admired the patriotic fervour of both England's soldiers and their staunchest opponents: Owain Glyndwr and William Wallace.[39] Perhaps the most Anglophobic poem in *Welsh Melodies* is 'Chant of the Bards Before their Massacre by Edward I', in which the defiant bards invite 'the death-stroke' from the barbaric English so 'The children of song may not languish in chains' (1st Number, p. 60).[40] While patriotism is not a cosmopolitan attribute, respect for the patriotism of other nationalities can be. Hemans's commitment to international nationalism helps to explain how she can write both jingoistic poems praising England's military victories and sympathetic portrayals of England's enemies without perceiving a contradiction. And her cosmopolitanism also manifests itself in her respect for cultural artifacts of foreign nations: in *Modern Greece*, for example, she declares that the Elgin marbles have the power to inspire a 'British Angelo'.[41]

Clearly, Hemans's bardic ideology, which incorporates transcultural values, a semi-mystical reverence for nature, and a respect for patriotism, has little in common with Byron's morally relative and culturally hybrid cosmopolitanism. By the 1820s Hemans's verse had become much more popular among English readers than Byron's, and her poem to Byron, 'The Lost Pleiad' (1825), reflects on the famous exile's inability to connect with his native culture during the last years of his life. As Jerome McGann notes, Hemans wrote 'The Lost Pleiad' in 1823, the year before the poet died. Thus 'the poem isn't an elegy for his death but an elegiac meditation on the meaning of his life, and specifically on the diminishment his fame underwent in the last few years of his life'.[42] In 'The Lost Pleiad' Hemans compares Byron to Merope, whose star faded because she married a mortal. She takes the epigraph to the poem, 'Like the lost Pleiad seen no more below', from Byron's *Beppo* (1818; line 112), a product of his Italian acculturation. The Byronic narrator of *Beppo* presents himself as 'A broken Dandy lately on [his] travels' (line 410) and is humorously tolerant of the Italian custom of allowing married women to commit adultery with a 'Cavalier Servente' (line 285). Hemans's use of this quotation links the cultural relativism of *Beppo* to the dramatic decline in Byron's popularity as a poet. He is, like Merope, 'exil'd' ('The Lost Pleiad', line 8) and 'unmark'd' (line 2), and no one mourns his disappearance: 'They rise in joy, the starry myriads burning – / The shepherd greets them on his mountains free; / And from the silvery sea / To them the sailor's watchful eye is turning – / Unchang'd they rise, they have not mourn'd for thee' (lines 11–15).[43] Although the ancient bards are cosmopolitan in some ways, they retain their traditional values and 'patriot-feelings'. In contrast, Byron seems to Hemans to be estranged from his country and his bardic inheritance, and this estrangement may explain his loss of fame. His star may once have been 'peopled by some glorious race', but if this race once existed they are now no more; perhaps they were smitten 'with decay' (lines 19–20). 'The Lost Pleiad' is a cautionary poem, a warning to Hemans's contemporary bards not to follow Byron's example: 'Bow'd be our hearts to think of what *we* are, / When from its height afar / A world sinks thus – and yon majestic heaven / Shines not the less for that one vanish'd star!' (lines 21–5). Her writings suggest that it would be far better to model oneself after the ancient bards who 'are free throughout the world', who gather 'in the face of the sun, and in the eye of light', who follow their bardic principles, and who base their identity on natural sites and their heroic ancestors. The Welsh harp, Hemans vows in 'The Harp of Wales: Introductory Stanzas, Inscribed to the Ruthin Welsh Literary Society', will never be silenced: 'power was *thine* – a gift in every chord! / Call back that spirit to the days of peace, / Thou noble harp! thy tones are not to cease!'[44]

CHAPTER 12

Luttrell of Arran *and the Romantic invention of Ireland*

Malcolm Kelsall

There are two references to Charles Lever in Declan Kiberd's *Inventing Ireland* (1995), one to 'bad stage Irish melodrama' and the other to 'the ironies of master-servant relationship'. Cairns and Richards passed him by in *Writing Ireland* (1998) and Seamus Deane in *Strange Country* (1997). The notorious dismissive conjunction 'Lever and Lover' remains as effective for modern post-colonialism as it did for Romantic nationalism. Yet Lever is a novelist who is the direct heir of Edgeworth and Scott, who was seen by his contemporaries as a social critic comparable with Dickens and Trollope, and, as a regional novelist, he foreshadows the Romantic pessimism of Hardy. As an historical phenomenon his prolific output constitutes a massive cultural presence. His omission from cultural history is a speaking absence.

The importance of *Luttrell of Arran* (1865), at least, was recognised by W. J. McCormack in *Ascendancy and Tradition* (1985), and, thus, Lever's place in a 'tradition' of Burkean Romanticism (interpreted from the retrospective viewpoint of Yeats). But McCormack's context leads him ultimately to fit *Luttrell of Arran* into a proto-Yeatsian pattern of 'Ascendancy' landlordism and Gaelic peasantry, and he interprets the novel as an allegory of 'ascendancy culpability'. Terry Eagleton subsequently, in *Crazy John and the Bishop* (1998), merely imbricates *Luttrell of Arran* in a pattern of cultural emigration (previously analysed by Deane, and Daniel Corkery before him) in which the Irish exile 'remains at home but in a state of deep disaffection from it'. Lever is (conventionally) smacked on the wrist for his 'geniality'.[1]

Although Bareham, Kreilkamp and Jeffares, among others, have begun a re-evaluative process, it is from the margins of Irish cultural studies, and, in a short essay, there is no room here to reconstitute the historical significance of Lever.[2] There is a prima facie case, however, to read one novel, *Luttrell of Arran*, with the intrinsic respect one would extend to any other substantive work of art, without apologetics, and in a context not dominated by nationalist tradition and its post-colonialist legacy. Within the remit of the current collection of essays, the rootedness of the novel in an originary Burkean Romantic conservatism may be taken (post McCormack) as self-evident (although the Burkean elements are more complex and polysemous than McCormack's thesis permits). Equally, the Romantic Unionist regionalism of Scott may be presumed (post Lukács). Luttrell himself is a Byronic figure, or, rather, the Byronic revolutionary as he might have been if he had survived to a disenchanted old age; and the novel's heroine, Kate Luttrell, acquires, in the conclusion, Wordsworthian associations.

But specific Romantic affinities are not the main concern of this essay. The two dominant romantic themes of the novel are so widely diffused in literature in English (and in European culture post Fichte and Herder) that source and allusion criticism would lose the wood for the trees. *Luttrell of Arran* is concerned with two fundamental Romantic subjects: land and folk. But land and folk here are interpreted in a Romantic context which (as far as Lever is concerned) antedates that invention which may be subsumed in the (albeit amorphous) generalisation 'Irish Romantic nationalism'. The novel is set (in substantial measure) in what became one of the sacred places of the Gaelic nation. If anywhere in Ireland had been untouched by the corrupting influence of the 'Saxon' it was the Aran Islands, that last refuge of the undefiled 'Celt'. This was the racial heartland which nourished (or starved), in uncontaminated poverty, the racially pure *Volk*, whose very poverty, sufferings and heroic powers of resistance symbolised the inextinguishable flame of nationhood. The high-water mark of that myth might date from Yeats's demand to Synge in the 1890s that he visit the islands to express a life never expressed before, and Flaherty's elegiac reconstruction in the 1930s of a life now lost. It is a tradition still preserved by writers like Declan Kiberd, and has been savaged by Martin McDonagh.[3]

Luttrell of Arran indicates the lateness of this idealisation of the *Heimat*. Lever's heroine, Kitty O'Hara/Kate Luttrell, having chosen the islands as her home, antedated Synge by about forty years when she wrote an account of the unexpressed life she found there. But her London publisher (in the novel) rejects her manuscript as being of no interest to Victorian society, and although Kitty is a lover of her native land, the thought of an Irish publisher never crossed her mind. Although one of the major topoi of the emergent Romantic nation is central to Lever's novel, it is, as yet, without nationalist signification.

Kitty herself is a yet more important signifier in the invention of 'Ireland'. She is rechristened Kate Luttrell of Arran, replacing the original Byronic Luttrell of the novel's title. She becomes, symbolically, the embodiment of the *Volk* and the Gaelic *Heimat*. She is, thus, a proto Cathleen Ni Houlihan waiting in the wings of history for her cue, but not yet the creature of Irish nationalism.

The novel, accordingly, stands in an extraordinary position to the cultural history of nationalism in Ireland. Two crucial signifiers are present in the choice of the place and the protagonist, but they are rooted in a different symbolic order. That the novel is symbolic, there can be little reasonable doubt. By 1865 Lever had mastered the late Dickensian mode. His notorious carelessness in constructing his melodramatic plots may be the product of inartistic haste, but may equally show his lack of interest in the conventions of the 'well-made' novel. Mere plot can resolve nothing in the political problems with which he is concerned. Accordingly, the story line of *Luttrell of Arran* is scarcely worth the summary, although so little is known of Lever, that some indication is necessary.

Conventionally Lever uses two 'stage Englishmen' to introduce Ireland to the reader, one, Sir Gervaise Vyner, representing old blood; the other, George Grenfell, being a scion of new money. Their Romantically 'picturesque' tour to the west brings them into contact with two branches of the same family. Inishmore, in the Aran Islands, has become the retreat of 'Luttrell of Arran', a former United Irishman and aristocratic revolutionary. Disappointed in his sanguine (become sanguinary) hopes of the French Revolution, he has withdrawn into an ultra-Byronic (or Manganesque) misanthropy to his desert island. He has an only son, Harry (a good English name) who, early in the story, excited by the prospect of freedom in the New World, disappears in pursuit of adventure overseas (Byron redivivus in post-Jeffersonian America). The main narrative, now, concerns another branch of the family, the 'Irish cousin' (to adopt a phrase from Somerville and Ross), Kitty O'Hara, the daughter of a physical-force Fenian clan on the mainland. The well-trained reader of nineteenth-century fiction will expect that (some hundreds of pages later) Kitty and Harry will marry, and they do. But the long-frustrated courtship with which the novel is primarily concerned is not this, but one between Kitty and old Sir Within Wardle, an aristocrat of the old school, whose ambitious ward Kitty becomes at his castle in Wales. It is a January and May tale of 'great expectations' disappointed. When the unnatural marriage does not take place, Kitty returns to her uncle on Inishmore (on the way surviving an attempted rape by means of a false marriage to a villainous Englishman, Adolphus Laderelle, who is aided by a corrupt Fenian, Tim O'Rorke). Old Luttrell dies; Kitty is about to accompany her grandfather, who is being transported to Australia for killing a sheriff's officer in a fight over repossession; but her grandfather dies also. Young Luttrell has returned to inherit his impoverished patrimony, and, in the last pages of the novel, Harry and Kitty contrive the expected 'happy' ending.

Lever had long-since moved beyond being a writer of picaresque fiction. Even in banal summary it is apparent that this is a polysemous novel, divided between the generations: the old, dying world of Burkean conservatism and Byronic revolt on the one hand, and, on the other, a new world struggling to define selfhood and place. It is divided also between classes (the old aristocracy and the labouring poor) and between ideologies (English improvement – by Vyner – of the agricultural order or terrorist violence). Inevitably, also, it is divided between 'England' and 'Ireland' as different landscapes, histories and points of view. It is, ultimately, a darkly pessimistic fiction. The marriage between Kitty and Harry suggests some sort of protoYeatsian resolution for the dilemmas of the Irish situation in the marriage of old, aristocratic blood with improved peasant stock, but the very haste of the ending suggests little confidence. The best the new order will be able to do is to marginally alleviate poverty, ignorance and its concomitant violence.

Perhaps it is Lever's pessimism about the future condition of Ireland which nationalist sentiment found difficult to accept. But, in that respect, he is in good company. Synge's portrayal of the cult of violence in the west also proved offensive. Likewise, O'Casey's satires on the ideology of physical-force nationalism made him persona non grata. Similarly, Lever does not offer the nostrum 'kill the Saxon' as the simple solution to the problems of Ireland. But that violent 'remedy' is not suppressed. On the contrary. Kitty is a member of a Fenian sept, and the nascent IRA (in the person of O'Rorke) presents to the reader an anti 'colonial' doctrine as hard-line as any nationalist might wish:

'Liberty, first of all, darling,' said he . . . 'tis the birthright of the man as he steps on his native earth; 'tis the first whisper of the human heart, whether in the frozen regions of eternal snow, or the sun-scorched plains of the tropic. 'Tis for sacred liberty our fathers fought for seven centuries, and we'll fight seven more.

> Erin go Bragh is a nation's cry
> 'Tis millions that sing it in chorus,
> And to that tune, before we die,
> We'll chase the Saxon before us.'
> (pp. 339–40)[4]

O'Rorke is given extensive opportunity to express his opinions in the novel and the poverty of the people provides ample material justification for him. (Symbolically, he lives at a spot called 'Vinegar Hill', the site of the rebels' defeat in the rising of 1798.) But any reader attuned to the discourse of O'Casey nowadays will pick up the windy rhetoric of O'Rorke. It is presented by Lever as the mindless mantra of old-style Jacobinism, now yoked to racial hatred. It is also a cloak for criminality. What O'Rorke knows is that patriotism is the last refuge of the scoundrel. You can make money by violence. In the symbolic order of the novel, O'Rorke's participation (for gain) with an Englishman in the attempted rape of Kitty is a signifier that physical-force Fenianism is an act of violence perpetrated on the body of the very nation which the patriot claims to liberate. It is no wonder, therefore, that the generation of Collins and Pearse would not read Lever. No gunman wanted to be told that he was raping his own country.

But how do you express the homeland; how embody it in a unificatory symbol? It might seem numinously vague to state that it is, in this novel, a landscape and the body of a woman. But the definition of the *Heimat* in terms of the native soil, and the symbolisation of that nurturing earth in the person of a woman, have been standard elements in the invention of the Romantic nation. It would be redundant to multiply examples. But Lever's characters, and the novelist himself, are exploring something inchoate and recalcitrant within what is, in the abstract, a conventional Romantic topos. Although the stage Englishman, Vyner, who opens the novel, is wrong about 'Ireland' (stage Englishmen always are) yet his perspective on the landscape is culturally mainstream. His visionary outlook is shaped by an Anglocentric picturesque Romanticism (as it were, he expects to find a Wordsworthian Lake District) and underpinned by sound Whig/liberal economic principles (his purpose is to buy an estate and 'improve' both the tenants and the landscape).

What a glowing picture of a country he drew; what happiness, what peace, what prosperity. It was Arcadia, with a little more rain and a police force. There was no disturbance, no scarcity, very little sickness, religious differences were unknown, a universal brotherhood bound man to man, and imparted to the success of each all the sentiment of a general triumph. (p. 78)

Unlike O'Rorke's rhetoric (to which some nationalist bosoms may still return an echo) no one is likely to believe Vyner's vision of Ireland. But if the sceptical reader is expected to be wiser than Vyner, what does it tell one of the condition of Ireland that one should instantly scoff at words like 'peace', 'prosperity', 'brotherhood' (*Alle Menschen werden Brüder*), or the idea that there might be an end to religious division? If this is 'English' romanticism (Vyner's function in the novel) it is an idealistic vision not to be summarily dismissed as 'unIrish'.

More complex than this simple satire of good intentions is the long passage describing the landscape which Vyner desires to buy. He awakens one morning to see for the first time his potential demesne:

As he opened his eyes, the view that met them startled him. It was one of those vast stretches of landscape which painters cannot convey. They are too wide, too boundless for picture. The plain which lay outstretched before him, rising and falling like a vast prairie, was unmarked by habitation – not a hovel, not a hut to be seen. Vast groups of rocks stood out here and there abruptly, grotesque and strange in outline, as though giants had been petrified in the act of some great conflict, the stunted trees that crowned the summits serving as feathers on the helmets. A great amphitheatre of mountain girded the plain, save at one spot, the gap of Glenvallah, through which, as his map told him, his road on that morning lay. (p. 84)

This might be a passage from Scott or Fenimore Cooper. It is, accordingly, not mere description, but emblematic. What is described is, paradoxically, beyond representation. It has escaped the bounds of picturesque English Romanticism and the boundary of any form of human civilisation. It is even beyond the compass of the English language. It is a vast 'prairie' which Vyner sees before him. Thus, Ireland has become the yet unexplored terrain of North America. It is not a merely casual comparison, for the parallel between the American and the Irish wilderness is a thematic preoccupation of the early chapters of the English journey to the west. Vyner and Grenfell have already compared the natives with the hostile Sioux (p. 13), a motif taken up in the first description of Harry Luttrell who first boards Vyner's (aptly named) yacht, 'The Meteor,' in the manner, and with the appropriate weapon of an Indian (pp. 25–6). This is a wild west beyond the reach of the law, for here there can be no leases nor landlords (p. 87), and where any attempt to collect the landlord's rent will leave his 'scalp' dangling at the waist of the war-painted savage (pp. 32, 92). Like the North American colonist, on the frontier of civilisation, Vyner has equipped himself with a 'map' (the product of the Unionist Ordnance Survey?), but the map (with its claim to scientific order) is at odds with the imaginative impact of the land. For what Vyner's imagination perceives is an area of cataclysmic and primordial struggle, 'as though giants had been petrified in the act of some great conflict'. From time immemorial (O'Rorke's seven centuries are not long enough) this land has been the site of destructive warfare, now petrified as natural. It is not surprising that Vyner's imagination works in this way. The place where he has been residing is O'Rorke's dwelling at 'Vinegar Hill'. His host is an unreconstructed Fenian. The place from whence the Englishman has come is Inishmore, where he had found an 'iron-bound shore' and 'semi-savage natives'. He is at the very frontier of European civilisation. The message he received from Luttrell on Inishmore was to 'go back and build model cottages in Norfolk' for, in Indian territory, 'all the privilege your purchase will confer, will be to feed us in times of famine, and be shot at when prices rise' (p. 45). The primordial violence of Ireland makes it a land uncontainable either by Vyner's English picturesque aesthetic or his liberal ethic.

It would be easy at this juncture to apply the discourse of post-colonialism to the novel. Here, as usual, is Ireland as a 'colony' and the English as misguided colonists. But that would be a merely procrustean reading. What the text is doing in pairing O'Rorke and Vyner in a common satire is to foreclose the two major historical alternatives seeking to make 'Ireland' at this time: the Jacobinical, racialist violence of O'Rorke (kill 'Saxons' and liberate 'the Gael') and the liberal policies of improvement and concession expressed by Vyner's dream of an Arcadian estate. Both end in a form of Burkean 'Terror': in O'Rorke's case, the revolutionary violence of the rapist, and, with Vyner, an image of the 'Sublime' landscape where aesthetic Terror is expressive of immemorial and intractable historical violence.

For Lever, what is intractable in Ireland (the social reality behind the symbolic structures) is, quite simply, poverty: the enormous gap between the rich and the poor. Lever is at one with his contemporary Disraeli, there are two nations. But, in Ireland, the fundamental social problem (common throughout the Union) is aggravated by race and language. In a rare passage *in propria persona* Lever unites his conservative, one-nation, theme with the racial issue:

'One half the world knows not how the other half lives,' says the adage; and there is a peculiar force in the maxim when applied to certain remote and little-visited districts in these islands, where the people are about as unknown to us as though they inhabited some lonely rock in the South Pacific.

While the great world, not very far off, busies itself with all the appliances of state and science... these poor creatures drag on an existence rather beneath than above the habits of savage life. Their dwellings, their food, their clothes, such as generations of their fathers possessed; and neither in their culture, their aspirations, nor their ways, advanced beyond what centuries back had seen them.

Of that group of islands off the north-west coast of Ireland called the Arrans, Innishmore is a striking instance of this neglect and desolation. Probably within the wide sweep of the British islands there could not be found a spot more irretrievably given up to poverty and barbarism. Some circular mud hovels, shaped like beehives, and with a central aperture for the escape of the smoke, are the dwellings of an almost naked, famine-stricken people, whose looks, language, and gestures mark them out for foreigners if they chance to come over to the mainland.

This passage opens the novel. Nothing could be further from the kind of signification which Romantic nationalism attached to the Gaeltacht. On the contrary, the 'us' with whom Lever identifies his text are the inhabitants of the 'great world' of 'the British islands'. We are the people of a great state, for whom the appliance of science is a sign of civilisation. In contradistinction, the 'foreigners' of the Aran islands belong to the world of 'barbarism' sunk beneath 'the habits of savage life'. When Lever compares the islanders with the inhabitants of 'some lonely rock in the South Pacific', he is not seeing the islanders as the oppressed people of an alien, evil empire, but, rather, as being so remote from our knowledge that even our science is unaware of them. Rather than their culture being a national treasure suppressed by colonialism (the nationalist position), it is historically regressive. Where civilisation has touched these people, it has died. This is shown later in the novel in the derelict Abbey of Inishmore (Luttrell's home). Here the detritus of Gaelic culture is represented by a kind of Jeffersonian Indian Hall, or museum of relics that the misanthropic United Irishman has shored against his ruins. What use are these signifiers, 'the ghost of a civilisation long dead and buried' (p. 298) among a 'famine-stricken people'?

This is an utterly bleak and pessimistically conceived post-famine symbolic landscape. A reader of Carleton or Synge might challenge Lever on matters of sociological detail in this 'wrong end of the telescope' view of things, but sociological accuracy is not the issue. This landscape is 'famine-stricken' both literally and spiritually. It lacks the aliment of civilisation. But whence might such aliment come? The liberal English Romantic, Vyner, rightly learns that capital investment here is impractical. There are no model capitalists in Lever such as Disraeli offers in the persons of Millbank or Trafford, whose progressive industrial estates revitalise the social welfare of the old, ideal feudal order. As for the popular, nationalist, alternative to capitalism – Irishmen shooting Englishmen – that leaves nineteenth-century Ireland in the Dark Ages of inter-tribal warfare.

Lever had no final solution to the Irish problem. But had anyone else in the nineteenth century? At least he had the honesty to be pessimistic. Spiritually he belongs with those late Romantics of what Shelley called (in the preface to *The Revolt of Islam*) 'the age of despair' which followed the Enlightened dream in the bloody realities of the revolutionary wars of the Napoleonic era. In Ireland, the aftermath of that despair, Lever suggests, lasted longer (it is embodied in the dying United Irishman, Luttrell). If there is a way out of the negativity of this despair, it is by way of a kind of spiritual regeneration of the people. In that respect, he belongs with 'young Ireland' although, given his conservatism and his affinities with Disraeli, one might claim him rather as a 'Young Briton'. What kind of symbolic ideal might embody the spiritual nation? It is a vital question, for the imagination may release the mind from the fury and the mire of recalcitrant reality and offer, at least in Shelleyan mode, some form of symbol of what might be. Or, put another way, in Ireland, metahistory, the way things are perceived, can make real history.

Hence the role of Kitty O'Hara/Kate Luttrell in this fiction. The story of the Irishwoman's relationship with the Englishman, Sir Within Wardle (who keeps her as his ward within his castle) is far more than a psychological romance of January and May, although the psychology of the story is extremely well done. But, at the symbolic level, Lever is reworking one of the perennial myths of Irish history, perhaps best known from Swift's story of the 'injured lady'. 'Ireland' is a vulnerable woman, and 'England' is a powerful, masculine figure who threatens her. Except, in Lever's recension of the myth, Kate, rather than being seduced, desires some form of union with the English Other, and the tale makes clear why this should be so.

The movement of the story from Ireland to 'England' is from wilderness to civilisation, from the ignorance of savagery to sophisticated culture, and from poverty to riches. It is a movement also of temporal recession back to the Burkean idealisation of the ancient social order (what has been called 'the return to Camelot').[5] Once out of the hovel, Kate responds with quickened intelligence and passion to the riches and the splendour of an alien culture. The savage woman (of Fenian blood) is, accordingly, transformed into a queen.

It is not merely that she had grown into a tall and graceful girl, but that one by one the little traits of her peasant origin had faded away, and she looks, and seems, and carries herself with all the air of a high-born beauty. In her lofty brow, her calm features, her manner, in which a quiet dignity blends with a girlish grace, and, above all, in her voice singularly sweet-toned as it was, might be read every sign of that station that men distinctively call the 'best'. (p. 237)

This is a transformation analogous to the more famous metamorphosis of Yeats's Cathleen Ni Houlihan. but, in Lever, what Sir Within Wardle's young ward has chosen is the 'grace' and the 'best' of Burkean civilisation, not Pearsean blood-sacrifice. It is a powerful, transformatory force for good, and, by civilising her, it potentially empowers her. She need only marry Sir Within to become the mistress of all 'the glorious prerogative of wealth, that marvellous power that culls from life, one by one, every attribute that is pleasure-giving, and surrounds daily existence with whatever can charm or beguile', or, in a word, she can enter 'Paradise' (p. 167).

Yet, as the text makes clear, it is a beguilement and a charm. Sir Within Wardle's wonderful castle is like one of Spenser's enchanted palaces. It attracts and yet is full of signs of danger. Although the ancient castle has become a modern country house, and the country house, as Grenfell claims, is 'the best thing we have in England; and, indeed, the best thing the world has anywhere' (p. 403), yet, its origin as a fortress (it is in Wales) is a constant reminder that the roots of this civilisation lie in conquest (Lever, like O'Rorke, has a memory seven centuries long). That conquest now, at least in 'mainland' Britain, is no more than a memory. But the very antiquity of the castle makes it, in some respects, the parallel of Luttrell's old Abbey on Inishmore. Both represent dead (or dying) culture reduced, in Sir Within Wardle's case, to mere 'connoisseurship'. Witness the tour of the castle, by which Kate is 'entranced' (a word which again suggests a quasi-Spenserian allegory).

He showed them his armoury – mailed suits of every time and country, from the rudely shaped corselets of Northern Europe, to the chased and inlaid workmanship of Milan and Seville; and with these were weapons of Eastern fashion, a scimitar whose scabbard was of gold, and a helmet of solid silver amongst them; and, last of all, he introduced them into a small low-ceilinged chamber, with a massive door of iron concealed behind one of oak. This he called his 'Gem-room;' and here were gathered together a variety of beautiful things, ranging from ancient coins and medals to the most costly ornaments in jewellery; jewelled watches, bon-bon boxes of the time of Louis XIV; enamelled miniatures in frames of brilliants of various foreign orders, which, though not at liberty to wear, he treasured as relics of infinite worth. (p. 195)

The suits of armour, and the European and imperial wars they signify, belong to an outmoded culture whose violence is aestheticised (but not concealed) by connoisseurship. It is a culture which cannot cross the frontier to the modernity of the nineteenth century. The reference to 'the time of Louis XIV' places Sir Within as the last remnant of the ancient social order (just as Luttrell is the last remnant of another, Byronic, order in Ireland). The artifacts, which cannot be worn, and the old man showing them are both 'relics'. Indeed, Sir Within, before he dare appear in public, has to be made presentable by cosmetics which apply a simulacrum of youth to the decrepitude of age. To adapt Paine's criticism of Burke (and Sir Within belongs to the golden Versailles of Burke's imagination) we admire the plumage, but perceive the dying bird.

Although, allegorically, Sir Within resembles a kind of Archimago, nonetheless, Lever generates strong sympathy for the old-fashioned po-litesse and wit and taste of the old man, who is deeply affectionate towards

Kate. And Kate herself is deeply attracted by what the old man has to offer, partly because she is selfish (Ireland covets English wealth and culture) but partly also because he wins her affection. This is an extraordinarily rich psychological study, and the more complex the misalliance becomes, the more complex also the resonances of Kate's role.

In a clearly symbolic passage Kate has a proleptic dream which she recounts to Sir Within:

I thought a great queen, who had no child of her own, had adopted me, and said I should be her daughter, and in proof of it she took a beautiful collar from her throat and fastened it on mine. (p. 197)

She has been exploring the treasures of the house. She has been particularly entranced by 'a massive necklace of emeralds and brilliants... labelled, "A present from the Emperor to Marie Antoinette on the birth of the Dauphin."' She sees herself in her dream, accordingly, as a new queen, identifying herself with a woman who was the most hated figure of the *Ancien Régime* in Europe, but also the woman whom Burke had celebrated as the 'morning star' of the age of chivalry. (It is a typical Leverian irony.) Sir Within makes Kate's dream in some measure reality, for he gives her the necklace: '"You see so much is true," said he, pointing to the massive emerald drop that hung upon her neck.' He does not perceive, but the reader of an Irish novel will, that the symbolic emerald is green, the colour of Ireland. The true reading of the dream is that the 'great queen' without a child of her own is Ireland, and the daughter she has adopted is Kate. But this is a vision not yet understood and which may not be fulfilled. For the entranced Kate at this juncture is about to deny her nationality. She will tell Grenfell, '"I have seen next to nothing of Ireland; far too little to have caught up...any traits of her nationality"' (p. 255), and once her nationality has been disowned, the 'unfortunate lady' is ripe for an English misalliance.

That 'union' does not take place. But it is part of the tragedy of the novel that Kate's removal from 'within' the 'ward' ends in 'hate'. The bitterness of her break with her guardian/lover is the nadir of the novel, for, psychologically, Kate comes close to resembling a failed Becky Sharp (an adventuress on the make disappointed of her prey) and (allegorically) it suggests that one reason for Ireland's hatred of England is the inability of the weaker party to screw all that it desires out of the other. She risks falling into a void where she can be neither wife nor daughter to Sir Within (p. 309), and *déracinée* and *déclassée*, she cannot belong in Ireland either. Thus, Lever does not palliate the difficulty of her return to the 'barbarism' and 'savagery' of the Aran Islands, nor the difficulties of her working out of her new role as Luttrell's 'Kate of Arran'. (Can one imagine Oscar Wilde taking root on Inishmore, or even Synge settling down to a life of kelp and curraghs?) Yet, had Kate remained merely the peasant daughter of an alienated Fenian family, although she would have been integrated with the *Volk*, her potential would have been unfulfilled. Her 'English' education within the charmed circle of Burkean chivalry has transfigured her. When she visits her grandfather in prison, the old man's imagination reinterprets her earlier dream of the queen and the emerald necklace:

'Merciful Mother! Blessed Virgin! is it yourself is come to comfort me?' cried he, as he dropped on his knees, while the tears streamed down his hard and wrinkled cheeks. 'Oh, Holy Mother! Tower of Ivory! do I see you there, or is my ould eyes deceivin' me?' (p. 378)

The confusion in the syntax here obviously blends Kate with the queen of heaven, the Virgin Mary. A greater 'queen' even than Ireland has claimed Kate as her own. Perhaps less obvious, but typical of Lever's ironies, is the function of the question: 'or is my ould eyes deceivin' me?' What is dream and what is reality in Irish history? Can a woman like Kate really carry the weight of signification with which her grandfather invests her?

Of course not. But by her return to her people 'from another sphere' (p. 460) she is changed, changed utterly. This is shown partly through the symbolic language of natural description. She learns to love that Irish landscape which had proved so alien and intractable to English eyes earlier in the novel:

The season was the autumn, and the wild hills and mountains were gorgeous in all the brilliant colour of the ever varied heaths. In the little clefts and valleys, too, where shelter favoured, foxgloves and purple mallows grew with rare luxuriance, while on every side was met the arbutus, its crimson berries hanging in festoons over rock and crag. The sudden, unexpected sight of the sea, penetrating by many a fissure, as it were, between the mountains, gave unceasing interest to the wild landscape, and over the pathless moors that she strayed, not a living thing to be seen, was the sense of being the first wayfarer who had ever trod these wastes. (p. 328)

It is these moors now, not an 'English' demesne, which she calls 'Paradise', and, compared with her English dream, a 'real' place (pp. 467 and 323). She has become, as it were, an Irish Dorothy Wordsworth who has found her own 'deep, abiding place', and who is in love with and organically in relationship to actualities and the intimate details of the pathless wilderness. That intimate detail is the aesthetic correlative of her 'real' commitment to her own people, the eternal *Volk*: 'They were there, toiling ever on, no hope of any day of better fortune, no thought of any other rest than the last long sleep of all' (p. 323). But the function of Kate is to alleviate that toil by practical acts of reform: the construction of a schoolhouse so that the next generation may learn like herself; a hospital; an inn to encourage the tourist trade; the purchase of seed potatoes and hemp at competitive prices... All these are little things in relation to 'the Irish problem' addressed by governments and gunmen. But her acts resemble the tiny details of the landscape she learns to love, these tiny acts are targeted at the very essence of the Irish problem (the gross poverty of the people) and Kate knows what the people need, because she is one of them. (She is, as it were, midway between the Wordsworths' 'home at Grasmere' and the coming of *The Irish Homestead*.) Mere dreams? Lever's text certainly raises the question whether Kate is (unfortunately) unique. It was a 'pathless' landscape into which she had strayed, penetrating the 'fissures' of things where no wayfarer had gone before her. If that were not irony enough, this Irish landscape which she has learned to love is seen in an autumn light. If Autumn come, can Winter be far behind?

Lever's subsequent closure of the fiction is hasty, but, as David Lodge pointed out in his own 'two nations' novel, *Nice Work*, nineteenth-century social fiction is frequently merely conventional in its ending (a convention which, in postmodern fashion, he knowingly imitates). So Kate abruptly marries young Harry Luttrell, and the peasantry happily celebrate their ancient lord who has returned to his people and who has united himself with peasant stock (pp. 482–3). *Mutatis mutandis* it is the kind of conventional ideology which one might parallel (following McCormack) in Lever's progenitor Edgeworth or successor Yeats. But, equally conventionally, one might draw parallels with the late Romanticism of 'the return to Camelot' and the marriages across race and class of Disraeli's 'state of England' novels.

But Lever is more complex than mere plot summary may indicate. Both Harry Luttrell (who quit Ireland early in the novel in the company of a republican citizen of the United States of America) and Kate (who has been educated in Romantic chivalry outside Ireland) represent something beyond the great hate in a little room of introverted Irish history. Although both break from the narrow mould of nationalist culture, they are not free from history. Thus Luttrell's name carries with it a dark message, which Lever is at pains to explain: the family crest is a heart rent in two, and the motto *La Lutte réelle*, the struggle is real (p. 155). It is an appropriate motto for a divided Ireland struggling to heal and reinvent itself. On the other hand, the ultimate 'message' of the novel, from the peasant Kate, to the landlord class, which she has joined, might seem unambiguously straight: 'We belong to our people' (p. 471). If Lever had left it like that, one might fairly complain that his conclusion is banal, But the words, in fact, are not Kate's. She cites her source: ' "We belong to our people", as Elizabeth said'. Lever's Cathleen Ni Houlihan quotes a Tudor monarch, and identifies her own role with that of the arch coloniser, Elizabeth! Does Lever here turn a dark irony on the English queen's utterance? Or does he express the ultimate union of England and Ireland in a common historical culture? Which question cannot be answered. Hence *La Lutte réelle* of polysemous history.

CHAPTER 13

Contemporary Northern Irish poets and Romantic poetry

Michael O'Neill

I

One might begin an essay that will sketch a general picture, before looking in more detail at Seamus Heaney's and, to a lesser degree, Derek Mahon's poetry, with James Joyce laying in to 'romanticism' (with a small 'r'): 'in realism you are down to facts on which the world is based: that sudden reality which smashes romanticism into a pulp. What makes most people's lives unhappy is some disappointed romanticism, some unrealizable or mis-conceived ideal.'[1] To the degree that Romantic poetry embodies the pursuit of an 'unrealizable or misconceived ideal', it tends to provoke opposition in contemporary Northern Irish poets, aware, among other things, of the political havoc caused by abstract idealism. John Montague, for instance, forcing himself in 'Tim' to 'drink / from the trough of reality', declares in *The Rough Field* that 'No Wordsworthian dream enchants me here / With glint of glacial corrie, totemic mountain'.[2] Still, Romantic poetry, as inau-gurated by *Lyrical Ballads*, itself seeks to 'choose incidents and situations from common life', albeit with a 'certain colouring of imagination', and by means of 'a selection of language really used by men'.[3] Moreover, who is more alert to the way the 'ideals' may be 'misconceived' than poets such as Keats and Shelley? With some justice, Aidan Day contends that *Alastor* can be read as 'a demonstration of the solipsistic emptiness of an inward-looking spiritual orientation', even if it is the case that Shelley has an 'inward' sympathy with the Poet's need to image 'to himself the Being whom he loves'.[4]

The capacity of Romantic poetry to enact and criticise longing and desire is part of its fascinating doubleness: as a movement that implies art is at once autonomous and shaped by historical circumstance, that licenses transcendental questing while valuing the meanest flower that blows, and that gives a new status to the self even as it frequently investigates the self's relationship with society, Romanticism affords subsequent poets an important model. To adapt Basil Bunting on Pound's *Cantos*, the Romantic poets are like the Alps and take some getting round.[5] Northern Irish poets, in particular, have found it valuable to wrestle with the angel of Romantic poetry. They may rebel against the apparent bardic self-importance of a Wordsworth, but the ancestral features are observable in the younger faces. Tom Paulin, for instance, shares something of the early Auden's scepticism about the political meanings of Romantic individualism ('"Lord Byron at the head of his storm-troopers!"'), and he is happy to endorse Hazlitt's adverse judgements on Shelley and Coleridge.[6] Yet the close of 'Inishkeel Parish Church' compresses into itself a Romantic-influenced glimpse of freedom, 'an enormous sight of the sea, / A silent water beyond society'.[7] If Larkin, with his 'enormous yes' or his undeceived gaze through high windows, is more immediately to the fore here, Shelley's Julian (in *Julian and Maddalo*), a lover of 'waste / And solitary places' (*SPP*, lines 14–15), is in the background, as is Wordsworth's 'Immortality Ode', with its rollingly expansive metaphor of the 'immortal sea' (166) discerned by the soul 'in a season of calm weather' (164).[8]

Again, for all the resistance quoted above, Montague's *The Rough Field* shows the lure of Wordsworthian impulses and poetic practices as it drama-tises and enacts circlings, leadings-on and near returns. As Robert F. Garratt argues, 'Montague protests too much'. Garratt goes on to point out how '[r]eferences to a Wordsworthian preoccupation with memory, with childhood experiences, and with the role of the imagination are sprin-kled throughout various sections of *The Rough Field*'.[9] However, it is note-worthy that Montague's phrasing in the lines quoted above echoes, not Wordsworth, but Yeats: the Yeats who in a gesture of disenchantment with dream asserts in 'The Circus Animals' Desertion', 'It was the dream it-self enchanted me'.[10] In an act of simultaneous repression and evocation, Montague repudiates Wordsworth but brings to light the hold over his imagination of Yeats's phrasing, and replays his great if problematic Irish forebear's drama of self-reflexive poetic 'enchantment', a drama that has its origins, in turn, in Yeats's complex debt to the Romantic tradition.[11]

In the uses made by contemporary Northern Irish poets of the Roman-tic inheritance, Romanticism's own splits and divisions are multiplied and refracted. A tension at the heart of Romanticism concerns the role of imag-inative 'colouring', to borrow Wordsworth's word, already quoted. The idea of a 'plain sense of things', in Wallace Stevens's phrase, is, ultimately, a notion impossible to divorce from a Romantic context. In 'The Plain Sense of Things', Stevens offers a post-Romantic elegy for High Romanti-cism ('The great structure has become a minor house'), but he implies the continuing relevance of the Romantic through his insistence that the 'absence of imagination had / Itself to be imagined'. Earlier poems by Stevens such as 'Tea at the Palaz of Hoon' and 'The Snow Man' are opposite sides of a coin minted by Wordsworth and Coleridge, most prodigally in their lyric exchanges of 1802. 'Tea at the Palaz of Hoon' affirms an inventive scenario in, and as a result of, which 'I was myself the compass of that sea'. 'The Snow Man' seeks to imagine 'Nothing that is not there and the nothing that is'.[12] In his recent selected poems, Heaney sets side by side his own equivalents to these poems: 'Thatcher', in which the thatcher, a surrogate for, as well as anti-self of, the poet, leaves onlookers 'gaping at his Midas touch', and 'The Peninsula', a poem of emptied vision, which begins, 'When you have nothing more to say', and ends with a glimpse of 'things founded clean on their own shapes'.[13] This latter vision may seem the opposite of Romantic imaginings; but if it is an opposite, it is one brought into being by a dialectical turn against Romanticism.

In fact, the Romantics often prize otherness, discovered in the wrestle for primacy between language and experience. Even Shelley, aware of the mind's propensity to project feeling, begins his lyric cry of dejection with delighted, if strangely emotionless, notations of the external: 'I see the waves upon the shore / Like light dissolved in star-showers, thrown' ('Stanzas Written in Dejection', lines 12–13). There, Shelley mimes an uninvolved seeing, but he betrays his imaginative involvement with the scene through a simile that expresses a yearning for a vision of connectedness. That kind of dramatic struggle stiffens the linguistic sinews of Romantic poetry, and it reappears in the work of Seamus Heaney, who moves towards a poetry that (as Heaney describes Blake's practice in 'The Secret Rose') offers 'an open invitation into its meaning rather than an assertion of it'.[14]

In 'Glanmore Sonnets', Heaney echoes Wordsworth's *The Prelude* at the start of the second sonnet:

> Sensings, mountings from the hiding places,
> Words entering almost the sense of touch,
> Ferreting themselves out of their dark hutch . . .

The lines plait references to Books I and XI of *The Prelude* (quoted from the 1805 version): Book I's 'Trances of thought and mountings of the mind' (line 20) and Book XI's 'hiding-places of my power' (line 335).[15] Both Wordsworthian passages deal with inspiration, and Heaney's poem follows suit, celebrating his own imaginative 'mountings from the hiding places'. But if Wordsworthian 'sense' uses empirical perception as the springboard for visionary intuition – of, for example, 'unknown modes of being'

(*The Prelude*, 1. 420) –, Heaney's 'sensings' combine the physical and imaginative. His words enter 'almost the sense of touch', a reclamation of the sensuous that is forcibly corroborated by the third line's image of words 'Ferreting themselves out of their dark hutch'. In a further twist, however, 'Ferreting themselves' combines the startlingly literal (the words turn into ferrets) and the intellectually metaphorical (the words tug into existence a new sense of their own workings), a twist that shows how false it is to simplify Heaney solely into a celebrant of the physical. A Wordsworthian connection, in all its complexity, is proudly trumpeted here. In the sequence's third sonnet, however, Heaney turns self-consciously on such dreams of literary affinity, puncturing a faltering comparison between himself and his wife and 'Dorothy and William' as his wife 'interrupts: / "You're not going to compare us two…?" '

One might generalise from the interplay between these two sonnets and argue that the longing for Romantic authority pervades Heaney's work, as does the ironic opposition to that longing. Other poets intensify such opposition. Paul Muldoon's *Madoc* (1990) plays beguiling games with Coleridge's and Southey's Pantisocratic dreams. In one poem, for instance, he invokes Lacan as the presiding philosophical spirit in a conjuring up and dismissal of Coleridge's 'The Eolian Harp': 'The wraith pokes its tongue in Southey's ear – / "Rhythm in all thought, and joyance everywhere" – / before leaving only a singe on the air'. In keeping with Muldoon's two-faced ironies, the Coleridgean affirmation at once mocks Southey and is, in turn, subjected to mockery. A few pages later in '[*Quine*]', as if to deflate the poetic inspiration figured in the Romantic poem, Muldoon grants his Coleridge – on the day of his death – only a vision of 'scrub / and salt-flats' in conjunction with 'A tinkle on an Aeolian harp'. This 'tinkle' introduces a relationship with the natural that is hardly numinous:

> July 25th, 1834. A tinkle on an Aeolian harp
> across the scrub
> and salt-flats.
>
> Coleridge props himself up under a canopy of gnats
> and returns their call to a pair of chickadees;
> 'Quiddities. Quiddities. Quiddities.'[16]

The repetition of 'Quiddities' in this bathetic context annuls its sense; any Aristotelean respect for reality it conveys is ironised by Muldoon's elegant incongruities of phrasing and rhyme.

Irony is often, in fact, a feature of Northern Irish poetry's relationship with Romanticism. Given historical differences and cultural dissonance, it could scarcely be absent. But pinpointing irony's presence and activity can be difficult. Ciaran Carson interweaves phrases from Keats's 'Ode to a Nightingale' in 'The Irish for No'.[17] Here Carson sets sectarian atrocities against Keatsian sensuous luxuriance, and shows an alertness to the resulting cultural (and physical) 'Mish-mash. Hotch-potch'. Neil Corcoran finally reads the Keatsian echoes as bound up with allusions to Heaney in such a way as to discredit both poets: 'in the dark of contemporary social and political attrition', Corcoran writes, 'Carson finds Heaney's poetic of late Romantic expansiveness wanting'. It is a seemingly plausible reading in the light of passages such as the following:

> The stars clustered thick as blackberries. They opened
> the door into the dark.
> *The murmurous haunt of flies on summer eves.* Empty
> jam-jars.
> Mish-mash. Hotch-potch.

Early Heaney ('Blackberry-Picking' and 'Door into the Dark') is at once evoked and squashed here. Yet whether Heaney himself uncomplicatedly espouses a 'poetic of late Romantic expansiveness' in, say, 'Blackberry-Picking' is questionable; that poem faces up to the processes of rotting and souring clear-sightedly held at bay in, for example, Keats's 'To Autumn'. Corcoran is, in fact, more complexly persuasive when, earlier in his analysis, he argues that Carson's use of Keats's poem works 'almost uninterpretably'. For one thing, to quote the Ode is to recall an ideal of aesthetic finish; to the degree that Carson aims at shaping his lines, such a recollection draws the Belfast poet into artistic complicity with his Romantic forebear. For another, the intertextual play to which such '*bricolage* of reference', as Corcoran describes it, releases Carson's imagination to engage in free, though quietly tense, association.[18]

Carson's poem opens with the question at the close of Keats's 'Ode to a Nightingale': '*Was it a vision, or a waking dream?*' The effect of this quotation, comfortably swallowed in the maw of a long line borrowed from C. K. Williams, is both mocking, since what follows is an overheard quarrel, and a point of entry into Carson's decidedly post-Romantic, postmodern poetic world. Yet his hallucinatory jumble of narrative hints draws a kind of ersatz dignity from the Keatsian affiliation; this affiliation reappears later when we learn that 'The casements / Were wide open' and that 'We were debating, / Bacchus and the pards and me', and when Keats's own doubting but empowering question, '*I cannot see what flowers are at my feet*', is brought into play. Such intertextuality, unresolvable in thematic terms, demands for its understanding a mock-heroic, labile poetics of quotation that allows for the precursor texts to be honoured even as they are being subverted. In this poem the Keatsian quotations bear on, even as they are undone by, the poem's grim allusions to atrocity. Carson's own style has enough commerce with surreal associationism for his initial borrowing of Keats's final question to take on self-reflexive relevance. The Keatsian quotations are not simply juxtaposed with an undercutting demotic idiom; they slide and seep into the new world of the poem, as when Carson writes, 'so the harbour slips away to perilous seas as things remain unsolved'. The poem's own relation with Keatsian Romanticism seems itself to be 'unsolved', to be, in the poem's last words, 'debating whether *yes* is *no*'.[19]

'Debating whether *yes* is *no*' might describe a common and sophisticated response made by Northern Irish poets to the intricate affirmations of Romantic poetry: a kind of post-Romantic irony, adding to Romantic irony's ability to assert and undercut in the name of creative freedom the awareness that any such freedom is caught up in the coils of textual associations. So, at the end of 'A Lighthouse in Maine', Derek Mahon happens on a lighthouse 'shining / In modest glory like // The soul of Adonais'.[20] For the Shelleyan splendour recalled there, Mahon's cunningly down-at-heel three-line stanzas contrive a low-key epiphany. Though 'The soul of Adonais' seems deliberately incongruous, the kind of incongruity that would occur to a literary sensibility, the sense of discovery − as the famous phrase resonates in a line to itself after a stanza break − is strong. Mahon is saying that the lighthouse has as much right to attention as 'The soul of Adonais', even as he complicates any notion of unmediated contact with the object by virtue of his poetic activity. 'Modest glory' may be a diminished version of Shelley's 'white radiance of Eternity' (line 463), but it is present, in the here and now, invoked in a spirit of anti-transcendental commitment to the earthly. As Mahon has said earlier in the poem,

> The north light
> That strikes its frame
>
> Houses is not
> The light of heaven
> But that of this world.

Even here, though, any hint of anti-Romantic polemic checks itself in that last phrase's glancing recollection of 'the very world which is the world / Of all of us, the place in which, in the end, / We find our happiness, or not at all' (*The Prelude*, x. 725–7). Generally, this looking back to and backing off from the Romantics, played out in many poems, illuminates the dilemma and achievement of poets from Northern Ireland. The Shelleyan vision of poets in *A Defence of Poetry* as 'the unacknowledged legislators of the World' (*SPP*, p. 508) may arouse an instinctive defensiveness in these poets, yet they can never wholly abandon this vision in their search for images and rhythms adequate to the condition of contemporary history.

2

Writing about his translation of *Beowulf*, Seamus Heaney focuses, in particular, on what he calls 'the liminal situation of the literary translator, the one standing at the frontier of a resonant original, in awe of its primacy, utterly persuaded, and yet called upon to utter a different yet equally persuasive version of it in his or her own words'.[21] In Heaney's own relationship with English Romantic poetry, especially that of Wordsworth, there is something of this liminality, except for the fact that Heaney's relationship is that of the inventor, often in search of corroboration. As already suggested, Heaney's dealings with Wordsworth are pervasive. In his essay 'The Makings of a Music' he contrasts Wordsworth's music with Yeats's. Wordsworth's music reveals, according to Heaney, 'a wise passiveness, a surrender to energies that spring within the centre of the mind'; Yeats's verse suggests 'the music of energy reined down, of the mastered beast stirring' (*P*, pp. 63, 73).

Heaney is describing two kinds of Romanticism, neither of which is straightforwardly available to him because he grew up, as he puts it, in 'Singing School', with a colonised sense of having 'no rights on / The English lyric'. Intriguingly, that poem has as an epigraph four and a half lines from *The Prelude* beginning (in Heaney's quotation), '*Fair seedtime had my soul, and I grew up / Fostered alike by beauty and by fear*' (1, 305–6). After this epigraph suggestive of affinity and contrast, the poem proper opens with a wryly assertive nod towards the Patrick Kavanagh of 'Epic': 'Well, as Kavanagh said, we have lived / In important places'. The poem confirms, albeit ambivalently, that initial note of assertion about the poet's links with a home-grown tradition represented by Kavanagh. Heaney brings out the lived experience of growing up in a place where, among other things, 'the leather strap / Went epileptic in the Big Study' and the poet as a young man was harassed by policemen 'pointing / The muzzle of a Sten gun in my eye'. That is what it is really like, the poet seems to be saying, to be 'Fostered... by fear', and, in a sense, Wordsworth serves as an ironised reference point.

If the poet's 'act / Of stealth' – apparently, the throwing of biscuits over the school fence one night in September 1951 – recalls the boat-stealing episode in *The Prelude*, Book 1, Heaney turns his back on the inwardness celebrated by Wordsworth. Heaney pointedly truncates his original, the boat-stealing being for Wordsworth an 'act of stealth / And troubled pleasure' (388–9). 'Troubled', as often in Wordsworth, hints at an imaginative disturbance that is ultimately affirmative, and he concludes the episode with a darkly empowering vision of 'huge and mighty Forms that do not live / Like living men' (lines 425–6), described as 'the trouble of my dreams' (line 427). Heaney, by contrast, eschews any 'dim and undetermined sense / Of unknown modes of being' (*The Prelude*, I. 419–20) (here, at any rate) for a more socially constrained consciousness of the 'ministry of fear'. Later, in the sequence's final poem, 'Exposure', Heaney will lay claim to a tentatively lyrical state of poetic autonomy, a state that has exacted sacrifices, but is alive to possibilities. What weighs with Heaney are his 'responsible *tristia*', as, very much the post-Romantic, he, like the birches, is 'Inheriting the last light'. Unable to 'come on meteorite', he is no trumpeter of a prophecy, merely a cautious stroller 'through damp leaves, / Husks, the spent flukes of autumn'. Politically and personally, Heaney has taken cover, even as he risks exposure; feeling 'Every wind that blows', he does not command any Shelley-like wind to scatter his words among mankind. And yet, for all the poem's sense of loss – the poet has missed 'The comet's pulsing rose' – it does more in that just-quoted line, the last in the work, than recall 'The diamond absolutes'. It recreates them by virtue of a phrase that, tapping Shelleyan and Yeatsian symbolic energies, makes present what has been missed.

Heaney, then, at the end of 'Singing School' reaffirms a precarious sense of continuity with Romantic lyric self-belief. The Wordsworthian music heard in 'The Makings of a Music' accords more with early Heaney's exploration of what Neil Corcoran calls 'an enlargement of consciousness . . . enacted in some interchange between mind and nature'.[22] In poems such as 'Personal Helicon' Heaney writes a poetry that meshes surrender to childhood experience with subsequent adult awareness. In addition, he is capable of a meta-poetic dimension. So, that poem concludes:

> Now, to pry into roots, to finger slime,
> To stare, big-eyed Narcissus, into some spring
> Is beneath all adult dignity. I rhyme
> To see myself, to set the darkness echoing.

It would be absurd to find Wordsworth everywhere in such passages. The wit of 'big-eyed Narcissus' is hardly characteristic of the Romantic poet (who is not without his own forms of humour), while the poem of Wordsworth most brought to mind by the final sentence – *The Prelude* – studiously

avoids 'rhyme'. But Heaney has, very adroitly, and yet without too knowing
a self-consciousness, succeeded in making his poem at once 'personal' and
in touch with tradition, with the springs of Helicon. The poem enacts its
relationship with tradition in lines such as – and especially – 'Others had
echoes, gave back your own call / With a clean new music in it'. At the
self-referential level, this formulation suggests how Heaney would like to
relate to his precursors.

   Behind the poem's end one can also hear an echo of Wordsworth's lines
about echoing, which Heaney meditates on in 'The Makings of a Music'.
The Wordsworthian lines are these: 'My own voice cheered me, and, far
more, the mind's / Internal echo of the imperfect sound; / To both I listened,
drawing from them both / A cheerful confidence in things to come' (*The
Prelude*, I. 64–7; quoted from Heaney's essay). Heaney comments: 'even
though he is listening to the sound of his own voice, he realizes that this
spoken music is just a shadow of the unheard melody, "the mind's internal
echo" ' (*P*, p. 63). Wordsworth is mediated here through Keats's 'Ode on
a Grecian Urn', where Keats appears at his most aesthetically attuned to
language and its limits: an appropriate mediation, considering that one
finds, sketched in Heaney's prose, a hint of the poetically self-aware turn
inwards of the end of 'Personal Helicon', which adds to Wordsworthian
listening an act of seeing the self, brought about in and by the process
of poetic composition ('I rhyme / To see myself'). Such self-seeing is both
qualified appositionally and extended by the subsequent move 'to set the
darkness echoing'. Heaney's stance at the close is more ambiguous than
Wordsworth's in the just-quoted lines about 'the mind's / Internal echo'.
Wordsworth's 'cheerful confidence in things to come' has given way to a
less evidently 'cheerful' desire to set the darkness echoing. And yet Heaney
actively wishes to 'set' going a process that will bring him into contact with
a 'darkness' that might be within and outside the self, but lies beyond the
conscious will. In this balance between the active and passive, Wordsworth's
example and influence are detectable.

   But if *The Prelude*'s interplay between self and world has shaped Heaney's
poetic procedures, one senses that, with Wallace Stevens, he would wish to
claim that 'while ... I come down from the past, the past is my own and not
something marked Coleridge, Wordsworth, etc.... My reality-imagination
complex is entirely my own even though I see it in others'.[23] Yet full independence shows at moments of maximum assimilation. By the time of
The Government of the Tongue (*GT*), Heaney has internalised Wordsworth
to the point where he is able to draw, in his criticism, with ingenuity and
insight on the self-referring dimension of the Boy of Winander section

from *The Prelude*. The passage, in part, describes the poet as a young boy mimicking the cry of the owls until he is rewarded for his pains by their answering call. In Heaney's essay on Sylvia Plath, the passage is used to illustrate three stages of poetic development: the initial pleasure in managing to 'get it right', the second stage of eliciting 'actual cries' when 'scale-practising' passes into a living 'poetry of relation', and a third stage in which 'the workings of the active universe, to use another phrase from *The Prelude*, are echoed far inside him'. Wordsworth's lines reinforce Heaney's self-image as a poet driven by the quest for 'direct contact... with the image-cellar, the dream-bank, the word-hoard, the truth-cave – whatever place', as he puts it, making peace with a troublingly magnificent precursor, 'a poem like Yeats's "Long-Legged Fly" emerges from'.[24] One can regard Heaney as seeing his career conforming to the three stages he draws from the Boy of Winander passage: early work, mid-career work such as the 'Glanmore Sonnets' in which the poet takes stock and asks 'What is my apology for poetry?', and finally more recent work that seeks 'to try to make space... for the marvellous as well as for the murderous', in Heaney's words from his Nobel Prize acceptance-speech, printed as 'Crediting Poetry' in *Opened Ground* (p. 458).

It is typical of Heaney's wary even-handedness that this attempt is heralded in a dialectically contrary way by aspects of *Field Work*, a volume angry, as 'Oysters' has it, that 'my trust could not repose / In the clear light, like poetry or freedom / Leaning in from the sea'. Even in 'Crediting Poetry' the 'marvellous' does not oust its alliterative partner and ideological opponent, 'the murderous'. Still, nothing is more Romantic in Heaney than his struggle to credit poetry with absolute value in itself and a kind of collateral ethical value. Shelley's already quoted claim in *A Defence of Poetry* that 'Poets are the unacknowledged legislators of the World' haunts Heaney's thinking on this subject. His 'The Unacknowledged Legislator's Dream', the first piece in the second part of *North* (1975), appears to reject the Romantic poet's claim. (Though the poem appears to be a prose-poem, the margins are not always justified on the right-hand side, so I shall indicate its 'line-breaks'.) The speaker begins with a reference to Archimedes' assertion that 'he could move the world if he could / find the right place to position his lever'.[25] Appropriately, Shelley quotes the original of this assertion as epigraphs to *Queen Mab* and *Laon and Cythna*, two revolutionary works. In Heaney's piece, the speaker dreams of undermining 'the masonry / of state and statute', but ends up in a prison cell. Yet the close veers between self-mockery (hubristic dreams have been put in their place) and the threat or promise of further action ('I jump on the concrete flags to / test them').

The final sentence sets up a challenge to the reader – 'Were those your eyes just now at the hatch?' – that takes one back to Shelley. *A Defence of Poetry*'s account of how poetry changes lives, not by communicating the writer's 'conceptions of right and wrong' (*SPP*, p. 488), but by mobilising the reader's imagination, is not far from Heaney's position in an essay such as 'The Interesting Case of Nero, Chekhov's Cognac and a Knocker'. Here Heaney argues that through poetry the tongue, 'ungoverned', 'gains access to a condition' that, 'while not being practically effective, is not necessarily inefficacious' (*GT*, p. xxii). Heaney stresses poetry's offer of release from the poet's 'predicaments', an emphasis that aligns itself with Shelley's wish to 'familiarize the more highly refined imagination' of his readers with 'beautiful idealisms of moral excellence' (*GT*, p. xxii; *SPP*, p. 135). Certainly the two poets share the conviction that direct familiarisation of the reader's (and poet's) imagination with 'beautiful idealisms', where that phrase implies no sentimental escapism but the mind's finest hopes, is a central and 'potentially redemptive' part of the poet's task (*GT*, p. xxii). For all their differences, both Shelley and Heaney seek to imagine states when 'hope and history rhyme', as the Irish poet puts it in section IV of 'Voices from Lemnos'. It is in *Seeing Things*, in particular, that one of Shelley's Promethean legacies, the envisioning of spiritual realities, comes to the fore. As often, Heaney consciously has Yeats in mind; but Shelley is one of Yeats's singing masters. When in 'Squarings', xxii, Heaney asks a series of queries about the whereabouts of 'spirit', and concludes, 'set questions for the ghost of W. B.', it is possible to glimpse, in the background, the poetic cosmos of spirit-echoes in *Prometheus Unbound*, act II.

But it is Wordsworth who provides the steadiest Romantic focus for Heaney's thinking about the rival claims of poetry and politics, thinking that has animated much of his finest poetry. In 'Frontiers of Writing', a lecture delivered in 1993, he recalls an earlier essay 'Place and Displacement', in which he 'found an English literary parallel which nicely illuminated the typical case of the poet from the minority in Ulster'. This parallel was Wordsworth, dislocated and alienated after his country had gone to war upon Revolutionary France. Heaney finds heartening the very thing some recent critics have found reason to fault: Wordsworth's turn to and use of poetry to describe 'a consciousness coming together through the effort of articulating its conflict and crises'.[26] This formulation might describe much of Heaney's own efforts to articulate conflict yet in doing so to heal trauma.

For Stan Smith, such healing follows a path from Wordsworthian predicament to Keatsian negative capability. Smith is responding shrewdly to the idiom of Heaney's 1984 'Place and Displacement' lecture (delivered as a Pete Laver Lecture), in which Heaney describes poetic development in this way: the writer is 'displaced from a confidence in a single position by his disposition to be affected by all positions, negatively rather than positively capable'.[27] But to pursue Heaney's debt to Romanticism in terms of switched allegiances would be to simplify. Wordsworth certainly does not drop away. In *The Spirit Level*, 'Tollund' brings to mind his earlier piece, 'The Tollund Man', which broods on ancient and contemporary atrocity, and seeks unavailingly a healing music or poetic formula when the poet asserts, 'I could risk blasphemy, / Consecrate the cauldron bog / Our holy ground'. As the long sentence unwinds of which these quoted words are the opening, we find ourselves taken back towards, rather than away from, the violence. Heaney is in Yeatsian territory, the world of 'Meditations in Time of Civil War' and '1919' (much of Heaney's own contact with Romanticism is fruitfully mediated through his response to Yeats). 'The Tollund Man' concludes thus: 'Out there in Jutland / In the old man-killing parishes / I will feel lost, / Unhappy and at home'. The fineness of this derives from the refusal to resolve tensions out of which the poem is made.

In 'Tollund', Heaney writes a poem that implicitly answers his earlier piece. We are not exactly in the world of 'Tintern Abbey' since Heaney is not describing a return visit (a central feature of 'The Tollund Man' was that its mood was proleptic, anticipatory). Yet, like Wordsworth's poem, Heaney has found his way through to a new and uncomplacent serenity, and one might wish to apply to his poem his words about Kavanagh's 'Innishkeen Road:' 'The poet's stance becomes Wordsworth's over Tintern Abbey, attached by present feelings but conscious that the real value of the moment lies in its potential flowering, its blooming, in the imagination' (Heaney, 'From Monaghan to the Grand Canal: the Poetry of Patrick Kavanagh', *P*, p. 117). He does so by revisiting less a place than a poetic career. Heaney's poem begins with a memory of standing 'a long time out in Tollund Moss' in a landscape at once 'Hallucinatory and familiar'. The adjectives yoke together heterogeneous perspectives, and bespeak the poet's need and ability to straddle two worlds and various opposites: Ireland and Jutland, imagination and memory, invention and reality. The Jutland world is one with which he is still 'at home', though he is no longer 'unhappy'. Rural Derry does not seem far away from the 'swept and gated farmyard', and yet Jutland is quickly regarded as providing the setting for a literary fiction in the third stanza: 'It could have been a still out of the bright / "Townland of Peace", that poem of dream farms / Outside all contention'. That notion sounds desirable, but possibly illusory, and the poem

immediately turns away from any immersion in a pastoral that might, in
Keats's terms, turn cold. The run-on lines assert a freedom from encase-
ment in artistic dream, and the poem discovers – in a way that is a source
of encouragement – that 'Things had moved on'.

This moving-on shows, for Heaney, in the fact that the imagined landscape in one of his great lyric triumphs reveals traces of change. Not only
has a 'standing stone' 'been resituated and landscaped', but also there are
now 'tourist signs' 'In Danish and in English'. In the earlier poem the poet's
linguistic alienation is stressed, as he says the names, 'Watching the pointing hands / Of country people, / Not knowing their tongue'. In the later
work, 'we' (Heaney and his wife, one presumes) are 'at home beyond the
tribe'. With chastened hopefulness, the poem likens them to 'ghosts who'd
walked abroad / Unfazed by light, to make a new beginning'. In its self-
conscious angling of earlier work, 'Tollund' reminds us that one bequest
of Romanticism is the evolving and shaped literary career.

3

In his study of American Modernist poetry, Albert Gelpi argues for a 'sub-
tler continuity between Romanticism and Modernism beneath the avowed
discontinuity'. Continuity does not preclude difference: 'For the Romantics', Gelpi writes, 'absolute experience predicated aesthetic failure, but
the Modernists could postulate the absolute only as an ultimate gauge of
technical achievement'.[28] Gelpi's terms help to clarify the inheritance and
choices available to poets who are, in turn, post-Romantic and writing after
Modernism. Derek Mahon's awareness of the dilemmas facing and opportunities open to the poet results in a light-wristed, gravely witty stance;
Mahon is a poet who likes his Romanticism at a remove, refracted through
Symbolist or Decadent prisms, through the lyric purity of a Jaccottet, or
through a mocking echo of Stevens's late-Romantic 'rage for order': 'somewhere beyond the scorched gable end and the burnt-out buses / there is
a poet indulging / his wretched rage for order – / or not as the case may
be'. The poet's 'posture is grandiloquent and deprecating', and Mahon's
own deprecating grandiloquence suggests his desperately ironic relationship to the Romantic tradition. The cold beauty and arrested perfection
of Keats's 'Ode on a Grecian Urn' give way in Mahon's terminal vision to
'The Apotheosis of Tins'. Here, the tins speak for a condition of derelict,
parodically aesthetic freedom 'from the historical nightmare', as the poem
offers a mock-celebration of their 'saintly / devotion to the notion of per-
manence / in the flux of sensation / and crisis'.[29]

More recently, however, Mahon's allusions to Keats demonstrate that the Romantic poet has become one of his exemplary figures. The seventh stanza of 'Ode to a Nightingale' (starting, in Mahon's text, '*Thou was not born for death, immortal Bird!*') stands at the head of the epigraphs to *The Hudson Letter* (1995). In loose-knit sections, full of allusions, echoes and literary revisitings, the poem describes Mahon's life in America and celebrates 'the resilience of our lyric appetite' (1).[30] The Keatsian epigraph stands in enigmatic and suggestive relationship to the sequence. Though the bird is not 'born for death', the poet of *The Hudson Letter* feels mortality pressing upon him. In the final section 'The Small Rain' (xviii) Mahon writes in elegiac mode, 'the friends and contemporaries begin to go'. Part of the pathos of Keats's stanza is the gap yet link between art, figured as immortal bird-song, and human suffering, plangently embodied in the image of 'the sad heart of Ruth'. Mahon wears his own 'sad heart' very much on his sleeve – and 'at night to lie', as he puts it, 'empty of mind, heart hammering'; and yet his poem's endless weaving in and out of other texts suggests a frail trust in poetry as able to embrace, if not offer a stay against, existential confusion. '*Now more than ever seems it rich to die*', he writes in xviii, borrowing Keats's line from stanza vi of the 'Ode to a Nightingale', 'into an oceanic, a molecular sky'. 'Molecular' sets up a scientific friction with the consciousness-drowsing 'oceanic', and the poem is in no mood to find salvation in any naive reprise of Romantic lyricism. Nevertheless, 'the secret voice of nightingale and dolphin' is included in the poem's final litany of what constitutes essential compass-points of poetic perception – along with 'the homeless, no rm. at the inn', and typically of Mahon, 'the gaseous planets'.

Nature may betray the heart that loved her, but the poem finishes with a plea, 'Take us in; take us in!', that one might think is covertly uttered by many contemporary Northern Irish poems in their cunning, heartfelt solicitations of Romantic poetry. Though it is quoted playfully at the head of 'Sappho in "Judith's Room"' (section xiii), Susan Sontag's recommendation that 'in place of a hermeneutics we need an erotics of art' comes close to a manifesto for Mahon in *The Hudson Letter*. The 'erotics of art' include, for the author of this work, a belated, melancholy and yet energised and energising responsiveness to Romantic poetry.

Notes

1 ROMANCING THE CELT

1 *The Songs of Charles Dibdin* (London: G. H. Davidson, 1847), vol. I, p. 310.
2 There is a nice irony here in that the great medieval document vaunting Scottish martial prowess, 'The Declaration of Arbroath' (1320), boasts that the modern Scots have driven out earlier ethnic groups from their land.
3 Stuart Piggott, *Celts, Saxons and the Early Antiquaries* (Edinburgh: 1966 O'Donnell Lecture, 1967), p. 11.
4 Matthew Arnold, 'On the Study of Celtic Literature', in R. H. Super (ed.), *The Complete Prose Works of Matthew Arnold* (Ann Arbor, MI and Toronto: University of Michigan Press, 1960–78), vol. III, pp. 341, 361.
5 See Arnold's usage of the term in his essay 'John Keats' (1880), in *The Complete Prose Works of Matthew Arnold*, vol. IX, p. 214.
6 Richard Wendorf and Charles Ryskamp (eds.), *The Works of William Collins* (Oxford: Clarendon Press, 1979), pp. 56–63. Page references to this edition are hereafter given after quotations in the main text.
7 Howard D. Weinbrot, *Britannia's Issue: the Rise of British Literature from Dryden to Ossian* (Cambridge University Press, 1993), see especially pp. 403–566.
8 John Home, *Douglas*, ed. Gerald D. Parker (Edinburgh: Oliver and Boyd, 1972):

> Who has not heard of gallant PIERCY's name?
> Ay, and of DOUGLAS? Such illustrious foes
> In rival Rome and Carthage never rose!
> From age to age bright shone the British fire,
> And every hero was a hero's sire.
> ('London' Prologue, lines 4–8, p. 19)

9 Walter Scott, *Waverley*, ed. Andrew Hook (London: Penguin, 1972), p. 135.
10 Burns *Poems and Songs*, ed. James Kinsley (London: Oxford University Press, 1971), Poem no. 62 (pp. 80–90). Line references from this edition follow quotations in the text.
11 See 'The Vision', lines 109–14 (and Burns's note) in *Poems and Songs*, p. 84.
12 Murray Pittock, *Inventing and Resiting Britain: Cultural Identities in Britain and Ireland 1685–1789* (Basingstoke: Macmillan, 1997), pp. 153–6.

13 Peter Quennell records Byron's seemingly extreme reaction to criticism by the *Edinburgh Review*: 'Hobhouse puts it on record that, when the *Edinburgh Review* published its savage criticism of *Hours of Idleness*, the poet was "very near destroying himself"', Quennell, *Byron: the Years of Fame* (London: Faber and Faber, 1935), pp. 25–6.

14 Theobald Wolfe Tone, *Memoirs, Journals and Political Writings* compiled T. W. Tone, 1826, ed. Thomas Bartlett (Dublin: Lilliput Press, 1998), p. 132.

15 Katie Trumpener, *Bardic Nationalism: the Romantic Novel and the British Empire* (Princeton: Princeton University Press, 1997), p. 11.

16 Here Franklin continues to contribute to a growing interest in and recognition of Jones as an important influence on English Romantic writing beyond 'influencing the way in which India is represented in the poetry of the period' (Michael Rossington, 'Poetry by Burns, Cowper, Crabbe, Southey and other Male Authors', in Michael O'Neill (ed.), *Literature of the Romantic Period* (Oxford: Clarendon Press, 1998), p. 202). See, for example, Jerome McGann's brief but suggestive discussion of Jones's poetry in *The Poetics of Sensibility: a Revolution in Literary Style* (Oxford: Clarendon Press, 1996, pp. 128–31) and Martin Priestman's rather longer discussion of his work in *Romantic Atheism: Poetry and Freethought, 1780–1830* (Cambridge: Cambridge University Press, 1999), pp. 22–6, 48–55, 69–73, 77–9) as one of three eighteenth-century poets 'who... stand behind Romanticism in ways which deserve greater acknowledgment' (p. 45).

17 Jerome McGann, *The Romantic Ideology: a Critical Investigation* (Chicago, IL: Chicago University Press, 1983), p. 1.

18 Ibid., p. 89.

19 Kirsteen Daly, 'Worlds Beyond England: *Don Juan* and the Legacy of Enlightenment Cosmopolitanism', *Romanticism* 4.2 (1998), p. 190.

20 McGann, *Romantic Ideology*, pp. 87, 89.

21 Ibid., p. 90. In Hemans's poetry we find a striking example of what Trumpener describes as the 'newfound popularity' of all things Bardic in England which 'endangered the Bardic tradition in a new way' (*Bardic Nationalism*, p. 6). Indeed, Trumpener offers an excellent, if unsubstantiated, outline of precisely the kind of Romantic 'displacement' that Brewer's analysis of Hemans spotlights.

22 Lynda Pratt, 'Revising the National Epic: Coleridge, Southey and *Madoc*', *Romanticism* 2.2 (1996), pp. 149–63.

23 Weinbrot, *Britannia's Issue*, p. 3.

24 Murray G. H. Pittock, *Inventing and Resisting Britain*; Robert Crawford (ed.), *The Scottish Invention of English Literature* (Cambridge: Cambridge University Press: 1998) and Colin Kidd, *Subverting Scotland's Past: Scottish Whig Historians and the Creation of an Anglo-British Identity 1689–c. 1830* (Cambridge: Cambridge University Press, 1993).

25 Linda Colley, *Britons: Forging the Nation 1707–1837* (New Haven and London: Yale University Press, 1992), p. 8.

26 Benedict Anderson, *Imagined Communities* (London and New York: Verso, 1983, revised and extended 1991), p. 5.

27 Gilles Deleuze and Felix Guattari, *A Thousand Plateaus: Capitalism and Schizophrenia*, trans. Brian Massumi (London: Athlone, 1988); Anderson, *Imagined Communities*; James Whittaker, *William Blake and the Myths of Britain* (Basingstoke and London: Macmillan, 1999).

28 Here Franklin offers an Anglo-Welsh frame within which to consider what Trumpener calls 'the depoliticisation' of Evans's 'A Paraphrase of the 137th Psalm, Alluding to the Captivity and Treatment of the Welsh Bards by King Edward I'. For Trumpener, the blunting of 'the full political force of' Evans's 'original' is the result of the poem's 'departing from its original mode of paraphrase... for another (the redeployment of tropes proposed by another contemporary poet)' (*Bardic Nationalism*, p. 9). Franklin's larger Anglo-Welsh context for that departure is perhaps pointed to by the fact that the 'contemporary poet' is Gray, but it is not explicitly acknowledged, or explored, by Trumpener.

29 This is to foreground the influence of English politics, but, as Weinbrot has pointed out, eighteenth-century Celtic self-inventions could and did reinvent the Celtic past according to a wide range of English cultural values. Macpherson's Ossian poems, for example, 'draw on Scottish Celtic nostalgia', but 'also tap deep veins of English sentiment, disgust with classical brutality, love of Old Testament poetry, and enchantment with British-Druid-Bardic mystical imaginative life and language' (Weinbrot, *Britannia's Issue*, p. 8).

30 Another way of tracing this history would be to focus on the history of the Bard in British literature. See, for example, Weinbrot's discussion of Gray's use of the Bard as a symbol of British national identity (*Britannia's Issue*, pp. 389–401).

2 SIR WILLIAM JONES

1 William Bolts, *Consideration on Indian Affairs* (London: J. Almon, 1772), p. vi. See the General Introduction to Michael J. Franklin (ed.), *Europe Discovers India: Key Indological Sources of European Romanticism*, 6 vols (London: Ganesha Press, 2001).

2 Consider James Mill's comparison of Highlanders and Hindus in their mingling of fiction and reality, in *The History of British India*, abridged by William Thomas (Chicago: University of Chicago Press, 1975), p. 567. The Celt Macpherson was also destined to know the Indian, becoming in 1781 Agent of the Nawab of Arcot, with an interest in the East Indian business of Sir John Macpherson (Governor-General of India 1785–6), his relative and Jones's friend.

3 See her Introduction to Howard Gaskill (ed.), *The Poems of Ossian and Related Works* (Edinburgh: Edinburgh University Press, 1996).

4 Thomas Percy thought 'cold European imaginations' might benefit from the strength and exoticism of Eastern metaphor, see *The Song of Solomon, newly translated from the original Hebrew: with a Commentary and Annotations* (London: R. and J. Dodsley, 1764), pp. xxii–xxiii.

5 'Un Traité sur la poësie orientale' (1770); *A Grammar of the Persian Language* (1771); *Dissertation sur la Litérature orientale* (1771); 'An Essay on the Poetry of the Eastern Nations' (1772); *Poeseos Asiaticae Commentarium, Libri Sex, cum Appendice* (1774).

6 Elizabeth Montagu to James Beattie, 5 September 1772, quoted in Garland Cannon (ed.), *The Letters of Sir William Jones*, 2 vols (Oxford: Oxford University Press, 1970), vol. I, p. III. Hereafter referred to as *Letters*.

7 W. Carew Hazlit (ed.), *The History of English Poetry from the Twelfth to the Close of the Sixteenth Century* (1774–81) (London: Reeves and Turner, 1871), vol. I, p. 116.

8 See my *Sir William Jones* (Cardiff: University of Wales Press, 1995), pp. 21–2, 106–10.

9 'On the Poetry of the Eastern Nations', see my *Sir William Jones: Selected Poetical and Prose Works* (Cardiff: University of Wales Press, 1995), p. 333. Hereafter referred to as *Selected Works*.

10 Hugh Blair, *A Critical Dissertation on the Poems of Ossian* (1763). Howard D. Weinbrot's thesis traces a pacifist rhetoric in mid-century poetry rejecting classical literature's militaristic imperialistic values and seeking inspiration in Hebrew and Celtic literature; see *Britannia's Issue: the Rise of British Literature from Dryden to Ossian* (Cambridge: Cambridge University Press, 1993), esp. pp. 477–571.

11 *Edinburgh Review* 6.12 (July 1805), 462.

12 See Edward Snyder, *The Celtic Revival in English Literature 1760–1800* (Cambridge, MA: Harvard University Press, 1923), pp. 17–33; Saunders Lewis, *A School of Welsh Augustans* (1924; rpr. Bath: Firecrest, 1969).

13 In 1761 Richard Morris visited Macpherson at Teddington and wrote to Lewis that 80 members of Jesus College, Oxford had enrolled in the Cymmrodorion Society, see John H. Davies (ed.), *The Letters of Lewis, Richard, William and John Morris 1728–1765*, 2 vols (Aberystwyth: privately published by the editor, 1907), vol. II, p. 362. Richard and Lewis Morris were nevertheless continually disappointed by the commitment of the membership.

14 The mixture of the pragmatic and the speculative which was to be found in the Morris Circle amongst men who pursued their intellectual interests during hard-earned moments of leisure was also a hallmark of the members of the Asiatick Society of Bengal, founded by Jones on 15 January 1784.

15 Quoted in Prys Morgan, *The Eighteenth Century Renaissance* (Llandybie: Davies, 1981), p. 14.

16 Anna Maria Jones (ed.), *The Works of Sir William Jones*, 13 vols (London: Stockdale and Walker, 1807), vol. I, pp. 2–3 (hereafter referred to as *Works*). William Jones senior was himself fascinated by Welsh antiquities, purchasing Moses Williams's library from his widow, and employing Richard Morris to catalogue it. At his death he bequeathed it to his former pupil, the Earl of Macclesfield, and the precious manuscripts remained inaccessible in boxes at Shirburn Castle.

17 The district is rich in associations with both the Druids and the British saints, see Camden's *Britannia*, ed. Edmund Gibson (London: F. Collins, 1695), col. 675; Henry Rowlands, *Mona Antiqua Restaurata. An Archaeological Discourse on the Antiquities, Natural and Historical of the Isle of Anglesey, the Ancient Seat of the British Druids* (Dublin: Aaron Rhames, 1723).

18 See *Celtic Remains* (London: Parker, 1878), p. xliii. In similar patriotic vein, Evan Evans rails against English antiquaries 'blinded with prejudice, bloated with pride, and cankered with envy', as he manipulates arguments to counter Camden's rejection of the Brutus genealogy; see 'A Short View of the State of Britain' (1785), in D. Silvan Evans (ed.), *Gwaith y Parchedig Evan Evans* (Caernarfon: Humphreys, 1876), pp. 255–301, 284.

19 Morris's ethnological syncretism brings together the Old Testament, the classics and the Triads in an attempt to forge an ancient lineage for the Welsh; see *Celtic Remains*, pp. vii–xiii.

20 James Clifford, 'Of Other Peoples: Beyond the Salvage Paradigm', in Hal Foster (ed.), *Discussions in Contemporary Culture* (Seattle, LA: Bay Press, 1987).

21 Hugh Owen (ed.), *Additional Letters of the Morrises of Anglesey (1735–1786)*, 2 vols (London: Hon. Soc. of Cymmrodorion, 1947–9), vol. I, p. 291.

22 *Works*, vol. I, p. 78.

23 *Letters*, vol. II, p. 652.

24 Ibid., p. 649.

25 Letter to Edward Richard, 8 August 1758, *Additional Letters of the Morrises*, vol. I, p. 349.

26 *Gwaith y Parchedig Evan Evans*, p. 128.

27 *Some Specimens of the Poetry of the Antient Welsh Bards* (London: R. and J. Dodsley, 1764), p. ii. For a convenient translation, see Charlotte Johnston, 'Evan Evans: Dissertatio De Bardis', *National Library of Wales Journal* 22 (1981), 64–91.

28 *Letters of Lewis, Richard, William and John Morris*, vol. II, p. 544; Aneurin Lewis (ed.), *The Correspondence of Thomas Percy and Evan Evans* (Baton Rouge, LA: Louisana University Press, 1957), pp. 121–2.

29 The copyright brought him twenty pounds (see *Myvyrian Archaiology*, vol. I, p. xii). He failed to get eight pounds from the Cymmrodorion for his valuable dissertation on the bards.

30 Lewis, *Correspondence of Thomas Percy*, p. 131.

31 From Sir Roger Mostyn's gardens 'we had the most magnificent view my eyes ever beheld, and almost the finest my imagination, warm as it is, could conceive. We had on one side a prospect of the isle of Anglesea, the ancient Mona, where my ancestors presided over a free but uncivilised people' (*Letters*, vol. I, pp. 198–9).

32 *Letters*, vol. II, p. 529.

33 For a consideration of Jones's antipathy towards the despotic power of landlords, see my 'Accessing India: Orientalism, anti-"Indianism" and the Rhetoric of Jones and Burke', in Tim Fulford and Peter Kitson (eds.), *Romanticism and Colonialism* (Cambridge: Cambridge University Press, 1998), pp. 48–66, 49–51.

34 Attending a service in St David's Cathedral, Evans was 'surprised to find it performed in English in so remote a corner. I suppose our clergy think that the vulgar have no souls, just as we are taught by travellers that the Turks suppose of the ladies. No great inducement to either to behave well' (Letter to Benjamin Davies, 18 June 1781, National Library of Wales [hereafter NLW] M S. 5497).

35 'But know their rights, and knowing dare maintain' (line 14) was stamped by the radical Thomas Spence on a political token; see *Selected Works*, p. 78.

36 *Gwaith y Parchedig Evan Evans*, p. 182. Morris replied: 'What can you expect from Bis–ps or any officers ignorant of a Language which they get their living by, and which they ought to Cultivate instead of proudly despising. If an Indian acted thus, we would be apt to Call him Barbarous. But a Sc–t or Sax–n is above Correction' (*Additional Letters of the Morrises*, vol. II, p. 623).

37 *Gwaith y Parchedig Evan Evans*, pp. 51–2.

38 Ibid., p. 247.

39 *Selected Works*, pp. 54–5.

40 Ibid., p. 58.

41 Later, as a Cymmrodorion in Calcutta and 'warmly interested in British antiquities and literature', Jones remained mindful of his Celtic heritage, promising an old circuit colleague 'a General Epistle to the Druids of the Tivy'. He was consulted in India by Richard Morris Jr. on the best mode of publication for Lewis Morris's *Celtic Remains* (see *Letters*, vol. II, pp. 692–3, 876–7); *Additional Letters of the Morrises*, vol. II, pp. 781–2.

42 Jones, *Selected Works*, p. 402; see also 'A Speech on the Reformation of Parliament', ibid., pp. 390–1.

43 Preserved in the Pennant Collection, NLW ms. 2598C.

44 See Emyr Wyn Jones, *Yr Anterliwt Goll: Barn ar Egwyddorion y Llywodraeth... Gan Fardd Anadnabyddus o Wynedd* (Aberystwyth: Llyfrgell Genedlaethol Cymru, 1984), and, by the same author, *Diocesan Discord: a Family Affair, St Asaph 1779–1786* (Aberystwyth: printed for the author, 1988). Evans was the officiating clergyman when Thomas Edwards ('Twm o'r Nant', 1739–1810) married Elizabeth Hughes in Llanfair Talhaearn on 19 February 1763. They became friendly and Evans fostered his interest in Welsh literature.

45 'A Specimen of the Critical History of the Celtic Religion and Learning', in *A Collection of Several Pieces of Mr. John Toland*, 2 vols (London: J. Peele, 1726), vol. I, pp. 1–183.

46 William Stukeley relied upon Samuel Bochart for the theory that the Phoenician-Egyptian Hercules, who 'conversed with *Abraham*' first colonised Britain, but developed his own anachronistic theory that these tin-seeking Tyrians also built magnificent temples like Stonehenge, where the Druids practised the patriarchal religion of the Phoenicians; see *Stonehenge, a Temple Restored to the Druids* (London, 1740), p. 1. This genealogy was accessible to metropolitan English poetry such as Richard Glover's *London: or, the Progress of Commerce* (1739), which stressed the noble ancestry of British commerce, or Henry James Pye's *Naucratia; or Naval Dominion* (1798), a paean to imperial sea-power.

47 Joseph Leersen, 'On the Edge of Europe: Ireland in Search of Oriental Roots, 1650–1850', *Comparative Criticism* 8 (1986), 91–112, 100.

48 Charles Vallancey, *An Essay on the Antiquity of the Irish Language, Being a Collation of the Irish with the Punic Language. With a Preface proving Ireland to be the Thule of the Ancients. Addressed to the Literati of Europe* (Dublin: S. Powell, 1772), p. 3.

49 *A Letter from Dr Stukeley to Mr MacPherson, on his Publication of Fingal and Temora. With a Print of Cathmor's Shield* (London: Richard Hett, 1763), pp. 14, 11.

50 See Norman Vance, 'Celts, Carthaginians and Constitutions: Anglo-Irish Literary Relations, 1780–1820', *Irish Historical Studies* 22 (1981), 216–38.

51 Vallancey, *Essay on the Antiquity of the Irish Language*, pp. 251–72.

52 'According to him, when silly people gave me the surname of *Persian*, they in fact called me *Irishman*. Do you wish to laugh? Skim the book over. Do you wish to sleep? Read it regularly' (*Letters*, vol. II, pp. 768–9). The following day, 11 September 1787, Jones wrote to congratulate the eminent Irish antiquarian Joseph Cooper Walker on his *Memoirs of the Irish Bards* (1786), adding, in a in more diplomatic mode: 'When you see Colonel Vallancey, whose learned work I have read through twice with great pleasure, I request you to present him with my best remembrance. We shall soon I hope see faithful translations of Irish histories and poems. I shall be happy in comparing them with the Sanscrit, with which the ancient language of Ireland had certainly an affinity' (*Letters*, vol. II, pp. 770–1). Two years later, on 17 September 1789, Jones was again writing from Crishna-nagur to Walker, and, in the context of praising Walker's research and arranging subscriptions for Charlotte Broke's distinguished verse-translations of ancient Irish texts [*Reliques of Ancient Irish Poetry* (1789)], asserted that 'Col. Vallancey's translation [probably *Comparaison de la langue punique et de la langue irlandoise* (1787)] will interest me highly' (*Letters*, vol. II, pp. 841–2).

53 Jones, *Selected Works*, p. 361.

54 'Celtomania and Indomania run together at a rather profound level. For British ethnologies from General Vallancey onward seem to show that an openness to the one tends to go with an openness towards the other, and that, contrarily, anti-Irish feeling on the part of the English and the Scots tends to go with hostility towards the Indians and, as well, towards the claims of language to show a relationship among them' (Thomas Trautmann, *Aryans and British India* [Berkeley, Los Angeles, London: University of California Press, 1997], p. 96).

55 Vallancey's successors, such as Sir William Betham, Roger O'Connor, Henry O'Brien and Thomas Moore were slow to abandon the Phoenician vision even though it had been overtaken by the Indo-European model; they employed the impetus of the Calcutta research to embroider the significance of the similarity between 'Iran' and 'Erin', or to correlate the phallic shape of Ireland's round towers and Hindoo pagodas; see Leersen, 'On the Edge of Europe', 103–12.

56 John Pinkerton, *A Dissertation on the Origin and Progress of the Scythians or Goths. Being an Introduction to the Ancient and Modern History of Europe* (London: G. Nicol, 1787), p. 123.

57 Jones, *Works*, vol. II, pp. 431–2; *Letters*, vol. I, p. 85.
58 Jones, *Works*, vol. II, p. 452. Jones tentatively suggests a parallel between the Irish Ogham alphabet and the Sanskrit texts called Āgama; see 'Sixth Anniversary Discourse' in *Works*, vol. III, pp. 123–4.
59 Jones completed half of a projected series of eighteen 'Hymns to Hindu Deities' which with their emphases upon the seminal and amniotic waters of creation, upon creativity and the nature of perception, focussed Romantic attention on the analogies between God's action in the formation of the world and the poet's act of creation. Jones's prefatory Argument to 'A Hymn to Nárávena' (1786) with its valuable insights into the substantial overlap of the artistic and the religious, the philosophic and the literary, is a seminal document in the history of Romanticism; see my *Sir William Jones*, pp. 95–105.
60 Jones, *Works*, vol. II, pp. 445–6.
61 Pope's projected epic, 'Brutus', was also to include Druidical elements.
62 Thomas Maurice, whose efforts to reconcile the Hindu Trimurti with the Christian Trinity were reliant upon Jones's research, claimed: 'The celebrated order of Druids, anciently established in this country were the immediate descendants of a tribe of Brahmins' (*Indian Antiquities*, 7 vols [London: printed for the author by H. L. Galabin, 1793–1800], vol. VI, pt. I, pp. 19–20).
63 Many antiquarians saw the Druids' teachings as superior to the Greeks and Romans in their advocacy of the soul's immortality. William Borlase claimed that the Druids taught Pythagoras metempsychosis; see *Antiquities, Historical and Monumental of the County of Cornwall*, (London: W. Bowyer and J. Nichols 2nd edition, 1769), p. 97.
64 There is little pan-Celtic solidarity as the Druid rallies the attendant spirits in their battle against a powerful coalition of 'the HINDU god of battles' and the ancestral enemy, the Gauls. *Works*, vol. II, pp. 447–9.
65 Ibid., p. 453. This is the second of four stanzas which Jones appended to his later plan.
66 According to David Ludden: 'Today, Orientalism is most defensible on the ground that people in India and elsewhere believe its imagery to represent the truth about themselves' ('Orientalist Empiricism: Transformations of Colonial Knowledge', in Carol Breckenridge and Peter van der Veer [eds.], *Orientalism and the Postcolonial Predicament* [Philadelphia, PA: University of Pennsylvania Press, 1993], pp. 250–78, 271).
67 *Additional Letters of the Morrises*, vol. II, p. 457.
68 See Trautmann, *Aryans and British India*, pp. 77–80.

3 THE CRITICAL RESPONSE TO OSSIAN

1 The standard work on Macpherson is Fiona Stafford's *The Sublime Savage: James Macpherson and the Poems of Ossian* (Edinburgh: Edinburgh University Press, 1988). For a broad view of the field see also the collections Howard Gaskill (ed.), *Ossian Revisited* (Edinburgh: Edinburgh University Press, 1991)

and Fiona Stafford and Howard Gaskill (eds.), *From Gaelic to Romantic: Ossianic Translations* (Amsterdam: Rodopi Press, 1998).

2 S. H. Monk, *The Sublime: a Study of Critical Theories in Eighteenth-Century England* (1935; Ann Arbor, MI: University of Michigan Press, 1960), p. 126; Jerome J. McGann, *The Poetics of Sensibility: a Revolution in Literary Style* (Oxford: Clarendon Press, 1996), p. 33.

3 See 'Macpherson's Ossian and the Ossianic Controversy: a Contribution towards a Bibliography', *The Bulletin of the New York Public Library*, 30.6 (June 1926), pp. 424–39, 30.7 (July 1926), pp. 508–24; John J. Dunn, 'Macpherson's Ossian and the Ossianic Controversy: a Supplementary Bibliography', *The Bulletin of the New York Public Library*, 75.9 (November 1971), pp. 465–73.

4 See, for example, Gaskill's 'Herder, Ossian and the Celtic', in Terence Brown (ed.), *Celticism* (Amsterdam: Rodopi Press, 1996), pp. 257–71, 257–8, for this process whereby 'Ossian has been shunted into a forgotten siding of German literary history' (p. 257).

5 John Butt, *The Age of Johnson 1740–1789*, ed. (and completed by) Geoffrey Carnall (Oxford, 1977), p. 7.

6 Gaskill, 'Ossian, Moritz and the Joy of Grief', *Colloquia Germanica* 28 (1995), pp. 101–25, 101–2; John J. Dunn, 'Coleridge's debt to Macpherson's Ossian', *Studies in Scottish Literature* 7.1 and 2 (July–October 1969), pp. 76–89; pp. 88–9.

7 William Wordsworth, *Wordsworth's Literary Criticism*, ed. W. J. B. Owen, (London: Routledge, 1974), p. 208.

8 Fiona Stafford, '"Dangerous Success": Ossian, Wordsworth and English Romanticism' in *Ossian Revisited*, pp. 49–72 (hereafter page references to this work follow quotations in the main text); John Robert Moore, 'Wordsworth's Unacknowledged Debt to Macpherson's Ossian', *PMLA* 40 (1925), pp. 362–78.

9 F. J. Lamport, 'Goethe, Ossian and *Werther*', in Stafford and Gaskill (eds.), *From Gaelic to Romantic*, pp. 97–106.

10 Robin Flower, *Byron and Ossian* (Nottingham: Byron Foundation Lecture, 1928), p. 4. Hereafter page references to this work follow quotations in the main text.

11 David Fuller, *Blake's Heroic Argument* (London: Croom Helm, 1988), pp. 21, 23.

12 James Douglas Merriman, *The Flower of Kings: a Study of the Arthurian Legend in England between 1485 and 1835* (Lawrence, KA: University Press of Kansas, 1973), p. 149. Hereafter page references to this work follow quotations in the main text.

13 For the Celtic elements in Chrétien's Arthurian world (such as the Joyous Garde episode at the finale of *Erec et Enide*) see Eugene Vinaver's classic *The Rise of Romance* (Oxford: Clarendon Press, 1971). Gawain owes the peculiar fluctuations in his strength (a feature found as late as Malory) to his buried origins as Celtic sun deity.

14 To object that Tennyson's Arthur is more Christ than Ayrian is, I think, to put the cart before the horse.

15 *James Macpherson's Fingal (1792)*, ed. and intro. Jonathan Wordsworth (Poole, 1996), unpaginated.

16 For this breakdown see John J. Dunn, 'The Influence of Macpherson's *Ossian* on British Romanticism' (unpublished PhD thesis, Duke University, 1965), pp. 107–8. Hereafter page references to this work follow quotations in the main text.

17 Howard Gaskill notes that interest in *Ossian* in France and Germany did not peak until the 1800s (with five complete German translations between 1806 and 1811). See his 'Ossian at Home and Abroad', *Strathclyde Modern Language Studies* 8 (1988), pp. 5–27, 7.

18 See also Dunn, 'Influence of Macpherson's *Ossian*', for discussion of the confusion of opinion over literary merit with opinion over authenticity. The understanding of Southey's use of *Ossian*, he claims, has particularly suffered from this (p. 162).

19 'On Poetry in General' (1818), in P. P. Howe (ed.), *The Complete Works of William Hazlitt* (London: J. M. Dent, 1930), vol. v, pp. 1–18, 18.

20 Scott to Anna Seward, (? September 1806), in H. J. C. Grierson (ed.), *The Letters of Walter Scott 1787–1807* (London: Constable, 1932), pp. 320–4, 320–1.

21 See Cecil Y. Long and Edgar F. Shannon (eds.), *Letters of Alfred, Lord Tennyson* (Oxford: Clarendon Press, 1982–90), vol. III, p. 99n.

22 Andrew Hook, '"Ossian" Macpherson as Image Maker', *The Scottish Review* 36 (November 1984), pp. 39–44, 39.

23 Price, 'Ossian and the Canon in the Scottish Enlightenment' in Gaskill (ed.), *Ossian Revisited*, pp. 109–27, 126. Hereafter page references to this work follow quotations in the main text.

24 Katie Trumpener, *Bardic Nationalism: the Romantic Novel and the British Empire* (Princeton NJ: Princeton University Press, 1997), p. 109.

25 See Larry Leroy Stewart's 'Ossian in the Polished Age: the Critical Reception of James Macpherson's *Ossian*' (unpublished PhD thesis, University of Michigan, 1971) for the evolving debate over *Ossian*'s epic status. Various figures who were happy to accept a fragmentary, lyric *Ossian* were less willing to accept a 'Northern Homer' on scholarly and ideological grounds.

26 See Gaskill, 'Ossian at Home and Abroad', p. 17 for this point.

27 Stuart Curran, *Poetic Form and British Romanticism* (Oxford University Press, 1986), pp. 158–9.

28 I owe my awareness of this to Dr Howard Gaskill.

29 See James Malek, 'Eighteenth-Century British Dramatic Adaptations of Macpherson's *Ossian*', *Restoration and Eighteenth-Century Theatre Research* 14 (1975).

30 *The Airs, Duets, Chrouses, and Argument, of the New Ballet Pantomime (Taken from Ossian) called Oscar and Malvina; or, the Hall of Fingal* (1791), p. 14.

31 Dunn, 'Coleridge's Debt', p. 76, 81.

32 See for examples of these new directions: Fiona Stafford, *The Last of the Race: the Growth of a Myth from Milton to Darwin* (Oxford: Clarendon Press, 1994); Susan Manning, 'Ghost-Writing Tradition: Henry Mackenzie,

Burns and Macpherson', *Scotlands* 4.1 (1997), pp. 86–107; also Joep Leersen, 'Ossianic Liminality: between Native Tradition and Preromantic Taste' and Dafydd Moore, 'James Macpherson and William Faulkner: a Sensibility of Defeat', both in Stafford and Gaskill (eds.), *From Gaelic to Romantic*, pp. 1–16; pp. 183–215.

33 Peter Murphy, *Poetry as an Occupation and Art in Britain 1760–1830* (Cambridge: Cambridge University Press, 1993), pp. 5, 47–8.

34 Dáithí Ó hÓgáin, *Fionn mac Cumhaill: Images of the Gaelic Hero* (Dublin: Gill and Macmillan, 1988), p. 315.

35 Hook '"Ossian" Macpherson as Image Maker', p. 39; Murray G. H. Pittock, *The Myth of the Jacobite Clans* (Edinburgh: Edinburgh University Press, 1995), p. 118.

36 Hook, ' "Ossian" Macpherson as Image Maker', p. 39. For a convenient example of the '*Ossian* as cultural imperialism' line see Peter Womack's *Improvement and Romance: Constructing the Myth of the Highlands* (Basingstoke and London: Macmillan, 1989).

37 For example, see Hook '"Ossian" Macpherson as Image Maker'; Pittock, *The Myth of the Jacobite Clans* and also his *Inventing and Resisting Britain: Cultural Identities in Britain and Ireland 1685–1789* (London: Macmillan, 1997), pp. 156–8; Fiona Stafford, 'Primitivism and the "Primitive" Poet: a Cultural Context for Macpherson's *Ossian*' in Brown (ed.), *Celticism*, pp. 79–96.

38 For corroboration of this point see, for example, Martin Prochazka, 'Ossian Revived: Macpherson's "Ossian Poems" and Historical Aspects of Czech Romantic Culture', *Ceska Literatura* 14.1 (1993), pp. 25–47; Stephen Cristea, 'Ossian v. Homer: an Eighteenth-Century Controversy; Melchior Cesarotti and the struggle for Literary Freedom', *Italian Studies* 24 (1969), pp. 93–111; Paul Dukes, 'Ossian and Russia', *Scottish Literary News* 3.3 (November 1973), pp. 17–21.

39 I should acknowledge the debt the stimulation of my thinking on both sides of this issue owes to an exchange of views with Dr Cairns Craig of the University of Edinburgh.

4 BLAKE AND GWENDOLEN

1 'Advertisement of Exhibition of Paintings', in Geoffrey Keynes (ed.), *Blake: Complete Writings* (Oxford: Oxford University Press, 1966) (hereafter referred to as K), p. 560. All quotations from Blake's poetry are taken from this edition and are followed in the main text by plate, line and page references. See also Morton D. Paley, *The Continuing City: William Blake's 'Jerusalem'* (Oxford: Clarendon Press, 1983), pp. 54–7.

2 Such evidence as there is for this can be most usefully reviewed in G. E. Bentley, Jr, *Blake Records* (Oxford: Clarendon Press, 1969), pp. 398–400.

3 Jason Whittaker, *William Blake and the Myths of Britain* (London: Macmillan, 1999), p. 1.

4 Ibid., pp. 1–2.

5 See in particular Whittaker, *Blake*, pp. 60–79, on the history of the bards and the origins of languages.

6 See my 'Blake: Social Relations of Poetic Form', *Literature and History* 8 (1982), pp. 182–205.

7 Work which should culminate in a book provisionally titled *Blake Astray*.

8 See W. H. Stevenson (ed.), *Blake: the Complete Poems* (London: Longman, 2nd edn, 1989), p. 713.

9 Gilles Deleuze and Félix Guattari, *A Thousand Plateaus: Capitalism and Schizophrenia*, trans. Brian Massumi (London: Athlone Press, 1988), p. 12 (hereafter refered to as 'D and G'). Subsequent references to this work are given after quotations in the main text.

10 See Freud, *The Interpretation of Dreams* (1900), in James Strachey et al. (eds.), *The Standard Edition of the Complete Psychological Works of Sigmund Freud* (London: Hogarth Press, 1953–74), vol. v, pp. 522–5.

11 On this Deleuze and Guattari refer us back to Ssu-ma Ch'ien, *The Records of the Grand Historian*, trans. Burton Watson (New York: Columbia University Press, 1961), vol. ii, pp. 155–93.

12 See *Jerusalem*, lines 10, 20; K, p. 629.

13 On Gwendolen, see also Whittaker, *Blake*, pp. 226–9; and Morton D. Paley, 'William Blake, the Prince of the Hebrews, and the Woman Clothed with the Sun', in M. D. Paley and Michael Phillips (eds.), *William Blake: Essays in Honour of Sir Geoffrey Keynes* (Oxford: Clarendon Press, 1973), pp. 288–90.

14 See *Jerusalem*, lines 71, 23; K, p. 710.

15 See Kathleen Raine, *Blake and Tradition* (Princeton, NJ: Princeton University Press, 1968), vol. i, p. 267, on Annandale and the closed western gate; also Joseph Campbell, *The Masks of God: Creative Mythology* (New York: Viking Press, 1968), pp. 418–19.

16 See also Deleuze and Guattari's source, Ibn Khaldûn, *The Muqaddimah: an Introduction to History*, trans. Franz Rosenthal (Princeton, NJ: Princeton University Press, 2nd edn, 1967).

17 See Jung, 'The Relations Between the Ego and the Unconscious' (1945), in *Two Essays on Analytical Psychology*, trans. R. F. C. Hull (London: Routledge and Kegan Paul, 1953).

18 Perhaps here too we might find another approach to the physical and hieratic mysteries of Blake's *alter ego*, 'William Bond' (see K, pp. 434–6).

19 See: Benedict Anderson, *Imagined Communities: Reflections on the Origin and Spread of Nationalism* (London and New York: Verso, 2nd edn, 1991); John Breuilly, *Nationalism and the State* (Manchester: Manchester University Press, 2nd edn, 1985).

20 On loss, see my *Gothic Pathologies: the Text, the Body and the Law* (London: Macmillan, 1998), passim.

5 THE WELSH AMERICAN DREAM

1 Quoted by Brian Little, *The City and the County of Bristol: a Study in Atlantic Civilisation* (London: Wener Laurie, 1954), p. 216.

2 Joseph Cottle, *Reminiscences of Samuel Taylor Coleridge and Robert Southey* (London: Lime Tree Bower Press, 1970).

3 David Aers, 'Coleridge and the Egg that Burke Laid', *Literature and History* 9.2 (Autumn, 1983), pp. 152–63, p. 159.

4 See Richard Holmes, *Coleridge: Early Visions* (London: Hodder and Stoughton, 1989), p. 89.

5 On the Madoc legend I am chiefly indebted to the excellent Gwyn A. Williams, *Madoc: the Making of a Myth* (London: Eyre Methuen, 1979). See also the masterly demolition of the myth by Thomas Stephens, *Madoc: an Essay on the Discovery of America by Madoc ap Owen Gwynedd in the Twelfth Century* (London and New York: Longman, Green and Co., 1893), and the defence of it by Richard Deacon, *Madoc and the Discovery of America, Some New Light on an Old Controversy* (London: Frederick Muller, 1966).

6 On Edward Williams, see, in English: Prys Morgan's perceptive short biography, *Iolo Morganwg* (Cardiff: University of Wales Press, 1975); Geraint H. Jenkins's essay 'Facts, Fantasy and Fiction: the Historical Vision of Iolo Morganwg' (Aberystwyth: University of Wales Centre for Advanced Welsh and Celtic Studies, Paper no. 12, 1997). Though the author died before completing the projected three volumes, the fullest scholarly study remains (in Welsh): G. J. Williams, *Iolo Morganwg – Y Gyfrol Gyntaf* (Caerdydd: Gwasg Prifysgol Cymru, 1956).

7 On possible links between Williams and Blake, see Arthur Johnson, 'William Blake and the Ancient Britons', *National Library of Wales Journal* 22 (1981/2), pp. 304–20.

8 National Library of Wales (hereafter NLW) 13222C, fo. 469; Kenneth Curry (ed.), *New Letters of Robert Southey* (New York and London: Columbia University Press, 1965), vol. I, p. 394 (hereafter *NLRS*).

9 See Morgan, *Iolo Morganwg*, p. 58. Southey's heavy reliance on Warrington in the 1794 manuscript of the poem is noted by Kenneth Curry, in his 'Southey's *Madoc*: the Manuscript of 1794', *Philological Quarterly* 22.4 (October, 1943), pp. 347–69, p. 349.

10 Ian Haywood, 'The Making of History: Historiography and Literary Forgery in the Eighteenth Century', *Literature and History* 9.2 (Autumn, 1983), pp. 139–51; see also, Paul Baines, *The House of Forgery in Eighteenth-Century Britain* (Aldershot: Ashgate, 1999). Neither of these studies deals specifically with Edward Williams, however.

11 This was noted in the *Analytical Review* 18 (1794), pp. 196–200, p. 197.

12 Little, *City and County of Bristol*, p. 221.

13 'Letters addressed to Iolo Morganwg or connected with him' (NLW 21285E, fo. 846).

14 My information on Bristol's role as a metropolis is taken from W. E. Minchinton, 'Bristol – Metropolis of the West in the Eighteenth Century', *Transactions of the Royal Historical Society* 5.4 (1954), pp. 69–89.

15 Ibid., p. 83. See also, Gwyn A. Williams, 'Druids and Democrats: Organic Intellectuals and the First Welsh Radicalism', in Raphael Samuel and Gareth

Stedman Jones (eds.), *Culture, Ideology and Politics: Essays for Eric Hobsbawm* (London, Boston, Melbourne and Henley: Routledge and Kegan Paul, 1982), pp. 246–76, p. 248.

16 Aers, 'Coleridge and the Egg that Burke Laid', p. 159.

17 On Williams's linguistic interests, see Richard M. Crowe, 'Iolo Morganwg – An Eighteenth-Century Welsh Linguist', in Cyril J. Byrne, Margaret and Pádraig Ó Siadhail (eds.), *Celtic Language and Celtic Peoples: Proceedings of the 2nd North American Congress of Celtic Studies* (Halifax: St Mary's University Press, 1992), pp. 305–14.

18 Morgan, *Iolo Morganwg*, p. 4; Williams, 'Druids and Democrats', p. 270.

19 Morgan, *Iolo Morganwg*, p. 9.

20 NLW M62/988.

21 On Williams and the cult of Druidism in Glamorgan, see Roy Denning, 'Druidism at Pontypridd', in Stewart Williams (ed.), *Glamorgan Historian* 1 (Cowbridge: Brown and Sons, 1963), pp. 136–45.

22 Williams, 'Druids and Democrats', p. 263.

23 This poem compares America to 'the promis'd land' and the Welsh to 'Israel's Sons' (lines 33–4), and puts Madoc's story forward as the stuff of *British* epic: 'Were Homer now alive to hear of this, / He'd write his Madocks, burn his Odysses' (lines 87–8).

24 Quoted by Geraint H. Jenkins, '"A Rank Republican [and] a Leveller": William Jones, Llangadfan', *Welsh History Review* 17 (1994–5), pp. 365–86, p. 83.

25 See 'On the Discovery of America' (NLW 21393C), and 'The Discovery of America' (NLW 21394D). For a detailed analysis of Edward Williams's accumulation of evidence for Madoc's discovery of America, see Williams, *Madoc*, pp. 118–40.

26 See letter of 28 March 1792 to Mrs Bowdler, 'Letters addressed to Iolo Morganwg or connected with him' (NLW 21285E, fo. 806).

27 'Iolo Morganwg Miscellaneous Papers B' (NLW21393C, fo. 24).

28 Ibid., NLW 21394E, fo. 6.

29 Ibid., fo. 8.

30 See his letter to his wife on 11th February 1790, 'Letters addressed to Iolo Morganwg or connected with him', NLW 21285E, fo. 805.

31 See John T. Griffith, *Rev. Morgan John Rhys: the Welsh Baptist Hero of Civil and Religious Liberty of the Eighteenth Century* (Carmarthen: W. M. Evans and Son, 1910), p. 23, and Gwyn A. Williams, *The Search for Beulah Land: the Welsh and the Atlantic Revolution* (London: Croom Helm, 1980).

32 'Iolo Morganwg Miscellaneous Papers B', NLW 21394E, fo. 8.

33 Ibid., fo. 9.

34 Ibid.

35 *Poems, Lyrical and Pastoral* was reviewed in the *Analytical Review* 18 (1794), pp. 196–200; *British Critic* 4 (1794), p. 424; *Critical Review* 11 (1794), pp. 168–75; *Gentleman's Magazine* 64.2 (1794), pp. 1113–14; *Monthly Review* 13 (1794), pp. 405–14; *New Annual Register* 15 (1794), p. 252; *Scots Magazine* 56 (1794), p. 273.

36 'Letters addressed to Iolo Morganwg or connected with him', NLW 21285E, fo. 826

37 E. P. Thompson, *Witness against the Beast: William Blake and the Moral Law* (Cambridge: Cambridge University Press, 1993), p. 59. Cf also his plan to 'prove that all Church establishments or in other words all systems of Church and Kingdom, are, as if with might and main, preaching <u>Christianity</u> out <u>of the world</u>' (Letter 19 February 1794, NLW MS 21285E, fo. 850).

38 Robert Hole points out that the repeal of the Test and Corporation Acts was the overriding aim of Priestley and his followers, for previous Toleration acts had granted liberty of conscience to Trinitarian Dissenters, but Unitarians were excluded until 1812. The religious argument dominated British political debate at this juncture. See Robert Hole, *Pulpits, Politics and Public Order in England 1760–1832* (Cambridge: Cambridge University Press, 1989), p. 120–6.

39 Many accounts of the Madocian Indians mention their possession of Bibles they can no longer read, so that the possibility of educating them as missionaries to the other Indians is mentioned by Evan Evans (1731–88), 'Cwrtmawr 34B', NLW, fo. 17–20; later, Edward Williams proposes a non-exploitative Mission to enlighten the natives on the 'charms of that *Angel Peace*', NLW 21394E.

40 Elijah Waring, *Recollections and Anecdotes of Edward Williams, the Bard of Glamorgan or Iolo Morganwg, B.B.D.* (London: Charles Gilpin, 1850), p. 108. Williams also broke with his brothers who emigrated to the West Indies because they became slave owners.

41 *NLRS*, I, p. 332.

42 Lynda Pratt, 'Revising the National Epic: Coleridge, Southey and *Madoc*', *Romanticism* 2.2 (1996), pp. 149–63. See also her 'Naval Contemplation: Poetry, Patriotism and the Navy 1797–1799', *Journal for Maritime Research*: Royal Observatory Greenwich web site (December 2000), pp. 1–15; and 'The Pantisocratic Origins of Robert Southey's *Madoc*: an Unpublished Letter', *Notes and Queries* 244.1 (March 1999), pp. 34–9. I am grateful to Dr Pratt for reading and commenting on a draft of this chapter.

43 To John May, 3 September 1799, in *Selections from the Letters of Robert Southey, edited by his son-in-law, John Wood Warter* (London: Longman, 1856), vol. I, p. 82.

44 See Kenneth Curry (ed.), *The Contributions of Robert Southey to the Morning Post* (Tuscaloosa: University of Alabama Press, 1984). His preoccupation with Wales in 1798 is shown by poems such as 'St. David's day – 1 March 1798'; 'Llanthony Abbey' – 5 December 1798; 'Inscription for Cardiff Castle' – 19 September 1798; 'Inscription for a monument in the vale of Ewias' – 21 December 1798; 'Ode: in Vain the Travell'r Seeks Aberffraw's Tow'rs' – 31 December 1798.

45 *The Poetical Works of Robert Southey* (London: Longman, 1841), vol. V, p. 3. There are no substantial changes from the first edition of 1805, therefore all quotations are henceforth from this edition, abbreviated as *PWRS*. References follow quotations in the main text.

46 I am indebted to Paul Jarman for pointing out to me that this section of the poem was, in fact, a late addition to the poem rather than a remnant of Southey's early pacifism as might have been supposed.

47 See Geoffrey Carnall, *Robert Southey and his Age: the Development of a Conservative Mind* (Oxford: Oxford University Press, 1960), pp. 78–9.
48 *Letters of Robert Southey*, vol. i, p. 324.
49 Jenkins, 'A Rank Republican [and] a Leveller', p. 381.
50 Both reviews are reprinted in Lionel Madden (ed.), *Robert Southey: the Critical Heritage* (London and Boston, MA: Routledge and Kegan Paul, 1972), pp. 105–6.
51 Williams, *Madoc*, p. 67.
52 See Gwyn A. Williams, 'Romanticism in Wales', in Roy Porter and Mikuláš (eds.), *Romanticism in National Context* (Cambridge: Cambridge University Press, 1988), pp. 9–36, p. 33.
53 *Letters of Robert Southey*, vol. i, p. 242.
54 'Letters addressed to Iolo Morganwg or connected with him', NLW 21285E, fo. 898.

6 WORDSWORTH, NORTH WALES AND THE CELTIC LANDSCAPE

1 Mark Reed, *Wordsworth. The Chronology of the Early Years, 1770–1799* (Cambridge, MA: Harvard University Press, 1967), p. 119 and Appendix vii, pp. 315–17.
2 Mary Moorman, *William Wordsworth, a Biography. The Early Years, 1770–1803* (Oxford: Clarendon Press, 1957), p. 91.
3 Dorothy Wordsworth (DW) to Jane Pollard, 26 June 1791, in E. de Selincourt (ed.), *The Letters of William and Dorothy Wordsworth: the Early Years, 1787–1805*, rev. Chester L. Shaver (Oxford: Clarendon Press, 1967), p. 51.
4 *A Description of the Scenery of the Lakes in the North of England* (London: Longman, 1823), p .8.
5 Moorman, *Early Years*, p. 161.
6 G. B. Hill (ed.), *Boswell's Life of Johnson*, rev. L. F. Powell (Oxford: Clarendon Press, 1934), vol. v, pp. 441, 442.
7 Ibid., p. 452.
8 Ibid., p. 590.
9 Samuel Johnson, *Lives of the English Poets*, ed. G. B. Hill (Oxford: Clarendon Press, 1945), vol. iii, p. 438–9.
10 William Powell Jones, *Thomas Gray, Scholar* (Cambridge, MA: Harvard University Press, 1937), pp. 84–5 and pp. 90–9.
11 Ibid., p. 93.
12 For an account of the composition of the poem, and its interruption, see Roger Lonsdale (ed.), *The Poems of Thomas Gray, William Collins, Oliver Goldsmith* (London and Harlow: Longman, 1969), pp. 177–200.
13 P. Toynbee and L. Whibley (eds.), *Correspondence of Thomas Gray* (Oxford: Clarendon Press, 1935), p. 502.
14 Simon Schama, *Landscape and Memory* (London: Fontana Press, 1995), p. 470.
15 Moorman, *Early Years*, pp. 128, 135.

16 William Mason, *The Poems and Letters of Thomas Gray* (London: R. Priestley, 1820), p. 242.

17 Henry Penruddocke Wyndham, *A Tour through Monmouthshire and Wales, Made in the Months of June and July, 1774. And in the Months of June, July and August, 1777* (London, 2nd edn, 1781).

18 Ibid., p. 126, p. 13.

19 Nicholas Owen, *A History of the Island of Anglesey* (London, 1775), p. 11. Owen's description is echoed in Sharon Turner's *History of the Anglo-Saxons* (see note 29). Turner makes it clear that druidical punishment could have disastrous consequences: 'Whoever disobeyed their decree, was interdicted from their sacrifices, which with them was the severest puishment. An interdicted person was deemed both impious and wicked; all fled from him, and avoided his presence and conversation, lest they should be contaminated by the intercourse. He was allowed no legal rights. He participated in no honours.'

20 Thomas Pennant, *A Tour in Wales* (London, 2nd edn, 1784), vol. I, p. 1.

21 Ibid., vol. II, p. 172.

22 Reed, *Chronology, 1770–1799*, p. 316. Reed's Appendix VII, on 'Wordsworth's Early Travels in Wales', is the most comprehensive account of the facts and dating problems of the poet's visits in 1791 and 1793.

23 Moorman, *Early Years*, pp. 238–9.

24 See Kenneth Woodbridge, *Landscape and Antiquity, Aspects of English Culture at Stourhead, 1718 to 1838* (Oxford: Clarendon Press, 1970); M. W. Thompson (ed.), *The Journeys of Sir Richard Colt Hoare through Wales and England, 1793–1810* (Stroud: Alan Sutton, 1983).

25 E. Relph, *Place and Placelessness* (London: Pion, 1976), p. 17.

26 Quotations from *The Prelude* are taken from the 1850 text, which in places (such as the begining of Book XIV) contains phrases that are important for the argument. Book and line references follow quotations in the text.

27 Moorman, *Early Years*, p. 224.

28 W. J. B. Owen and Jane Worthington Smyser (eds.), *Concerning the Convention of Cintra. The Prose Works of William Wordsworth* (Oxford: Clarendon Press, 1974), vol. I, p. 328.

29 Sharon Turner, *A History of the Anglo-Saxons* (London, 1799–1805, 4th edn, 1823), vol. I, pp. 319–21. The story of the sack of Ancient Bangor is also found in Bede's *Ecclesiastical History*, but there it is seen as a fight between the Celtic Christians and the English (Augustinian) Christians, and there is no mention of Taliesin. See (ed.) Bertram Colgrave and R. B. Mynor's *Bede's Ecclesiastical History of the English People* (Oxford: Clarendon Press, 1969), p. 141.

30 DW to Lady Beaumont, 18 September 1824, in de Selincourt (ed.), *The Letters of William and Dorothy Wordsworth: the Later Years* (Part 1), rev. Alan G. Hill (Oxford: Clarendon Press, 1978), p. 273. Wordsworth described Jones as 'very rubicund in Complexion and weigh[ing] about 17 stone, and would, as they said, make 3 good hermits for the Vale of which he is Curate' (ibid., p. 277). Curiously, Bede's *Ecclesiastical History* at one point makes it clear that hermits

were very important in Welsh Christianity (Colgrave and Mynors (eds.), *Bede's Ecclesiastical History*, p. 137n).
31 *Letters of William and Dorothy Wordsworth: the Later Years*, p. 278.
32 DW to John Kenyon, 4 October 1824, ibid., p. 281.
33 WW to Jane Marshall, late November 1824, ibid., p. 289.

7 THE FORCE OF 'CELTIC MEMORIES'

1 Matthew Arnold, 'On the Study of Celtic Literature', in R. H. Super (ed.), *The Complete Prose Works of Matthew Arnold* (Ann Arbor, MI: University of Michigan Press, 1960–78) vol. IX, p. 373.
2 Jerome J. McGann (ed.), *The Complete Poetical Works of Lord Byron* (Oxford: Clarendon Press, 1980–93), vol. VII, p. 44. All quotations from Byron's poetry are taken from this edition (hereafter referred to as *Works*). Canto (where appropriate) and line references follow quotations in the main text.
3 Leslie A. Marchand, *Byron: a Biography* (London: John Murray, 1957), vol. I, p. 42.
4 Leslie Marchand (ed.), *Byron's Letters and Journals* (London: John Murray, 1973–94), (hereafter referred to as *BLJ*) vol. IV, p. 146.
5 How much Gaelic was spoken there at that time, I have found difficult to ascertain. It would certainly have been spoken but 'by the 1790s Gaelic was fast giving way to English throughout the north-east central Highlands'. Nevertheless the Gaelic language was 'very generally spoken throughout the whole parish of Crathie and Braemar' [Deeside] in 1842. Byron would have heard some Gaelic in Aberdeen itself. There was a Gaelic chapel opened in 1795. Previously some Gaelic services had been held in St Nicholas. In 1839, the Gaelic Parochial district 'contained 1,486 persons'. But there was an increasing use of English in these chapels. Certainly some Gaelic texts were printed in Aberdeen and, by 1815, there were two Gaelic schools. See Charles W. J. Withers, *Gaelic in Scotland 1698–1981* (Edinburgh: John Donald, 1984), pp. 197, 199, 201, 203, 256, 308.
6 *Works*, vol. I, p. 33.
7 Ibid., p. 393.
8 E.g. 'For Nature then an English audience felt—' (*English Bards and Scotch Reviewers*, line 116).
9 *Works*, vol. I, p. 409.
10 Thomas Moore, *Life of Lord Byron* (London: John Murray, 1853), vol. I, p. 19. He did, it seems, visit Scotland once again when he was fifteen. See J. M. Bulloch, *The House of Gordon* (Aberdeen, 1903), vol. II, p. 142.
11 Karl Elze, *Lord Byron* (London: John Murray, 1872), p. 9. He gives no authority for this statement and it is not in Moore's *Life* or other obvious sources. Elze is usually careful in his statements though and it is plausible enough. Certainly he was entered in the Aberdeen School Register as 'Geo. Bayron Gordon' (Bulloch, *House of Gordon*, vol. II, p. 141). Elze also gives, from Moore, a story from Byron's childhood opposed to my emphasis which is that Byron gave

another boy a drubbing as he had promised 'for that he was a Byron and would never belie his motto "Trust Byron"' (p. 23).

12 Bulloch, *House of Gordon*, vol. II, pp. 127–8.

13 Moore, *Life of Lord Byron*, vol. I, p. 10.

14 Bulloch, *House of Gordon*, vol. II, p. 125.

15 Benita Eisler, *Byron: Child of Passion, Fool of Fame* (London: Hamish Hamilton, 1999), p. 24. No source is given, perhaps taken from Elze who also gives no source.

16 *BLJ*, vol. VII, p. 61.

17 16 October 1820, in *BLJ*, vol. VII, p. 204. A few days later, he writes again to Murray, 25 October 1820, and reveals that the claims in the earlier letter are all wrong for 'Sir John Gordon was not of Gight' (*BLJ*, vol. VII, p. 212). He explains it thus: 'I must have made all these mistakes in recollecting my mother's account of the matter . . . She had a long list of ancestors like Sir Lucius O'Trigger'. Not withstanding this disclaimer, we note that Byron had gone to the trouble of immediately looking up the reference to verify whether one of his ancestors was involved in Scott's historical fiction.

18 *BLJ*, vol. VII, p. 204.

19 *Works*, vol. I, p. 373, n. 25.

20 Leslie Marchand, *Byron: a Portrait* (London: John Murray, 1971), p. 366. By the terms of the will Byron took the Noel arms. As in his own mother's case, this was done to preserve the family name in the case of female inheritance.

21 *Works*, vol. I, p. 5, 33.

22 See note 13.

23 Ernest J. Lovell Jr (ed.), *Medwin's Conversations of Lord Byron* (Princeton, NJ: Princeton University Press, 1966), p. 59.

24 E. H. Coleridge (ed.), *Byron's Works* (London: John Murray, 1899–1904, revised and enlarged, 1922), vol. V, p. 578, n. 1.

25 In 1822, Byron wrote: 'my heart warms to the Tartan . . . or to anything of Scotland which reminds me of Aberdeen and other parts not so far from the Highlands' (letter to Walter Scott, 12 January 1822, in *BLJ*, vol. IX, p. 87). The reference is to chapter 49 of *The Heart of Midlothian*. 'the dress which he himself chiefly wore at Cephalonia was a tartan jacket' (Moore, *Life of Lord Byron*, vol. I, p. 35). Byron wore the 'old' Gordon tartan which is not exactly the same as the present one, but even the 'old' tartan was itself part of a notional revival of Highland costume which gathered pace in the early nineteenth century.

26 'In yonder Grave a Druid lies'. The first line of Collins's 'Ode occasion'd by the Death of Mr. Thomson'.

27 See line 7 of 'To Samuel Rogers', *Works*, vol. III, p. 13.

28 A. L. Owen, *The Famous Druids: a Survey of Three Centuries of English Literature on the Druids* (Oxford: Clarendon Press, 1962). There is one discarded reference in Byron's poetry that does endorse the customary poetic associations of the word. There is an unrecorded and uncancelled reading in the original draft MS of *The Prophecy of Dante*, Canto III, line 68 which reads:

Tuneful   thy Druids
<Numerous>shall be <th<eir>y numbers.

Although Byron never adopted it in his fair copy, it remains uncancelled in the first draft. I am most grateful to Andrew Nicholson for this point.

29 *English Bards and Scotch Reviewers*, line 741: *Hints from Horace*, line 696.
30 Walter Scott, *Rob Roy* (London: John Nimmo, 1893), vol. I, p. 55.
31 'Celtic ancestors' has to be understood in a general sense which is that of the time. Scott, for instance, often uses the word 'Highlander' and 'Celt' interchangeably. The Gordons did not stem from North East Highlands and were in origin, ironically enough, Anglo-Norman just like the Byrons. See J. A. Rennie, *The Scottish People* (London: Hutchinson, 1960), p. 128.
32 His direct ancestors, certainly throughout the eighteenth century, were not Catholic but all branches of the Gordons numbered many Catholics amongst them and were often Jacobites.
33 'Ah! You were destined to die at Culloden' ('Lachin Y Gair', line 27). Byron notes: 'whether any perished in the Battle of Culloden, I am not certain; but as many fell in the insurrection, I have used the name of the principal action, "pars pro toto"' (*Works*, vol. I, p. 373, n. 27).
34 *BLJ*, vol. I, p. 114.
35 Section xxi of *The Field of Waterloo* contains all these references. I quote from Logie Robertson (ed.), *The Poetical Works of Sir Walter Scott* (London: Oxford University Press, 1917).
36 *Childe Harold's Pilgrimage*, III, line 253.
37 *Works*, vol. II, p. 303.
38 T. S. Eliot, *On Poetry and Poets* (London: Faber, 1957), p. 202.
39 Marchand, *Byron: a Portrait*, p. 241.
40 Edgar Johnson, *The Great Unknown* (London: Hamish Hamilton, 1970), vol. II, p. 1098.
41 *BLJ*, vol. I, p. 131.
42 3 May 1814, in ibid., vol. IV, p. 113.
43 Andrew Noble, 'Byron: Radical, Scottish Aristocrat', in Angus Calder (ed.), *Byron and Scotland* (Edinburgh University Press, 1989), p. 38.
44 *Works*, vol. III, p. 459, n. 233.
45 Ibid., p. 416, n. 1.
46 Ibid., n. 2.
47 Murray G. H. Pittock, *The Myth of the Jacobite Clans* (Edinburgh University Press, 1995), p. 37.

8 SHELLEY, IRELAND AND ROMANTIC ORIENTALISM

1 In the absence of a new edition of *Laon and Cythna* at the time of writing, all references to the poem are to Harry Buxton Forman (ed.), *The Works of Percy Bysshe Shelley in Verse and Prose* (London: Reeves and Turner, 1880), which is hereafter abbreviated as (S). 'The Tombs', 'On Robert Emmet's Tomb', 'To the Republicans of North America', 'The Devil's Walk' and 'The Ocean

Rolls Between Us' are quoted from Geoffrey Matthews and Kelvin Everest (eds.), *The Poetry of Percy Bysshe Shelley* (London and New York: Longman, 1989–), hereafter abbreviated as (SP). *An Address to the Irish People, Proposals for an Association of Philanthropists* and *Declaration of Rights* are quoted from E. B. Murray (ed.), *The Prose Works of Percy Bysshe Shelley* (Oxford: Clarendon Press, 1993–), hereafter (SPW). Shelley's letters are quoted from Frederick L. Jones (ed.), *The Letters of Percy Bysshe Shelley* (Oxford: Clarendon Press, 1964), hereafter (SL). All quotations from these works are followed by references in the main text.

2 In Shelley's Irish lyric, 'The Ocean Rolls Between Us' (1812), Ireland is described in very similar terms: 'O thou Ocean / Whose multitudinous billows overlash / Erin's green isle...' (1–3).

3 Marilyn Butler, 'Plotting the Revolution: the Political Narrative of Romantic Poetry and Criticism', in Kenneth R. Johnston, Gilbert Chaitain and Herbert Marks (eds.), *Romantic Revolutions: Criticism and Theory* (Bloomington, IN: Indiana University Press, 1990), pp. 133–58, 135.

4 Nigel Leask, *British Romantic Writers and the East: Anxieties of Empire* (Cambridge: Cambridge University Press, 1992); Mohammed Sharafuddin, *Islam and Romantic Orientalism: Literary Encounters with the Orient* (London and New York: I. B. Tauris, 1994). I am indebted to both these works notwithstanding the differences of emphasis and interpretation to be found in this chapter.

5 In this discussion, the terms 'Orient' (and to a certain extent 'Ireland') are used to denote what Edward Said famously calls 'a discursive phenomenon, internally consistent and self-perpetuating' (Edward Said, *Orientalism* [New York: Vintage, 1991], p. 5).

6 Michael O'Neill, *Percy Bysshe Shelley: a Literary Life* (London: Macmillan, 1989), p. 22.

7 P. M. S. Dawson, *The Unacknowledged Legislator: Shelley and Politics* (Oxford: Clarendon Press, 1980), pp. 134–66.

8 Marianne Elliott, *Partners in Revolution: the United Irishmen and France* (New Haven, CT and London: Yale University Press, 1982), pp. 282–323.

9 Hampshire County Record Office 38M49/5/42. See Elliott, *Partners in Revolution*, p. 313.

10 Timothy Webb, '"A Noble Field": Shelley's Irish Expedition and the Lessons of the French Revolution', in Nadia Minerva (ed.), *Robespierre and Co.: atti della ricerca sulla Letteratura Francese della Revoluzione* (Bologna: Edizione Analisi, 1990), vol. II, pp. 553–76. I am particularly indebted to Webb's ground-breaking work in this field.

11 Webb, '"A Noble Field"', p. 573.

12 Leask, *British Romantic Writers and the East*, pp. 113, 114.

13 Constantin Volney, *Les Ruines, ou méditation sur les révolutions des empires* (Paris: Canongette et Campagnie, 1830), p. 243. Translation mine.

14 Leask, *British Romantic Writers and the East*, p. 89.

15 In their respective studies of Romantic Orientalism, both Leask and Sharafudin read Moore's *Lallah Rookh* as an allegory of Irish nationalism.

Unfortunately, Sharaffudin's more extensive analysis is let down by a tendency to confuse Robert Emmet with Wolfe Tone: 'He [Moore] was unable to participate in the 1798 rebellion, which cost Emmet his life, because of illness... It is certainly possible to see in the Ghebers doomed revolt a shadow of the 1798 rebellion, and, in the fate of its dashing heroic chieftain, Hafed, an echo of Robert Emmet' (Sharaffudin, *Islam and Romantic Orientalism*, pp. 171, 173).

16 I would like to thank Melissa Fegan for drawing this reference to my attention.

17 R. N. C. Vance, 'Texts and Traditions: Robert Emmet's Speech from the Dock', *Studies* 71 (Summer, 1982), pp. 185–91. Despite their inclusion in many subsequent editions of his speech, Vance argues that Emmet may never have actually uttered these famous lines about Ireland as a nation.

18 Thomas Jefferson Hogg, *The Life of Percy Bysshe Shelley* (London and New York: George Routledge and Sons, 1906), p. 366.

19 'The reference is apparently, in part at least, to Lord Castlereagh, who represented the "legioned west" (Great Britain) at the Congress of Vienna' (Kenneth Neil Cameron, *Shelley: the Golden Years* [Cambridge, MA: Harvard University Press, 1974], p. 336).

9 BYRON AND THE 'ARIOSTO OF THE NORTH'

For Jane Stabler and Peter Cochran.

1 Leslie Marchand (ed.), *Byron's Letters and Journals*, 13 vols. (London: John Murray, 1973–94), (hereafter referred to as *BLJ*), vol. v, p. 266. See also *Childe Harold*, iv, stanza 40 in *Lord Byron, The Complete Poetical Works*, ed. Jerome J. McGann (Oxford: Clarendon Press, 1980–93), vol. ii, p. 137.

2 See especially Andrew Rutherford (ed.), *Byron: the Critical Heritage* (London: Routledge and Kegan Paul, 1970), pp. 40, 57, 59–60, 66, 99, 154, and John O. Hayden (ed.), *Scott: the Critical Heritage* (London: Routledge and Kegan Paul, 1970) (hereafter referred to as *SCH*), pp. 270–1.

3 John Gibson Lockhart, *Life of Sir Walter Scott* (London: Adam and Charles Black, 1893), p. 309.

4 *Letters of Sir Walter Scott*, ed. H. J. C. Grierson, 12 vols. (London: Constable, 1932–7), see especially vol. iii, pp. 99, 114–15, 123, 135, 136–39, 217–18 and 396.

5 See for example, Scott, *Letters*, vol. iii, p. 457 and 478–9.

6 *BLJ*, vol. ii, p. 193 and vol. iii, p. 168.

7 *English Bards and Scotch Reviewers*, lines 153–88 and n. in vol. i, pp. 234–5 of Jerome J. McGann (ed.), *Lord Byron: The Complete Poetical Works*, 7 vols (Oxford: Clarendon Press, 1980–93). All quotations from Byron's poetry are taken from this edition (hereafter referred to as *Works*). Canto (where appropriate) and line references follow quotations in the main text.

8 *Works*, vol. i, p. 402.

9 *Hints from Horace*, lines 79–86 (*Works*, vol. i, p. 292).

10 Ibid., lines 403–10 (*Works*, vol. i, p. 304).

11 *SCH*, pp. 47 and 49.

12 This and the following three quotations are taken from the Holland House Papers in the British Library (Add. MSS. 51639), fo. 9.

13 Ibid., fo. 128.

14 Ibid., fo. 146–48.

15 Ibid., fo. 150.

16 *BLJ*, vol. III, p. 168.

17 Ibid., p. 209 and 219–20 (see also p. 250).

18 *Works*, vol. III, p. 149.

19 *BLJ*, vol. I, p. 227.

20 *Childe Harold*, II, stanzas 55–60 and 62, lines 1–5 (*Works*, vol. II, pp. 61–3).

21 *Works*, vol. II, pp. 192–3.

22 J. Logie Robertson (ed.), *The Poetical Works of Sir Walter Scott* (Oxford University Press, 1909) (hereafter *SPW*), pp. 3–4.

23 *SPW*, p. 1.

24 Ibid., p. 585. *The Bridal of Triermain* was first printed anonymously and without the Introduction in the *Edinburgh Annual Register* (1809). It was first published under Scott's name and with the Introduction in 1813.

25 Ibid., p. 585.

26 Ibid., p. 586.

27 See n. 21 above.

28 *The Island* (1823), II. xii, lines 290–93 (*Works*, vol. VII, p. 44; see also p. 145 for Byron's own note to these lines).

29 E. T. Cook and Alexander Wedderburn (eds.), *The Works of John Ruskin* (London, 1903–12), vol. XXXIV, p. 331 (Ruskin's emphasis).

30 Ibid.

31 *The Vision of Don Roderick* (1811), III. xvi (*SPW*, p. 609).

32 Scott, *Novels and Tales* (Edinburgh: Constable. 1825), vol. X, ch. iv, pp. 86–7.

33 *BLJ*, vol. III, p. 218.

34 *Childe Harold*, IV, stanzas 108, 45 and 46 (*Works*, vol. II, pp. 160 and 139).

35 *Childe Harold*, III, stanzas 179, 180 and 94 (*CPW*, vol. II, pp. 184 and 155).

36 *The Age of Bronze* (1823), I, lines 1–4 (*Works*, vol. VII, p. 1).

37 *The Field of Waterloo* (1815) (*SPW*, p. 627).

38 *The Antiquary* (1816), vol. II, ch. ix, pp. 230–1.

39 *Works*, vol. V, p. 476.

40 Ibid., pp. 614–15.

41 See Andrew Nicholson (ed.), *The Manuscripts of the Younger Romantics. Lord Byron. Volume X. Don Juan Cantos XIV and XV Manuscripts* (New York and London: Garland Publishing, 1995), pp. 94–5 and 151–2.

42 For fuller details, see Andrew Nicholson (ed.), *Byron: the Complete Miscellaneous Prose* (Oxford : Clarendon Press, 1991) (hereafter *CMP*), pp. 354–5.

43 *Works*, vol. V, p. 606.

44 *The Lay of the Last Minstrel*, IV. xxiv: 'Either receive within thy towers / Two hundred of my master's powers, / Or straight they sound their warrison, / And storm and spoil thy garrison' (*SPW*, p. 27).

45 W. E. K. Anderson (ed.), *The Journal of Sir Walter Scott*, rev. edn (Edinburgh: Canongate, 1998), p. 316.
46 See his section 'De l'Arioste' under 'Epopée' in his *Dictionnaire philosophique*, 14 vols. (1816), vol. VII, pp. 102–12 (quotation from pp. 102–3).
47 *CMP*, p. 160.
48 See *BLJ*, vol. VIII, p. 13.
49 *Works*, vol. V, pp. 441–2.
50 *Works*, vol. II, p. 169.
51 *De Divinatione*, I. xxxi. 66: 'furor appellatur, cum a corpore animus abstractus divino instinctu concitatur' (it is called frenzy when the mind is abstracted from the body and inspired by divine influence).
52 *Macbeth*, III. ii. 13 (the emphasis is Byron's).
53 *The Lay of the Last Minstrel*, VI. ii: 'Land of brown heath and shaggy wood, / Land of the mountain and the flood, / Land of my sires!' (*SPW*, p. 39).

10 SCOTT AND THE BRITISH TOURIST

1 Jeremy Black, *The British Abroad: the Grand Tour in the Eighteenth Century* (Stroud: Alan Sutton, 1992), pp. xi, 3, 4, 7, 9. Hereafter page references to this work will follow quotations in the main text.
2 See Paul Monod, 'Pierre's White Hat', in Eveline Cruickshanks (ed.), *By Force or By Default?* (Edinburgh: John Donald, 1989).
3 Murray G. H. Pittock, *Celtic Identity and the British Image* (Manchester: Manchester University Press, 1999), pp. 36, 75–6 (hereafter page references to this work will follow quotations in the main text); Jean-Jacques Rousseau, *Du Contrat social*, ch. 1. For Skene, see especially Clive Dewey, 'Celtic Agrarian Legislation and the Celtic Revival: Historicist Implications of Gladstone's Irish and Scottish Land Acts 1870–1886', *Past and Present* (August 1974), pp. 30–70, pp. 50, 52.
4 Final chorus of *Hellas* in *The Works of P. B. Shelley* (Ware: Wordsworth, 1994), p. 270.
5 *Michael*, from *Lyrical Ballads*.
6 Robert Southey, 'The Death of Wallace' and *Madoc*, in *Poetical Works* (London: Longman, 1845), pp. 128, 313–416.
7 Katherine Jean Haldane (now Haldane Grenier), 'Imagining Scotland: Tourist Images of Scotland 1770–1914' (unpublished PhD thesis, University of Virginia, 1990), pp. 6, 9 (hereafter page references to this work will follow quotations in the main text). For discussion of *Gemeinschaft/Gesellschaft*, see Murray G. H. Pittock, *Scottish Nationality* (Basingstoke: Palgrave, 2001), p. 7 n. 21.
8 John Glendening, *The High Road: Romantic Tourism, Scotland and Literature, 1720–1820* (Basingstoke: Macmillan, 1997), p. 7.
9 John R. and Margaret M. Gold, *Imagining Scotland: Tradition, Representation and Promotion in Scottish Tourism since 1750* (Aldershot: Scolar Press, 1995), p. 55.

10 Malcolm Andrews (ed.), *The Picturesque: Literary Sources and Documents* (Mountfield: Helm Information, 1994), vol. I, p. 9. Hereafter page references to this work will follow quotations in the main text.

11 Edmund Burke, A *Philosophical Enquiry into the Origin of our Ideas of the Sublime and the Beautiful*, ed. James T. Boulton (1958; London: Routledge and Kegan Paul, 1987), pp. xxx, xxxv–xxxvii, xlii.

12 Bartan Thurber, 'Scott and the Sublime', in J. H. Alexander and David Hewitt (eds.), *Scott and his Influence* (Aberdeen: Association for Scottish Literary Studies, 1983), pp. 87–98, p. 93; see also Marinell Ash, 'A Past "Filled with Living Men": Scott, Daniel Wilson and Scottish and American Archaeology', ibid., pp. 432–42, p. 433.

13 Carl Paul Barbier, *William Gilpin* (Oxford: Clarendon Press, 1963), pp. 99, 115, 123–4, 144. Hereafter page references to this work will follow quotations in the main text.

14 H. J. C. Grierson with Davidson Cook, W. M. Parker and others (eds.), *The Letters of Sir Walter Scott* (London: Constable, 1932), vol. III, p. 240 and vol. XII, p. 329; Andrews, *Picturesque*, vol. III, p. 60. Scott was studying Price in 1811 and 1813.

15 Karl Kroeber, *Romantic Landscape Vision: Constable and Wordsworth* (Madison, WI: University of Wisconsin Press, 1975), p. 136.

16 William Ruddick, 'Sir Walter Scott's Northumberland', in Alexander and Hewitt, *Scott and his Influence*, pp. 20–30 (p. 21). Hereafter page references to this work will follow quotations in the main text.

17 William Vaughan, *Romanticism in Art* (1978; London: Thames and Hudson, 1994), p. 38.

18 Alexander M. Ross, '"Waverley" and the Picturesque', in Alexander and Hewitt, *Scott and his Influence*, pp. 99–108, p. 99 (hereafter page references to this work will follow quotations in the main text); Michel Baridon, 'Philosophic Light and Gothic Gloom: Landscape and History in Eighteenth-Century Scotland', in Jennifer J. Carter and Joan H. Pittock (eds.), *Aberdeen and the Enlightenment* (Aberdeen: Aberdeen University Press, 1987), pp. 218–37, p. 233.

19 Dr Gill Hughes, email of 6 March 2001 to the author; *Edinburgh Evening Courant* 14, 18 April 1814.

20 John O. Hayden (ed.), *Scott: the Critical Heritage* (London: Routledge and Kegan Paul, 1970), p. 57.

21 Tobias Smollett, *The Expedition of Humphrey Clinker*, ed. Peter Miles (London: J. M. Dent, 1993), p. 246.

22 Peter Lord, *Words with Pictures: Welsh Images and Images of Wales in the Popular Press, 1640–1860* (Aberystwyth: Planet, 1995), pp. 27, 67; *Gwenllian: Essays on Visual Culture* (Llandysul: Gomer Press, 1994), p. 103.

23 Sir Walter Scott, *Waverley*, ed. Andrew Hook (London: Penguin, 1985). Page references to this edition follow quotations in the main text.

24 S. C. Kaines Smith, *An Outline History of Painting in Europe to the end of the Nineteenth Century* (London and Boston, MA: Medici Society, n.d.), pp. 181–4.

25 Adam Ferguson, *An Essay on the History of Civil Society*, ed. Franz Oz-Salzberger (Cambridge University Press, 1995 [1767]), pp. 105.

26 Jana Davis, 'Landscape Images and Epistemology in "Guy Mannering"', in Alexander and Hewitt, *Scott and his Influence*, pp. 119–28, p. 119.

27 Sir Walter Scott, *The Bride of Lammermoor*, ed. W. M. Parker (1906; London: J. M. Dent, 1988), p. 81; *The Heart of Midlothian*, ed. Claire Lamont (Oxford University Press, 1982), p. 151. Hereafter page references to these editions will follow quotations in the main text.

28 Sir Walter Scott, *Redgauntlet*, ed. Kathryn Sutherland (Oxford University Press, 1985), p. 32; *Old Mortality*, ed. Angus Calder (1975; Harmondsworth: Penguin, 1987), p. 462. Hereafter page references to these editions will follow quotations in the main text.

29 *The Poetical Works of Sir Walter Scott, Bart* (Edinburgh: Adam and Charles Black, 1853), pp. 247, 279. All quotations from Scott's poetry are taken from this edition. Page references follow quotations in the main text.

30 Hogg's poem, first printed in *The Spy*, pits 'Saxon' against 'Scot' (James Hogg, *The Spy*, ed. Gillian Hughes [Edinburgh: Edinburgh University Press, 2000]).

31 E. de Selincourt (ed.), *Journals of Dorothy Wordsworth* (London: Macmillan, 1941), vol. I, pp. 207, 214, 252, 268, 272, 332, 390, 399.

32 Stephen Gill, *William Wordsworth: a Life* (1989; Oxford: Oxford University Press, 1990), pp. 25, 26, 37, 214, 217, 255, 261, 275, 297.

33 Thomas Deegan, 'Walter Scott and the American Western Film', in Alexander and Hewitt, *Scott in Carnival* (Aberdeen: Association for Scottish Literary Studies, 1993), pp. 569–80, p. 576.

34 Pittock, *Scottish Nationality*, p. 86; James Anderson, *Sir Walter Scott and History* (Edinburgh: Edina Press, 1981), p. 4.

35 Murray G. H. Pittock, *The Invention of Scotland* (London: Routledge, 1991), pp. 103, 108.

36 William Secord, *Dog Painting: the European Breeds* (Woodbridge: Antique Collectors' Club, 2000), p. 89.

37 John Prebble, *The King's Jaunt* (London: HarperCollins, 1988), pp. 19, 103, 131.

38 William Donaldson, *The Highland Pipe and Scottish Society 1750–1950* (East Linton: Tuckwell Press, 2000), p. 112 n., p. 153.

39 Sydney and Olive Checkland, *Industry and Ethos: Scotland 1832–1914* (London: Edward Arnold, 1986), p. 28. Hereafter page references to this work will follow quotations in the main text.

40 Angus Calder, *Revolving Culture: Notes from the Scottish Republic* (London and New York: I. B. Tauris, 1994), p. 88 for *Marmion's* sales.

41 J. H. Alexander, 'To Visit or not to Visit ? The Yarrow Question in the "Lay" and "Marmion"', in Alexander and Hewitt, *Scott and his Influence*, pp. 31–40, p. 31.

42 Charles Jedrej and Mark Nuttall, *White Settlers: the Impact of Rural Repopulation in Scotland* (Luxembourg: Harwood, 1996), pp. 15, 17, 24.

43 David McCrone, Angela Morris and Richard Kiely, *Scotland – the Brand* (Edinburgh: Edinburgh University Press, 1995), p. 91.

11 FELICIA HEMANS,BYRONIC COSMOPOLITANISM AND THE ANCIENT WELSH BARDS

1 'A Farewell to Wales', in *The Poetical Works of Mrs Hemans* (London: Frederick Warne, 1900), p. 474.
2 Peter W. Trinder, *Mrs Hemans* (Cardiff: University of Wales Press, 1984), p. 3.
3 Ibid., p. 30.
4 Jane Aaron, 'The Way Above the World: Religion and Gender in Welsh and Anglo-Welsh Women's Writing, 1780–1830', in Carol Shiner Wilson and Joel Haefner (eds.), *Re-Visioning Romanticism: British Women Writers, 1776–1837* (Philadelphia, PA: University of Pennsylvania Press, 1994), pp. 111–27, pp. 125–6. Citing Francis Jeffrey's October 1829 review of Hemans's *Records of Woman* and *The Forest Sanctuary*, Susan J. Wolfson discusses the 'happy Englishing of world literature' and the 'able broadcasting of English standards', present in Hemans's poems set in foreign cultures (Susan J. Wolfson, '"Domestic Affections" and "the Spear of Minerva": Felicia Hemans and the Dilemma of Gender', in Wilson and Haefner, *Re-Visioning Romanticism*, pp. 128–66, p. 132.
5 Tricia Lootens, 'Hemans and Home: Victorianism, Feminine "Internal Enemies", and the Domestication of National Identity', *PMLA* 109.2 (March 1994), p. 239, quoting from Hazlitt's discussion of patriotism.
6 Nanora Sweet, 'History, Imperialism, and the Aesthetics of the Beautiful: Hemans and the Post-Napoleonic Moment', in Mary A. Favret and Nicola J. Watson (eds.), *At the Limitis of Romanticism: Essays in Cultural, Feminist, and Materialist Criticism* (Bloomington, IN: Indiana University Press, 1994), pp. 170–84, p. 173.
7 See *Don Juan*, X, line 17. All quotations from Byron's poetry are taken from Jerome J. McGann and Barry Weller (eds.), *Lord Byron: the Complete Poetical Works* (Oxford: Oxford University Press, 1980–91). Hereafter line references follow quotations in the main text.
8 T. S. Eliot, 'Byron', in M. H. Abrams (ed.), *English Romantic Poets: Modern Essays in Criticism* (London: Oxford University Press, 2nd edn, 1975), pp. 261–74, p. 262.
9 Leslie Marchand (ed.), *Byron's Letters and Journals* (London: John Murray, 1973–82), vol. II, p. 94. All quotations from Byron's letters are taken from this edition (hereafter *BLJ*). Volume and page references follow subsequent quotations in the main text.
10 Jane Aaron, 'The Way Above the World', p. 126.
11 *Stanzas to the Memory of the Late King* (London: John Murray, 1820), p. 6.
12 Henry F. Chorley, *Memorials of Mrs Hemans with Illustrations of her Literary Character from her Private Correspondence* (London: Saunders and Otley, 1836), vol. I, p. 156.

13 Of course, Byron also situated poems in places he had not visited: consider, for example, the Russian section of *Don Juan* and *The Island*, which recounts the South Pacific adventures of the *Bounty* mutineers.

14 Chorley, *Memorials of Mrs Hemans*, vol. II, p. 22.

15 Ernest Bernhardt-Kabisch, *Robert Southey* (Boston: Twayne Publishers, 1977), pp. 110–11. Some Welsh scholars question the theory that the twelfth-century Welsh bards were heavily influenced by Druidism (the twelfth century is when Madoc is supposed to have sailed for America). See John Rhys and David Brynmor-Jones, *The Welsh People: Chapters on their Origin, History and Laws, Language, Literature and Characteristics* (1923; New York: Greenwood Press, 1969), p. 255.

16 Kenneth Curry (ed.), *New Letters of Robert Southey* (New York: Columbia University Press, 1965), vol. I, p. 395.

17 Rev. Robert Williams, *A Biographical Dictionary of Eminent Welshmen, from the Earliest Times to the Present, and Including Every Name Connected with the Ancient History of Wales* (London: Longman, 1852), p. 309.

18 Robert Southey, *Madoc* (London: Longman, Hurst, Rees and Orme, 1805), vol. I, pp. 109, p. viii.

19 Trinder, *Mrs Hemans*, p. 30.

20 Felicia Hemans and John Parry, *A Selection of Welsh Melodies, with Symphonies and Accompaniments by John Parry, and Characteristic Words by Mrs Hemans* (London: J. Power, 1822), 1st Number, p. 45.

21 E. D. Evans, *A History of Wales 1660–1815* (Cardiff: University of Wales Press, 1993), p. 235.

22 See her note to 'Taliesin's Prophecy' (*Welsh Melodies*, 1st Number, p. 37), quoted later in this essay.

23 *The Siege of Valencia; a Dramatic Poem. The Last Constantine: with Other Poems* (London: John Murray, 1823). Page references to this edition follow quotations in the main text.

24 *Cambro-Briton*, June 1822, quoted in Trinder, *Mrs Hemans*, pp. 31–2.

25 Chorley, *Memorials of Mrs Hemans*, vol. I, p. 92.

26 Ibid., pp. 98–9.

27 Trinder, *Mrs Hemans*, p. 33.

28 *Poems. England and Spain. Modern Greece* (New York: Garland, 1978). Page references to this edition follow quotations in the main text.

29 Quotations from Wordsworth's poetry are taken from Stephen Gill (ed.), *The Oxford Authors: William Wordsworth* (Oxford: Oxford University Press, 1984). Book and line references follow quotations in the main text.

30 See *The Siege of Valencia*, p. 312–13; *Welsh Melodies*, 2nd Number, p. 52.

31 Anne K. Mellor, *Romanticism and Gender* (New York: Routledge, 1993), p. 135.

32 Chorley, *Memorials of Mrs Hemans*, vol. I, p. 87.

33 'To Wordsworth', in *Records of Woman: with Other Poems* (London: T. Cadell, 1827), p. 580.

34 Lootens, 'Hemans and Home', p. 247–8.

35 Williams, *Biographical Dictionary of Eminent Welshmen*, p. 477.

36 R. R. Davies, *The Revolt of Owain Glyn Dwr* (Oxford: Oxford University Press, 1995), pp. 144, 326.

37 Ibid., pp. 325–6.

38 Lootens, 'Hemans and Home', p. 239.

39 See Hemans's prize-winning poem, *Wallace's Invocation to Bruce. A Poem* (Edinburgh: William Blackwood, 1819).

40 Some of the poem's sting is taken away by Hemans's footnote, which asserts 'This sanguinary deed is not attested by any historian of credit' (*Welsh Melodies*, 1st Number, p. 60).

41 See *Modern Greece: a Poem* (London: John Murray, 1817), p. 50 and Sweet, 'History, Imperialism, and the Aesthetics of the Beautiful', p. 178.

42 Jerome J. McGann, *The Poetics of Sensibility: a Revolution in Literary Style* (Oxford: Clarendon Press, 1996), p. 160.

43 'The Lost Pleiad', in Jerome J. McGann (ed.), *The New Oxford Book of Romantic Verse* (Oxford: Oxford University Press, 1993), pp. 696–7.

44 *Poetical Works of Mrs Hemans*, p. 57.

12 LUTTRELL OF ARRAN

1 Declan Kiberd, *Inventing Ireland: the Literature of the Modern Nation* (London: Jonathan Cape, 1995; London: Vintage Books, 1996), pp. 33, 73; David Cairns and Shaun Richards, *Writing Ireland: Colonialism, Nationalism and Culture* (Manchester: Manchester University Press, 1988); Seamus Deane, *Strange Country: Modernity and Nationhood in Irish Writing since 1790* (Oxford: Clarendon Press, 1997); W. J. McCormack, *Ascendancy and Tradition in Anglo-Irish Literary History from 1789 to 1939* (Oxford: Clarendon Press, 1985), p. 212; Terry Eagleton, *Crazy John and the Bishop and Other Essays on Irish Culture* (Cork University Press, 1998), p. 247. My concern is with Lever's place in recent Irish cultural studies, and not with histories of the Irish novel.

2 T. Bareham (ed.), *Charles Lever: New Evaluations* (Gerrards Cross: Colin Smythe, 1991); A. Norman Jeffares, *Images of Invention: Essays on Irish Writing* (Gerrards Cross: Colin Smythe, 1996); Vera Kreilkamp, *The Anglo-Irish Novel and the Big House* (New York: Syracuse University Press, 1998). See also Thomas O'Keefe, 'Maria Edgeworth and Charles Lever: the Big House and the Garrison', *Eire* 19 (1977), pp. 81–92; Christopher Morash, 'Reflecting Absent Interiors: the Big House Novels of Charles Lever', in Otto Rauchbauer (ed.), *Ancestral Voices: the Big House in Anglo-Irish Literature* (Hildesheim: Georg Olms Verlag, 1992), pp. 61–76; Julian Moynahan, *Anglo-Irish: the Literary Imagination in a Hyphenated Culture* (Princeton, NJ: Princeton University Press, 1994); Walter Rix, 'Charles Lever: the Irish Dimension of a Cosmopolitan', in Heinz Kosok (ed.), *Studies in Anglo-Irish Literature* (Bonn: Bouvier Verlag Herbert Grundmann, 1982), pp. 54–64.

3 See Kiberd's chapter 'Irish Literature and History', in R. F. Foster (ed.), *The Oxford History of Ireland* (Oxford University Press, 1992) in which the islands

are represented as the home of a native tradition of proto-feminism and proto-anarcho-socialism in comparison with non-Gaelic capitalism, and John Wilson Foster, 'Certain Set Apart: the Western Island in the Irish Renaissance', *Studies* 66 (1977), pp. 263–7. Compare McDonagh's current *The Lieutenant of Inishmore* which (literally) puts a cleaver through Synge's *The Playboy* via Tarantino.

4 Charles Lever, *Luttrell of Arran* (London: Chapman and Hall, 1865). All quotations are taken from this edition, and page references follow quotations in the main text.

5 See M. Girouard, *The Return to Camelot* (New Haven, CT: Yale University Press, 1981).

13 CONTEMPORARY NORTHERN IRISH POETS

1 Joyce to Arthur Power, quoted from James Joyce, *Ulysses*, ed. Jeri Johnson (Oxford University Press, 1993), pp. xxiii–xxiv.

2 John Montague, *Collected Poems* (Loughcrew: Gallery Press, 1995).

3 William Wordsworth, 'Preface' (1802), in Michael Mason (ed.), *Lyrical Ballads* (London: Longman, 1992), p. 59.

4 Aidan Day, *Romanticism* (London: Routledge, 1996), p. 160; Preface to *Alastor* quoted from Donald H. Reiman and Sharon B. Powers (eds.), *Shelley's Poetry and Prose* (New York: Norton, 1977), p. 69. All quotations from Shelley's work are taken from this edition (hereafter referred to as *SPP*), and line references follow quotations in the main text.

5 'There they are, you will have to go a long way round / if you want to avoid them', writes Bunting in 'On the Fly-Leaf of Pound's *Cantos*' in Basil Bunting, *Collected Poems* (Oxford University Press, 1978).

6 Auden's 'Letter to Lord Byron', quoted from Tom Paulin (ed.), *The Faber Book of Political Verse* (London: Faber, 1986). For Paulin's agreement with Hazlitt's critical views of Coleridge and Shelley, see his *The Day-Star of Liberty: William Hazlitt's Radical Style* (London: Faber, 1998).

7 Quoted from Paul Muldoon (ed.), *The Faber Book of Contemporary Irish Poetry* (London: Faber, 1986).

8 Larkin's 'enormous yes' comes from 'For Sidney Bechet'. I also allude to the end of 'High Windows'. Quotations from Larkin's poetry are taken from Philip Larkin, *Collected Poems*, ed. Anthony Thwaite (London: Marvell Press and Faber, 1988). Wordsworth is quoted from Stephen Gill (ed.), *The Oxford Authors: William Wordsworth* (Oxford University Press, 1984), and line references follow quotations in the main text.

9 Robert F. Garratt, *Modern Irish Poetry: Tradition and Continuity from Yeats to Heaney* (Berkeley, CA: University of California Press, 1986), p. 217.

10 Quoted from Edward Larrissy (ed.), *W. B. Yeats* (Oxford: Oxford University Press, 1997).

11 For Yeats and Romanticism, see: Harold Bloom, *Yeats* (London: Oxford University Press, 1970); George Bornstein, *Yeats and Shelley* (Chicago, IL:

University of Chicago Press, 1970); George Bornstein, *Transformations of Romanticism in Yeats, Eliot, and Stevens* (Chicago, IL: University of Chicago Press, 1976).

12 Quoted from Wallace Stevens, *Collected Poems* (London: Faber, 1955).

13 Quoted from *Opened Ground: Poems 1966–1996* (London: Faber, 1998), as are all Heaney's poems, unless otherwise indicated.

14 'The Fire i' the Flint: Reflections on the Poetry of Gerard Manley Hopkins', in Seamus Heaney, *Preoccupations: Selected Prose 1968–1978* (London: Faber, 1980), p. 83; hereafter referred to as *P* in main body of the text.

15 For discussion of Heaney's response to Wordsworth, see: Neil Corcoran, *Seamus Heaney* (London: Faber, 1986); Michael R. Molino, 'Heaney's "Singing School": a Portrait of the Artist', *Journal of Irish Literature* 16.3 (1987), pp. 12–17; Michael Parker, *Seamus Heaney: the Making of the Poet* (Basingstoke: Macmillan, 1993); Helen Vendler, *Seamus Heaney* (London: Faber, 1998); Simon Dentith, 'Heaney and Walcott: Two Poems', *Critical Survey* 11.3 (1999), pp. 92–9. See also Heaney's selection of Wordsworth's poems (with a suggestive introduction) in *The Essential Wordsworth* (New York: Ecco, 1988). For a fine, wide-ranging discussion of the overall topic dealt with in my essay, see Patricia Horton's unpublished PhD thesis 'Romantic Intersections: Romanticism and Contemporary Northern Irish Poetry' (Queen's University of Belfast, 1996).

16 Paul Muldoon, *Madoc: a Mystery* (London: Faber, 1990).

17 Quoted from Ciaran Carson, *The Irish for No* (1987; Newcastle upon Tyne: Bloodaxe, 1988).

18 Neil Corcoran, 'One Step Forward, Two Steps Back: Ciaran Carson's *The Irish for No*', in Neil Corcoran (ed.), *The Chosen Ground: Essays on the Contemporary Poetry of Northern Ireland* (Dufour: Seren, 1992), pp. 215, 214.

19 See also Mary Fitzgerald-Hoyt, 'Grounding Keats's Nightingale: Ciaran Carson's *The Irish for No*', *Canadian Journal of Irish Studies* 19.2 (1993), pp. 76–80.

20 Quoted from Derek Mahon, *Selected Poems* (1990; London: Penguin in association with Oxford University Press, 1993).

21 Seamus Heaney, 'The Drag of the Golden Chain', *Times Literary Supplement*, 12 November 1999, p. 14.

22 Corcoran, *Seamus Heaney*, p. 47.

23 Holly Stevens (ed.), *Letters of Wallace Stevens* (New York: Knopf, 1966), p. 792, quoted from Carlos Baker, *The Echoing Green: Romanticism and the Phenomena of Transference in Poetry* (Princeton, NJ: Princeton University Press, 1984), p. 279.

24 'The Indefatigable Hoof-Taps: Sylvia Plath', in Seamus Heaney, *The Government of the Tongue* (1988; London: Faber, 1989), pp. 154, 159, 163; hereafter referred to as *GT* in main body of the text.

25 Quoted from Seamus Heaney, *North* (London: Faber, 1975).

26 Seamus Heaney, *The Redress of Poetry* (London: Faber, 1995), p. 189.

27 Heaney is quoted from Stan Smith, 'Seamus Heaney: the Distance Between', in Corcoran, *The Chosen Ground*, p. 45.

28 Albert Gelpi, *A Coherent Splendor: the American Poetic Renaissance, 1910–1950* (1987; Cambridge: Cambridge University Press, 1990), pp. 2, 4–5.
29 These two poems are quoted from Derek Mahon, *Poems 1962–1978* (Oxford: Oxford University Press, 1979).
30 Quotations are from Derek Mahon, *The Hudson Letter* (Loughcrew: Gallery, 1995).

Bibliography

Aaron, Jane, 'The Way Above the World: Religion and Gender in Welsh and Anglo-Welsh Women's Writing, 1780–1830', in Carol Shiner Wilson and Joel Haefner (eds.), *Re-Visioning Romanticism: British Women Writers, 1776–1837* (Philadelphia, PA: University of Pennsylvania Press, 1994).

Aers, David, 'Coleridge and the Egg that Burke Laid', *Literature and History* 9.2 (Autumn, 1983).

Airs, Duets, Chrouses, and Argument, of the New Ballet Pantomime (Taken from Ossian) called Oscar and Malvina; or, The Hall of Fingal (London: T. Cadell, 1791).

Alexander, J. H., 'To Visit or not to Visit? The Yarrow Question in the "Lay" and "Marmion"', in J. H. Alexander and David Hewitt (eds.), *Scott and his Influence* (Aberdeen: Association for Scottish Literary Studies, 1983).

Anderson, Benedict, *Imagined Communities: Reflections on the Origin and Spread of Nationalism* (London and New York: Verso, 1983, revised and extended 1991).

Anderson, James, *Sir Walter Scott and History* (Edinburgh: Edina Press, 1981).

Andrews, Malcolm (ed.), *The Picturesque: Literary Sources and Documents* (Mountfield: Helm Information, 1994).

Arnold, Matthew, 'John Keats', in *The Complete Prose Works of Matthew Arnold*, vol III, ed. R. H. Super (Ann Arbor, MI and Toronto: University of Michigan Press, 1962).

'On the Study of Celtic Literature', in R. H. Super (ed.), *The Complete Prose Works of Matthew Arnold*, vol IX (Ann Arbor and Toronto: University of Michigan Press, 1973).

Ash, Marinell, 'A Past "Filled with Living Men": Scott, Daniel Wilson and Scottish and American Archaeology', in Alexander and Hewitt (eds.), *Scott and his Influence*.

Baines, Paul, *The House of Forgery in Eighteenth-Century Britain* (Aldershot: Ashgate, 1999).

Baker, Carlos, *The Echoing Green: Romanticism and the Phenomena of Transference in Poetry* (Princeton, NJ: Princeton University Press, 1984).

Barbier, Carl Paul, *William Gilpin* (Oxford: Clarendon Press, 1963).

Bareham, T., (ed.), *Charles Lever: New Evaluations* (Gerrards Cross: Colin Smythe, 1991).

Baridon, Michel, 'Philosophic Light and Gothic Gloom: Landscape and History in Eighteenth-Century Scotland', in Jennifer J. Carter and Joan H. Pittock (eds), *Aberdeen and the Enlightenment* (Aberdeen: Aberdeen University Press, 1987).

Beatty, Bernard, 'Byron and the Paradoxes of Nationalism', in Vincent Newey and Ann Thompson (eds.), *Literature and Nationalism* (Liverpool: Liverpool University Press, 1991), pp. 152–61.

Bentley, G. E., Jr., *Blake Records* (Oxford: Clarendon Press, 1969).

Black, Jeremy, *The British Abroad: the Grand Tour in the Eighteenth Century* (Stroud: Alan Sutton, 1992).

Blair, Hugh, *A Critical Dissertation on the Poems of Ossian* (1763).

Blake, William, *Blake: the Complete Poems* ed. by W. H. Stevenson (London: Longman, 2nd edn, 1989).

Blake: Complete Writings, ed. Geoffrey Keynes (Oxford: Oxford University Press, 1966).

Bloom, Harold, *Yeats* (London: Oxford University Press, 1970).

Bolts, William, *Consideration on Indian Affairs* (London: J. Almon, 1772).

Borlase, William, *Antiquities, Historical and Monumental of the County of Cornwall*, (London: W. Bowyer and J. Nichols, 2nd edn, 1769).

Bornstein, George, *Transformations of Romanticism in Yeats, Eliot, and Stevens* (Chicago, IL: University of Chicago Press, 1976).

Yeats and Shelley (Chicago, IL: University of Chicago Press, 1970).

Boswell, James, *Boswell's Life of Johnson*, ed. G. B. Hill, rev. L. F. Powell (Oxford: Clarendon Press, 1934).

Breckenridge, Carol, and van der Veer, Peter (eds.), *Orientalism and the Postcolonial Predicament* (Philadelphia, PA: University of Pennsylvania Press, 1993).

Breuilly, John, *Nationalism and the State* (Manchester: Manchester University Press, 2nd edn, 1985).

Bulloch, J. M., *The House of Gordon* (Aberdeen, 1903).

Bunting, Basil, *Collected Poems* (Oxford University Press, 1978).

Burke, Edmund, A *Philosophical Enquiry into the Origin of our Ideas of the Sublime and the Beautiful*, ed. James T. Boulton (1958; London: Routledge and Kegan Paul, 1987).

Burns, Robert, *Poems and Songs*, ed. James Kinsley (London: Oxford University Press, 1971).

Butler, Marilyn, 'Plotting the Revolution: the Political Narrative of Romantic Poetry and Criticism', in Kenneth Johnston, Gilbert Chaitin and Herbert Marks (eds.), *Romantic Revolutions: Criticism and Theory* (Bloomington: Indiana University Press, 1990).

Butt, John, *The Age of Johnson 1740–1789*, ed. (and completed by) Geoffrey Carnall (Oxford, 1977).

Byron, George Gordon, *Byron's Letters and Journals*, ed. Leslie A. Marchand (London: John Murray, 1973–82).

Byron's Works, ed. E. H. Coleridge (London: John Murray, 1899–1904, revised and enlarged, 1922).

Byron: the Complete Miscellaneous Prose, ed. Andrew Nicholson (Oxford: Clarendon Press, 1991)

The Complete Poetical Works of Lord Byron, ed. Jerome J. McGann (Oxford:
Clarendon Press, 1980–93).

*The Manuscripts of the Younger Romantics. Lord Byron. Volume x. Don Juan Cantos
XIV and XV Manuscripts*, ed. Andrew Nicholson (New York and London:
Garland Publishing, 1995).

Medwin's Conversations of Lord Byron, ed. Ernest J. Lovell (Princeton, NJ:
Princeton University Press, 1966).

Cairns, David, and Richards, Shaun, *Writing Ireland: Colonialism, Nationalism and
Culture* (Manchester: Manchester University Press, 1988).

Calder, Angus, *Revolving Culture: Notes from the Scottish Republic* (London and
New York: I. B. Tauris, 1994).

Camden, William, *Britannia*, ed. Edmund Gibson (London: F. Collins, 1695).

Cameron, Kenneth Neil, *Shelley: the Golden Years* (Cambridge, MA: Harvard
University Press, 1974).

Campbell, Joseph, *The Masks of God: Creative Mythology* (New York: Viking Press,
1968).

Carnall, Geoffrey, *Robert Southey and his Age: the Development of a Conservative
Mind* (Oxford: Oxford University Press, 1960).

Carson, Ciaran, *The Irish for No* (1987; Newcastle upon Tyne: Bloodaxe, 1988).

Checkland, Sydney and Olive, *Industry and Ethos: Scotland 1832–1914* (London:
Edward Arnold, 1986).

Chorley, Henry F., *Memorials of Mrs Hemans with Illustrations of her Literary
Character from her Private Correspondence* (London: Saunders and Otley,
1836).

Clifford, James 'Of Other Peoples: Beyond the Savage Paradigm', in Hal Foster
(ed.), *Discussions in Contemporary Culture* (Seattle: Bay Press, 1987).

Colgrave, Betram and Mynors, R. B. (eds.), *Bede's Ecclesiastical History of the English
People* (Oxford: Clarendon Press, 1969).

Colley, Linda, *Britons: Forging the Nation 1707–1837* (New Haven and London:
Yale University Press, 1992).

Collins, William, *The Works of William Collins*, eds. Richard Wendorf and Charles
Ryskamp (Oxford: Clarendon Press, 1979).

Corcoran, Neil, 'One Step Forward, Two Steps Back: Ciaran Carson's *The Irish for
No*', in Neil Corcoran (ed.), *The Chosen Ground: Essays on the Contemporary
Poetry of Northern Ireland* (Dufour: Seren, 1992).

Seamus Heaney (London: Faber, 1986).

Cottle, Joseph, *Reminiscences of Samuel Taylor Coleridge and Robert Southey*
(London: Lime Tree Bower Press, 1970).

Crawford, Robert (ed.), *The Scottish Invention of English Literature* (Cambridge:
Cambridge University Press, 1998).

Cristea, Stephen, 'Ossian v. Homer: an Eighteenth Century Controversy; Melchior
Cesarotti and the Struggle for Literary Freedom', *Italian Studies* 24 (1969),
pp. 93–111.

Crowe, Richard M., 'Iolo Morganwg – An Eighteenth-Century Welsh Linguist', in Cyril J. Byrne, Margaret and Pádraig Ó Siadhail (eds.) *Celtic Language and Celtic Peoples: Proceedings of the 2nd North American Congress of Celtic Studies* (Halifax: St. Mary's University Press, 1992).

Curran, Stuart, *Poetic Form and British Romanticism* (Oxford University Press, 1986).

Curry, Kenneth, 'Southey's *Madoc*: the Manuscript of 1794' in *Philological Quarterly* 22.4 (October, 1943).

Daly, Kirsteen, 'Worlds Beyond England: *Don Juan* and the Legacy of Enlightenment Cosmopolitanism', *Romanticism* 4.2 (1998).

Davies, R. R. *The Revolt of Owain Glyn Dwr* (Oxford: Oxford University Press, 1995).

Davis, Jana, 'Landscape Images and Epistemology in "Guy Mannering"', in J. H. Alexander and David Hewitt (eds.), *Scott and his Influence* (Aberdeen; Association for Scottish Literary Studies, 1983).

Dawson, P. M. S., *The Unacknowledged Legislator: Shelley and Politics* (Oxford: Clarendon Press, 1980).

Day, Aidan, *Romanticism* (London: Routledge, 1996).

Deacon, Richard, *Madoc and the Discovery of America, Some New Light on an Old Controversy* (London: Frederick Muller, 1966).

Deane, Seamus, *Strange Country: Modernity and Nationhood in Irish Writing since 1790* (Oxford: Clarendon Press, 1997).

Deegan, Thomas, 'Walter Scott and the American Western Film', in J. H. Alexander and David Hewitt (eds), *Scott in Carnival* (Aberdeen: Association for Scottish Literary Studies, 1993).

Deleuze, Gilles, and Guattari, Felix, *A Thousand Plateaus: Capitalism and Schizophrenia*, trans. Brian Massumi (London: Athlone, 1988).

Denning, Roy, 'Druidism at Pontypridd', in Stewart Williams (ed.), *Glamorgan Historian* 1 (Cowbridge: Brown and sons, 1963).

Dentith, Simon, 'Heaney and Walcott: Two Poems', *Critical Survey* 11.3 (1999).

Dewey, Clive, 'Celtic Agrarian Legislation and the Celtic Revival: Historicist Implications of Gladstone's Irish and Scottish Land Acts 1870–1886', *Past and Present* (August 1974).

Dibdin, Charles, *The Songs of Charles Dibdin* (London: G. H. Davidson, 1847).

Donaldson, William, *The Highland Pipe and Scottish Society 1750–1950* (East Linton: Tuckwell Press, 2000).

Dukes, Paul, 'Ossian and Russia', *Scottish Literary News* 3.3 (November 1973), pp. 17–21.

Dunn, John J., 'Coleridge's Debt to Macpherson's Ossian', *Studies in Scottish Literature* 7.1 and 2 (July–October 1969).

'Macpherson's Ossian and the Ossianic Controversy: a Contribution towards a Bibliography', *The Bulletin of the New York Public Library* 30.6 and 7 (June, July 1962).

'Macpherson's Ossian and the Ossianic Controversy: a Supplementary Bibliography', *The Bulletin of the New York Public Library* 75.9 (November 1971).

'The Influence of Macpherson's *Ossian* on British Romanticism' (unpublished PhD thesis, Duke University, 1965).

Eagleton, Terry, *Crazy John and the Bishop and Other Essays on Irish Culture* (Cork University Press, 1998).

Eisler, Benita, *Byron: Child of Passion, Fool of Fame* (London: Hamish Hamilton, 1999).

Eliot, T. S., 'Byron', in M. H. Abrams (ed.), *English Romantic Poets: Modern Essays in Criticism* (London: Oxford University Press, 2nd edn, 1975).

Elliott, Marianne, *Partners in Revolution: the United Irishmen and France* (New Haven, CT and London: Yale University Press, 1982).

Elze, Karl, *Lord Byron* (London: John Murray, 1872).

Evans, E. D., *A History of Wales 1660–1815* (Cardiff: University of Wales Press, 1993).

Evans, Evan, *Gwaith y Parchedig Evan Evans* (Caernarfon: H. Humphreys, 1876).

Some Specimens of the Poetry of the Antient Welsh Bards (London: R. and J. Dodsley, 1764).

Ferguson, Adam, *An Essay on the History of Civil Society*, ed. Franz Oz-Salzberger, (Cambridge: Cambridge University Press, 1995.

Flower, Robin, *Byron and Ossian* (Nottingham: Byron Foundation Lecture, 1928).

Foster, John Wilson, 'Certain Set Apart: the Western Island in the Irish Renaissance', *Studies* 66 (1977).

Franklin, Michael, 'Accessing India: Orientalism, anti-"Indianism" and the Rhetoric of Jones and Burke', in Tim Fulford and Peter Kitson (eds.), *Romanticism and Colonialism*, (Cambridge University Press, 1998).

Sir William Jones (Cardiff: University of Wales Press, 1995).

Franklin, Michael J. (ed.), *Europe Discovers India: Key Indological Sources of European Romanticism*, (London, 2001).

Fuller, David, *Blake's Heroic Argument* (London: Croom Helm, 1988).

Garratt, Robert F., *Modern Irish Poetry: Tradition and Continuity from Yeats to Heaney* (Berkeley, CA: University of California Press, 1986).

Gaskill, Howard, 'Herder, Ossian and the Celtic', in Terence Brown (ed.), *Celticism* (Amsterdam: Rodopi Press, 1996).

'Ossian at Home and Abroad', *Strathclyde Modern Language Studies* 8 (1988).

'Ossian, Moritz and the Joy of Grief', *Colloquia Germanica* 28 (1995).

Gaskill, Howard (ed.), *Ossian Revisited* (Edinburgh: Edinburgh University Press, 1991).

Gelpi, Albert, *A Coherent Splendor: the American Poetic Renaissance, 1910–1950* (1987; Cambridge: Cambridge University Press, 1990).

Gill, Stephen, *William Wordsworth: a Life* (1989; Oxford: Oxford University Press, 1990).

Girouard, M., *The Return to Camelot* (New Haven, CT: Yale University Press, 1981).

Glendening, John, *The High Road: Romantic Tourism, Scotland and Literature, 1720–1820* (Basingstoke: Macmillan, 1997).

Glover, Richard, *London: or, the Progress of Commerce* (London, 1739).

Gold, John R. and Margaret M., *Imagining Scotland: Tradition, Representation and Promotion in Scottish Tourism since 1750* (Aldershot: Scolar Press, 1995).

Gray, Thomas, *Correspondence of Thomas Gray*, eds. P. Toynbee and L. Whibley (Oxford: Clarendon Press, 1935).

The Poems and Letters of Thomas Gray, ed. William Mason (London: R. Priestley, 1820).

The Poems of Thomas Gray, William Collins, Oliver Goldsmith, ed. Roger Lonsdale (London and Harlow: Longman, 1969).

Griffith, John T., *Rev. Morgan John Rhys: the Welsh Baptist Hero of Civil and Religious Liberty of the Eighteenth Century* (Carmarthen: W. M. Evans and Son, 1910).

Haldane, Katherine Jean, 'Imagining Scotland: Tourist Images of Scotland 1770–1914' (unpublished PhD thesis, University of Virginia, 1990).

Hayden, John O. (ed.), *Scott: the Critical Heritage* (London: Routledge and Kegan Paul, 1970).

Haywood, Ian, 'The Making of History: Historiography and Literary Forgery in the Eighteenth Century', *Literature and History* 9.2 (Autumn, 1983).

Hazlit, W. Carew (ed.), *The History of English Poetry from the Twelfth to the Close of the Sixteenth Century* (1774–81; London: Reeves and Turner, 1871).

Hazlitt, William, *The Complete Works of William Hazlitt*, ed. P. P. Howe (London, 1930).

Heaney, Seamus, 'The Drag of the Golden Chain', *Times Literary Supplement*, 12 November 1999.

'The Indefatigable Hoof-Taps: Sylvia Plath', in *The Government of the Tongue* (1988; London: Faber, 1989).

North (London: Faber, 1975).

Opened Ground: Poems 1966–1996 (London: Faber, 1998).

Preoccupations: Selected Prose 1968–1978 (London: Faber, 1980).

The Redress of Poetry (London: Faber, 1995).

Hemans, Felicia, *Modern Greece: a Poem* (London: John Murray, 1817).

Poems. England and Spain. Modern Greece (New York: Garland, 1978).

Records of Woman: With Other Poems (London: T. Cadell, 1827).

The Poetical Works of Mrs Hemans (London: Frederick Warne, 1900).

Stanzas to the Memory of the Late King (London: John Murray, 1820).

The Siege of Valencia; a Dramatic Poem. The Last Constantine: with Other Poems (London: John Murray, 1823).

Wallace's Invocation to Bruce. A Poem (Edinburgh: William Blackwood, 1819).

Hemans, Felicia, and Parry, John, *A Selection of Welsh Melodies, with Symphonies and Accompaniments by John Parry, and Characteristic Words by Mrs Hemans* (London: J. Power, 1822).

Hoare, Richard Colt, *The Journeys of Sir Richard Colt Hoare through Wales and England, 1793–1810* ed. M. W. Thompson (Stroud: Alan Sutton, 1983).

Hogg, James, *The Spy*, ed. Gillian Hughes (Edinburgh: Edinburgh University Press, 2000).

Hogg, Thomas Jefferson, *The Life of Percy Bysshe Shelley* (London and New York: George Routledge and Sons, 1906).

Hole, Richard, *Pulpits, Politics and Public Order in England 1760–1832* (Cambridge: Cambridge University Press, 1989).

Holmes, Richard, *Coleridge: Early Visions* (London: Hodder and Stoughton, 1989).

Home, John, *Douglas*, ed. Gerald D. Parker (Edinburgh: Oliver and Boyd, 1972).

Hook, Andrew, '"Ossian" Macpherson as Image Maker', *The Scottish Review* 36 (November 1984).

Horton, Patricia, 'Romantic Intersections: Romanticism and Contemporary Northern Irish Poetry' (unpublished PhD thesis, Queen's University of Belfast, 1996).

Hoyt, Mary Fitzgerald, 'Grounding Keats's Nightingale: Ciaran Carson's *The Irish for No*', *Canadian Journal of Irish Studies* 19.2 (1993).

Jedrej, Charles, and Nuttall, Mark, *White Settlers: the Impact of Rural Repopulation in Scotland* (Luxembourg: Harwood, 1996).

Jeffares, A. Norman, *Images of Invention: Essays on Irish Writing* (Gerrards Cross: Colin Smythe, 1996).

Jenkins, Geraint H., '"A Rank Republican [and] a Leveller": William Jones, Llangadfan', *Welsh History Review* 17 (1994–5).

'Facts, Fantasy and Fiction: the Historical Vision of Iolo Morganwg' (Aberystwyth: University of Wales Centre for Advanced Welsh and Celtic Studies, Paper no. 12, 1997).

Johnson, Arthur, 'William Blake and the Ancient Britons', *National Library of Wales Journal* 22 (1981/2).

Johnson, Edgar, *The Great Unknown* (London: Hamish Hamilton, 1970).

Johnson, Samuel, *Lives of the English Poets*, ed. G. B. Hill (Oxford: Clarendon Press, 1945).

Johnston, Charlotte, 'Evan Evans: Dissertatio De Bardis', in *National Library of Wales Journal* 22 (1981).

Jones, Emyr Wyn, *Diocesan Discord: a Family Affair, St Asaph 1779–1786* (Aberystwyth: printed for the author, 1988).

Yr Anterliwt Goll: Barn ar Egwyddorion y Llywodraeth . . . Gan Fardd Anadnabyddus o Wynedd (Aberystwyth: Llyfrgell Genedlaethol Cymru, 1984).

Jones, William, *The Letters of Sir William Jones*, ed. Garland Cannon (Oxford: Oxford University Press, 1970).

Sir William Jones: Selected Poetical and Prose Works, ed. Michael Franklin (Cardiff: University of Wales Press, 1995).

The Works of Sir William Jones, ed. Anna Maria Jones (London: Stockdale and Walker, 1807), 13 vols.

Jones, William Powell, *Thomas Gray, Scholar* (Cambridge, MA: Harvard University Press, 1937).

Joyce, James, *Ulysses*, ed. Jeri Johnson (Oxford University Press, 1993).

Kabisch, Ernest Bernhardt-, *Robert Southey* (Boston: Twayne Publishers, 1977).

Kaines Smith, S. C., *An Outline History of Painting in Europe to the end of the Nineteenth Century* (London and Boston, MA: Medici Society, n.d.).

Khaldûn, Ibn, *The Muqaddimah: an Introduction to History*, trans. Franz Rosenthal (Princeton, NJ: Princeton University Press, 2nd edn, 1967).

Kiberd, Declan, *Inventing Ireland: the Literature of the Modern Nation* (London: Jonathan Cape, 1995; London: Vintage Books, 1996).

'Irish Literature and History', in R. F. Foster (ed.), *The Oxford History of Ireland* (Oxford University Press, 1992).

Kidd, Colin, *Subverting Scotland's Past: Scottish Whig Historians and the Creation of an Anglo-British Identity, 1689–c.1830* (Cambridge: Cambridge University Press, 1993).

Krielkamp, Vera, *The Anglo-Irish Novel and the Big House* (New York: Syracuse University Press, 1998).

Kroeber, Karl, *Romantic Landscape Vision: Constable and Wordsworth* (Madison, WI: University of Wisconsin Press, 1975).

Lamport, F. J., 'Goethe, Ossian and *Werther*', in Stafford and Gaskill, *From Gaelic to Romantic*.

Larkin, Philip, *Collected Poems*, ed. Anthony Thwaite (London: Marvell Press and Faber, 1988).

Leask, Nigel, *British Romantic Writers and the East: Anxieties of Empire* (Cambridge: Cambridge University Press, 1992).

Leersen, Joep, 'On the Edge of Europe: Ireland in Search of Oriental Roots, 1650–1850', *Comparative Criticism* 8 (1986).

'Ossianic Liminality: between Native Tradition and Preromantic Taste', in Stafford and Gaskill, *From Gaelic to Romantic*.

Lever, Charles, *Luttrell of Arran* (London: Chapman and Hall, 1865).

Lewis, Saunders, *A School of Welsh Augustans* (1924; rpr. Bath: Firecrest, 1969).

Little, Brian, *The City and the Country of Bristol: a Study in Atlantic Civilisation* (London: Wener Laurie, 1954).

Lloyd, A. L., *The Famous Druids: a Survey of Three Centuries of English Literature on the Druids* (Oxford: Clarendon Press, 1962).

Lockhart, John Gibson, *Life of Sir Walter Scott* (London: Adam and Charles Black, 1893).

Lootens, Tricia, 'Hemans and Home: Victorianism, Feminine "Internal Enemies", and the Domestication of National Identity', *PMLA* 109.2 (March 1994).

Lord, Peter, *Gwenllian: Essays on Visual Culture* (Llandysul: Gomer Press, 1994).

Words with Pictures: Welsh Images and Images of Wales in the Popular Press, 1640–1860 (Aberystwyth: Planet, 1995).

Macpherson, James, *The Poems of Ossian and Related Works*, ed. Howard Gaskill (Edinburgh: Edinburgh University Press, 1996).

James Macpherson's Fingal (1792), ed. Jonathan Wordsworth (Poole, 1996).

Madden, Lionel, (ed.), *Robert Southey: the Critical Heritage* (London and Boston, MA: Routledge and Kegan Paul, 1972).

Mahon, Derek, *Poems 1962–1978* (Oxford: Oxford University Press, 1979).

Selected Poems (1990; London: Penguin in association with Oxford University Press, 1993).

The Hudson Letter (Loughcrew: Gallery, 1995).

Malek, James, 'Eighteenth-Century British Dramatic Adaptations of Macpherson's *Ossian*', *Restoration and Eighteenth-Century Theatre Research* 14 (1975).

Manning, Susan, 'Ghost-Writing Tradition: Henry Mackenzie, Burns and Macpherson', *Scotlands* 4.1 (1997).

Marchand, Leslie A., *Byron: a Biography* (London: John Murray, 1957).

Maurice, Thomas, *Indian Antiquities* (London: printed for the author by H. L. Galabin, 1793–1800).

McCormack, W. J., *Ascendancy and Tradition in Anglo-Irish Literary History from 1789 to 1939* (Oxford: Clarendon Press, 1985).

McCrone, David, Morris, Angela, and Kiely, Richard, *Scotland – the Brand* (Edinburgh: Edinburgh University Press, 1995).

McGann, Jerome J., *The Poetics of Sensibility: a Revolution in Literary Style* (Oxford: Clarendon Press, 1996).

  The Romantic Ideology: a Critical Investigation (Chicago: Chicago University Press, 1983).

McGann, Jerome J. (ed.), *The New Oxford Book of Romantic Verse* (Oxford: Oxford University Press, 1993).

Mellor, Anne, *Romanticism and Gender* (New York: Routledge, 1993).

Merriman, James Douglas, *The Flower of Kings: a Study of the Arthurian Legend in England between 1485 and 1835* (Lawrence, KA: University Press of Kansas, 1973).

Mill, James, *The History of British India*, abridged by William Thomas (Chicago: University of Chicago Press, 1975).

Minchinton, W. E., 'Bristol – Metropolis of the West in the Eighteenth Century', *Transactions of the Royal Historical Society* 5.4 (1994).

Molino, Michael R., 'Heaney's "Singing School": a Portrait of the Artist', *Journal of Irish Literature* 16.3 (1987).

Monk, S. H., *The Sublime: a Study of Critical Theories in Eighteenth-Century England* (1935; Ann Arbor, MI: University of Michigan Press, 1960).

Monod, Paul, 'Pierre's White Hat', in Eveline Cruickshanks (ed.), *By Force or By Default?* (Edinburgh: John Donald, 1989).

Montague, John, *Collected Poems* (Loughcrew: Gallery Press, 1995).

Moore, Dafydd, 'James Macpherson and William Faulkner: a Sensibility of Defeat', in Stafford and Gaskill, *From Gaelic to Romantic*.

Moore, John Robert, 'Wordsworth's Unacknowledged Debt to Macpherson's *Ossian*', *PMLA* 40 (1925).

Moore, Thomas, *Life of Lord Byron* (London: John Murray, 1853).

Moorman, Mary, *William Wordsworth, a Biography. The Early Years, 1770–1803* (Oxford: Clarendon Press, 1957).

Morash, Christopher, 'Reflecting Absent Interiors: the Big House Novels of Charles Lever', in Otto Rauchbauer (ed.), *Ancestral Voices: the Big House in Anglo-Irish Literature* (Hildesheim: Georg Olms Verlag, 1992).

Morgan, Prys, *Iolo Morganwg* (Cardiff: University of Wales Press, 1975).

  The Eighteenth Century Renaissance (Llandybie: Davies, 1981).

Morris, Lewis, *Celtic Remains* (London: Parker, 1878).

Morris, Lewis, Richard, William and John, *Additional Letters of the Morrises of Anglesey (1735–1786)*, ed. Hugh Owen (London: Hon. Soc. of Cymmrodorion, 1947–9).

  The Letters of Lewis, Richard, William and John Morris 1728–1765, ed. John H. Davies (Aberystwyth, pub. 1907).

Moynahan, Julian, *Anglo-Irish: the Literary Imagination in a Hyphenated Culture* (Princeton, NJ: Princeton University Press, 1994).

Muldoon, Paul, *Madoc: a Mystery* (London: Faber, 1990).

Muldoon, Paul (ed.), *The Faber Book of Contemporary Irish Poetry* (London: Faber, 1986).

Murphy, Peter, *Poetry as an Occupation and Art in Britain 1760–1830* (Cambridge: Cambridge University Press, 1993).

Noble, Andrew, 'Byron: Radical, Scottish Aristocrat', in Angus Calder (ed.), *Byron and Scotland* (Edinburgh University Press, 1989).

Ó hÓgáin, Dáithí *Fionn mac Cumhaill: Images of the Gaelic Hero* (Dublin: Gill and Macmillan, 1988).

O'Keefe, Thomas, 'Maria Edgeworth and Charles Lever: the Big House and the Garrison', *Eire* 19 (1977).

O'Neill, Michael, *Percy Bysshe Shelley: a Literary Life* (London: Macmillan, 1989).

Owen, Nicholas, *A History of the Island of Anglesey* (London, 1775).

Paley, Morton D., *The Continuing City: William Blake's 'Jerusalem'* (Oxford: Clarendon Press, 1983).

'William Blake, the Prince of the Hebrews, and the Woman Clothed with the Sun' in M. D. Paley and Michael Phillips (eds.), *William Blake: Essays in Honour of Sir Geoffrey Keynes* (Oxford: Clarendon Press, 1973).

Parker, Michael, *Seamus Heaney: the Makings of the Poet* (Basingstoke: Macmillan, 1993).

Paulin, Tom, *The Day-Star of Liberty: William Hazlitt's Radical Style* (London: Faber, 1998).

Paulin, Tom (ed.), *The Faber Book of Political Verse* (London: Faber, 1986).

Pennant, Thomas, *A Tour in Wales* (London, 2nd edn, 1784).

Percy, Thomas, *The Song of Solomon, newly translated from the original Hebrew: with a Commentary and Annotations* (London: R. and J. Dodsley, 1764).

Percy, Thomas and Evans, Evan, *The Correspondence of Thomas Percy and Evan Evans*, ed. Aneurin Lewis (Baton Rouge: Louisana University Press, 1957).

Piggott, Stuart, *Celts, Saxons and the Early Antiquaries* (Edinburgh: 1966 O'Donnell Lecture, 1967).

Pinkerton, John, *A Dissertation on the Origin and Progress of the Scythians or Goths. Being an Introduction to the Ancient and Modern History of Europe* (London: G. Nicol, 1787).

Pittock, Murray G. H., *Celtic Identity and the British Image* (Manchester: Manchester University Press, 1999).

Inventing and Resisting Britain: Cultural Identities in Britain and Ireland, 1685–1789 (Basingstoke: Macmillan, 1997).

Scottish Nationality (Basingstoke: Palgrave, 2001).

The Invention of Scotland (London: Routledge, 1991).

The Myth of the Jacobite Clans (Edinburgh: Edinburgh University Press, 1995).

Pratt, Lynda, 'Naval Contemplation: Poetry, Patriotism and the Navy 1797–1799', *Journal for Maritime Research*: Royal Observatory Greenwich web site (December 2000).

'Revising the National Epic: Coleridge, Southey and *Madoc*', *Romanticism* 2.2 (1996).

'The Pantisocratic Origins of Robert Southey's *Madoc*: an Unpublished Letter', *Notes and Queries* 244.1 (March 1999).

Prebble, John, *The King's Jaunt* (London: HarperCollins, 1988).

Price, John Valdimir, 'Ossian and the Canon in the Scottish Enlightenment', in Gaskill, *Ossian Revisited*.

Priestman, Martin, *Romantic Atheism: Poetry and Freethought, 1780–1830* (Cambridge: Cambridge University Press, 1999).

Prochazka, Martin, 'Ossian Revived: Macpherson's "Ossian Poems" and Historical Aspects of Czech Romantic Culture', *Ceska Literatura* 14.1 (1993).

Punter, David, 'Blake: Social Relations of Poetic Form', *Literature and History* 8 (1982).

Gothic Pathologies: the Text, the Body and the Law (London: Macmillan, 1998).

Pye, Henry James, *Naucratia; or Naval Dominion* (London, 1798).

Quenell, Peter, *Byron: the Years of Fame* (London: Faber and Faber, 1935).

Raine, Kathleen, *Blake and Tradition* (Princeton, NJ: Princeton University Press, 1968).

Reed, Mark, *Wordsworth. The Chronology of the Early Years, 1770–1799* (Cambridge, MA: Harvard University Press, 1967).

Relph, E., *Place and Placelessness* (London: Pion, 1976).

Rhys, John, and Brynmor-Jones, David, *The Welsh People: Chapters on their Origin, History and Laws, Language, Literature and Characteristics* (1923; New York: Greenwood Press, 1969).

Rix, Walter, 'Charles Lever: the Irish Dimension of a Cosmopolitan', in Heinz Kosok (ed.), *Studies in Anglo-Irish Literature* (Bonn: Bouvier Verlag Herbert Grundmann, 1982).

Ross, Alexander M., '*Waverley* and the Picturesque', in J. H. Alexander and David Hewitt (eds.), *Scott and his Influence* (Aberdeen: Association for Scottish Literary Studies, 1983).

Rossington, Michael, 'Poetry by Burns, Cowper, Crabbe, Southey, and other Male Authors', in Michael O'Neill (ed.), *Literature of the Romantic Period* (Oxford: Clarendon Press, 1998).

Rowlands, Henry, *Mona Antiqua Restaurata. An Archaeological Discourse on the Antiquities, Natural and Historical of the Isle of Anglesey, the Ancient Seat of the British Druids* (Dublin: Aaron Rhames, 1723).

Ruskin, John, *The Works of John Ruskin*, (eds.) E. T. Cook and Alexander Wedderburn (London, 1903–12).

Rutherford, Andrew (ed.), *Byron: the Critical Heritage* (London: Routledge and Kegan Paul, 1970).

Said, Edward, *Orientalism* (New York: Vintage, 1991).

Schama, Simon, *Landscape and Memory* (London: Fontana Press, 1995).

Scott, Walter, *Novels and Tales* (Edinburgh: Constable, 1825).

Old Mortality, ed. Angus Calder, (1975; Harmondsworth: Penguin, 1987).

Redgauntlet, ed. Kathryn Sutherland (Oxford University Press, 1985).

Rob Roy (London: John Nimmo, 1893).

The Antiquary, ed. David Hewitt (Edinburgh: Edinburgh University Press, 1995).

The Bride of Lammermoor, ed. W. M. Parker (1906; London: J. M. Dent, 1988)

The Heart of Midlothian, ed. Claire Lamont (Oxford University Press, 1982).

The Journal of Sir Walter Scot, ed. W. E. K. Anderson (Oxford University Press, 1972).

The Letters of Walter Scott 1787–1807, ed. H. J. C. Grierson (London: Constable, 1932).

The Poetical Works of Sir Walter Scott, ed. J. Logie Robertson (London: Oxford University Press, 1917).

Waverley, ed. Andrew Hook (London: Penguin, 1972; 1985).

Sharafuddin, Mohammed, *Islam and Romantic Orientalism: Literary Encounters with the Orient* (London and New York: I. B. Tauris, 1994).

Shelley, Percy Bysshe, *Shelley's Poetry and Prose*, eds. Donald H. Reiman and Sharon B. Powers (New York: Norton, 1977).

The Letters of Percy Bysshe Shelley, ed. Frederick L. Jones (Oxford: Clarendon Press, 1964).

The Poetry of Percy Bysshe Shelley, ed. Geoffrey Matthews and Kelvin Everest (London and New York: Longman, 1989–).

The Prose Works of Percy Bysshe Shelley, ed. E. B. Murray (Oxford: Clarendon Press, 1993–).

The Works of Percy Bysshe Shelley in Verse and Prose, ed. Harry Buxton Forman (London: Reeves and Turner, 1880).

Smollett, Tobias, *The Expedition of Humphrey Clinker*, ed. Peter Miles (London: J. M. Dent, 1993).

Smith, Stan, 'Seamus Heaney: the Distance Between', in Neil Corcoran (ed.), *The Chosen Ground: Essays on the Contemporary Poetry of Northern Ireland* (Bridgend: Seren Books, 1992).

Snyder, Edward, *The Celtic Revival in English Literature 1760–1800* (Cambridge, MA.: Harvard University Press, 1923).

Southey, Robert, *Madoc* (London: Longman, Hurst, Rees and Orme, 1805).

New Letters of Robert Southey, ed. Kenneth Curry (New York and London: Columbia University Press, 1965).

Selections from the Letters of Robert Southey edited by his son-in-law, John Wood Warter (London: Longman, 1856).

The Contributions of Robert Southey to the Morning Post (Alabama: University of Alabama, 1984).

The Poetical Works of Robert Southey (London: Longman, 1845).

Stafford, Fiona, ' "Dangerous Success": Ossian, Wordsworth and English Romanticism', in *Ossian Revisited* (Edinburgh University Press, 1991).

Introduction, in Howard Gaskill (ed.), *The Poems of Ossian and Related Works* (Edinburgh: Edinburgh University Press, 1995).

'Primitivism and the "Primitive" Poet: a Cultural Context for Macpherson's *Ossian*' in Terence Brown, *Celticism* (Amsterdam: Rodogi, 1996).

The Last of the Race: the Growth of a Myth from Milton to Darwin (Oxford: Clarendon Press, 1994).

The Sublime Savage: James Macpherson and the Poems of Ossian (Edinburgh Press, 1988).

Stafford, Fiona and Gaskill, Howard (eds), *From Gaelic to Romantic: Ossianic Translations* (Amsterdam: Rodopi Press, 1998).

Stephens, Thomas, *Madoc: an Essay on the Discovery of America by Madoc ap Owen Gwynedd in the Twelfth Century* (London and New York: Longman, Green and Co., 1893).

Stevens, Wallace, *Collected Poems* (London: Faber, 1955).

Letters of Wallace Stevens, ed. Holly Stevens (New York: Knopf, 1966).

Stewart, Larry Leroy, 'Ossian in the Polished Age: the Critical Reception of James Macpherson's *Ossian*' (unpublished PhD thesis, University of Michigan, 1971).

Stukeley, William, *A Letter from Dr Stukeley to Mr MacPherson, on his Publication of Fingal and Temora. With a Print of Cathmor's Shield* (London: Richard Hett, 1763).

Sweet, Nanora, 'History, Imperialism, and the Aesthetics of the Beautiful: Hemans and the Post-Napoleonic Moment', in Mary A. Favret and Nicola J. Watson (eds.), *At the Limitis of Romanticism: Essays in Cultural, Feminist, and Materialist Criticism* (Bloomington, IN: Indiana University Press, 1994).

Tennyson, Alfred, *Letters of Alfred, Lord Tennyson*, eds. Cecil Y. Long and Edgar F. Shannon (Oxford: Clarendon Press, 1982–90).

Thompson, E. P., *Witness against the Beast: William Blake and the Moral Law* (Cambridge: Cambridge University Press, 1993).

Thurber, Bartan, 'Scott and the Sublime', in J. H. Alexander and David Hewitt (eds.), *Scott and his Influence* (Aberdeen: Association for Scottish Literary Studies, 1983).

Toland, John, *A Collection of Several Pieces of Mr. John Toland* (London: J. Peele, 1726).

Tone, Theobald Wolfe, *Memoirs, Journals and Political Writings compiled by T. W. Tone, 1826*, ed. Thomas Bartlett (Dublin: Lilliput Press, 1998).

Trautmann, Thomas, *Aryans and British India* (Berkeley, Los Angeles, London: University of California Press, 1997).

Trinder, Peter W., *Mrs Hemans* (Cardiff: University of Wales Press, 1984).

Trumpener, Kate, *Bardic Nationalism: the Romantic Novel and the British Empire* (Princeton: Princeton University Press, 1997).

Turner, Sharon, *A History of the Anglo-Saxons* (London, 1799–1805, 4th edn, 1823).

Vallancey, Charles, *An Essay on the Antiquity of the Irish Language, Being a Collation of the Irish with the Punic Language. With a Preface proving Ireland to be the Thule of the Ancients. Addressed to the Literati of Europe* (Dublin: S. Powell, 1772).

Vance, Norman, 'Celts, Carthaginians and Constitutions: Anglo-Irish Literary Relations, 1780–1820', *Irish Historical Studies* 22 (1981).

Vance, R. N. C., 'Texts and Traditions: Robert Emmet's Speech from the Dock', *Studies* 71 (Summer, 1982).

Vaughan, William, *Romanticism in Art* (1978; London: Thames and Hudson, 1994).

Vendler, Helen, *Seamus Heaney* (London: Faber, 1998).

Vinaver, Eugene, *The Rise of Romance* (Oxford: Clarendon Press, 1971).

Volney, Constantin, *Les Ruines, ou méditation sur les révolutions des empires* (Paris: Canongette et Campagnie, 1830).

Voltaire, François, *Dictionnaire Philosophique*, (1816).

Waring, Elijah, *Recollections and Anecdotes of Edward Williams, the Bard of Glamorgan or Iolo Morganwg, B.B.D.* (London: Charles Gilpin, 1850).

Webb, Timothy, '"A Noble Field": Shelley's Irish Expedition and the Lessons of the French Revolution', in Nadia Minerva (ed.), *Robespierre & Co: atti della ricerca sulla Letteratura Francese della Revoluzione* (Bologna: Edizione Analisi, 1990).

Weinbrot, Howard D., *Britannia's Issue: the Rise of British Literature from Dryden to Ossian* (Cambridge University Press, 1993).

Whittaker, James, *William Blake and the Myths of Britain* (Basingstoke and London: Macmillan, 1999).

Williams, G. J., *Iolo Morganwg – Y Gyfrol Gyntaf* (Caerdydd: Gwasg Prifysgol Cymru, 1956).

Williams, Gwyn A., 'Druids and Democrats: Organic Intellectuals and the First Welsh Radicalism', in Raphael Samuel and Gareth Stedman Jones (eds.), *Culture, Ideology and Politics: Essays for Eric Hobsbawm* (London, Boston, Melbourne and Henley: Routledge and Kegan Paul, 1982).

Madoc: the Making of a Myth (London: Eyre Methuen, 1979).

'Romanticism in Wales', in Roy Porter and Mikuláš (eds.), *Romanticism in National Context* (Cambridge: Cambridge University Press, 1988).

The Search for Beulah Land: the Welsh and the Atlantic Revolution (London: Croom Helm, 1980).

Williams, Robert, *A Biographical Dictionary of Eminent Welshmen, from the Earliest Times to the Present, and Including Every Name Connected with the Ancient History of Wales* (London: Longman, 1852).

Withers, Charles W. J., *Gaelic in Scotland 1698–1981* (Edinburgh: John Donald, 1984).

Wolfson, Susan J., '"Domestic Affections" and "the Spear of Minerva": Felicia Hemans and the Dilemma of Gender', in Carol Shiner Wilson and Joel Haefner (eds.), *Re-Visioning Romanticism: British Women Writers, 1776–1837* (Philadelphia, PA: University of Pennsylvania Press, 1994).

Woodbridge, Kenneth, *Landscape and Antiquity: Aspects of English Culture at Stourhead, 1718 to 1838* (Oxford: Clarendon Press, 1970).

Womack, Peter, *Improvement and Romance: Constructing the Myth of the Highlands* (Basingstoke and London: Macmillan 1989).

Wordsworth, Dorothy, *Journals of Dorothy Wordsworth*, ed. E. de Selincourt (London: Macmillan, 1941).

The Letters of William and Dorothy Wordsworth: the Later Years (Part 1), rev. Alan G. Hill (Oxford: Clarendon Press, 1978).

Wordsworth, William, *A Description of the Scenery of the Lakes in the North of England* (London: Longman, 1823).

Wordsworth, William, *The Essential Wordsworth*, ed. Seamus Heaney (New York: Ecco, 1988).

Lyrical Ballads, ed. Michael Mason (London: Longman, 1992).

The Letters of William and Dorothy Wordsworth: the Early Years, 1787–1805, ed. E de Selincourt; rev. Chester L. Shaver (Oxford: Clarendon Press, 1967).

The Oxford Authors: William Wordsworth, ed. Stephen Gill (Oxford: Oxford University Press, 1984).

The Prose Works of William Wordsworth, eds. W. J. B. Owen and Jane Worthington (Oxford: Clarendon Press, 1974).

Wordsworth's Literary Criticism, ed. W. J. B. Owen, (London, 1974).

Wyndham, Henry Penruddocke, *A Tour through Monmouthshire and Wales, Made in the Months of June and July, 1774. And in the Months of June, July and August, 1777* (London, 2nd edn, 1781).

Yeats, W. B., *The Oxford Authors: W. B. Yeats*, ed. Edward Larrissy (Oxford: Oxford University Press, 1997).

Index